URBAN NETWORKS
IN CH'ING CHINA AND
TOKUGAWA JAPAN

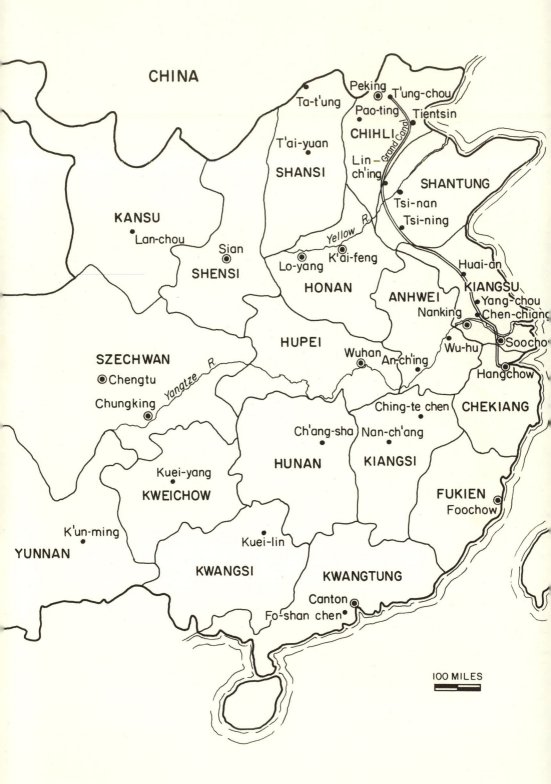

JAPAN

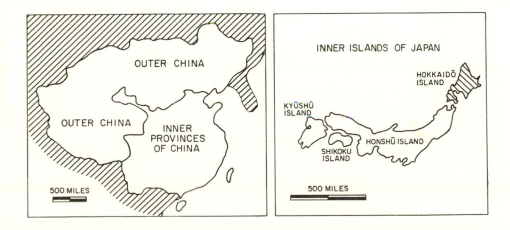

JAPAN SEA

TŌHOKU

Sendai

Kanazawa

CHŪGOKU   CHŪBU   KANTŌ

Yamaguchi   KINKI   Kyoto
Hiroshima   Kamakura   Edo
Hakata   Osaka Nagoya
Nagasaki   SHIKOKU   Sakai
Kumamoto

KYŪSHŪ
Kagoshima

100 MILES

OUTER CHINA

OUTER CHINA   INNER
PROVINCES
OF CHINA

500 MILES

INNER ISLANDS OF JAPAN

HOKKAIDŌ
ISLAND

KYŪSHŪ
ISLAND

HONSHŪ ISLAND

SHIKOKU
ISLAND

500 MILES

GILBERT ROZMAN

URBAN NETWORKS
IN CH'ING CHINA AND TOKUGAWA JAPAN

PRINCETON UNIVERSITY PRESS PRINCETON, NEW JERSEY

CONTENTS

TABLES

DIAGRAM

MAPS

ACKNOWLEDGMENTS

This book began as a paper presented in various forms to seminars on Chinese and Japanese social structure, on Tokugawa history, and on urban sociology and then appeared as a dissertation. The effort as well as the guidance has been consistently interdisciplinary, and my aim in reworking the material into a book has continued to be to devise a method of comparison that would apply first of all to China and Japan, and subsequently to other premodern societies.

Starting with the view that understanding differences requires a method of demonstrating similarities, I have erected an urban bridge from the cities of China to those of Japan, showing first similarities and then differences between patterns of settlement. The bridge is intended not only to provide a way of movement between China and Japan, but also between sociology and history, disciplines which have been as artificially separated through intentional seclusion and indifference as were Ch'ing China and Tokugawa Japan. Our narrow perspectives of historical societies must be widened by the awareness that the kinds of questions one asks about a country are a function not only of detailed knowledge of that country, but also of available knowledge of other countries. By comparing two stable and well-documented countries, I seek to raise a new set of questions.

A number of professors have assisted me in writing this book. I am grateful above all, to Marion J. Levy, Jr. and to Frederick W. Mote. They first taught me sociology and Chinese history, respectively, and continued to be my principal advisers many years later as this book took shape. These two men have set standards for theory and for sinology that have constantly inspired me. I am indebted also to Marius B. Jansen for helpful comments concerning research on Japan

ACKNOWLEDGMENTS

and to Gerald Breese for introducing me to urban sociology and to both of them for reading this manuscript critically. Other readers who have helped shape parts of this volume are John W. Hall, Tetsuo Najita, Ezra Vogel, and C. K. Yang. Assistance in securing materials was provided by G. William Skinner, Endymion Wilkinson, Shiba Yoshinobu, and Yamane Yukio. Generous support for research came from the Foreign Area Fellowship Program. All of this help has made the writing of this book more satisfying.

Princeton, New Jersey   GILBERT ROZMAN
January 1972

CHRONOLOGY

B.C.	China	Japan	Capitals China	Capitals Japan
2000				
1800				
1600			Cheng-chou	
1400	Shang: -1100		An-yang	
1200				
1000				
800	Western Chou: -770		Lo-yang	
600				
400	Eastern Chou: -221			
200	(Warring States): -221			
0	Ch'in: -206		Ch'ang-an	
	Western Han -A.D. 8		(Sian)	

A.D.	China	Japan	China	Japan
100	Eastern Han: -220		Lo-yang	
200				
300	Six Dynasties: -580			
500	Sui: -618		Ch'ang-an	
600		Yamato: -710		Heijō
700	T'ang-906	Nara: -784		(Nara)
800				
900	Five Dynasties: -960	Heian: -1185		Heian
1000	Northern Sung: -1127		K'ai-feng	(Kyoto)
1100				
1200	Southern Sung: -1280	Kamakura: -1336	Lin-an	Kamakura
1300	Yuan: -1368		(Hangchow)	and Kyoto
1400		Muromachi	Peking	
1500	Ming: -1644	(Ashikaga):		Kyoto
		-1477	Nanking and	
1600		Sengoku: -1600	Peking	
1700	Ch'ing: -1911	Tokugawa: -1868		Edo
1800			Peking	and Kyoto
1900	Republic: -1949	Meiji: -1912	Nanking	Tokyo (Edo)
	People's Republic:			
	1949—	Taishō: -1926	Peking	
		Shōwa: 1926—		

ANNOTATIONS

1-6 market: a market which is open on the 1st and 6th days of each 10-day period; i.e., 6 days each 30-day month. Similarly 2-7 refers to the 2nd and 7th days; 3-8 to the 3rd and 8th days, etc. . . .

2/10 market: a market which is open twice each 10 days, normally at 5-day intervals, e.g., a 1-6 market is a 2/10 market. Similarly 1/10 refers to a market which is open once each 10 days, 3/10 to 3 times each 10 days, etc. . . .

10/21: notation used only in Tables in Chapters 4 and 5; indicates that the number of markets rose from 10 at an earlier date to 21 at a later date.

DIAGRAM

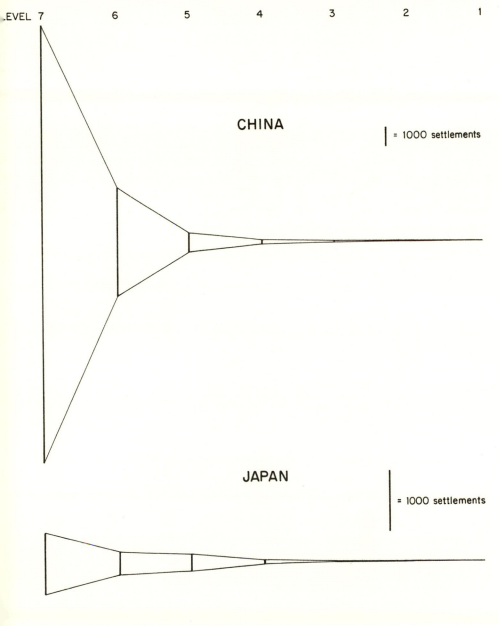

LEVEL 7   6   5   4   3   2   1

CHINA

| = 1000 settlements

JAPAN

| = 1000 settlements

SCALE: JAPAN = 3X CHINA

Central Places in China and Japan

URBAN NETWORKS
IN CH'ING CHINA AND
TOKUGAWA JAPAN

GENERAL INTRODUCTION

Urban distributions reflect stages of societal development. Until societies reached a certain level of complexity and differentiation, cities did not exist. Recent levels of urbanization soaring above 60 and 70 percent of the population in advanced industrial societies reflect man's conquest of increasing portions of his material environment. In the interim, between the time cities were first established by men who knew primitive agriculture and the beginning of the Industrial Revolution less than two hundred years ago, the proportion of people living in cities was small. Yet, over thousands of years cities were being continually transformed as premodern (before 1800) societies were changing. A society with many levels of cities and 10 percent of its population urban was in many respects different from one with just 2 percent of its people in a small number of cities. Data on variations in the percentage of the population residing in cities as well as on variations in the distribution of cities within countries form the starting point for a comparison of societies. Changing cities and networks of cities reveal changing societies.

Urban distributions in premodern China and Japan should be the concern of four subfields (1) historical sociology,[1] (2) urban sociology, (3) Chinese history, and (4) Japanese history. From sociologists and those in related specialties, I sought useful approaches for comparing premodern societies. Unfortunately, those who have borrowed models from experience elsewhere in the world, hoping to apply them to China and Japan, have generally failed to add to our knowledge about the course of development in these two countries before the mid-nineteenth century. They have not considered that the rate at which new levels of cities are added may be an index of

3

societal change nor have they made much effort to find similar indices of development. Renewed interest in comparing societies during the past two decades is a hopeful sign that improved periodizations of societies will appear, but useful strategies are still nearly nonexistent.

Ignorance is widespread not only about the general place of Chinese and Japanese development among premodern societies, but also about the comparative state of premodern cities in China and Japan. The urban sociologist is usually concerned with the history of individual cities, not with the history of networks of cities. He rarely asks how city plans are meaningful representations of their societies and generally ignores how a map of all cities divided according to their population levels is a spatial depiction of a society.[2] Neither Max Weber in *The City* nor Gideon Sjoberg in *The Pre-industrial City*, the two authors to whom most westerners turn for a general discussion of premodern cities, provides a framework for comparing the stages in Chinese and Japanese city development. The former concentrated on showing the absence of bourgeois self-government in Chinese and Japanese cities and the latter minimized the urban presence in both countries. Others who see premodern societies as essentially static have failed to distinguish between Chinese or Japanese cities in different periods. We still have little knowledge of the scale and significance of cities in premodern China and Japan in which, after all, roughly two-fifths of the world's urban population lived before 1800.

For the sociologist comparing premodern societies, the historian's contributions are manifold. The historian is expected to have found all useful data on a particular country, to have made it readily available and usable, and to have tentatively interpreted its significance for that country. Especially since World War II Japanese scholars have approached this ideal. Not only historians, but geographers, economists, and sociologists also have contributed extensively to the study of premodern Japanese cities. With this book I hope to narrow the gap between Western and Japanese knowledge of Tokugawa cities and to begin to remedy the absence of comparisons between these cities and others in the premodern world.

In contrast to the wealth of materials distilling the history of cities in Japan, Chinese cities have received little attention from twentieth century Chinese scholars. The only recourse for me was to turn directly to materials written during the Ch'ing period for most of my information. Japanese research on Chinese history facilitated this effort. Of course, Western sources on the histories of both China and Japan provided me with the necessary background for materials written in Chinese and Japanese.

Of the four sources on which this interdisciplinary study depends, Japanese history is the least uncertain. Enumerations of city populations in Tokugawa Japan were more plentiful than in Ch'ing China. Yet, data are still too sparse and reliability too uncertain to warrant the precise calculations that a sociologist prefers. What follows are estimates. Where figures are found in historical materials, I am not certain that they are the results of careful investigations. They must be used with caution. But to ignore them is to prefer ignorance over partial knowledge. It is more useful to determine what probably prevailed.

For both Ch'ing China and Tokugawa Japan I have placed cities into levels with ranges in population, e.g., 3,000 to 10,000 or 300,000 to 900,000, etc. Even where it is impossible to determine the correct population of a city (by which I mean an urbanized area, not necessarily corresponding to a legally defined unit), it is usually possible to indicate to which level the city belonged. As I point out in the introduction to Part II, estimates of the proportion of Japanese living in cities are likely to be more accurate than estimates for China. Not only superior population figures but also the wealth of detail on individual cities in Japan make that country easier to study.

In writing about premodern cities in two societies, I postpone until another occasion a further comparison of cities in other societies. My first priority is to focus on these two examples. For purposes of analysis Chinese society was superior to other societies in continuity, in size, in the wealth of continuous historical materials left to posterity, and, I would add, in its level of economic development before the seventeenth century. Japanese society was also large-scale and exceptional. The rate of change there was faster than in China. Extensive study of materials from the Tokugawa period provides an excellent foundation for comparative research. Moreover, as early as a century prior to the Industrial Revolution, Japan may have been the only society, with the possible exception of Western European countries, to surpass China in economic development. Together late premodern China and Japan should be regarded not just as one corner of Asia, but as one-third of the world in population, as probably more than one-third of the world in production, and as approximately two-fifths of the world in urban population.

Around 1800 the human population of the earth stood between 900 million and 1 billion, approximately 4 percent of the people lived in cities with more than 10,000 inhabitants.[3] About 12 million or one-third of these urban dwellers lived in China. It is conceivable that for at least 2,000 years as many as one-third or even at times one-half of all city residents had been Chinese. Eight or nine locations in China had been the sites of cities with populations probably in excess of 800,000 at some time prior to 1800. The world's premodern urban history was mainly a Chinese phenomenon.

While China stood out in total urban population, Japan was the more dramatic case. With 3 percent of the world's population, Japan in the late eighteenth century contained more than 8 percent of the people in cities of more than 10,000. It is likely that Japan was the only large-scale premodern society outside of Europe with more than 10 percent of its population in cities of this size. Moreover, the sudden increase in Japan's urban population in the century and a half prior to the early 1700s may well have had no parallel in world history before industrialization.

Similarities are striking. Peking and Edo were probably the two largest cities in the world, having populations in excess of 1 million. Wuhan, Soochow, and Osaka were three of the world's great ports. Nanking and Kyoto were renowned centers of craft and artistic traditions. In short, China and Japan can be classified together as highly developed premodern societies. Their differences, however, are also revealing. China's urban activities were more dispersed. The Japanese lived in larger cities than Chinese urban residents. In this respect Tokugawa Japan was a more centralized society and it was also a more urbanized society. By 1700 the proportion of Japanese in cities climbed to at least twice the figure for the Chinese. And by the early nineteenth century periodic marketing was on the decline in Japan while it continued to expand in China. Development of Japan's urban network was rushing forward ahead of its neighbor's.

The Ch'ing and Tokugawa periods are the obvious choices for a comparison of premodern China and Japan. These were stable periods when change came gradually rather than by violent upheaval. By the beginning of these periods the long process of completing the seven-level hierarchy of cities identified in Chapter 1 was complete. Extrapolating from the emergence of the seven levels of cities, I propose that China and Japan were closest to each other in development during the seventeenth and eighteenth centuries. A "close up" on this time span should show Japan catching up and overtaking China in the proportion of its population in cities and in other respects as well. For both countries data on these periods are far more plentiful than on earlier periods. Finally, these periods conveniently overlap more than two centuries. Coincidentally, the Tokugawa Bakufu and the Ch'ing dynasty following forty-four years behind, each lasted for about 268 years. For two and two-thirds centuries they persisted as both the culmination of the relatively slowly evolving premodern social patterns of their respective countries and as the foundation for different responses to the radically transforming forces introduced from the modernizing and colonizing Western powers.

Sociologists and historians alike have neglected general discussions of Chinese and Japanese premodern cities. Until now there have been no knowledgeable comparisons of Chinese or Japanese cities with each other or with cities in other countries. There has been almost no attempt to devise a general procedure for studying the course of urbanization in China or Japan. Regional variations in cities have been largely ignored. The place of cities in the social structure is woefully misunderstood. This book is intended to focus attention on these important topics and to suggest new ways in which they may be treated.

PART

✻ *I* ✻

PART I: INTRODUCTION

The first three chapters treat general aspects of spatial distributions in China and Japan. Chapter 1 traces the development of cities in Chinese and Japanese history, including the presentation of a generalized framework in the form of a hierarchy of seven levels of central places which enables comparison of stages of urban development. Chapter 2 presents a survey of the social structure supporting the cities of the Ch'ing and Tokugawa periods, treating a number of topics that are important for an understanding of urban networks. Chapter 3 centers on one kind of spatial distribution—the movement of resources through marketing. By the eighteenth century marketing, even more than administration, was the foundation for urban growth.

These three chapters are intended to provide a coordinated approach to comparing premodern societies. Using the framework developed in Chapter 1, we should be able to identify precisely the point of urban development reached century by century in various countries. From the readings of urban indicators, we can start to trace the course of social change to determine to what extent the level of urbanization is a measure of centralization, of economic development, or of other indices that should be used for premodern societies. By beginning with calculations for China and Japan of the number of levels of the seven-level hierarchy present in each century and of the rate at which new levels were being added prior to 1600, I have introduced measurements which I hope will prove useful in comparing other societies too.

Chapter 2 is an initial effort to develop an approach to the general study of social structure in advanced premodern societies, centering on graphs showing the number of cities at various population levels. Societies such as Tokugawa Japan were characterized by a narrow-based pyramid, having relatively few small marketing centers with populations of less than 3,000 supporting a correspondingly large number of cities with populations exceeding 30,000 or 300,000. The relative concentrations of urban residents in cities at various levels was markedly different in Ch'ing China with its wide-based pyramid. Evidence for China and Japan is presented to show that such societal characteristics as the distribution of social classes and the degree of orderliness in a city plan are related to this index of concentration. Future research should be directed at determining in greater detail which aspects of societies relate to the shape of the urban pyramid.

Finally, central place theories as devised by geographers, urban sociologists, and others offer a promising approach for integrating the study of marketing patterns with research on periodization and on spatial aspects of social structure. The rates at which periodic markets are added and then later eliminated provide evidence of the pace of increasing efficiency in the organization of space. This is discussed by E.A.J. Johnson in the *Organization of Space in Developing Countries*, published in 1970 by Harvard University Press. Analysis of marketing in Chapter 3 is the third approach used in Part I which deserves a prominent place in the study of premodern societies.

✵ *1* ✵

CITIES IN CHINA AND JAPAN PRIOR TO
THE CH'ING AND TOKUGAWA PERIODS

Cities have existed for more than 5,000 years. Originating in the Near East (in Mesopotamia and later in the Nile river valley), they appeared in India and then in China almost 4,000 years ago. The spread of cities in East Asia from their origin in the northwest of present-day China has continued to this century. While, on the one hand, the Chinese have created cities as they have extended their control of the Asian mainland and nearby islands, on the other hand, neighboring peoples have established cities based on the Chinese model. The Japanese were one of the peoples most influenced by the achievements in China, and began to build Chinese-style cities in the seventh century A.D. By the time the Chinese had already completed two-thirds of their premodern urban experience, the Japanese were just building their first cities.

Premodern history can be seen as successive additions of new levels of cities. Note the seven levels of cities given in Table 1. The appearance of cities at each of these levels and the number of levels present are taken to be indicators of the state of urban development. Before the seventeenth century A.D. cities had existed in China for 3,400 to 3,500 years and in Japan for 900 to 1,000 years. Throughout its brief urban history, Japan was gaining on China by adding new levels of cities at a faster rate. During the seventeenth century the urban network of Japan finally caught up with that of China; all seven levels were now present in both countries.

The varying order in which these seven levels of central places appeared in China and Japan indicates differences in their respective processes of urbanization and social change. The hierarchy of cities in China, but not in Japan, was nearly intact at the top when the bottom levels (6 and 7) were added. This may help explain how Chinese marketing settlements were readily integrated into the existing city system while the society remained stable. In contrast, the appearance of levels 6 and 7 in Japan was the beginning of a spurt in urban growth corresponding to a major transformation of Japanese society. More will be said in the summary at the end of

TABLE 1

Definitions of Levels of Central Places, by Function[a]

Level	Definition
1	National administrative center
2	Capitals of a divided or a decentralized dynasty or a regional center in a united country
3	Elevated administrative center—e.g., a provincial capital—or an intermediate port linking a city at level 1 or 2 to distant areas
4	Second lowest administrative center—e.g., a prefectural capital—or a major regional port
5	Lowest administrative center—e.g., a district capital
6	Intermediate marketing settlement, serving as a nexus between nearby level 7 markets
7	Standard marketing settlement, differing from an ordinary village because of the presence of a periodic market

[a]Note that definitions for the levels of central places used in this chapter are based on functions, whereas definitions first given in Chapter 2 for the seven-level hierarchy in the Ch'ing and Tokugawa periods are based on populations.

this chapter about the consequences of different patterns of building a complete seven-level hierarchy.

The history of cities in China and Japan can be usefully divided into four stages. The first stage is here called ancient China and ancient Japan, periods ending in the 220s B.C. and the A.D. 710s respectively. The earliest Chinese cities were Shang dynasty aristocratic complexes and the centers of fiefs in Shang and Chou dynasty China (level 2). Emerging out of the transformation of Chou feudalism were state capitals (level 2) and *hsien* (district) cities (level 5). The first Japanese cities were also at level 2—temporary capitals built and then quickly abandoned. With the exception of close ties joining cities at level 5 with their parent centers at level 2, cities at this early stage of urban history were generally administered independently, with only loose connections between them.

Stage two in the development of cities lasted in China until the A.D. 750s and in Japan until the 1180s. These were imperial periods when long-standing capitals were built in unified China and Chinese-style capitals were introduced in Japan. The number of levels of cities present in China was first three (levels 1, 4, and 5 or 2, 4, and 5) and then four (levels 1, 3, 4, and 5). In contrast, the Japanese imperial center (level 1 or level 2) existed in an environment of few supporting cities at level 5 and later at level 3. The rising commercial economy of absentee landlords, especially in Japan, meant that the imperial government was losing some of its control over the agricultural surplus and correspondingly over cities.

I have termed stage three middle imperial China (— 1360s) and feudal Japan (— 1470s). This was the time when levels 6 and 7 were added in China and Japan. Divergent paths of development indicated by the designations "imperial" and "feudal" were reflected in the existing levels of cities. In China there were five or six levels, including levels 4 and 5 as outposts of central control over emerging commercial growth in levels 6 and 7. In Japan there were three or four levels, but levels 4 and 5 were absent. Central control was lacking.

Ming China (— 1640s) and Sengoku Japan (— 1600s) are singled out as the fourth stage. With the appearance of levels 1 and 2 together in China all seven levels were now present. Administrative divisions, marketing patterns, city walls, and transportation networks were all essentially the same as in the following Ch'ing period. Urban growth proceeded rapidly in Japan—two levels were added and finally the seventh level followed in the early seventeenth century. New planned cities were a physical expression of a recentralized society in Japan.

By dividing history into these four stages, I have tried to identify times when the urban networks of the two countries were most similar. It can be shown that in many respects the history of cities in Japan paralleled earlier developments in China. In the eighth century Japan was 1,000 years behind China in establishing an imperial capital. In the thirteenth century China's lead had been narrowed to 500 years as periodic markets blossomed in Japan. The gap between the urban networks in the two countries continued to narrow through the sixteenth century when China and Japan were about to enter the final phase of their premodern journey roughly equal in urban endowment.

Ancient China

The early development of Chinese cities presumably followed a common progression. With the beginning of agriculture, settlements advanced from hidden clusters of dwellings to shifting villages and finally to permanent farming villages. As improvements in farming techniques spread, larger settlements became possible. By 1850 B.C. in northern Honan province centers emerged among groups of mutually dependent settlements. Concentrations of ceremonial objects uncovered in walled areas testify to the existence of aristocratic complexes whose members had charge of administration, the redistribution of goods and services, and the performance of religious rites for people in the vicinity.[1]

In the centuries after the origin of cities in China walled cities (level 2) served as the seats of prominent lineages. The more important the city, the higher stood its ruler in the hierarchy of Shang dynasty lineage heads. The royal family at the top of the hierarchy resided in the capital city. Of the seven or more capital cities of the Shang period, the best known are Cheng-chou, built about 1650 B.C., and An-yang, the capital after 1400. Rulers in these capitals commanded the allegiance of lineage heads in cities throughout the agricultural areas of north-central China.

Effective control of a local area in highly ritualized Shang China and in early Chou China depended on establishing in a city symbols associated with lineage power. Chang Kwang-chih has described how the walled nucleus of the city was built as a planned unit in which importance was attached to the "construction of the ancestral temples and the placement of the lineage treasures in them."[2] Specialized craft quarters and farming settlements supplying products and labor to the rulers surrounded the planned core of the city. The presence of a wall around the palace and ceremonial centers and the size of the wall were physical manifestations of the spiritual achievement of the ancestors of the ruling lineage. By revering the accumulated achievements of his ancestors the head of each lineage demonstrated his right to rule. Carefully ordering the symbols of rule in the city was an important step in controlling the surrounding territory.[3]

Change in the ruling lineages occurred in approximately 1100 B.C. when the Chou people from Shensi province conquered the Shang territory. Placing their capital farther west, the Chou divided control over a larger area than the Shang had ruled by investing relatives and other warriors with land. The levels of Chou walled cities ranged from the *kuo*, with the temples of the supreme lineage of the state, to the *tu*, with the temples of the grand lineages, to the *tsung-yi*, with the temples of aristocratic lineages.[4] The lords of the tu and the tsung-yi, as vassals of the Chou rulers in the kuo, built rectangular walled cities on level plains near the center of transport of their fiefs. From these cities they provided military support for the Chou claim to territory while ruling the fiefs as their own private property. These three kinds of cities should not be conceived as three levels in a hierarchy of administrative centers, but rather as the centers of separate loosely related fiefs.

By the time the Chou capital was moved to Lo-yang in Honan province during the eighth century B.C. the importance of the capital in the sprawling Chou empire was weakening. Already city-building had been extended to the territories of many provinces of present-day China. Development centered in the mid-Yellow river valley, followed by other areas nearby, and south along rivers connecting to the Yangtze river. In the next few centuries notable cities would appear south of the Yangtze as well. Traditional ties of family relationships and feudal loyalties were losing their effectiveness in binding the lords of separate fiefs together. Although acknowledging the hegemony of the Chou ruler, local lords fought to increase the size of their own domains. Two new kinds of cities developed out of the transformation of Chou feudalism: state capitals and hsien cities.

During the centuries of internecine wars and shifting administrative boundaries victorious lords set up state capitals (level 2) to consolidate control of larger areas. New classes of ministers (*tai-fu*) and warrior-officials (*shih*) congregated in these cities. In addition, artisans and merchants began to gather outside of the walled enclosures. As early as the Shang dynasty groups of craftsmen who concentrated on bronze-casting for the narrow needs of the small number of aristocracy had lived near cities. Now iron was becoming available for more widespread use. Artisans made tools for the rulers to supply large-scale irrigation projects and to distribute to peasants for improved agricultural production. More intensive agriculture was essential for increasing the rulers' incomes, which in turn sustained growing city populations. Rulers depended upon merchants for importing goods not available locally such as salt and luxury items. A second wall was added to expanding state capitals.[5] As before, the palaces and temples were located within the inner walled area, while the added outer wall enclosed new residential zones and areas of crafts and commerce.

To administer expanded territories lords introduced hsien cities (level 5). As the old rules of warfare were abandoned the distance between privileged lineages in the cities and peasants in the countryside was narrowed.[6] Reliance on conscription of peasants became a feature of the military system. Officials in hsien cities organized corvée and military services and sent some tax revenues to their rulers in the state capitals. Construction of networks of roads and canals improved movement and transport between hsien cities and state capitals. Located at communications nexus and at the center of lowland areas, hsien cities provided a means for direct control of local areas from the state capitals. Despite changes in rulers the sites chosen for these local cities were practically continuously occupied until the imperial unification in 221 B.C. and thereafter for 2,000 years.[7] Hsien cities served as nearly constant rungs in the developing hierarchy of cities.

The Warring States period, an era of longer and larger wars, began in about 450 B.C. Development of increasingly populous state capitals corresponded to the growing wealth and territory under successful lords. Large states had capitals with tens of thousands of inhabitants.[8] As the number of state capitals fell, the number of hsien cities increased. Since wars were no longer battles on the open plain but were more and more a series of seiges of cities culminating in the seige of the capital city, granaries, some farm land, a water supply, and a larger population had to be supported within the walls. Thus, in the Warring States period, the inner wall was gradually neglected while the outer wall became the center of defense.

The changing structure of the Chinese city was only in part a reflection of its increasingly diversified population, of more bureaucratic administrative practices, and of defenses against new military tactics. Chinese cosmology even before Confucius was developing toward an acceptance of reality in which man was expected to act harmoniously in order for all the elements of the universe to function together smoothly. Reacting to the breakdown in the customs of Chou society, Confucius helped to universalize ethical conduct, which he attributed to the Chou aristocracy, as harmonious. He valued rituals as devices which insured that ethics were applied.[9] From at least the third century B.C. those influential in carrying on the traditions of Confucius' teachings stressed the use of rituals to organize man's life. The ritualization of society included planning cities so that important elements were arranged according to preconceived regularities. Choosing the site, laying out the city, placing the palace and administrative offices, and specifying areas for marketing activities were all the concern of the developing corpus of rituals.[10] During the Han dynasty, the guide to city planning in the *Chou Li* incorporated many of the structural features of Warring States cities. This book, together with the body of city-building skills passed down among artisans, preserved methods of arranging cities all the way to the Ch'ing period.

Ancient Japan

Agricultural settlements developed about 2,000 years later in Japan than in China. During the last centuries B.C. the number and size of settlements increased as simple techniques of cultivation were introduced. The extension of Han dynasty influence to nearby Korea was the source of more rapid change in Japan. Wet-field rice cultivation and the use of iron tools spread initially from China to northern Kyūshū island and by the first century A.D. large villages existed over much of Honshū island as well. These villages were less self-sufficient and had more division of labor than the earlier hunting and gathering communities in Japan.[11]

During the first centuries A.D. hundreds of small states were formed in Japan. The foundation of each state was an *uji*, a union of people within adjoining settlements through kinship or fictive kinship ties. From the third century A.D. the custom of erecting large earthen burial mounds for former uji leaders indicated that within many states a great capacity existed for mobilizing labor and material resources.

From the third to the fifth centuries rulers of the Yamato state unified uji throughout Japan. A court formed around the palace of the Yamato ruler. Gathered there were Buddhist temples, Shinto shrines, and aristocrats upon whom graded ranks were conferred. In contrast to China—where even if a city had to be moved a short distance it retained the same name and identity—the Yamato court locations changed with every new ruler without leaving any evidence of large settlements. Although the efforts of the Yamato court succeeded in reducing warfare and in integrating the uji of Japan, a city had not yet developed at the court's location.

The Yamato state was reorganized in the seventh century. Much had been learned in preceding centuries from embassies sent to China, from Chinese and Korean immigrants, and from Japanese returning from the Chinese colonies in Korea. Craft skills and a written language had been introduced from China. Finally, the establishment of the *ritsuryō* system after 645 raised the position of the Yamato ruler to the head of an imperial system based on Chinese techniques of land distribution and administration. Increased control of resources by members of the imperial court and officials associated with it was reflected in the development of capital cities.

Between the years 645 and 710 many capital cities (level 2) were constructed and soon abandoned. Some sites were probably outgrown by the influx of population into the capital. Prominent families, particularly from the Kinki region in which the capitals were located, moved to the cities seeking official position and influence. Representatives of temples and shrines, who as well as titled family heads, managed to keep some private land holdings, also sought recognition at court. Most prominent families continued, however, to keep a rural residence. Some capitals were probably abandoned as being too far from the areas in the Kinki region (especially in Yamato kuni) in which these influential families were concentrated.[12] Perhaps the two most famous of the early short-lived capitals were Naniwa (Osaka) and Fujiwara.[13] The planned city of Heijō (Nara) was entered in 710, marking a transition to the development of more permanent capitals.

Early Imperial China

In the process of unifying China under its first emperor in 221 B.C. the Ch'in armies destroyed many of the capitals of rival states. The founder of the dynasty personally inspected cities, determining which were to be destroyed and which were to remain. The country was divided up into *chün* (a political division containing two or more hsien) and hsien. Representatives of the central government settled in the administrative centers of each of these divisions. Prominent families were required to move to the new Ch'in capital at Hsien-yang in Shensi province. Great mobilizations for building and conquests characterized the brief Ch'in dynasty, but when Emperor Shih Huang-ti died civil war quickly followed. The capital city was burned with the fall of the empire.

The founder of the Han dynasty set up a new capital in about 200 B.C. at Ch'ang-an in Shensi province. At first, approximately two-thirds of the large Han empire was divided into independently administered kingdoms, but within a century Han rulers successfully reunited China under central control. Ch'ang-an became the first long-standing capital (level 1) of imperial China.

The city of Ch'ang-an was the center for three types of commodity distribution: taxes, monopolies, and private commerce. Most important were incoming taxes in kind to support the military, the court, and the bureaucracy. Supplies were needed for costly military campaigns and for numerous troops stationed around the city area to defend against nomadic intrusions from the northwest. At times conflict over the control of revenue entering the capital pitted officials against each other and against the inner-court relatives and eunuchs upon whom the emperor often relied. Craftsmen and merchants were dependent on selling their products in exchange for the redistribution of government revenues in the nine markets supervised by officials inside and outside the city wall. More than in later dynasties, the population of the capital was dependent on government revenue.

Government monopolies were reestablished during the Han period. Particularly important were monopolies on salt and iron, goods produced in limited areas and required by large numbers of people. Monopolies on these goods brought in revenue to the capital and also gave officials control over the supply of two essential military needs.

The third form of distribution was private commerce. Luxury items intended for the government-supported population of Ch'ang-an arrived over new trade routes from distant areas of the Asian mainland. Most famous was the Silk Route from Central Asia. Long-distance commerce was too costly to serve the daily needs of the populace, which could only afford necessities brought from areas near Ch'ang-an or made within the city to be sold in the official markets. Those in the city who were neither government employees nor their servants depended on merchants to supply such basic items as grains and firewood and to some extent they supplied themselves, cultivating vegetables on plots within the large area enclosed by the city wall.

Compared to other premodern periods the Han dynasty was a time of considerable expansion of the population of China and of the area in which Chinese lived. Most of the hsien capitals which existed in Ch'ing China were established by the end of the Han dynasty. In north China many of the chün (level 4) and hsien capitals were former cities now rebuilt as part of the expanded administrative network. New cities appeared in Hopei province to the northeast and along waterways connecting to the Yangtze in central and south China. Even in Kwangtung, in far southeastern China, twenty-two hsien capitals were founded.[14] A census of the year A.D. 2 gave the population of the enlarged territory of Han China as 60 million.

It is likely that Han period hsien cities were isolated from each other. In areas of China where population was still sparse, scattered villages within the hsien had poor communications with the local city. Chinese settlers may have been attracted to the hsien city and villages in its vicinity while non-Chinese peoples avoided official exactions in remote areas. The military outposts in hsien cities best protected nearby areas.

Officials sent to hsien capitals in north China often came into conflict with the heads of powerful local families, striving to avoid taxes and to protect dependent peasants from corvée duties. To the extent that titled families with hereditary rights and tax exemptions brought together land as their private military bases, hsien officials were limited in control only to the land holdings outside of these bases. Eventually, deteriorating tax revenues meant weakened control of central cities, especially from the late Han period.

In the first century A.D. the Eastern Han dynasty reunited China with Lo-yang as its capital. The Western Han capital of Ch'ang-an had reached roughly 250,000 in population and Lo-yang was probably somewhat smaller.[15] To support these capitals and secondary capitals, as Lo-yang had been in the Western Han, canals were constructed linking Ch'ang-an to the Yellow river and both cities to grain producing areas further east in China. Many large chün and hsien cities appeared along these transport routes.[16] Lo-yang itself was an important transport center on the Yellow river.

Cosmology was given a new role in Han China. It was believed that magical power had aided in the rise of the dynasty and an elaborate system of correlative thinking emerged. In city planning numerology played a part in determining the number of wards into which the city was divided and greater significance came to be attached to geographical symmetry.[17] The more extreme symbolism reappeared only rarely in cities of later dynasties, but the building of carefully planned cities divided into rectangular areas remained a model in China—a model rigidly applied in imperial Japan. The cities of Heijō and Heian more closely fit the ideal T'ang dynasty city than any actual Chinese city.[18]

Cities rose and fell during the more than three centuries of intermittent warfare and short-lived dynasties from the third century A.D.[19] After the migration of large numbers of Chinese south many of the great Yangtze area cities first prospered. Nomads devastated the cities of north China and then settled there, seeking with Chinese help to recreate the prosperous cities of old. Some of their centers of government became large capital cities (level 2). Lo-yang, the capital of the Northern Wei dynasty which ruled all of northern China, was larger in size and population than the capitals of the Han dynasty.

The example of Northern Wei Lo-yang is illustrative of the changing capitals of post-Han China.[20] The spread of large land holdings brought an influx into capital cities of absentee landlords, independently supplied from their own lands, yet more dependent on commercial exchange than the wealthy in Han capitals.[21] Northern Wei rulers were more congenial to private commercial activities than had been Chinese rulers. In each direction from the market areas in Lo-yang appeared streets with stores grouped by specialties. Craftsmen gathered in the city to produce luxuries for the wealthy landlords as well as for officials. Buddhist temples appeared as conspicuous centers of consumption. In other respects the capital retained Han features. For instance, the gates to the closed residential wards (*fang*) were still locked at night.

China was reunited in the late sixth century under the Sui dynasty. Establishing the capital once again in Ch'ang-an, the Sui built a great canal enabling the newly developed wealth of the Yangtze area to be transported to the capital. Land was divided under the equal-field system, providing an improved fiscal foundation in comparison to previous dynasties. Nonetheless, large holdings continued to supply private resources for the consumption of representatives of powerful families and temples.

The three centuries of T'ang China can be conveniently divided into two periods. From the middle of the eighth century city controls became less rigid and marketing and urban population became less concentrated. These changes mark the beginning of the period I have chosen to call middle imperial China. The conditions of the early T'ang dynasty are more clearly seen in continuity with those prevailing in the Han dynasty.

A hierarchy of four levels of cities was nearing completion in the seventh and eighth centuries. More than 1,200 hsien cities existed at level 5. Total hsien population varied considerably, but generally must have been less than 80,000. Normally, the officially controlled market in the hsien city was the only market to serve these people. Highly self-sufficient villages in the rest of the hsien sent grains, cloth, and other taxation in kind. Some of these goods were distributed as pay to officials in the city, who would sell what they did not consume in the market. Other tax revenue was also sold locally or sent to nearby soldiers, but much of it was forwarded to officials in cities higher in the hierarchy. Villagers also provided corvée, which was still of great importance in local administrative efforts.

Chou (prefectural) cities and remaining chün cities were T'ang dynasty level 4 centers. Officials stationed in each chou city governed a number of hsien (five hsien was the average). A chou city ordinarily had one official market serving a larger local concentration of population than the hsien market. The principal chou cities were transportation centers on important rivers along which taxes in kind were shipped.

Tao (circuit) cities were first established in the T'ang dynasty. The number of tao into which China was divided varied, but generally there were more than ten tao, each of which had a principal administrative center. Chengtu in Szechwan and Canton in Kwangtung were tao capitals (level 3) known as great centers of regional or foreign trade. The gradual rise of tao cities must be seen in connection with the development of some of these same centers as capitals of short-lived dynasties before the Sui period and with the growing commercial prosperity of cities which were not capitals.

At the top of the hierarchy of cities were the primary capital of Ch'ang-an and the secondary capital of Lo-yang. In the seventh century the plan of these cities showed the clear supremacy of administrative controls over the movement of services and resources. As in the Han period, a strict system of wards persisted in T'ang Ch'ang-an, providing control of movement at night and at times of civil disorder. Most of the more than 100 wards in Ch'ang-an measured between 500 and 1,000 yards per side with about 2,000 households located within. Lo-yang also contained more than 100 wards, but in a total area about two-thirds the size of Ch'ang-an, indicating that the wards were probably less populous.[22]

Although in some respects the ward system had changed from the

Han period to the T'ang period, cities continued to be highly ordered. Whereas Han wards had only one gate, T'ang wards generally had four. Moreover, certain residences of aristocrats and temples in the city could now have a private gate to the street. In the two T'ang capitals commercial activity was confined to two or three market areas, the officials of which sought to supervise thousands of shops grouped by specialty. The gridiron street plan into which the capitals were divided—rectangular wards surrounded by intersecting main streets—likewise reflected the orderliness of the early T'ang city.[23]

Imperial Japan

Headquarters of ruling uji (such as the one of the Yamato court) had developed as the principal settlements of Japan during the centuries preceding the Taika Reform of 645. The needs of the ruling uji were not met by a large concentrated population, but by dispersed subordinates. The uji rulers did not have imposing walls built to focus attention on the temporary seats of their rule. Finally, in the seventh century the process of consolidating the many uji centers became evident in a succession of short-lived capitals. A small court of hereditary nobles moved with the transferring capitals, but much of their wealth continued to be spent at rural residences.

The eighth century capital of Heijō (level 1) reached a population of 200,000.[24] In a country having about 10 percent of the peak population of Han or T'ang China, the sudden emergence of a large capital city deserves careful attention. One explanation might be found in geographical differences between the two countries. Although Japan had a much smaller population, a far greater percentage of its people had close transportation ties to the capital region. A comparison might be made with the large capitals of independent states in preimperial China which also had a high concentration of urban population in one city. In contrast, resources from many areas of imperial China could not be sent to any one city without enormous costs; consequently, more local cities were needed to improve the central government's control of labor and production.

As transportation improved, it became possible to supply larger capital cities. Given the state of the transportation network in eighth century Japan, it is likely that Heijō was overwhelmingly dependent on just the Kinki region and adjoining provinces. Similarly Han Ch'ang-an and Lo-yang were not able to receive many supplies from most areas of China, and only when the rich Yangtze valley became linked by canal to Ch'ang-an, did its population during the T'ang period probably exceed 1 million.[25] The Japanese capital of Heian (Kyoto) in the ninth and tenth centuries grew to as many as ½ million people, benefiting also from improved transportation ties.[26]

The sudden development of large capitals in Japan suggests that the requisites for a centralized imperial system—which took 1,600 years in forming after the appearance of the first city in China—had, in fact, been forming in preurban Japan. Borrowing from China required an advanced social foundation on which to build. Presumably because such a foundation did exist in Japan, Heijō and Heian were comparable not to Chinese cities shortly after the beginning of urban development in China, but to Ch'ang-an in the Han period and even in the T'ang period. If more information were available about preimperial Japan, we would undoubtedly find exceptional characteristics for a preurban people.

Following the example of Chinese institutions, Japanese divided their country into two levels of local units. At the bottom level were *gun* whose capitals ought not to be considered cities since they were not closely incorporated into the administrative network and could have contained no more than a few hundred people, most of whom were engaged in agriculture. The heads of prominent local families were often recognized as gun leaders, responsible to officials at the next administrative level in *kokufu* cities (level 5). From the beginning Japanese demonstrated the propensity to extend administration down to smaller units than existed in China.

Once the Chinese-style capital was introduced in Japan it existed in an environment where there was a near absence of local cities. Kokufu cities contained the largest concentrations of population outside of the imperial capital. The three principal islands of Japan were divided into more than 60 *kuni*, the capital of each of which was called its kokufu.[27] The kokufu were generally located at central points on plains; many were river or ocean ports. The closer a kokufu was to the imperial capital, the greater was its scale and importance. Dazaifu in northern Kyūshū was an exception: government organs were placed there to control foreign relations with Korea and China as well as to provide administration for all of Kyūshū, including eight other kokufu. For a time the kokufu city second to Dazaifu was remote from the capital in the opposite direction. It was a predominantly military city in northeast Honshū island where the Ainu minority was being driven north by the Japanese.

The plan of the imperial capital and of the kokufu cities as well was largely borrowed from China. Heian, which replaced Heijō and the short-lived city of Nagaoka as capital, most clearly demonstrated the Chinese model. This city was a rectangle of about ten square miles which was completely filled by a grid plan. Unlike Chinese cities it did not have a large outer wall. The structural element in it which was most obviously Chinese was what John Hall has described as "a series of walled enclosures within walled enclosures."[28] Three areas interrupted the monotonous pattern of walled rectangular wards: a large rectangular area in the north-central sector of the city which embraced the palace compound, official buildings and other structures containing the ceremonial and material possessions of the court, and two large marketing areas in the east and west which were similar to the markets of T'ang Ch'ang-an.

From the tenth to twelfth centuries the system of land division and allotments degenerated, thereby in turn undermining the basis of the flow of manpower, tax grain, and other goods to the capital. Private means of control came to eclipse the elaborate central bureaucracy in Heian. Titled officials and representatives of temples and shrines competed to acquire increasing amounts of tax-free land for themselves which they organized into manors called *shōen*. Heian remained a large capital because absentee shōen lords concentrated there. Nevertheless, as the relationship between the imperial government and the shōen lords was changing, this city (now at level 2 because the country was decentralized) was also gradually transformed.

The shift from exchange under state agencies to exchange primarily under shōen lords in Heian affected the structure of the city. Ward divisions broke down. Prior to this time strict market controls had resembled those in early imperial China, i.e., laws for markets placed them under officials who supervised prices and weights, graded goods according to type, recorded standard prices every ten days and compiled annual records.[29] Now marketing broke out of the confines of officially delineated and regulated areas. Streets with shops were concentrated in new areas of the city. Craftsmen organized into guilds under the protection of a temple head or of a prominent lord. Bands of *bushi* (samurai) moved into Heian as supporters of their shōen lords. In short, strong personal bonds replaced official controls in the organization of Heian.

Although a shōen lord residing in Heian received goods directly from his estates, even if he owned estates in diverse areas of the country, he was unlikely to be able to supply all of his needs. Instead the lord had to rely on urban markets where he could buy goods from other shōen and sell some of his own surplus. One of the attractions of Heian was the high quality of crafts produced there. Only continuous and substantial support from his shōen enabled a lord to purchase these luxuries. The dependence of the capital on private supplies of goods and the growth in the consumption of luxuries in Heian are comparable to developments in Northern Wei Lo-yang and other post-Han capitals. As central governments in both China and Japan were weakening in their ability to tax great landlords, they were losing their ability to order the capital city as well.[30]

Parallel to the decline of imperial control within the capital occurred a breakdown in the administration of local areas. Kokufu cities were disappearing. Since shōen representatives did not send goods to these outposts of central government, the storehouses, public buildings, and other structures of the kokufu became unnecessary. Within unitary sections of shōen, roads were constructed to the residences of representatives of absentee lords; however, the distribution of shōen was so fragmented that no city could appear to replace the kokufu. Some ports (level 3) developed where sizable quantities of shōen goods passed through en route to Heian, but these were collection points close to central cities and far from most localities. The presence of scattered craftsmen and merchants demonstrated that functions previously concentrated in the kokufu and new ones related to growing amounts of commerce and currency were now dispersed over the countryside. Not until the thirteenth century did these functions begin to be consolidated in new types of cities.

Middle Imperial China

The eighth century is commonly identified as a transitional period in Chinese history. The T'ang rulers temporarily lost Ch'ang-an and Lo-yang in the rebellion of the middle of the century. However, once these cities were restored officials enacted fundamental reforms in response to changing economic conditions. They replaced per capita taxes with taxes primarily based on land ownership and thus transformed large estates from tax-exempt refuges to tax-paying holdings. As taxation in cash began to replace taxation in kind in the course of the next few centuries, a growing agricultural surplus came to be sold in local markets. From the middle of the eighth century new taxes were also imposed on commerce, yielding substantial revenues by the eleventh century.

A trend toward decentralization of marketing was apparent starting from the eighth century.[31] Not only were market places in the capital cities less enclosed, but also new areas of commercial activity appeared. As in late Heian Japan, the breakdown in marketing restrictions and the development of a freer street plan accompanied the conversion of large cities from dependence on the consumption of officials and a small aristocracy to dependence on a larger wealthy urban population anxious to purchase goods transported to the city in the least expensive manner and sold in free markets. A broadened base of choosing officials during the late T'ang and Sung periods reflected, and helped select entrants into, the expanding group of newly wealthy families.

Markets formed at two new kinds of locations beyond the walled cities: (1) outside one or more city gates and (2) in villages. The rising demand for food and the dwindling supply of land inside the city wall combined to spur commercial vegetable farming in the vicinity of cities. Other commercial crops were also arriving in increasing quantities to supply city dwellers. In response to these new patterns of supply, markets were founded at the gates of cities and gradually walls lost importance in delimiting the built-up areas of the city.

The expansion of commercial agriculture far from cities led to the development of rural periodic markets. At first, growing local commerce was transacted in chou and hsien cities where the only markets were located. Gradually during the T'ang dynasty rural markets formed at road junctions, along rivers, and at temples. These markets were periodic, meeting once or twice every ten days. Fairs, meeting once or twice a year, were also beginning to appear in some rural as well as urban locations. Villages with periodic markets had existed even before the T'ang dynasty, but the proliferation of hundreds of them from the eighth century became the basis for the development of new cities. These new marketing centers emerged as an omnipresent part of the hierarchy of central places in subsequent centuries.

The breakdown of T'ang administration accelerated the development of an infrastructure for marketing. During the ninth century, army officers formed independent provincial bases. Garrisons of troops called *chen* became the centers of military control in local areas. Since commanders trying to strengthen their control of supplies brought marketing functions to some chen, the term "chen" later often came to mean a nonadministrative city with marketing more active than in ordinary rural periodic markets (level 6 as opposed to level 7). The process of decentralization can be seen in the decline and then the fall of the T'ang capitals for provincial centers under governors and for short-lived capitals of regional dynasties and in the dispersal of marketing and population from chou and hsien cities to emerging chen.[32]

From the T'ang period to the Sung period important changes were taking place in the economic geography of China.[33] During the T'ang period the first substantial urbanization of the southeast coast appeared. Sea transport was improved between Canton and Yang-chou, connecting to the Yangtze river and to the Grand Canal. The chaotic conditions of the tenth century caused less disruption in south China. By the beginning of the Sung dynasty, the center of population as well as of agricultural production in China had shifted south near the Yangtze. During the Sung dynasty the predominance of the Yangtze region and further south was increased substantially by the application of new agricultural techniques better suited to the rich soil and climate there. Denied the prosperity of south China, non-Chinese dynasties occupying the north were doomed to relative poverty. Only beginning from the Yuan period did advances in sea transportation and the extension of the Grand Canal near the northern coast enable the rice surplus of the Yangtze regions to support a growing urban population in northern Shantung and Hopei provinces.

The distribution of commercial taxes in the eleventh century appears to be the best indication of the relative sizes of the cities in the Northern Sung dynasty.[34] Aside from certain minor taxes all commercial taxes were collected in 2,041 settlements. Of this total, four locations were in the four capital cities, 19 were in the capitals of the *lu* (which had replaced tao as provincial level units), at least 232 were in the chou cities and a small number of other higher order cities and the remainder of the tax collection points were in hsien capitals, in cities officially labeled chen and in other non-administrative commercial centers. A total of at least 7,000,000 *kuan* in taxes was collected in these settlements. Lawrence J. C. Ma's calculations show that 170 cities contributed taxes of at least 10,000 kuan and of these 63 cities exceeded 20,000 kuan.[35] Kawakami Kōichi gives the geographical distribution of 137 of the cities which provided more than 10,000 kuan.[36] Four lu with only 19 percent of the chou and 18 percent of the tax collection points contained 40 percent of these 137 cities. The fact that these lu were adjacent to each other in the Yangtze delta and near the Grand Canal demonstrates the more highly urbanized character of that region. Twenty-seven cities yielded taxes of more than 30,000 kuan each. Five bordered the Grand Canal and seven were directly connected to it. Four other cities were along sea routes, while nine were related to border defense in the north.

Commercial tax data can be used to indicate long-run changes in urban populations. At the principal national capital K'ai-feng, more than 100,000 kuan were collected annually. While the fact that K'ai-feng collected less than 2 percent of Sung taxes is clarified by our awareness that much government revenue entered the capital city independently, this amount arriving in K'ai-feng must have reflected a smaller percentage of urban population in the capital than for previous dynasties. Still, K'ai-feng's percentage of city population far exceeded the 4 percent of Ch'ing urban residents living in Peking. Even if Sung China had been 10 percent urban—an amount considerably higher than the percentage in cities in Ch'ing China— K'ai-feng, with 1 million people, would have contained as many as 10 percent of all city dwellers. T'ang Ch'ang-an, with as many residents as K'ai-feng despite a smaller national population probably held at least 15 percent of the urban dwellers. Thus, we see that in the course of Chinese history the proportion of urban dwellers who lived in the principal city was steadily decreasing.

Figures for the top 39 Sung cities apart from K'ai-feng show that they paid 21 percent of the total amount of commercial taxes. Similarly, Ch'ing dynasty population data accumulated in Chapter 5 reveal that the first 38 cities after Peking made up 20-25 percent of the urban total. If payment of commercial taxes was indeed an indication of city sizes during the Sung period, then the proportion of urban dwellers in large cities appears to have remained nearly constant from Sung to Ch'ing China.

Commercial taxes in the area around K'ai-feng ranged generally from 3,000-10,000 kuan per hsien city and from 500-2,000 kuan per chen. Only the chen with the highest tax exceeded the hsien city with the lowest tax in this area.[37] Figures for another chou further from K'ai-feng indicate that 37,000 kuan were collected in the chou city while the highest total for a hsien city was 6,500 kuan and the highest chen figure stood at 10,600 kuan.[38] The prosperity of certain chen is further suggested by the fact that 20 of the 170 principal tax collection points were in chen.

China's internal trade developed from a few luxuries and necessities for survival to widespread commerce in daily needs for the population of an increasingly complex society. Quantities of goods increased as shipping distances widened. Private trade involved not just wealthy landlords, but more and more peasants who directly participated in marketing activities. There was a growing interdependence of settlements; villages were brought into new relationships with hsien cities based on occupational specialization and commercial flow. Yet, during the Sung dynasty long-distance commercial traffic had not yet become an important factor in the development of cities in many provinces. The fact that scattered among the centers with high taxes along the Yangtze were ports with low taxes suggests that fewer goods traveled long distances than in the Ch'ing period.[39] Trade flowed into cities from nearby rural areas and, to a lesser extent, from nearby cities. Not until the Ming period did long-distance trade flourish into a national market.

K'ai-feng was located at the juncture of the Grand Canal with the Yellow river. Although the Yellow river had already become unusable for transportation, the location of a capital at K'ai-feng provided a link between the Yangtze delta reached by the Grand Canal and the great needs of the military in north China. Imports— mainly from the south and east—were consumed in the city, reexported, or manufactured into finished products for one of these two purposes.[40] The city had become part of a widening urban network and served less as a center of luxurious consumption than had previous capitals.

The structure of Sung cities varied with the level of the city. In K'ai-feng and the southern capital there were three walls. The western capital at Lo-yang had two walls, as did most chou cities.[41] Hsien cities generally had only one wall. Where there were two concentric rectangular walls, within the inner walled enclosure were primarily government offices and beyond—between the two walls— could be found commercial streets, periodic markets, residential wards, and some cultivated land. Most hsien cities were two miles or less in perimeter; chou cities were generally larger and lu cities and capitals were encircled by walls reaching up to ten miles or more in length.

The breakdown of the ward system in favor of fewer divisions continued during the Sung period. It was common for a city to be divided into about four *hsiang*, or quarters, e.g., north, south, east, and west or northeast, northwest, southeast, and southwest. Many hsiang later continued under a different name: from the middle of the Sung period the term *yü* became increasingly popular. Also from the Sung period street names were widely used to divide cities into administrative areas.[42] In contrast to walled administrative centers in which the four main streets connecting to the gates of the city often divided the city into four quarters, chen lacked walls and often had only one main street on both sides of which houses and stores were situated.

Private transportation of goods in the Sung dynasty for the first time rivaled public shipping.[43] Government revenues from the central and lower Yangtze regions made up a large part of the supplies of the capital cities and of the military on the borders in both the Northern and Southern Sung periods. In addition, public monopolies on such goods as salt, tea, and wine removed items from private trade. Yet, commercial shipments were growing in necessities including firewood, rice, and oil and in various luxury items.[44] Farmers near large cities in the Yangtze delta increasingly specialized in the production of foodstuffs and raw materials for urban consumption.

The lu in regions of more specialized agriculture generally contained more chen. Relatively undeveloped lu had as few as 19 chen, while others had more than 100. Szechwan lu (the one area for which tax information is not available) formed a separate commercial zone with comparatively numerous chen. The average number of chen per hsien was nearly 3 in Szechwan, but only between 1 and 1½ elsewhere.[45]

The fourth of the great Chinese capitals in which the population rose far above 500,000 and perhaps over 1,000,000 was Hangchow (Lin-an). Unlike Ch'ang-an, Lo-yang, and K'ai-feng, Hangchow was not located in northern China nor was it the capital of a dynasty which controlled as far north as the Yellow river. Supplies to Hangchow were plentiful owing to the proximity of the increasingly prosperous Yangtze delta. This city became the center of rapidly growing cities in many areas of central and south China. While new commercial and craft areas were being added to formerly predominantly administrative cities, resulting in many cases in built-up areas appearing just beyond the gates in the wall, the canals and waterways inside and outside the walls of Hangchow were also emerging as centers of transport and commerce.

Rival dynasties in the northeast or north of China existed throughout the Northern and Southern Sung periods. The Liao dynasty, ruling mainly beyond the Great Wall, had five capitals, including Peking. The Chin dynasty which occupied much more of China within the Great Wall made Peking (Ta-tu) its principal capital.[46] Even before the Mongols established Peking as the capital of a united China in the thirteenth century the city had become the center of tax revenue consumption from much of northern China.

The Yuan dynasty of the Mongols rerouted some of the rice surplus of the Yangtze delta to Peking. Supplying a capital so far northeast in China was accomplished by greatly lengthening the Grand Canal and by improving sea transport to north China. Yet, it is unlikely that Peking's population reached more than about one-half million. Nor was the capital as great a center of private trade as cities such as Hangchow and K'ai-feng during the Yuan dynasty. Similar to the capitals of minor non-Chinese dynasties, Peking was primarily a center of consumption by a large part of the ruling minority.

Unity under the Mongols helped to preserve most of the improvements in private trade which had been achieved in the south during the Sung period. The prosperity which Marco Polo observed in Yuan dynasty cities suggests that urban population quickly recovered after the decades of plunder and destruction caused by the Mongol invasion.

Feudal Japan

Kamakura and Kyoto were the two principal cities of Japan from the end of the twelfth century to the middle of the fourteenth century. Kyoto (at this time called Miyako rather than Heian) continued to be the largest city in Japan, the center of shōen lords who received and consumed there much of the surplus from their estates. The relatively unplanned structure of Kamakura reflected the increasingly feudal nature of Japanese society.[47] Administering feudal Japan, bushi crowded into Kamakura under a *shogun* whose headquarters was known as the *Bakufu*. Since the site of Kamakura was confining for the 100,000 to 200,000 inhabitants, many bands of bushi resided in valleys set back amidst the hills of the city.[48] Large temples were also scattered in the city's outlying valleys. Supplying the needs of the bushi and priests were artisans and merchants, who occupied the level coastal areas. Governmental controls persisted longer near the coast, where shops of the same occupation were required to concentrate in special areas. Nonetheless, the location of Kamakura far east of the seats of imperial administration separated it from the traditions of Chinese-style city planning.

The first substantial development of cities which were not primarily administrative occurred in Japan during the Kamakura period, as it had in T'ang China about 500 years earlier. Ports in the Kinki region developed as large cities, ranking next to Kyoto and Kamakura in size. Some ports such as Yodo, Ōtsu and Hyōgo (Kobe), which had previously functioned as transshipment points in the transport of taxes in kind to imperial ministries and of shōen goods to absentee lords, now acquired marketing significance as more and more shōen goods were sent commercially. Shōen lords found it more efficient to purchase products with cash received for the local sale of their estate revenues than to ship goods directly to their residences in Kyoto. At least equal to the new ports in commercial importance was Nara, a Kinki city with about 10,000 people, including many priests receiving a steady income from temple shōen. Areas near Kyoto and Nara favored by the proximity of cities became centers of specialized commercial agriculture, augmenting the demand for rice in the Kinki region. Absentee lords encouraged shōen administrators to increase income by producing foods and raw materials fetching the highest prices. Near cities vegetables were favored, while farther out—where local conditions permitted—raw materials needed for textile production were grown. For most areas, however, rice remained the most profitable crop. Rice markets prospered in Kyoto, Nara, and major ports.

Accompanying the growth of ports in the Kinki region, periodic markets, which met, as in China, one or two days in ten, were established in most areas of Japan. Markets formed at administrative centers within shōen and along water and land routes. Shōen goods were converted into cash in these markets, and large quantities of goods were then transported to intermediate port cities and sold there for higher prices corresponding to the more numerous population in the vicinity which was not self-sufficient. By the beginning of the fourteenth century, the commercialization of shōen agriculture had resulted in the widespread formation of periodic markets.[49]

New commercial areas developed not only in ports and in shōen but also at post stations on main roads and near the gates of famous temples and shrines. Post stations had existed in earlier periods in Japan as well as in China, and some of them developed as commercial centers in both countries as part of the widespread formation of periodic markets. Pilgrimages to temples increased in popularity during the Kamakura period, a time of mass acceptance of Buddhism. Market areas were established in front of the gates of some temples, leading to the name *monzenmachi*, literally a town in front of the gate. Monzenmachi became important in supporting their patron religious sects as income from shōen was falling.

In some ways the fourteenth century in Japan resembled the ninth and tenth centuries in China. Agricultural production was rising, local markets were springing up, and commercial spheres were forming, linking cities and periodic markets in villages. Chinese periodic markets were quickly incorporated into the hierarchy of central places; the brief independence of chen in the divisive decades of the Five Dynasties period was ended with Sung unification. In Japan conditions remained decentralized. While absentee lords became increasingly divorced from local areas, some found new sources of currency by taxing exchange in shōen periodic markets and by patronizing guilds of merchants and craftsmen in cities. Local exchange developed as wealthier peasants, local bushi, and shōen administrators purchased portions of the agricultural production to distribute themselves and for their own consumption.[50] For about three centuries this pattern of scattered urban activities in small communities typified feudal Japan.

Cities were becoming less orderly. No longer were roads carefully located as part of an overall plan nor were marketing areas clearly defined. The structure of cities reflected growing divisions in leadership. Bushi bands and armed priests joined nobles with reduced incomes owing to the loss of control over their shōen in confused patterns of urban control. Scattered craftsmen and merchants sought the protection of guilds, patronized by the powerful in return for services. Eventually guild leaders emerged as additional disputants for control of the city.

The rise of guilds as cooperative groups highly independent in the administration of urban areas is another similarity between post-T'ang China and Muromachi Japan, but on closer examination a difference is apparent. Especially during the fifteenth and sixteenth centuries Japanese guilds achieved a measure of self-government unknown in Chinese history. Forms of urban government approximated the "free" cities of feudal Europe, with administrators chosen or elected from the guilds or temples of the city. Until new patterns of central administration appeared toward the end of the sixteenth century, experiments in self-government were occurring in many Japanese cities.[51]

During the fourteenth and fifteenth centuries Japan was an unstable feudal society. After Kamakura was destroyed in 1334, the new Muromachi Bakufu centered in Kyoto was unable to provide as firm control over local administration. Gradually absentee owners were squeezed out in favor of local bushi, who consolidated control over previously fragmented shōen. Already in the thirteenth century, some so-called castles had been built at strategic points near mountain valleys or on the edges of plains. These were really more often similar to fortified houses than to the elaborate multistructured wooden complexes known as the castles of later Sengoku lords. Castles were of military importance for the small group living within, but did not yet form the nuclei of larger settlements. With the breakdown of the shōen system castle construction flourished. By the late fifteenth century a single kuni might have hundreds of castles as close as two to four miles apart in lowlands as well as in mountainous areas. Bushi lords competed for control of local lands, organizing networks of branch castles under one central castle.

While the local political head was moving from a shōen village to a castle, the local market was developing as an economic center independent of absentee lords and shōen boundaries. Locations of castles influenced market locations since bushi in castles needed markets to sell goods collected as taxes in kind. Over most of Japan markets were predominantly on the borders of plains in or near mountainous areas, but were not yet concentrated on the most efficient routes of transport. In the advanced Kinki region, however, markets were more centrally located because taxes were being converted to cash payments, causing peasants responsible for paying them to bring their goods to markets for exchange. By the end of the fifteenth century, castles and markets had proliferated throughout Japan, resulting in the separation of administrative and economic functions from the ordinary villages of the shōen and the enlargement of local commercial demand and exchange.

The principal cities of the Muromachi period continued to be Kyoto, Nara, and nearby ports, though not Kamakura. Weapons and luxury items made in these cities were increasingly sent to local concentrations of bushi, as consumption was decentralized from lords in big cities to bushi scattered over the countryside. The new consumers were still dependent on better quality products from Kinki area cities, producing an unprecedented rise in commerce from central cities to local areas. In return, local products continued to be sent to these cities. Intermediate ports in this enlarged two-way flow also grew as centers of new crafts to meet the needs of local bushi. Sakai in the Kinki area and Hakata in Kyūshū had more than 10,000 residents. Throughout Japan smaller ports expanded, facilitating market exchange. New transportation routes connected to the country's main artery, the Inland Sea, and to the overland traffic between the Japan Sea and Kyoto, linking the port of Tsuruga to Japan's greatest city via Lake Biwa.

Kyoto was practically destroyed in fighting at the end of the fifteenth century. The Muromachi Bakufu, which had been struggling for power in the city through customs controls, sumptuary laws, taxes on granaries and sake houses, and regulations on rice prices, now lost control over city administration.[52] In the decades that followed the Ōnin war of 1467-77 the emperor and court nobles (*kuge*) remained in Kyoto, but the city declined to one of the lowest population levels in its 700 year history. Kyoto's commercial elements had to compete with those in other cities to supply the emerging Sengoku *daimyo* (lords) scattered over Japan. Gradually in the sixteenth century Kyoto revived with a different position in a new hierarchy of cities.

Ming China

Organizing military and civilian forces was the first step in establishing a dynasty. The founder of the Ming dynasty extended his control by enlarging the area which his soldiers occupied. First came fighting off rivals, including the remnants of Yuan dynasty control. Then came setting up an administration in the last decades of the fourteenth century. Years of civil war were quickly replaced by demilitarized and recentralized patterns of administration. By 1400 the effects of war and bad government were remedied. The population of China was rising again to more than 100 million. Tax revenues were climbing to a new high as more land came under cultivation.[53] Administration was now more authoritarian than in the Sung period, but the small bureaucracy of approximately 12,000 civilian officials, 16,000 military officials, and 50,000 subofficials continued to rely on considerable self-government within the society.[54] The administrative classification of cities reached a form, which with some minor changes such as the division of a few *sheng* (provinces) and the addition of a small number of hsien was to be carried over until the waning decades of the Ch'ing period.

During the early years of the Ming dynasty the population was officially classified into three categories. Unlike the racially distinct four classes of the Yuan period, the Ming divisions separated military and artisan families from the rest of the population to provide hereditary services. Yet, both soldiers and craftsmen increasingly evaded service and registration of their families' supposedly fixed occupations. These categories were dropped by the Ch'ing period. For the most part we can think of Ming and Ch'ing China as an open society with rapid mobility into and out of the primarily administrative cities, where the bureaucracy was located.[55]

Nanking, which had frequently been a capital in periods of national disunity and remained a large city in the Yuan dynasty, served as the capital of China for the first decades of the Ming period. Then, from the beginning of the fifteenth century to the fall of the dynasty in 1644, the capital returned to Peking, while Nanking dropped to the position of secondary capital. The choice of a capital was not based on the level of economic development in the surrounding region, though good transportation ties to economically advanced areas of the country were essential, but on strategic factors.[56] Except for early Ming Nanking all the capitals of united China were located in the north where the threat of invasion was greatest. Moreover, capitals moved from west to east—from Ch'ang-an to Lo-yang to K'ai-feng to Peking—as the concentration of nomadic forces and of Chinese population shifted in that direction. During the Ming period defense of the empire required stationing great numbers of soldiers along the northern borders. Peking was ideally situated as an intermediate point in the line of supply from the rich agricultural areas of the country to the border garrisons. Prior to the Ming period Peking had not been under the firm control of a centralized Chinese government for more than 500 years, but as Chinese control was strengthened and lines of transport to the city were secured, the logic of moving the Ming capital to reunite the centers of military, civilian, bureaucratic, and court consumption prevailed.

Not only were the Ch'ing capital of Peking and the pattern of other administrative centers established in the Ming period, the transportation network between these cities was also greatly developed. The Grand Canal built during the Yuan dynasty served as the link between the consuming north and the producing south. Rice and luxuries of all kinds were transported on tens of thousands of ships from the Yangtze delta to Tientsin and on to T'ung chou just outside of Peking. Many cities spread along the Grand Canal: in Shantung Lin-ch'ing and Tsi-ning stood out; north of the Yangtze in Kiangsu were Huai-an and the salt center of Yang-chou; along the lower course of the Grand Canal were large chen—some with as many as 10,000 residents; and on opposite sides of the Kiangsu-Chekiang border were Soochow and Hangchow, which joined Nanking as the level 2 cities in the Yangtze delta with hundreds of thousands of inhabitants.[57]

Connecting to the Grand Canal were flourishing sea routes along the coast of southeast China and the even more heavily traveled course of the Yangtze river. Next to the rich lowlands in Kiangsu (part of Southern Chihli sheng in the Ming period) and Chekiang, the areas most advanced in commercial agriculture were scattered in Fukien and Kwangtung sheng along the southeast coast. Imports from foreign trade, semitropical fruits and sugar were shipped from Canton, Foochow, and other ports in this region to cities in the lower Yangtze delta. Up the Yangtze beyond Nanking the principal mart was Wuhan (a combination of three cities within a few miles of each other), the center of trade from Chungking and Chengtu farther west, Sian (Ch'ang-an) in the northwest, and Nan-ch'ang, Ch'ang-sha, and Ching-te chen in the south. Almost all of the major cities of China were readily reached from the Grand Canal, the southeast coast, or the Yangtze river and approximately half of the thirty largest cities in the country were situated along the three waterways.[58]

Land routes connected small cities throughout China and large cities especially in northern China. Small-scale local transport moved along roads uniting central places at levels 5 to 7. Busy post stations on these roads developed into marketing centers, although in the Ming period many of the stations were combined, with the result that those remaining were generally in hsien and chou cities. Middle-distance commerce passed between *fu* (level 4) and sheng cities (level 3). Cities at these levels were less populous where rivers were scarce and transport was costly. Exceptions were border cities such as Ta-t'ung, a center for trade with the Mongols and for shipments to Chinese military fortresses. The system for transporting grains to the northern garrisons required Shansi merchants to pay the enormous costs of supplying the soldiers by land in return for salt certificates, enabling them to distribute salt at monopoly prices in specified regions of China. After 1644, the main roads serving commercial and military transport as well as the principal Ming waterways remained without much change as the transportation network of Ch'ing China.

The Ming dynasty was the great age of wall-building. Large walls had taken on symbolic importance as reinforcements of the presence of effective government.[59] More than 1,000 walls ranging in length from over 1,000 miles (the Great Wall) to about 1 to 2 miles (most hsien city walls) were constructed or reconstructed during the Ming period.

Along with the middle of the Chou dynasty—when hsien cities first appeared—and the middle of the T'ang dynasty—which saw the spread of periodic markets outside of administrative centers—

the middle of the Ming dynasty merits our attention as a critical time in the development of Chinese society and cities. Four interrelated changes can be identified in the mid-Ming: (1) the sustained growth of agricultural production and population which lasted into the Ch'ing period, (2) the change in the tax system, (3) the development of handicrafts, and (4) the spread of central places.

The introduction of the sweet potato, the peanut, tobacco, and new strains of rice and tea enabled marginal lands to be cultivated and existing plots to be more intensely farmed, thus supporting a larger population and a more commercialized agriculture.[60] At first population growth was notable in north China, but by the middle of the Ch'ing period most sheng north of the rice belt were approaching their maximum populations before the twentieth century. It was chiefly in south and central China that improved agriculture spurred cumulative population growth. The six northernmost sheng (there were eighteen in all of China) which had previously contained most of China's populace dropped below 30 percent of the total population during the Ch'ing period.

Taxes for labor services were merged into the land tax creating the Single Whip system, which was the culmination of a process of change going back several centuries. Urban residents, now less fearful of taxes, unearthed their caches of money and enjoyed more ostentatious consumption.[61] Fixed statuses were freed, corvée was replaced by hired labor, and taxes were increasingly paid in currency.

The third noteworthy event of the mid-Ming period was the development of handicrafts. Nearly half of the city of Soochow was filled with looms. Textiles also were manufactured in large quantity in Nanking and Hangchow. Ching-te-chen pottery was an exceptional example of an industry in one city capable of supporting hundreds of thousands of urban residents. The tendency, first apparent during the Sung period, for commercial areas to develop outside of city gates continued. In rural areas of Kiangsu and other advanced provinces cottage industries spread, using the part-time labor of peasants, including women and children.

Finally, the Ming period should be remembered for the development of marketing settlements. Periodic markets spread from their earlier concentration in the Yangtze delta to new areas farther south, west, and north. Meanwhile in the Yangtze delta many periodic markets became daily markets, prospering as small, predominantly commercial cities.

The concentration of specialized agriculture and crafts in a few areas indicates that long-distance commerce was now much more important than in the Sung period. From the Chia-ching reign in the middle of the sixteenth century "sprouts of capitalism" were growing in China, to adopt one current cliché describing the phenomenon.[62] Domestic transport advanced to the point where the country by the seventeenth century formed a national market not just in luxury items, but even in such necessities as grain. Out-of-the-way inland periodic markets entered a wider network of transport for a mass market. Long-distance commerce expanded over large areas of China.

By the beginning of the seventeenth century a hierarchy of seven levels of cities existed in China. At the top was Peking. Next came Nanking and other regional centers. At level 3 were sheng capitals and at level 4 fu (prefecture) capitals, similar in number and jurisdiction to the chou of Sung China. Below at level 5 were hsien capitals; at level 6 chen or intermediate markets, and at level 7 ordinary periodic markets.

Sengoku Japan

The sixteenth century in Japan is known as the Sengoku period, a time of warring states which, as in the period's namesake 2,000 years earlier in China, were combining to form fewer and fewer administrative entities. The population of Japan was rising from near 15 to 18 million, probably not far below the total in China in the Warring States period. Moreover, the total urban population in cities with at least 5,000 people must have been roughly similar, the edge going perhaps to preimperial China, which was dotted with large state capitals. Yet, Japan in the sixteenth century was reaching a stage in city development comparable to Ming China. The widespread presence of periodic markets, the growth in long-distance commerce, the increasing proportion of craftsmen and merchants in city populations, to some extent even the reliance on self-government in organizations within cities were characteristics shared with Ming

China, not the Warring States of preimperial China. Japanese urban functions had reached their most decentralized state. The preconditions for sudden city growth, like those 1,000 years earlier, were again concealed. By the end of the sixteenth century Japan had entered perhaps the most remarkable period of urban development of any premodern country.

Identified with the Sengoku period was a new kind of city evolving in areas throughout Japan. *Jōkamachi*, or castle cities, were initially places to resist enemies and, gradually, also centers for the control and mobilization of the resources in the lord's domain. Reflecting indigenous conditions where authority coincided with local military power, the urban activities previously scattered over the domain were increasingly concentrated in the jōkamachi of the primary lord.

The origin of the jōkamachi may be traced back to the Kamakura period when Japanese cities were first built not according to a plan borrowed from China, but corresponding to personal bonds in a feudal society. As castles emerged during the fourteenth and fifteenth centuries, the tenuous control of absentee lords faded, while their former supporters strengthened independent local bases of power. After the divisive wars of the late fifteenth century, Sengoku daimyo arose, squeezing out absentee interests and struggling with each other to rule compact areas with more complete control. The various institutional innovations to provide these daimyo with a stronger hold on their vassals contributed to the development of castle cities.

Two prerequisites for the development of jōkamachi were the unification of local control vis-à-vis the outside and the consolidation of local bushi under a powerful lord. At the beginning of the sixteenth century land in local areas was divided among many claimants with varying degrees of control over its revenue. At the end of the century a single lord, the daimyo, had direct and nearly uniform control over an entire domain. The lands of absentee lords were largely confiscated. Bushi were gradually removed from villages and restricted to a fixed stipend. Gaining unquestioned administrative authority over villages, daimyo undertook land censuses to determine the productive potential of each village. Thorough knowledge of conditions in each village aided the daimyo's quest for firm control over a large part of local production.

The first jōkamachi already existed in the early Sengoku period. Outside the daimyo's castle were residences of his chief retainers, with groups of lower vassals attached to them, but ties between the daimyo and retainers were still weak. A lesser vassal might possess a larger house than one with a preferred status under the daimyo; the relation of the bushi to his daimyo was not yet the sole determinant of the former's income and style of life. Some of the lands of the chief retainers were located near the castle, in which case their subordinates were a combination of peasants and bushi, serving as tillers of the soil and warriors as the situation demanded. Bushi areas of these early jōkamachi resembled villages since their residences were mixed with peasant dwellings and fields.[63]

The early periodic markets had only a small number of participants, mainly individuals to whom a large amount of land was consigned and under whom many peasants tilled. As the productivity of labor increased, the number of people directly participating in the market economy grew. Also, as daimyo gave security to larger areas of land, marketing spheres were reorganized with a greater concentration of markets in areas of high productivity. Relatively developed marketing centers gradually acquired permanent stores. These level 6 nonadministrative cities were commonly called *zaikatachō*.

During the sixteenth century many market areas merged with castles.[64] At first craftsmen of products required for military preparation were the only commercial population in castle settlements. The distinction between bushi and jōkamachi artisans was unclear, since some of the craftsmen, and later merchants, given special responsibilities by the daimyo were organized into retainer bands. Gradually the commercial population established stores in castle settlements, striving to satisfy the daimyo's two imperatives: to develop crafts and trade in order to supply the growing bushi population in the castle area, and to strengthen central control over commercial activities within the domain. Just as the retainers in these early jōkamachi were dispersed, the merchants and artisans also were not yet grouped by occupation. Both the bushi and the commercial residents in the jōkamachi kept independent contacts with farmers in surrounding villages. Thus prosperity in the jōkamachi was limited by the fact that bushi still receiving goods directly from their own lands and perhaps farming some land had limited need for the commerce of a city.

Jōkamachi were steadily increasing in size during the sixteenth century. Growing concentrations of bushi in castle cities provided daimyo with greater control over their troops. For a time mainly the top retainers of the daimyo lived in residences near the capital while other principal retainers and most lower bushi lived in branch castles or in villages under the lord's control. But daimyo who were successful in expanding their domains required increasing numbers of bushi to join them in one central city. Abolishing branch castles was a continuous process contributing to the growth of the main castle settlements.

Early sixteenth century markets depended on bushi in nearby castles to provide protection. During the middle of the century, however, new policies were adopted by daimyo to free markets from the interference of bushi within the domain and from the exclusiveness of guilds (za) in the Kinki region.[65] Extending their control over domain economies, daimyo strengthened their military positions. Merchants and artisans freed from the exactions of nearby bushi became independent of all except the daimyo. New organs of control placed those active in markets within the domain subordinate to merchants inside the chō (commercial areas) of the jōkamachi. As markets were reorganized to meet the needs of daimyo, days when periodic markets met were adjusted so that overlapping days did not injure markets under the same lord. Rising opportunities in the chō of the jōkamachi attracted merchants and craftsmen from within and beyond the domain.

Frequently the daimyo possessed about one-quarter of the land in his domain and bushi held the rest, although the exercise of control by bushi came to be restricted as they transferred their administrative rights over the land to the daimyo in return for rice stipends.[66] The daimyo received for administrative and personal use taxes from lands scattered in areas of military importance and high productivity throughout the domain.

As daimyo increased their economic control over growing domains, they were able to obtain more currency for purchasing
weapons and other goods from the ports and principal cities of the
Kinki region. Craftsmen in these central cities now produced for the
entire country and transport flourished. Raw materials arrived in
Kinki cities from areas best endowed for their specialized production.[67] Somewhat in the pattern in the Yangtze delta during the
Ming period, the Kinki region filled with rural areas known for
particular kinds of commercial agriculture and with zaikatachō
where goods were processed. Typical daimyo did not appear in these
advanced areas; castles there were absorbed into marketing locations
and not vice versa.

The process of absorbing local castles and markets into one central
city slowed the increase in the number of central places. From the
thirteenth to the sixteenth centuries the number of such settlements
had risen rapidly. Harada Tomohiko estimates that the total number
of urban settlements climbed to between 500 and 600.[68] This figure
seemingly includes the early jōkamachi, major branch castles, ports,
periodic marketing settlements, and *jinaichō* (temple-centered commercial cities). Apart from Kyoto, which recovered in the sixteenth
century from its temporary nadir, and some ports, there was little
continuity in these "cities" which rose and fell as local conditions
fluctuated. The early jōkamachi generally were abandoned either
with the defeat of their lord or as the lord expanded his domain and
his central control over it. In the middle of the sixteenth century
cities were still small. Except for Kyoto, only large ports such as
Sakai and Hakata reached more than 20,000 population. Few other
cities exceeded 10,000. The largest jōkamachi of this period, including Odawara in the Kantō region, Fuchu in the Tōkai region, and
Yamaguchi in the Chūgoku region, had populations of roughly
10,000.[69] The rise from small urban settlements was just beginning.

From the middle of the sixteenth century more orderly jōkamachi
were developing. Reflecting the daimyo's need to closely control and
to protect the entire domain, castles were abolished in favor of one
castle city centrally located with good transportation ties to the most
productive areas of the domain and, if possible, to the Kinki region.
Relying on customs barriers to make the domain more unified and

self-sufficient, daimyo protected local crafts by excluding most outside goods not essential for military needs. Relatively closed domains may have hindered the growth of large cities for a time, but they spurred local development of communications and crafts. Protectionism favored the diffusion of advanced skills from Kinki area cities to emerging jōkamachi.

Oda Nobunaga and Toyotomi Hideyoshi preceded Tokugawa Ieyasu in unifying the lords of castle cities throughout Japan. Their policies laid the foundations for Tokugawa administrative divisions and urban control.[70] Nobunaga asserted control over many Kinki cities, repressing the self-governing commercial population of ports, which remained vital centers of interregional trade. Hideyoshi went further, placing the major ports including the newly flourishing cities of Osaka and Nagasaki directly under his control.[71] Later during the Tokugawa period certain ports and other strategic cities continued to be directly administered under the Bakufu independent of daimyo control.

The unifiers of Japan extended the subjugation of daimyo from military to commercial dependence. Holding essential commercial cities, they carried out policies designed to improve marketing relationships between areas throughout Japan. Daimyo could not control their domains as independent closed economies because more than 10 percent of the country's agricultural production came from Hideyoshi's holdings scattered in the midst of their own lands.[72] Distant daimyo were given land in the Kinki region to help meet expenses in the central cities. Most important, increasing obligations under Hideyoshi speeded the flow of tax revenues to Osaka to be exchanged for cash.

Replacing the short-lived castle city of Azuchi under Nobunaga, Hideyoshi built his jōkamachi first at Fushimi next to Kyoto and then at Osaka, while at the same time controlling Kyoto and rebuilding it into somewhat the form of a jōkamachi.[73] Although Tokugawa Ieyasu established his administrative center—sometimes called the largest of the jōkamachi—at Edo in the Kantō region and eliminated large daimyo such as those existing in the Chūgoku and Kantō regions under Hideyoshi, he continued to possess dispersed lands throughout the country, especially in the Kinki region where control was vital over the nexus of the emerging national market. As the temporary capital of Nanking in Ming China had served a useful function in the formation of a national market centered on the Yangtze delta, so too did the Sengoku administrative centers of Nobunaga and Hideyoshi in the advanced Kinki region play a role in overcoming earlier dispersion.

Late Sengoku jōkamachi city plans reflected the growing power of daimyo over their domains. During the last quarter of the sixteenth century the localism of bushi was greatly reduced. By 1600 only a small number of branch castles remained and even at these locations the bushi had lost much of their former independence. Correspondingly, bushi were no longer spread out throughout the jōkamachi. They were distributed according to rank in specified areas of new jōkamachi carefully planned and prepared in advance for the transfer from another jōkamachi.[74] Chō set aside for the commercial population were also finely divided, separating families according to their places of origin and their occupations. In these new cities merchants and artisans served mainly bushi consumers. Temples and shrines also were brought into special areas of the jōkamachi under daimyo control.

Both Osaka and Nanking were short-lived national administrative centers in advanced areas. In the 1580s a large castle was constructed in Osaka, symbolizing the central administration of Hideyoshi. Costs were assessed not only to the personal retainers of Hideyoshi, but also to daimyo throughout Japan. The transition from Osaka to Edo resembled the move from Nanking to Peking. Transport between much of Japan and Osaka continued to flourish and traffic along the route between the Osaka area and Edo developed rapidly as had traffic along the Grand Canal from the region dominated by Nanking to Peking two centuries earlier.

In the 1590s Edo, Osaka, and Kyoto were all entering a new era of prosperity. Hundreds of castle cities, some not yet in their final location, were developing throughout Japan. The consolidation of domains and the growth of the national market were progressing rapidly. City plans were revealing an orderly hierarchy of statuses. These trends reached maturity after the founding of a stable, centralized administration in 1600.

TABLE 2

Development of Central Places

	Ancient China / Ancient Japan	Early Imperial China / Imperial Japan	Middle Imperial China / Feudal Japan	Late Imperial China / Sengoku Japan
	1 2 3 4 5 6 7	1 2 3 4 5 6 7	1 2 3 4 5 6 7	1 2 3 4 5 6 7
China	x	x x x	x x x x x	x x x x x x
	x x	x x x	x x x x x	x x x x x x x
	(ca. 1850–220s B.C.)	(A.D. 750)	(-1360s)	(-1644)
Japan	x	x x	x x x	x x x x x
		x x	x x x x	x x x x x x
	(ca. A.D. 640s–710)	(-1180s)	(-1470s)	(-1600)

Summary

In the preceding pages I have divided the history of cities in China and Japan into four stages each, further noting developments requiring subdivisions within many of the stages. To clarify comparisons between the two countries, I have assumed that all cities fall within one of seven levels. Table 2 indicates the order in which central places at these levels appeared in each country.

The first cities were at level 2, the capitals of loosely united federations of kinship groups from various regions within the narrow boundaries of the country at that time. Cities at this level in China soon proliferated as fief centers. In contrast, during this first stage of Japanese history only one level 2 city was found at a time. From the beginning Japanese experienced city growth in more concentrated forms.

The fact that the earliest capitals of preimperial China formed at a time of less advanced social differentiation than in seventh century Japan may help explain the presence of walls encircling Chinese cities, but their absence in Japanese cities. Protecting the ruling lineages in early Chinese cities, walls symbolized a chasm between their members and the rest of the population that was wider than any in Japan. The long bronze age in China may have been the time when those controlling bronze artifacts separated themselves from the rest of the population. The bronze age was much shorter in Japan, where heads of uji waited long into the iron age before departing from the close proximity with their subjects afforded by rural residences. Another possibility is that early Chinese cities were rebuilt by conquerors, ruling alien peoples.[75] In any case, exercise of power became identified with urban living in China, but not in Japan.

Level 5 cities remained a nearly constant element of Chinese society for more than two thousand years. Even when individual hsien cities were destroyed, they quickly were rebuilt or others were founded to replace them. Hsien cities originated at a time when rising social mobility was undermining the previously acknowledged hegemony of certain early Chou families. Residing in these cities were officials loyal to the lord of a level 2 or a level 1 city, based on the lord's ability to draw into his administration people largely without independent sources of power. No social transformation similar to the one in mid-Chou China occurred in Japan. Except for roughly one or two centuries during the early Heian period, Japanese local officials were unable to assert their independence from eminent local families. Thus the transformation to an imperial state was never complete and kokufu cities (level 5) enjoyed only an ephemeral existence. Yet, continuity of leaders may have facilitated rapid development and made it possible to avoid the divisions that often slowed Chinese progress. The failure of kokufu cities in Japan enabled subsequent decentralization of urban activities as a shortcut to completing the hierarchy of seven levels of central places.

In China a large imperial capital was first built around 220 B.C., about 1,600 years after cities originated. Level 1 cities gave way to level 2 cities in periods of division only to reappear with the establishment of unified dynasties. In Japan a large imperial capital was suddenly built after less than a century of city-building. Incipient urban development must have lasted for many centuries before Japanese cities formally appeared. After roughly three centuries of existence, level 1 cities disappeared in Japan until the Tokugawa period, when the seven-level hierarchy was completed. The cyclical pattern of centralization as seen in the presence of level 1 cities had only two crests in Japan.

Of course, a basic condition for additional city formation is increased agricultural production. The agricultural surplus—and in emergencies even some of the food required for the subsistence of peasants—can be redistributed in various ways. At one extreme the peasant family could enlarge its consumption to eat up all that is grown. In this hypothetical case no specialized outside administrators exist and there are no cities. Although social differentiation may be widespread in villages, redistribution of the agricultural crops occurs without cities. Such was the case in Yamato Japan where the vestiges of social development that so dramatically gave rise to urban Japan were concealed.

Redistribution without cities may have been carried further in Japan than in China, but the dawning of the imperial age brought a new centralization of urban activities carrying the Japanese far from the extreme of the self-sufficient farming family. Early imperial China and imperial Japan approached another hypothetical extreme where a small number of lords and officials representing the central government appropriate all of the surplus. One large level 1 city developed in which merchants and artisans served a dense concentration of lords and officials. The limited commercial economy in the city was tightly controlled. Large capital cities in Han China and Heijō and Heian Japan corresponded, not to the agricultural surplus of the surrounding farm land, but to the inflow of goods from a central tax. The government was gathering the surplus and sending it, where possible, to the capital city. In China level 4 and 5 cities, developing gradually from preimperial cities, served to promote central administration locally. Similarly, level 5 cities existed in Japan at this time.

Similarities can be found in changing Chinese cities from the Han to the mid-T'ang periods and in Japanese cities from the tenth to the twelfth centuries. The imperial government was losing some of its control over the surplus. Now cities were being transformed with the rise of the commercial economy of absentee landlords. Some ports were developing into cities as shipments of agricultural goods to these landowners and growing luxury transport joined tax revenues en route to level 1 and 2 cities.

Comparisons also seem fruitful between thirteenth century Japan and eighth-ninth century China and between Muromachi Japan and Sung-Yuan China. Adding level 7 central places in the thirteenth century, the Japanese had already narrowed the Chinese lead to 500 years. Then in the fourteenth and fifteenth centuries the appearance of level 6 cities in Japan came only about 300 years later than in China. The addition of levels 6 and 7 should be regarded as an important transition in social history. Level 7 central places, appearing first, brought urban activities within the purview of ordinary villagers. Level 6 cities were needed to provide a closer link between level 7 and previously existing levels.

Unlike shipments of tax revenues which with difficulty can bridge the enormous gap between levels 1 and 5, commerce requires a more complete hierarchy of urban levels to flow smoothly. If level 7 central places exist without level 6 cities, then only a tenuous marketing link can be maintained between the countryside and the substantial cities of at least level 5. During the fourteenth century in Japan and the ninth and tenth centuries in China level 7 central places did exist bereft of level 6 intermediaries and widespread local instability dogged the scrambling efforts to join level 6 to level 7. Once central places at both of these levels had been founded, they provided a foundation for sustained commercial development.

Whereas in Japan there were only two levels of cities above levels 6 and 7 and both of these levels were remote, in China there were four previously established levels including levels 4 and 5. The presence of levels 4 and 5 in China restricted the possibilities for development of the emerging low-level central places. While the hierarchy of Chinese cities was nearly intact at the top when the bottom levels were added, in Japan levels 4-7 were added successively from the bottom up. Beginning in the thirteenth century these four levels plus level 1 appeared at the rate of one new level each century. Periodic markets in China first developed with two more levels of cities present than in Japan. Thus, although the feudal period in Japan was similar to the middle imperial period in China because levels 6 and 7 were added and because cities at higher levels acquired freer forms and commerce grew rapidly, the rate and sequence of change in the two countries was markedly different.

The rural-urban dichotomy prevailing throughout the Tokugawa period can be traced back to the long history of a few cities at high levels in an environment of few secondary cities. The distribution of Japanese settlements was bimodal; population was concentrated in ordinary villages and in large cities. In contrast, at least from the middle imperial period it is likely that a continuum, not a dichotomy, prevailed in China. As F. W. Mote has pointed out, walls around Ming and Ch'ing cities did not separate two styles of life. During the late dynasties there were no counterparts to the three cities which stood out as centers of the economy and civilization of Tokugawa Japan. Clearly no one city was as significant a center of Chinese civilization as was Kyoto in pre-Sengoku Japan.[76]

Departure from the countryside occurred in stages in Japan. Waves of migration are noticeable beginning with the assembling of kuge (aristocrats) in seventh century capitals and continuing until the gathering of bushi in Sengoku and early Tokugawa cities. In China those who lived in cities came and went, not leaving a city-identifying self-perpetuating urban elite. This difference persisted during the Ch'ing and Tokugawa periods, when Chinese cities were temporary abodes for the upwardly and downwardly mobile while bushi, daimyo, kuge, the imperial family, and select merchants and artisans maintained hereditary positions in specified Japanese cities. One consequence of the historic identification of certain strata with Japanese cities was the persistence of independent sources of authority in such feudal cities as Kyoto. Kuge, temple heads, and absentee lords during the Kamakura and Muromachi periods protected city residents by standing between them and the Bakufu. Even in their capital city Muromachi officials had to struggle to administer diverse urban residents.

The fact that Chinese periodic markets were integrated into the existing hierarchy of cities and Japanese markets were not is critical to an explanation of Ming and Sengoku differences. Locally powerful individuals in Japan used periodic markets to boost their personal positions, and subsequently the success of some of these individuals as bushi and daimyo contributed to the growth of the cities with which they were identified. A single central place could rise step by step from one level to another. In China, however, hsien cities rarely rose to higher levels and there was scant opportunity to shift from level 6 to level 5. From the Sung to Ming periods the power of the central government was growing, but the capacity to order and realign cities was falling. Social stability was kept at the expense of social control. In Japan the power of the central government was falling as cities became more disorderly, but society was being rebuilt. New cities replaced older ones. There was not even much continuity between the castle cities of Shugo daimyo (mainly fifteenth century), Sengoku daimyo, and Tokugawa daimyo.[77] Except in poor areas of Japan cities were not converted from one type of jōkamachi to another, but were replaced by newly built cities.

New planned cities in Japan were a physical expression of a centralized society. The continuation of Edo (Tokyo) as the largest city of Japan in the twentieth century was symbolic of the great continuity between modernizing Japan and its premodern Tokugawa antecedents. In contrast, the rise of a newly prosperous Chinese city, Shanghai, was an indication of the tortuous transition needed before rapid modernization could get under way. Similarly, the rise of the jōkamachi was a sign of a changed society as contrasted to the continuation of the hsien city in China. Twentieth century China needed a sharp break with the past before modernization would be possible and nineteenth century Japan did not. Japan in its feudal and Sengoku periods had already undergone rapid transformation. Differences between Ch'ing China and Tokugawa Japan were underscored by the greater dynamism in Japanese urban growth.

Table 2 reveals similarities and differences in the emergence of a seven-level hierarchy of central places in China and Japan. Level 2 cities could stand alone, but level 1 centralized capitals always were accompanied by level 5 local administrative centers. The addition of levels 3 or 4 signified an increasingly complex distribution of resources, an irrevocable step away from simple forwarding of tax revenues. Commercial growth was indicated first by the emergence of levels 6 and 7 and then by the growth of level 2 regional cities, coexisting with level 1 cities. It should be remembered that typical cities at any level did not necessarily remain constant in size and form throughout the long histories of these two countries. Fluctuation was most extreme in level 2 cities, which originated with small populations and then reappeared in post-Han China and in late

Heian and Kamakura Japan with hundreds of thousands of residents. In general the average population was rising from one stage of history to the next in cities at all levels.

The seven-level hierarchy is a paradigm for premodern development. The further a country had progressed in establishing these levels of cities, the more advanced its economy and society are likely to have been. Charting the appearance of each of the levels permits us to trace a country's development and to compare it to the process of change in other countries. With this approach we have seen that Japan was steadily catching up to China. After cities were founded in Japan they advanced at about twice the rate for cities in China.

Since there was relatively little change in the number and place names of the cities constituting the administrative hierarchy in China, the mistaken impression has been reinforced that Chinese society was virtually static. It is true that in terms of this hierarchy levels 4 and 5, which numbered more than 90 percent of all administrative cities, persisted in China from the Han period. And in comparison to Japan, Chinese cities did develop slowly, but the differences between the societies of Han and Ming China were substantial. The three levels of Han cities are indicative not only of a relatively underdeveloped premodern urban system, but also of an undifferentiated society corresponding to such an urban network. Without levels 6 and 7 regularized commerce could not exist in the countryside. Cities overwhelmingly reliant on tax revenues lacked the pluralism of Ming urban organizations. Without levels 6 and 7, the central capital loomed as a giant in a world in which its masters could subdue but not conquer. To centralize control over resource distribution a developed urban network is a necessary, although not sufficient, condition. The potentialities for centralization were enormously increased during the more than 1,000 years between the Han and Ming periods and in the corresponding interval between Heijō and Sengoku Japan. Comparisons between the societies and the urban networks of Ch'ing China and Tokugawa Japan will reveal how the leaders of Japan, but not of China, were able to utilize these broadened potentialities for establishing a centralized society.

2

SPATIAL DIVISIONS
IN SOCIAL STRUCTURE

During the Ch'ing and Tokugawa periods China and Japan reached the peak of their premodern city development. Yet, even in two such urbanized premodern societies, cities existed in a largely rural milieu. By the middle of the seventeenth century in China hundreds of thousands of villages enveloped more than ten thousand central places. The scale for Japan approximated one-tenth of the figures for China: at least one thousand central places were spaced among the tens of thousands of villages dotting the Japanese countryside. On the one hand, similar patterns of rural-urban relationships mirrored comparable levels of development. In both countries the hierarchy of central places was complete. After Edo emerged as the national administrative center above the regional cities of Osaka and Kyoto the lone hiatus in the hierarchy of cities inherited from Sengoku Japan was filled. In contrast to most countries where these seven levels had not completely formed, China and Japan resembled each other in their urban riches. On the other hand, marked differences existed between the centralized bureaucratic empire of China and the centralized feudal state of Japan. During the seventeenth to nineteenth centuries Japan's cities continued to develop rapidly in comparison to China's steady but pedestrian urban expansion. Although all seven levels were present in both countries, by the early nineteenth century the distribution of Japanese cities in many respects differed from the Chinese distribution. Higher levels of cities were overrepresented in Japan. Standard marketing settlements were exceptionally numerous in China. Differences between the systems of cities reflected varying spatial distributions within the two societies. In this chapter attention is focused on the differential distribution of cities at various levels and on corresponding aspects of social structure.

TABLE 3

Definitions of Levels of Central Places for
the Ch'ing and Tokugawa Periods, by Population[a]

Level		Population
1		about 1,000,000
2		300,000–899,999
3a		70,000–299,999
3b		30,000– 69,999[b]
4		10,000– 29,999
5		3,000– 9,999
6	Intermediate market	less than 3,000
7	Standard market	less than 3,000
	(or jōkamachi without a market)	

[a]Details about how the population figures used in this and subsequent chapters were obtained are presented in the introduction to Part II and in Chapters 4 and 5. Urban populations have been determined by estimating the number of residents in all settlements at levels 1 to 5 plus one-half the total for level 6. This low cut-off point for city populations is chosen for its applicability to premodern societies. Unless otherwise stated, data pertain to the first half of the nineteenth century.

[b]Level 3 is divided into 3a and 3b in order to keep this category from being too inclusive while preserving the division into seven levels comparable to those in Chapter 1.

The above definitions of the seven-level hierarchy of central places are to be used for Ch'ing China and Tokugawa Japan. They are a more precise extension of the levels given in Chapter 1 for periods when data on city populations had become relatively plentiful. The definitions used in Chapter 1, which do not require knowledge of urban population figures, have the advantage of permitting comparisons of many periods with widely varying populations. Those definitions are useful for comparing long periods of time in a single country or many countries, but they are not a fine enough tool for adequate treatment of late premodern China and Japan. For the Ch'ing and Tokugawa periods the second set of definitions presented above enables more exact specification of the distribution of cities.

The Geographical Setting

Geographical setting places limits on any society. By far the greatest part of the national product of large premodern societies is in the agricultural sector. The better the soil, the more sufficient and regular the water supply; the greater the access of usable water transport to areas of high agricultural productivity, the more advantage accrues to such societies. Yet, improvements in man's ability to control his setting—even in premodern periods—can alter and even reverse the advantages that the setting of one society gives over that of another. The Chinese and Japanese were unusually industrious in utilizing their relatively favorable settings.

The amount and location of arable land influences the pattern of cities. China and Japan are both mountainous, though mountains occupy a larger proportion of all land in Japan. The large northeastern plain in China (parts of Chihli, Honan, Shantung, and Kiangsu provinces) has no counterpart in Japan, where the largest plains in the Kantō and Kinki regions are equivalent in size to many smaller intermediate plains scattered over China. Thousands of tiny plains and valleys shape China and Japan. Ch'ing and Tokugawa cities were often found at the center of transportation routes across these plains and valleys.

Both China and Japan were highly stable territorial units during the Ch'ing and Tokugawa periods. Except for rebellions in the first decades of the dynasty and again in the nineteenth century and for foreign incursions after 1840, the eighteen inner provinces—where nearly all of the population and the production of China were concentrated—remained securely under one central government. In Japan the three principal islands experienced no significant military conflict after the first decades of the seventeenth century. Thus there is little ambiguity in the geographical setting of the two societies. In area Japan was approximately the size of a large Chinese province.

China and Japan were self-contained societies during the Ch'ing and Tokugawa periods. China was isolated from other societies by the tremendous territory encompassed outside of its inner provinces, an area from Tibet to Manchuria acting as a buffer with extremely sparse and mainly non-Chinese population. But the degree of isolation did not reach that of Japan. As a group of islands hundreds of miles from ports on the Asian mainland, Japan had never in historical times been invaded. In contrast, China had suffered many invasions and Ch'ing China was ruled by an alien people, the Manchus.

From about 1640 the policy of *sakoku* closed Japan, allowing limited trade with the Chinese and Dutch at an island in Nagasaki harbor and less significant trade with representatives of Korea, the Ryūkyūs and, although illegally, later Russia in outlying areas of the country. Chinese officials also succeeded in strictly regulating foreigners in the Ch'ing period. Unlike the Tokugawa Bakufu the Chinese did not seek to reduce foreign trade, yet, for about a century, they restricted it to Canton. Then in the nineteenth century foreign intrusions became common and the military supremacy of the first countries to begin industrialization produced a system of treaty ports, affecting the existing pattern of cities. Aside from the treaty ports and some cities altered during the brief period of railroad-building at the end of the Ch'ing dynasty, there was little foreign influence on conditions in most Chinese cities. Since my concern is with indigenous cities prior to the effects of contacts with the early modernizing societies, I will exclude cities in late nineteenth century China where extensive exogenous alterations occurred. There is no need to exclude Japanese cities since the arrival of American warships in the 1850s came too late to affect many Tokugawa cities, though it did contribute to the swift demise of the society.

Differences in the degree of homogeneity of the population were also largely determined by the extent of isolation of the two societies. In China lived ethnic and religious minorities of Mongols, Miao, Moslems, Tibetans, Chuang, Kam, Uighurs, and others. The distributions of these peoples varied, but they were generally found in the mountainous areas with little urban development. Moslems, however, formed significant urban communities known for their specialized occupations. Moreover, many Mongols were part of the banner population—the elite military corps which conquered China—residing as a privileged minority in Peking and several other large cities. Of course, Manchus had a special position as the conquering rulers. All Manchu families registered in banners. Some Manchus were stationed in the northeastern outer provinces which were the homelands of nomadic Manchus before they invaded China, but the majority of the banner population was urban. Thus Manchus were far more urban in their residence than any other ethnic group in China. Originally settling in Peking for military and administrative purposes, they came to be enticed by the luxuries of the capital. Similar to bushi in Japan, Manchus lost their martial spirit during more than two and one-half centuries of urban living. The only ethnic minority in Japan, the Ainu, had gradually been forced north onto the frontier island of Hokkaidō where they lived a separate existence away from urban Japan. Japanese *eta* and *hinin* were partly urban segregated minorities, but were not racially distinct.

Accessible transport must be regarded as a principal factor favoring Japan, especially in the late stages of premodern development. Improvements in ocean travel, particularly during the seventeenth century, united Japan in a proximity that could not possibly be attained in China until railroads were built. Nearly all of the twenty largest cities in Tokugawa Japan were located on the ocean's edge or a short distance away by river. Utilizing its comparative advantage in transportation routes, Japan had a powerful impetus for overtaking and surpassing China in interregional trade.

Administrative Divisions

Geography may set the limits, but man has many options for organizing within those limits. In both China and Japan most city dwellers lived in cities designated as administrative centers for the surrounding countryside. The levels of administrative partitions to a great extent determined the nation-wide pattern of cities. When a hsien was divided into two and a new city was designated to be a second hsien capital or when a *han* (domain) was reduced in size, its administrative center decreased in population. The distribution of cities was inextricably tied to the administrative divisions of the country.

Ch'ing China was divided into: (1) the imperial capital of Peking, (2) eighteen sheng (provinces), and (3) outer areas separately ad-

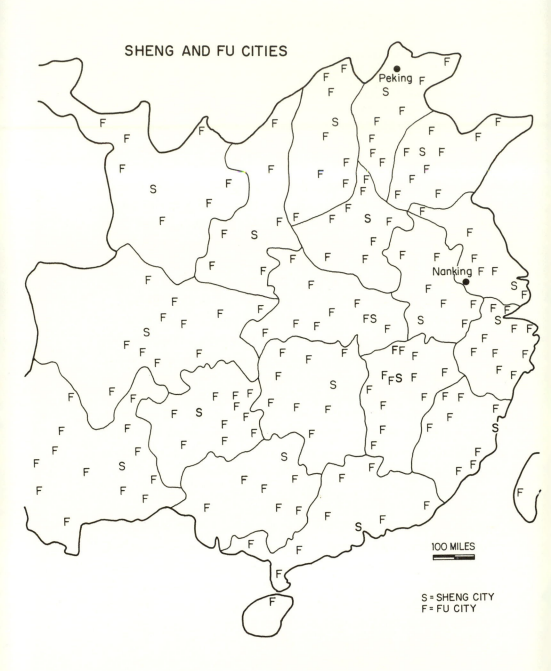

SHENG AND FU CITIES

S = SHENG CITY
F = FU CITY

100 MILES

ministered. Since regular administrative divisions did not apply to the outer areas until the last decades of the dynasty, these areas will be excluded from this discussion. Peking was located in Chihli—the sheng farthest northeast—and was split into two hsien in conformity with the prevalent pattern for large cities in China. The hsien administrations located inside the city served both urban and rural areas as elsewhere in China; however, in Peking's hsien, unlike most hsien centering on cities at levels 3b to 6, most of the residents were urban. Whereas typical hsien officials served populations which were 90-97 percent rural, Peking's administrators operated a primarily urban government.

During the seventeenth century there were only fifteen sheng, but three of these were divided by the early eighteenth century to give Hupei and Hunan in the central part of China, Anhwei and Kiangsu in the east-central region and Shensi and Kansu in the northwest. Late in the nineteenth century when additional sheng were added most boundaries of the original eighteen remained unaffected. Many of these eighteen sheng were geographical entities separated from adjoining sheng by mountain ranges or large rivers. Some sheng contained two or more distinct zones, e.g., a rice-producing south and a wheat- and millet-producing north or an eastern plain and western mountains. Usually the most populous city was the one designated the sheng capital. These eighteen sheng cities, together with Nanking, the secondary national capital in Kiangsu, and Peking stood out as the top twenty administrative centers of China.

Each sheng was divided into 7 to 13 fu (8-11 being most common).[1] A single city, which was usually the most populous in its administrative area, served as the fu city. Following the principle of labeling all cities by their highest administrative rank, I will not count as fu cities the approximately 10 percent of fu centers that served simultaneously as sheng cities. Similarly figures for hsien cities refer only to those cities where the hsien government represented the highest (and only) administrative presence. Although a single sheng capital always contained sheng, fu, and hsien administrative offices, it will only be counted as a sheng city. In the eighteen sheng we can count about 165 fu cities, most of which were centrally located in their administered areas. An idealized map of a fu would show a circle dotted with hsien and chou cities at a radius of approximately thirty miles from the fu city. Large fu consisted of a second more distant layer of hsien and chou cities. Of course, local conditions varied greatly and actual hsien and chou cities could be as close as 10 miles or as far as 100 or more miles from their parent city. If administrative functions had been entirely responsible for the population of a fu city, then the level of a city would have been a function of the number of administrative units inside the fu and of the total population within the fu. However, other factors which can roughly be lumped together as economic account for substantial variations in fu cities. Despite their wide range in population—often from about 10,000 to 50,000—fu cities generally ranked among the ten largest cities of the sheng in which they were located.

Directly beneath the administrative level of the sheng were not only fu cities, but also *chih-li chou* (administered or directly controlled chou). Strategic considerations underlay their choice since these were areas in which it was desired that administration would penetrate more deeply than in fu. Chih-li chou were common in some sheng, yet not present at all in others; the number of them varied widely from 0 to 10, with most sheng containing from 2 to 5. A chih-li chou consisted of a *pen* chou (including the chih-li chou city and surrounding area) and usually 2 to 4 hsien. Altogether approximately 65 administrative centers can be identified as chih-li chou cities. A few of these ranked among the ten largest cities in their sheng, but most fell slightly below the Top Ten, containing roughly 10,000 people.

Chou cities were placed directly under fu cities, while hsien cities were either under fu cities or chih-li chou cities. The chou administrative centers were more unevenly dispersed throughout China. In some sheng there were only 0, 1, or 2 chou, but in others more than 5 chou were distributed between various fu. Some fu contained more than 1 chou. Normally chou cities served larger administered areas than did hsien cities; consequently, the population of chou cities tended to be slightly higher. In all, China contained about 140-45 distinctly chou cities.

More than 70 percent of the administrative cities in China were hsien cities and an additional 10-15 percent of administrative centers acted as hsien capitals while simultaneously serving as seats of higher level administration as well. Some large cities were divided into two hsien and Soochow, the sheng city of Kiangsu, was even split into three hsien. Subtracting these hsien without separate cities and sheng and fu cities which doubled as hsien centers from the figure of nearly 1,400 hsien in Ch'ing China yields a total number of hsien cities slightly below 1,200.

About 50 cities with designations such as *t'ing* and *chih-li t'ing* also ranked as administrative centers. Usually they served areas which were larger but less developed than hsien. Many were found in mountainous parts of southwestern China, the least developed area in China's inner provinces and the area farthest from Peking. Rarely did such remote administrative units give rise to cities larger than small hsien cities. It is convenient for most purposes to treat these minor classifications as hsien cities, disregarding their separate identities.

Altogether there were roughly 1,600 local administrative units in China, including hsien, chou, and pen chou. The number of administrative cities was approximately 50-60 in small sheng and as high as 100 or more in large sheng.

Three commonly recognized parts within most of the 1,600 local areas were: (1) the inner walled city, (2) *kuan*—built-up areas around the city wall, and (3) villages with surrounding land. Located inside the walled city were government offices, residential areas, and main streets connecting the city center to gates in the wall.[2] Stores and open-air markets were found on the main streets either within the wall or in the kuan just outside the gates. Where a river flowed along one or two sides of the wall (often forming part of a surrounding moat), kuan commercial and residential areas frequently developed away from the gates parallel to the river. Beyond the kuan, villages were grouped according to zones, which were labeled by direction, e.g., north, south, east, and west. Large hsien contained more than 500 and in some cases more than 1,000 villages. Small hsien held only a few hundred or even fewer than 100 villages. Of course, not all of the settlements outside of the hsien city were ordinary villages. Approximately 3 percent of the settlements were loci of level 7 central places and nearly 1 percent stood out as level 6 cities.[3] Another 300-500 nonadministrative cities ranked at levels 3 to 5. In a minority of hsien at least one city was more populous than the hsien city. Such prosperous cities might have subadministrative offices, military garrisons, or post stations. The largest nonadministrative cities flourished as processing or marketing centers and many were ports.

Dividing Japanese cities by administrative levels is a more difficult task. Land was administered either under the Tokugawa Bakufu or under the daimyo of separate han. The customary division of daimyo into *shimpan* (Tokugawa branch families), *fudai* (lords allied with the Tokugawa family at the beginning of the seventeenth century), and *tozama* (lords allied only later, after the 1603 battle of Sekigahara) is not useful for comparing han internal conditions. A more fruitful basis for classifying territorial divisions is the *koku* figure (a measure of grain yield) for each of the 240-80 han. The official koku total for Japan in the latter half of the Tokugawa period was 25 or 26 million, though the actual figure must have reached 35-40 million.[4] Of the official amount approximately 7 million koku were directly under Bakufu control, 60 percent of which was *tenryō* land (Tokugawa family holdings) and the rest of which was land administered on behalf of *hatamoto* (direct vassals of the Tokugawa lord living in Edo). The remaining 18 million koku recorded for roughly 255 daimyo were divided as follows: 5 percent of the daimyo held more than 200,000 koku, with the largest daimyo in Kaga han (Chūbu region) holding 1.2 million; 13 percent of the daimyo ruled han of 100,000 to 200,000 koku; 34 percent of the daimyo held han of 30,000-100,000 koku; and 48 percent of the daimyo possessed han registered at 10,000 to 30,000 koku and of this last category two-thirds held below 20,000 koku. Substituting the somewhat more accurate koku total of 30 million for the official figure, the amounts can be revised as follows: Bakufu-controlled lands—8 million; lands of the 50 largest daimyo—15 million; and lands of other daimyo—7 million koku. The disparity in han koku figures was enormous. The combined registered koku yield of the more than 80 han between 10,000 and 20,000 koku reached only the level of the koku yield in the largest han.

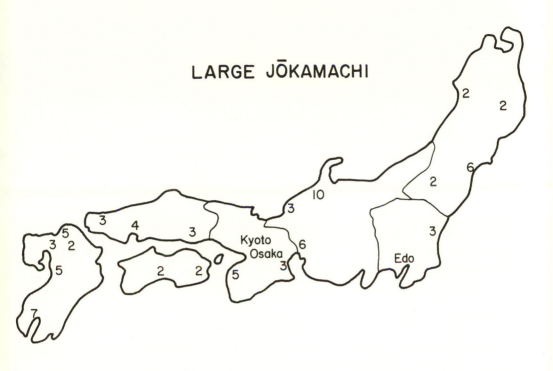

LARGE JŌKAMACHI

100 MILES

2 = 200,000 - 299,999 koku (official amount)
3 = 300,000 - 399,999 " "
4 = 400,000 - 499,999 " "
5 = 500,000 - 599,999 " "
6 = 600,000 - 699,999 " "
7 = 700,000 - 799,999 " "
10 = 1,000,000 - 1,100,000 " "

Seven regions into which Japan can be divided are: (1) Tōhoku, (2) Kantō, (3) Chūbu, (4) Kinki, (5) Chūgoku, (6) Shikoku, and (7) Kyūshū. When further specification is desired, it is common to split Chūbu into Hokuriku and Tōkai and Chūgoku into Sanyō and Sanin. Each of the seven regions was divided into kuni. While the island of Shikoku was comprised of only 4 kuni, the Kinki and Chūbu regions held 15 and 16 kuni, respectively. In all, Japan contained 72 kuni. The amount of koku per kuni varied greatly, from less than 100,000 to more than 1 million.[5] During the late Tokugawa period about half of all kuni contained between 200,000 and 500,000 koku. Kuni were further subdivided into gun, with 50 villages and 35,000 koku in a typical gun. Approximately ten gun made up a kuni. Small han consisted of only one gun or less, while large han contained an entire kuni or more. Sendai han, the largest in the Tōhoku region, sprawled over 20 gun and part of another gun and included 970 villages having an average of 620 official koku per village.[6] If the figures are corrected for the underestimation of koku, then the yield per gun in this han was more than 40,000 koku.

Tenryō and hatamoto lands were distributed predominantly in three regions: the Kantō region where Edo was located, the Kinki region with its advanced economy and large Bakufu-administered cities of Kyoto and Osaka and the Chūbu region where the Tokugawa family han was located before Tokugawa Ieyasu moved to Edo in 1590. Most Bakufu lands were administered by officials such as *daikan* and *gundai* who presided over lots of 60,000 or more koku each.[7] Having only temporary appointments without much independence from Bakufu controls and lacking vassals who could accompany them to their posts, these officials were unable to build cities. The tax which the daikan and gundai collected was forwarded directly to the large Bakufu-administered cities rather than spent partly in local jōkamachi as was the case in nearly all han.

While many of the largest han were located far from the Kantō and Kinki regions, small han were scattered strategically close to and in these two regions of Bakufu strength. Fifty-two of the smallest eighty-one han were found in the Kantō and Kinki regions. Some small han in other regions of Japan belonged to branch daimyo to whom the Bakufu had granted independence from daimyo of nearby large han. Also there were some instances of small daimyo typical of the sixteenth century who kept their domains through the Tokugawa period, though most daimyo were transferred from one han to another in the early period when Tokugawa power was being secured. Han sizes were frequently altered as daimyo moved to new han and a rise in official koku figures corresponded to the development of agricultural productivity. Eleven han could be identified with no city since their lords resided permanently in Edo where they received a specified amount of koku annually.[8] Jōkamachi of the smallest han differed little in size and commercial prosperity from villages. In the largest han, jōkamachi became urban centers second only to the triad of Bakufu central places among Tokugawa cities.

For most han the jōkamachi served both as the seat of administration and as the economic center. A handy rule of thumb is that the population in the jōkamachi equaled one-tenth the number of koku of the han.[9] In every jōkamachi a large proportion of land was occupied by the residences of bushi. Except in the smallest of these cities, there was also an area made up of chō, wards whose inhabitants were merchants and artisans called *chōnin*. Frequently, the third part of the jōkamachi consisted of temples and shrines, most near the periphery of the city.

Jōkamachi were often located at the center of transportation of the han, connecting the villages of the han to transport routes reaching all the way to Osaka and Edo. Generally, the more koku in the han, the more villages there were and also the more numerous were ordinary periodic markets (level 7) and zaikatachō (level 6). In many han the city second in size to the jōkamachi was an ocean or river port. However, a few of the largest ports including Nagasaki in the Kyūshū region and Sakai in the Kinki region were directly under Bakufu control. While some jōkamachi served as ports, others combined their central positions in han with post station functions. Along the busiest roads in Japan some of the largest post stations doubled as jōkamachi.

In Japan administrative order was concentrated at the two levels of the jōkamachi and the central Bakufu cities. In China it was distributed from hsien cities to Peking with varying levels in between.

Japanese looked primarily to Edo as the unifying administrative city. The system of *sankin kōtai*, whereby daimyo were obligated to spend every other year in alternate residence in Edo and to leave their families and some retainers there permanently, added a degree of centralization which did not so much interfere with the internal autonomy of each han as it limited the amount of resources which daimyo could afford to allow uncontrolled within the han. Under constant financial duress in Edo, daimyo were free to choose their own means for regaining solvency. While impoverished daimyo struggled to pay their debts, in China many magistrates became wealthy from less than a decade of service in a few posts. The hsien or chou magistrate who was appointed and faced replacement after three years or earlier was far more accountable for his actions, especially for encouraging the short-term revenue-producing activities and law-abiding obedience of local residents. Yet, the greater accountability in the imperial bureaucracy did not exclude unauthorized assessments. In contrast, the efficiency of administration in Japan did not permit irregular accumulation of private wealth. The fact that in Japan there were two administrative levels and in China four—usually from hsien to fu to sheng and on to the national capital—meant that the former's administrative task was easier.

Land Use

Cities depend above all on agricultural production. What crops are grown and what technology exists for growing them affects the amounts available to take from the countryside and to distribute to people not actually involved in agriculture. In China and Japan some land was used for growing vegetables, fruits, other foodstuffs, and raw materials for small-scale enterprises, but grain production was the lifeline of the two countries. In both countries, areas where rice was grown produced the largest surplus.

Both private and public land ownership existed in China. More than 90 percent of all arable land was owned privately by individual farmers or landlords. Most of the remaining land was divided into three forms of public use. About 60 percent of public lands provided revenues for garrisons of soldiers located throughout China.[10] As in previous dynasties the soldiers farmed much of this land themselves. Banner lands located near Peking made up about 25 percent of public land. Unlike lands belonging to bannermen in Manchuria and Mongolia, the lands in Chihli sheng were tilled by Chinese tenants who sent part of the harvest to bannermen living in Peking. Approximately 10 percent of public lands belonged to imperial estates, which were also concentrated near Peking, especially to the north and east. Imperial lands were divided into about 500 estates in 57 hsien and chou of Chihli sheng.[11] Particularly in this province a large number of villages included public as well as private land. The concentration of public lands near Peking resembled the preponderance of Bakufu lands in the vicinity of Edo. Patterns of land ownership indicate the special concern felt for the capital regions.

Private land in China was owned by heads of families who were under the administrative control of magistrates. Land was regularly bought and sold, in some places leading to the accumulation of large amounts under absentee landlords whose tenants worked on the land. If two or more sons survived when the family was divided— often at the death of the father—land was supposed to be parceled out equally. Even when the amount of the family's holdings was insufficient for such a division, the ideal of equal inheritance operated to reduce the wealth passed on to any one family branch. Although high mortality rates placing constraints on the survival of two or more sons limited actual property divisions, increasing population during the Ch'ing period did result in ever smaller holdings worked with more intensive labor inputs.

Japanese agriculture underwent a momentous change from the late Sengoku to the early Tokugawa periods. The decisive division between bushi and farmers, called the *heinō* split, was symbolized by regulations which, from the time of Hideyoshi, allowed only bushi to carry swords. Of more significance were the restrictions on where the bushi could live, limiting most of them to urban residences. Villages continued to send revenue, mostly indirectly passed on to these bushi, but the bushi no longer played an active role in village life. The Japanese village was consolidated as a unit without bushi interference and thus the villagers could be more tightly controlled by outside administrators. Farmers in Japan generally lacked freedom in choosing their village of residence, their occupation and even the crops they grew. In order to maintain tax revenues, daimyo in the seventeenth century devised policies virtually requiring that "once a rice farmer, always a rice farmer.[12]

Land under cultivation in China was counted in *mou* and in Japan in *chōbu*. These standards are equated as follows: 16 mou = 1 chōbu = 2.5 acres. The total number of mou rose from about 500 million at the beginning of the Ch'ing period to 950 in the mid-eighteenth century and on to more than 1.2 billion in the late nineteenth century.[13] Moreover, mean yields for all grains were rising from below 220 pounds to nearly 275 pounds per mou. In the southeast rice yields exceeded 300 pounds or even 400 pounds per mou, while yields for dry land grains in some northern provinces stood below 150 pounds per mou. Eighty percent of the cultivated acreage was in grain and in some provinces the percentage of land in grains was as high as 90 percent. During the seventeenth century grain output must have measured only about 40 million tons. By the late eighteenth century output had risen to 75 million tons. By the end of the Ch'ing period grain production reached well over 100 million tons with about half of that total from rice.

In Tokugawa Japan the cultivated acreage also doubled. The number of chōbu climbed from about 2 million at the beginning of the period to 3 million in the early eighteenth century and onward to more than 4 million (64 million mou) in the last decade of Tokugawa rule.[14] Most land was planted in rice with one chōbu yielding roughly 15 koku (1 koku = approximately 400 pounds). The rising use of fertilizers and commercialized dry-field crops contributed to the more intensive cultivation of a dwindling proportion of land for grains.

Bakufu and han lands were divided by their lords into villages each of which was assessed a taxable capacity based upon an estimate of the normal yield of land. Furthermore, the village head kept a record of the koku value of the production of each household. When the lord announced the tax rate—generally between 40-60 percent of the registered capacity of output—that percentage of each house's product was then owed to village officials to be forwarded to a representative of the daimyo. In contrast to China, little of the agricultural product was sent to absentee landlords in cities. Rents in cash or kind were paid to others in the village or its vicinity. Unauthorized deductions from tax revenues by those involved in the tax collecting process were also effectively controlled in Japan. Limiting the movement of goods into cities in these ways, the Japanese succeeded in making urban populations more dependent on government expenditures and on commerce.

Per capita consumption in Japan was generally at the level of about 3-4 *gō* of grain per day, which is the equivalent of one koku every 250-333 days. With equal distribution somewhat more than one koku would have been consumed annually by each Japanese. Similarly, in China, well over 400 pounds of grain per capita were consumed annually. For the early nineteenth century the total output of grains per village in both countries approximated 200,000 pounds.[15] If all had been eaten within the villages of production, then the average village population would have been about 350-450 in each country. Yet, not all produce was consumed locally. Redistribution occurred through taxes, rents, and the free market.

Amounts of land owned in both countries varied greatly. Particularly where redistribution is concerned, looking at the mean obscures actual patterns. Nonetheless, the mean figure provides a starting point. In China the mean family used about 15 mou of land, growing 3,500 pounds of grain. Family members required for their sustenance 2,200-2,500 pounds, owed about half of the remainder in taxes and exchanged some in the market, including enough to pay taxes owed in cash. Less land existed per capita in Japan. Although the population per amount of arable land was rising rapidly in late Ch'ing China and practically not at all in late Tokugawa Japan, Japan was still more densely settled. A Japanese family held about two-thirds of a chōbu, which also yielded 3,500 pounds of grain. Of this amount the family members ate, used for fodder, or saved for seeding at least 2,200 pounds. The largest part of the surplus went for taxes to the lord.

Variations in grain output were critical to redistribution in these societies. With the occasional exception of years plagued by extremely widespread famine, first priority was given to tax payments. Those farmers with unusually poor crops or whose land provided their families with only minimal consumption suffered from tax obligations. On the other hand, farmers whose lands proffered bounty harvests often kept large surpluses after taxes. Their options enabled hoarding until prices rose, usury to buy up additional acreage or to accumulate riches, and investment in local commerce and crafts. Both the rich and the poor were tempted by opportunities in cities. The poor could only hope to sell their labor. The rich might invest in a shop or in a shipment of goods to a place where higher prices would more than cover transport costs. While the rich sold their surplus grains to be forwarded to urban consumers, to rural grain-deficit areas, and, if the grain was of the right variety, to rice-wine producers, the poor struggled to subsist on a minimum of land.

In both China and Japan land use in the nineteenth century was markedly different from that in the seventeenth century. Although production still centered on grains, increasing populations permitted more intensive cultivation. Commercial crops such as cotton and tobacco had spread widely. New crops such as the sweet potato, peanuts, and maize enabled marginal lands to be cultivated in China. A critical question is: what happened to the rising agricultural output? In China it was mainly consumed in the village where it was produced or by landlords in nearby villages. Marketing did expand and official exactions must have risen, too, but they could not obtain a larger share of the output. The tripling of China's population was the basic change during the Ch'ing period. Chinese ate up their growing production. In Japan, however, after 1725 there was practically no change in population. While the amount of land per capita in China was falling, the ratio of cultivated land to people was increasing in late Tokugawa Japan.

Demographic Structure

Ch'ing and Tokugawa societies were both large-scale in terms of population. China was undoubtedly the most populous country in the world throughout this period, generally numbering about 30 percent of the world total. Japan's population numbered roughly one-tenth of China's, rising above this ratio in the seventeenth century and falling below it in the nineteenth. China's total rose from between 125 and 175 million at the beginning of the period to more than 200 million in the mid-eighteenth century, to 300 million at the beginning of the nineteenth century, and then to more than 400 million by the time of the T'ai-p'ing uprising in the 1850s.[16] Japan's total started around 18 million and rose to more than 30 million by the middle of the Tokugawa period.[17] There was little increase afterwards as the Japanese population fluctuated between 29 and 33 million. The increase in population was more sustained in Ch'ing China, but both periods represented remarkable cases of population growth for premodern societies.

At the turn of the nineteenth century the Chinese population was approximately 300,000,000 and the Japanese population was 30,-000,000. In both countries administrative units contained differing numbers of people. Chinese inhabitants were distributed approximately as follows: two sheng—30 million; seven sheng—20 million; five sheng—15 million; one sheng—10 million; and three sheng—5 million.[18] The average population of these eighteen sheng was 16-17 million. In Japan regions varied in population from 2 to 6 million, with three regions containing 5-6 million each and two regions holding 2-3 million each.[19] Hsien and chou varied in population from tens of thousands to more than 1 million. The range was similar for Japanese kuni, but the mean population per kuni was more than 400,000, at least twice the figure for hsien. Kuni generally contained fewer people than koku, but exceptions are noteworthy, e.g., densely settled Yamashiro kuni (Kyoto) and Settsu kuni (Osaka) contained about twice as many people as they held official koku. Likewise han population figures tended to be somewhat lower than figures for actual koku production.

Most Chinese and Japanese lived in stem or nuclear families with 3-6 members. A plausible age distribution is that 35-40 percent were below 15 years in age, 45 percent were between 15 and 44, 13-15 percent were between 45 and 64, and 3-4 percent were older than 65 years.[20] If we assume that work units apply roughly as follows: persons under 15 years of age = ⅓ unit; males 15-44 = 1 unit; females 15-44 = ½ unit*; persons 45-64 = ½ unit; and persons

---

* Because females were active in child birth, child-rearing, and housework, they were frequently unavailable for various forms of production.

over $65 = \frac{1}{10}$ unit, then the Chinese population of 300 million included 155-160 million units and the Japanese population of 30 million included 15.5-16 million work units. The ratio of work units to total family size was important in family prosperity. The 70 million families of China and the 7 million of Japan varied both in total size and in number of work units.

Families combined into larger units for some activities and administrative purposes. In China clans served as units of solidarity, particularly in the southeast. The single ideal of the extended family for all classes operated to bind close relatives together even without a formal organization. In Japan main family-branch connections contributed to intravillage and intracity groupings. Officially the *pao-chia* system in China divided families into groups of ten or eleven with a chosen family head representing not only his own family, but also the other ten families in his group. If all China had in fact been divided into this system, then 6 to 7 million pao would have existed. In Japan the system of *goningumi* grouped five families, providing more than 1 million subadministrative units. Varying numbers of these pao-chia and goningumi units comprised a village.

One difference between China and Japan is the fact that the Chinese were able to emigrate while Japanese were not. Especially in southeast China during the nineteenth century migration provided an escape from land scarcity. In contrast, the policy of sakoku in Japan completely closed the country to immigration or emigration.

Some population factors pertained particularly to cities. In both China and Japan an excess of males in prime ages provided a pool of migrants to large cities. A disproportionate part of the city population consisted of male migrants in their teens and early twenties, some of whom left their wives back home while working in the city and others—particularly the poorest men—who did not marry. Women of child-bearing ages who did live in cities were not distributed evenly among eligible males.[21] Concubines, geishas, entertainers, and prostitutes served men wealthy enough to have a wife. Cities did not replenish their numbers and required a constant stream of immigrants both to replace those leaving and to fill the gap between births and deaths.

Stratification

As in other premodern societies a highly skewed distribution of wealth, prestige, and other components of stratification characterized Ch'ing China and Tokugawa Japan. Emperors ruled both countries. The imperial family of Japan was not replaced through dynastic convulsions as in China, but remained for century after century generally quiescent in Kyoto, which after 1600 was the capital in name only. During the Tokugawa period the emperor, his family, and a small contingent of kuge lived in isolation from the actual administrators in Edo. Ideally the Manchu emperors both ruled and administered China. Living in the Forbidden City within the Inner City of Peking, they were surrounded by a large and lavish court. The intrigues and routines of the imperial family, the eunuchs, prominent bannermen, and officials provided the daily fare for an active emperor. The equivalent hub of administration in Japan was the shogun's court inside his castle complex in the center of Edo. Weak shogun, like weak emperors in China, relied heavily on councilors and members of cabinet-like bodies. Struggles for succession and promotion in Peking and Edo run through the histories of the periods.

Apart from the father-son tie the basic nexus of power and responsibility in China and Japan connected the family head and one individual designated as the head of a hsien or han. Magistrates administered hsien with less security and more immediate self-interest than daimyo had in han. The magistrate arrived as an outsider to provide impartial administration on behalf of the emperor. Often instead of refraining from favoritism among his subjects, the magistrate joined with his staff and subordinates to mulct the assets of the area. The bounty was spread among many: lowly runners receiving tens of taels of silver, the higher staff striving for hundreds, and the magistrate himself plundering thousands of taels each year in office. These gains were shared through gifts to higher officials, permitting many in the poorly paid bureaucracy to amass and protect great wealth. Tolerance of irregular assessments netted higher officials a steady income and sufficient revenue to carry on government activities until conditions changed in the nineteenth century. Whether unable or unwilling to reorder Chinese society in the prosperous first half of the Ch'ing period, the Manchu and Chinese authorities relied on an increasingly outmoded fiscal system.

Tax revenues served as a more important vehicle for the redistribution of income in Japan than in China. Generally, 30-60 percent of the inhabitants of a jōkamachi were *buke* (bushi and their families), whose source of income was government stipends. If only to supply these stipends, tax revenues arriving in the jōkamachi had to be considerable. In contrast, Chinese officials and soldiers comprised less than 10 percent of the population in most administrative cities. While quotas deliverable to the central government in China totaled about 4 million tons of grain or their equivalent—some 5-6 percent of the total grain output around 1800—revenue arriving in jōkamachi or sent to Osaka and Edo must have been 20 to 30 percent of the actual output in Japan.[22] I have suggested in Chapter 1 that the greater the proportion of city residents relying on salaries or stipends from tax revenues, the more opportunity officials had to order the city. If that was indeed the case, no wonder jōkamachi were highly ordered and hsien cities were not!

Ideally, China and Japan had contrasting class systems. Japanese classes were closed. A person was born and died in the same class. Practice of primogeniture and adopting out sons who did not inherit enhanced stability. Chinese classes were ideally open. Mobility upward and downward between classes met no officially approved obstacles. Entrance to the bureaucracy required successful performances in a series of competitive examinations open to practically everyone. In fact, the education and wealth essential for years and often decades of preparation limited access as did the lack of aspiration for education among many. Nevertheless, the examination path to success or frustration kept a constant flow of men into and out of the most prestigious occupations in Chinese society. Mobility was more restricted in Japan's administrations. Bushi receiving fixed stipends served as administrators for the Tokugawa shogun and for daimyo. Some scope existed for promoting men of ability among them despite the general practice of maintaining unaltered the stipend of a bushi and his descendants. Two alternate sources of talent, are dubbed by Marion J. Levy, Jr. "civil service by adoption" and "civil service by usury." The former brought talented youth into high administrative posts through inheritance once they were adopted by bushi who were qualified to hold such positions; the latter was a means by which wealthy merchants used loans to bushi to secure behind-the-scene influence. But, with rare exceptions, adopted sons rising to prominence were born in bushi families. Mobility within Japan's highest class contrasted with interclass mobility in China.

Even though open classes in China facilitated geographic and social mobility, conditions of scarcity resulted in a situation where practically each person rising on the social ladder did so at the eventual expense of another man who was falling. Upward mobility was generally blocked in an economy growing at a rate of about 1 percent per year. Similarly Japan's premodern economy did not permit high rates of mobility and closed classes posed a further barrier to movement, but, in fact, there was a considerable flow of peasants into minor merchant and artisan positions and a return flow as well.

While few in either country could enter the leisured elite, many were attracted to the life styles of the elite. In China, as in Japan, the status symbols of the elite were denied commoners, but sumptuary laws were difficult to enforce and, in fact, were largely ignored. By the nineteenth century access through purchase of degrees narrowed the gap between rich merchant and gentry in China.

There were four basic classes in China and Japan: (1) the elite of bushi and gentry, (2) the peasants, (3) the artisans, and (4) the merchants. The bushi class was larger proportionally than the gentry in China. Bushi totaled 6½ percent plus or minus 1 percent of the Japanese population. The nearly 450,000 bushi families lived mainly in jōkamachi and in Edo. Although variations were great, a typical distribution of bushi families found 70 percent in the han jōkamachi, 15-20 percent in Edo, and the remainder at various locations within the han. However, in a few han where bushi made up more than 10 percent of the total population, an unusually large percentage of them lived outside of the jōkamachi. China's gentry was less concentrated in large urban centers. Chang Chung-li's figures for the nineteenth century number the bureaucratic elite as around 100,000 households and the subelite as more than 1 million households.[23] Only the more than 10,000 officials in Peking and a somewhat larger number stationed in the 1,600 administrative centers of China were necessarily urban. Officials at home in mourning, retirement, or between assignments, those waiting for possible appointment, and most degree holders unlikely to be selected usually remained in the places where their families of orientation resided. A large proportion lived in villages and those who were from cities lived in nonadministrative ones as well as in places with officials on duty.

More than 200,000 households of bannermen should also be included in this count of China's elite. Although many of the commoners among the bannermen lived in rural areas outside of Peking, available figures indicate that at least half of all bannermen lived with their families in Peking, receiving at great cost to the government stipends of grain shipped from central, east-central, and northern provinces.[24] Smaller banner garrisons kept apart from the local populations in the walled-off areas of so-called Manchu cities within large Chinese cities. Bannermen were more urban than the rest of China's elite.

Bushi formed a much larger proportion of the Japanese population than the somewhat more than 1 percent of Chinese residents who were in the households of officials, other holders of high degrees and bannermen. Correspondingly, the 6-7 percent of the population living on bushi stipends received about 20 percent of Japan's income, a figure many times the proportion of China's income spent for government salaries and stipends. Bushi in Edo and bannermen in Peking forfeited geographic mobility in return for their stipends. It became increasingly difficult to live within fixed incomes in their urban environments. Particularly low-ranking bushi and bannermen were impoverished by their inability to keep the same percentage of the nation's wealth.

Based on their stipends bushi can be divided into four levels.[25] The top two levels with holdings—not revenue—of more than 1,000 koku and of more than 500 koku respectively consisted of about 5 percent of all bushi. The next one-third of the bushi in many han held more than 100 koku. And the bottom 60 percent had holdings of less than 100 koku. Bushi directly under the Bakufu numbered about 22,000 of whom 5,000 were hatamoto and the rest *gokenin*, inferior in rank. Hatamoto holdings ranged from 15 koku to 9,000 koku. At least two hundred hatamoto held 3,000 or more koku each; thus their lands added up to over 1 million koku. In contrast, smaller hatamoto holdings were split into many villages and each village was divided between many hatamoto. Hatamoto relinquished to Bakufu officials administrative and judicial rights over their lands. Similar variations in koku holdings prevailed among bushi under daimyo.

The Chinese gentry can be divided on the basis of examination degree and bureaucratic rank. The bureaucratic elite with their families consisted of somewhat over 400,000 people.[26] But most degree holders, who with their families numbered about 5 million people, had only lower degrees, not sufficient to qualify for government positions. In fact, those with little prospect for continued success in the examinations frequently had incomes as low as ordinary farmers. For bannermen, the elite of the Chinese military, membership in the twenty-four banners was equivalent to hsien or chou registration for the rest of the Chinese population.

Most Chinese and Japanese were members of families directly involved in agricultural production. A more precise figure for Japan places the number at 85 percent plus or minus 2 percent.[27] This includes roughly 2 percent of the population in fishing and marine activities and 1 percent in transport plus many urban laborers.

It should be noted that as many as 4 or 5 percent of the population officially listed as agricultural were "temporarily" working in cities. Of the 7 million families in Japan, approximately 6 million were farm families. The proportion of farmers in China was probably considerably higher. Indeed, some Chinese farmers actually lived permanently in cities, especially where vacant areas within the city wall were large enough to permit not only part-time vegetable gardening, but also full-time agriculture.

Yet, the proportion of farmers in the urban total of China as well as of Japan was small in cities at all levels from 1 to 4. It is likely that central places at level 5 may often have been inhabited by more than 10 percent who were practicing farmers, but only those at levels 6 and 7 were 50 percent agricultural or higher. For both countries if level 6 central places are treated as half urban (and level 7 central places as rural), the effect of farmers being mixed in with urban population figures is substantially diminished.

The higher value placed on farmers than on artisans and merchants in the four-tier ideal class hierarchies of China and Japan reflected the prior dependence on agricultural output of all in these societies. Dependence on agriculture for roughly 70 percent of the net national income produced meant that the effects of natural disasters penetrated throughout the society. Extreme low-points in the agricultural cycle were times of distress that government policy-makers could not ignore. Some years of poor harvests were not severe enough to shake the callous hearts of administrators, but at times of serious famines, government revenues had to bear part of the loss through remissions of taxes. Concern for stabilizing farm output and especially for preventing fluctuations in urban prices was recurrent in both countries.

The foundation of Japanese and Chinese society was the self-sufficient independent farmer who paid taxes, fed his family, used family labor to meet most needs, and marketed a small part of his crop to obtain cash to buy other nonluxury items at the market. Yet, variations among farmers drove many to one of two extremes. At one extreme fell the poor farmer. Unlike his neighbors, he could not afford any but the cheapest edible grains nor could he save for the important ceremonies of weddings and funerals. Unable to secure sufficient income from agriculture, his recourses were few: (1) to sell land or borrow with a mortgage on his remaining land; (2) to use the labor resources of his family in part-time rural work as hired hands or transport workers or to do put-out work for cottage industries; (3) to decrease the size of his family by adopting out a child, by selling him into some disguised form of servitude, or by infanticide; (4) to migrate to a city, but in times of famine urban prices would be high and the demand for labor low. In Japan the Tenmei (1781-1789) and Tempō (1830-1844) reform periods were ushered in by the arrival of waves of migrants to cities in conditions of severe famine. Even in times of relative calm farmers without land made up a large part of the migrants going to cities to make a living and fleeing from cities for want of success in that endeavor.

Large landowners also migrated to cities, but under different circumstances. In China the pattern of absentee landowners living in cities was widespread, though some family members generally remained at the country residence. After bushi had been removed from the Japanese countryside during the early Tokugawa period landowners remaining in rural areas found it difficult to leave. Japanese were not allowed to live as absentee landowners in cities except under unusual circumstances. During the late Tokugawa period, however, some rich farmers did succeed in entering cities. For example, individuals in the Kantō region who were successful in accumulating wealth through newly expanded commercial agriculture or through the omnipresent squeeze of usury, found new access to cities such as Edo.[28]

Differentiation among farmers was important not only for migration to cities, but also for supplying goods to cities. Whereas in Japan taxes served as the primary form of redistribution, in China the process of moving grains and other commodities from villages of origin was accomplished largely through inequalities in the form of rents and surpluses for marketing. Taxes in China were lower and less efficiently collected. Unlike Japan where about 6 percent of the population relied on stipends from tax revenues, in China salaries, and stipends to officials, bannermen and soldiers reached less than 2 percent of the people. After taxes farmers and landlords in China were generally left with more goods to market than their counterparts in Japan. No wonder level 7 settlements were relatively more numerous in China.

In order to clarify patterns of distribution in China and Japan I have made rough estimates of national income and some of its components, for the beginning of the nineteenth century. Table 4 presents these crude approximations, indicating—after the Chinese population had climbed to over 400 million, thirteen or fourteen times the Japanese figure—the ratio of Japanese to Chinese figures.

With an urban population of nearly 17 percent as opposed to 6-7 percent in China, Japan must have had a different breakdown of its national income roughly as indicated in this table.

Landowners were able to market larger surpluses in China. In the fertile rice-growing areas of East-central and Southeast China, the wealthiest landowners possessed as many as 10,000 mou or more of land. Altogether landowners in nineteenth century China parceled

TABLE 4

Estimates of National Income Produced[a]

(1 koku = approximately 3 taels)

Sources of Income	China (taels)	Japan (koku)[b]	Ratio of Totals for Japan & China (percent)
Agricultural production	1.4 billion	35 million	1:13 or 1:14
Secondary production	160 million	4 million	1:13 or 1:14
Tertiary production	440 million	11 million	1:13 or 1:14
Government revenues	?	12 million	(at least 1:10 and perhaps greater than 1:8)
To cities from countryside	250 million	15 million	(at least 1:7 and perhaps greater than 1:5)
Total	2.0 billion	50 million	1:13 or 1:14

[a]After an earlier draft of Table 4 had been drawn up, I found that E. S. Crawcour had made similar calculations for Japan based on more complete data for the 1860s. In revising this table I have used Crawcour's figures as a reference point, but I have decided, in accordance with Nakamura's work, that a higher proportion of the national income must have been produced by agriculture. See E. S. Crawcour, "The Tokugawa Heritage," in William W. Lockwood, *The State and Economic Enterprise in Japan,* (Princeton University Press, Princeton, 1965), 17–44, and James I. Nakamura, "Growth of Japanese Agriculture, 1875–1920," in the same volume, 249–324.

[b]Although koku was originally a measure for grain, it came to be used as a general standard of account.

out 300-400 million mou, which yielded 30-40 million tons of grain or their equivalent in cash. Considering that landowners tended to pay lower rates of taxes on the production of their lands and to own better quality land, even if they rarely ventured into large-scale investments in commercially profitable agriculture, the amount of their collective income could easily have exceeded 150 million taels. (The price of one picul of rice—133 pounds—was about one tael.) It is likely that 25 million Chinese tenant families paid at least the equivalent of 150 million taels after taxes to close to 3 million families of landowners.

In late Tokugawa Japan land holdings of more than 15 koku, and in extreme cases even exceeding 100 koku, provided a surplus for landowners to market, but the amount of rent—the equivalent of roughly 2 million koku—was a smaller percentage of the agricultural output than was 150 million taels or more in China. In short, these initial estimates assume that more than 10 percent of the Chinese agricultural product was distributed in the form of rents after taxes as opposed to approximately 5 percent in Japan. The Chinese urban population was more dependent on the flow of rents also because of the more widespread system of absentee landowners and because government revenues were more meager.

The middle farmer took a direct part in redistribution through commerce. Medium-sized holdings of from 8 to 15 koku in Japan generally provided small amounts to be converted in markets beyond what was necessary to obtain currency where taxes were partly owed in cash. By purchasing goods which originated in cities or which passed through cities at various levels, farmers returned the cash they received to urban areas. In addition, they journeyed to central places at various levels for shopping and entertainment. Through price differentials merchants made profits. Through differences in the costs of raw materials and finished crafts the artisans made a living. Most merchants and artisans were directly dependent on goods from the middle farmer and the landowner or on the marketing of tax revenues. Indirectly the margin for cities was provided by the labor of small farmers and tenants whose production exceeded their consumption.

The two classes ideally at the bottom of the basic hierarchy were artisans and merchants. Artisans were ideally above merchants, but merchants actually had greater opportunities for accumulating wealth. In both China and Japan these two classes together totaled less than 10 percent. More precisely for Japan the number of those

engaged primarily in craft and commercial activities stood at 7 percent ± 1 percent.[29] As would be expected, both merchants and
artisans were largely urban, living in cities of all sizes. Although
some level 7 settlements and other villages in which a few stores
were located had full-time merchant or artisan households, usually
in these settings such activities were not the primary occupation of
the household head, but rather were part-time supplements to farming. Particularly in the latter half of the Tokugawa period relatively
static city population figures did not reveal that these previously
urban classes were expanding as increasing numbers of farmers
engaged in village crafts and commerce. Decentralized commercial
development, as in the centuries before Sengoku and Tokugawa
consolidation, replaced rapid urban growth.

Merchants and artisans comprised about two-fifths of the urban
population in Japan; the figure was higher for China. In both countries these two groups included men of varying means. Those with
stores lived and worked at a single location. Artisans' shops lined city
streets. Their clientele ranged from the wealthiest who could afford
exquisitely crafted ornaments and ceramics to farmers who bought
tools for their work. Apprentices and journeymen worked in a
distinctly inferior relationship to foremen and shop bosses. Similarly,
itinerant merchants and peddlers were usually poor merchants. The
former were important in facilitating the flow of goods between
cities, traveling periodically between markets in central places. The
latter distributed goods within cities. Rich merchants bought and
shipped large consignments of goods, often over long distances.

In early Tokugawa Japan merchants and artisans migrated in
large numbers into growing jōkamachi and tenryō cities. The permanent exodus of many of these people along with bushi from the
villages contrasted with China where gentry, merchants, and artisans
often made money in cities and then returned to consume it in
village residences. Not only were Japanese chōnin separated from
farmers, but within the city they were segregated from bushi. The
chō were governed as a separate part of the city and limitations were
placed on intercourse between chōnin and bushi. To some extent
these barriers between the two largest components of Japan's urban
population gradually broke down. Poor chōnin managed to enter

bushi areas and impoverished bushi found part-time craft work in association with chōnin. Prevented from interclass mobility, wealthy merchants adopted patterns of consumption rivaling those of bushi. Sumptuary laws were newly applied in a vain attempt to keep merchants in inferior positions. Forced confiscations also interfered with attempts by chōnin to accumulate wealth.

Chōnin can be divided according to the street frontage allotted to their residences. For instance, figures for one chō in Hiroshima city indicate that there were 215 households, of which 67 were owners and the rest were rentiers.[30] The 67 owners possessed varying lengths of frontage: (1) two owners had lots exceeding 20 ken (1 ken = 6 feet); (2) eight others also can be classed as rich chōnin, having at least 7 ken each; (3) the remaining chōnin were divided almost evenly between middle chōnin with 4-6 ken (27), and (4) small chōnin with 3 ken or less (30).

Cities contained many who did not enjoy the fruits of an above-average income. Intense competition for scarce urban jobs and for the hundreds of thousands of shops in all of the cities of China and tens of thousands of shops in Japanese cities caused a rapid turnover. Intercity and intracity migration of people in transport, craft, and merchant activities was common. The short-term rentier or hired laborer was a phenomenon of a situation of low demand and potentially great supply. Rentiers made up more than 50 percent of the chōnin population of large jōkamachi in West Japan.[31] And in nineteenth century China short-term workers, fortunate enough to receive a full year's wages through one or more jobs, received only about 5-10 taels in pay, plus perhaps an allowance of grain.[32] This would have been sufficient to support the worker and to provide a little for his family back home in the village, but the danger was great that the worker would be laid off, especially during the off-season when wages were low and jobs were scarce. Long-term laborers had more security, but still ranked among the city's poor. Most worked for small enterprises and were dependent on the tremendous authority of their bosses. There were few large enterprises, notable exceptions being the silk and cotton plants in lower Yangtze cities, ceramics at Ching-te chen, and iron at Fo-shan (Kwangtung). The urban poor in China and Japan clung to the varied opportunities for employment in the city, knowing they could easily be dislodged. Only rarely did conditions lead to urban riots.[33] It was generally easier to organize violent protest in the countryside than in the cities of China and Japan.

A small part of the population in both countries is omitted from the usual breakdown into four classes. In Japan eta and hinin made up $1\frac{1}{2}$ percent, plus or minus $\frac{1}{2}$ percent.[34] The 100,000 families of eta and hinin were scattered in both urban and rural areas, but invariably in communities separated from the rest of the population. They engaged in occupations befitting pariahs; tanning and slaughtering were characteristically eta occupations. Similarly, in China these jobs were often done by a distinguishable minority, the Moslems. Although the status of Chinese in demeaning occupations was not as inescapably hereditary, those with socially unacceptable sources of income (prostitutes, actors, beggars, and others) could never be fully emancipated technically, within the lifetime of an individual, but practically speaking, people escaped the designations of base status, especially in larger cities. Moreover, even the law provided for the escape of their descendants. After the Yung-cheng reign in the early eighteenth century official stigma no longer aggravated the position of such social outcasts.[35] Other individuals in China excluded from the four classes because they were few in number were servants, priests, and most soldiers, government runners, and orderlies. The last three categories together comprised roughly 1 percent of the population. Both in China and Japan servants, priests and their families constituted only about $\frac{1}{2}$ percent of all inhabitants.

Detailed breakdowns of the population exist for specific areas in China and Japan. The exceptionally urban area of Tientsin hsien (Chihli) in 1846 was reported to have contained 84,440 households.[36] Retired officials and degree holders potentially awaiting appointments numbered 1.4 percent of household heads. Orderlies, runners, and other public employees, excluding those few whose residence was officially elsewhere and thus were stationed only temporarily in Tientsin, made up 3.4 percent. The commercial population counted 31.3 percent. Farmers numbered 54.2 percent and, as was typical of North China, a large proportion owned their own land. In addition, transport workers listed separately totaled 7 percent, indicative of the exceptional location of this hsien along the Grand Canal and sea routes linking Peking to Shantung and most sheng in China. Another 1 percent of the population in fishing, fruit gathering, and salt production also would be normally classified as agricultural. The remaining fractions of 1 percent included 309 priests and 294 beggars. Dividing Tientsin hsien into eight areas, Momose Hiromu finds that the 33,000 households in the city of Tientsin were exceptionally commercial.[37] Also unusual were two areas along the Grand Canal where more than 10 percent of the population was engaged in transport and 20 percent in commercial activities. Finally, more typical of patterns likely to prevail in other hsien were four of the eight areas in which 80-90 percent of the household heads were registered as farmers. (Further information on these eight areas is given below, pp. 172-74.)

The example of Hikone han (Chūbu) is instructive for Japan. In 1695 the population of the han was given as 260,000 and the koku figure as 300,000.[38] Of the population, 19,000 were bushi in the jōkamachi. The remaining castle city population consisted of 34 percent artisans and 62 percent merchants, together totaling 15,500, and 759 people living under the jurisdiction of shrine and temple directors. No separate figure was given for hired laborers.

Different processes were followed in the concentration of members of various strata in Chinese and Japanese cities. Gentry and commercial people in China were identified with their places of origin and regarded as temporarily making their abode in a given city.[39] In contrast, Japan's urban population had grown in cycles. During the Heijō and Heian periods kuge, officials and special craftsmen had converged on the capital city. With absentee lords and some bushi replacing officials at times, these classes continued to form the core of the urban population until the Sengoku period. Then a new wave of migrations to cities began. Kuge were reduced to a small number in Kyoto. Special craftsmen were losing their importance as luxury goods were eclipsed by more utilitarian items for mass consumption. The new city residents were bushi and chōnin, the former obliged to serve their lords wherever they were led and the latter generally lured by profitable opportunities. The bushi remained a stable component of the cities in which they lived. By the nineteenth century most could trace their families' lives in one city (or in Edo plus their jōkamachi) back many generations. The daimyo were raised in Edo and then spent less than half of their adult lives in the jōkamachi which they ruled. The imperial family and kuge living in Kyoto, the daimyo constantly returning to Edo, and the majority of bushi staying in specific castle cities all were self-perpetuating urban strata. Moreover, some privileged merchant and artisan families remained ascribed to their positions within jōkamachi. In contrast to these stable elements of city populations, peddlers, shopkeepers, and many other urban dwellers were as highly mobile in Japan as in China.

Transportation

Technology for moving goods and people changed slowly before the introduction of the railroad and the steamship. In China and Japan goods were generally shipped by ocean, river, canal, or lake. Where no water was navigable, pack animals or human porters bore goods along roads or trails. People also traveled over water, but more frequently movement was by horse or foot. Major highways in both countries served private trade and travel as well as the strategic traffic of civilian and military officials. Since land transportation was costly, it was generally confined to shipments of distances less than 100 miles, to luxuries whose few consumers could afford high costs, and to necessities needed only in small quantities. Bulk shipments of necessities such as grain arrived mainly by water. High transport costs contributed to the duplication of small-scale enterprises in separate cities. Rarely were daily needs produced in one city for export to another.

Water transport during the Ch'ing and Tokugawa periods can be divided into two types: (1) a small number of major routes and (2) numerous minor routes. The Pacific Ocean in its various guises from the Inland Sea to the Gulf of Tonkin provided interregional routes for domestic trade and small amounts of foreign trade. In China interregional transport was also carried along a number of major rivers and canals, including the Yangtze river from west to east and the Grand Canal from south to north. In Japan the main ocean routes bore such names as "eastern *mawari*" (around the Japan Sea) and "western mawari" (around the Inland Sea). Another route connected Osaka to Edo, completing the encirclement of the principal island of Honshū by sea traffic. While the above bodies of water served as the arteries in the two countries, lesser waterways existed in large numbers. Shipping to and from many of the cities of China and Japan and their rural hinterlands moved along these smaller water routes. Often a jōkamachi or major zaikatachō in Japan or a fu city or major chen in China was located at the juncture of two water routes. Minor waterways proved convenient carriers of commerce inside hsien and han.

The road systems of China and Japan centered on Peking and Edo respectively. The highest classification of roads in China was *kuan-lu*. Four main kuan-lu connected Peking to the northeast through the gateway of Shan-hai kuan (Chihli), to the west through T'ai-yuan (Shansi), to the central and south through Honan, and to the east and southeast through Shantung. Kuan-lu connected Peking to the sheng cities of every province and to military bases in northwest China. Also located along the routes of kuan-lu were many fu cities. Next ranked roads known as *ta-lu*, which linked additional fu cities as well as major chih-li chou cities to sheng cities. Small-scale roads and trails connected two or more hsien cities and served simultaneously as intra-hsien routes.

Post stations (*i*) were located about 25 miles apart along principal Chinese roads. These should not be confused with roadside stations (*p'u*), about 15,000 of which existed in China.[40] The p'u were spaced about 2-5 miles apart, usually in villages. Foot soldiers under a station head carried official papers by relay from p'u to p'u. The number of foot soldiers in outlying p'u might be as low as zero or one, while on main roads two to three men were common and in urban settlements often four to six men were assigned. But these numbers were too small to make much impact on the settlement. During the Ch'ing period i were frequently located in administrative cities or large chen. These posts had larger numbers of horses, animals, and men. The number of animals in a post provides a measure for the scale of the post. In Chihli sheng large posts had more than fifty horses and asses, middle posts had ten to forty-nine, and small posts had fewer than ten.[41] Although the number of men assigned to the post was generally only half the number of animals, these figures do indicate the relative importance of post functions in contributing to urban populations.

In China there were 1,780 posts: 1,634 for horses, 92 for boats, and 54 for both.[42] The most posts (331) existed in the strategic province of Kansu (including part of present-day Sinkiang) and the smallest number was found in Kwangtung, at the opposite extreme of China. Shantung province, which contained 139 posts and 1,054 p'u, was one of five sheng—all in northern China—in which a post was located in every hsien. In the south and west of China only a small number of hsien on main roads had posts. To the extent that posts contributed to urban development, they did so largely in the north of China.

Whereas many Chinese post stations had remained intact nearly continuously for centuries, Japan's system of posts had undergone many changes in the centuries of decentralization after the collapse of the imperial system. As domains were unified during the sixteenth century, customs barriers fell and roads were improved. By the early seventeenth century a centralized system of radial roads from Edo was superimposed over local han roads. Of the five main roads the most heavily traveled were the Tōkaidō and the Nakasendō (the former with 53 and the latter with 67 posts between Edo and the main Kinki cities). Posts on these roads stood much closer together than was common in China. Along the Tōkaidō, posts followed the coastal lowlands, each containing 100 men and horses. The more mountainous inland Nakasendō posts were second with 50 men and horses each, while posts along the other chief roads each had 25 men and horses.[43]

Besides the five main roads protected by the Bakufu there were many lesser roads in Japan. Some crossed Honshū Island, linking the Japan Sea side to the richer coast along the Inland Sea. Many connected to water transport or to the five main roads. New routes for private transport were developing during the Tokugawa period as alternatives to established roads and were often preferred for faster travel at lower cost.[44] Small post stations existed on many roads, but the quantity of overland transport and traffic was too small to give rise to cities. Unless a post was along a main road or in a settlement doubling as a jōkamachi or as a port, it was not likely to rank as high as level 6.

Roads served a more supplementary role in Japanese commerce. Long-distance transport benefited by plentiful sea ties. Ocean ports were usually on rivers leading inland. Only where water routes were unavailable was recourse made of roads for bulk shipments. The predominance of water routes in Japan was similar to the situation in Southeast and East-central China, not North or Northwest China. The larger proportion of Japan's national income transported over long distances should be seen in the light of more accessible water routes.

Cities as Systems

What was a city in late premodern China and Japan? It was a settlement fitting the definition for any level between 1 and 6. In area it measured between a few hundred square yards and twenty-five square miles. In population it contained between 500 and 1 million people. In function it was a center for trade ranging from a small periodic market and, perhaps, a few shops to a large daily market and thousands of shops. Cities were the foremost centers of consumption. The largest military garrisons, the highest paid officials, and the richest merchants and artisans all were characteristically urban. The upwardly mobile and the downwardly mobile moved in and out; while villagers rarely left their native places, cities were the hubs of social and geographic mobility.

During the centuries preceding modernization in many countries densely settled populations were troublesome for authorities. On the one hand, they could be organized by wealthy merchants to demand independent charters as free cities; on the other, they could be massed in opposition, taking the form of riots. Yet, Ch'ing and Tokugawa cities were extraordinarily stable, rarely posing either of these threats. Order was preserved by effective urban administration, and solidarity was served by self-governing organizations such as guilds and by stable family relationships. Cities were able to absorb large numbers without major dislocations in society.

The maintenance of urban order can be divided into two kinds of tasks. Certain activities had to be performed in order to maintain the city as an on-going unit. Important among these were fire control, water supply, and the prevention of excessive violence. All of these were the direct, though not exclusive, concern of urban administrators. Other activities related to the rapid turnover in city population. Three bases of cooperation within cities were: proximity of residence, a common place of origin, and a common occupation. When jōkamachi were being established, persons from various small cities were absorbed in different chō, often named for a unifying place of origin or occupation. But later the bonds of common origin and occupation weakened in Tokugawa cities and ties based on residences within the same chō spread. The same transformation did not occur in China. Propinquity within the city was secondary to *t'ung-hsiang* (from the same hsien) and *t'ung-hang* (from the same guild) in urban organization.

Formal administration penetrated further in Japanese cities. Ch'ing urban administration occurred as in the countryside under the magistrate and his staff, though the fact that the magistrate lived inside the city brought control closer. High degree holders had the most access to the magistrate. Representatives of organizations within the city dealt informally with members of the magistrate's staff. Like magistrates, daimyo had substantial executive and judicial power, but they also had much legislative power. Generally they ruled their cities through two or three separate administrations. Bushi were organized according to feudal bonds. Chōnin were placed under one high bushi—often called the *machitoshiyori*—who was assisted by low bushi called *yoriki* and *doshin*. Under the machitoshiyori groups of chō were administered by *nanushi*, headmen selected from wealthy chōnin. Privileged merchants and artisans active in the original construction of chō might pass on hereditary posts in chō administration, but other nanushi were elected. A third bushi official administered temple and shrine areas in large jōkamachi.

Organizations called *hui-kuan* were especially important in large Chinese cities. Hui-kuan first appeared in many areas of China in the two centuries before the Ch'ing period and then spread rapidly after 1700.[45] In nineteenth century Peking nearly 400 hui-kuan served as temporary lodgings for exam candidates and merchants and as community centers for many living within the city from the common areas of origin. Unlike other cities Peking received a great influx of candidates for the highest examination from areas all over China. Elsewhere in the country hui-kuan were centers more of merchants and craftsmen than of officials. Since hui-kuan housed such diverse activities as religious celebrations, recreational gatherings, mutual protection associations, and burial assistance, they could fulfill a variety of urban needs.

A contrast between ordered administrative cities and unplanned economic cities prevailed in both China and Japan. The similarity between the form of chen and zaikatachō is evidence of their common unplanned development as marketing centers along transport routes. These primarily economic cities usually stretched in long, narrow lots on both sides of one main road. Chen differed from primarily administrative cities in China, which were often walled in a rectangular form with intersecting streets in the center. Zaikatachō lacked castles and buke areas.

Jōkamachi and hsien cities were to some degree planned, but they differed in the extent of order imposed through planning. Whereas the ability of Chinese administrators to order cities had been falling for more than one thousand years, the Japanese had succeeded in reversing a similar trend with the construction of jōkamachi. Cities had been chosen anew, winning out over other locations on the basis of favorable situations and sites. In contrast, in China there was no radical redistribution of cities and no appearance of a new city plan to meet the conditions of a more developed society.

Even if Chinese cities were not reordered, the presence of a seat of government led to certain expectations about the form of the city. During the Ch'ing period many hsien cities were reconstructed and others were established in frontier areas receiving intensive new settlement as Taiwan (Fukien), Kweichow, and Yunnan. Expenses for building walls, moats, gates, towers, ramparts, administrative offices, and certain legitimating temples and granaries could run to hundreds of thousands of taels, collected usually by subscription. Especially costly was the city wall, imposing in its 1 to 2 mile circumference, 20 foot height, and thick layer of brick and stone materials around an inner core of pounded earth. The costs of repairing walls damaged by floods, earthquakes, or simple neglect called for extraordinary assessments on the inhabitants of a hsien.

The city wall was less a defensive necessity or a barrier between two life styles than a symbol of public order. Garrisons in cities remained in reserve while the troops scattered in mountain passes defended against small bands of outlaws. At the occasional times when large rebellious forces marched on the city, neither the wall nor the troops within could provide adequate resistance. The primary purpose of the wall was to signify that its urban site was the outpost of an authority which protected the existing form of society in China.

Jōkamachi were more separated from the countryside than were hsien cities. Many Japanese administrative cities were separately governed under officials responsible for urban affairs and were favored by laws ensuring commercial monopolies under resident chōnin. The plan of these cities revealed a clear contrast with rural Japan. The center of administration for the han was located inside the walled and moat-enclosed structures of the castle compound. The Chinese counterpart of the castle compound was the *yamen*, a series of courtyards in which the magistrate and part of his staff resided and government functions were concentrated. But the yamen was only one of many rectangular walled enclosures—usually in the northern half of the hsien city—and did not stand out as did the towers of the jōkamachi castle elevated on a bluff in a central area of the city. The greater physical eminence of the castle compound was indicative of the more active direction of urban and rural affairs emanating from there.

The second area of the jōkamachi to have no equivalent elsewhere in the han was the zone of *yashiki*, estates where bushi resided. Living in these secluded areas of the city, bushi enjoyed a separate existence from rural dwellers and from chōnin. In contrast, Chinese gentry (excluding bannermen) were neither separated from others in the city nor from contacts in the countryside and lived in areas scattered throughout the city. Differentiation among bushi was reflected in the size of their yashiki and in the distance between the yashiki and the castle. Yashiki closest to the castle were generally larger and were occupied by higher ranking bushi. Yashiki situated near the perimeter of built-up area contained mainly lower ranking bushi.

Chō were also distinctive areas unlike the rather arbitrarily separated yü (see above, p. 34) or other divisions in Chinese cities. Chō consisted of a number of rectangular blocks. Privileges were granted and duties imposed in terms of particular chō. Old chō became bastions of merchants and artisans exercising monopoly rights over the entire han. Serving as units into which crafts and commerce were organized, chō were the building blocks of Japanese cities.

Even the temples and shrines confined to special areas in jōkamachi contrasted in their relatively orderly deployment with Chinese urban religious structures. The clearly delimited zones of the jōkamachi reflected the centralization of administration and the limitations on commerce which favored a single city in each han. Only one castle was allowed per han after the early seventeenth century. The construction of new chō in urban areas outside jōkamachi was also tightly curtailed. Only when zaikatachō were regarded as indispensable to the prosperity of the jōkamachi did they too share in the protection granted by daimyo. The unwalled castle city appeared as a veritable model of orderliness in contrast to the walled Chinese city, which could not contain built-up areas sprawling outward in kuan and similarly haphazard growth within the wall.

Systems of Cities

Settlements vary in degree of urbanism; so any definition of cities must of necessity arbitrarily exclude places not far on the continuum from other places called urban. Ordinary villages in premodern societies can be easily eliminated from consideration as urban. It is, however, difficult to specify precisely the total number of natural villages since in both China and Japan some small villages were combined for administrative purposes. By the nineteenth century there were at a minimum 65,000 villages in Japan and 800,000 villages in China. In both countries at least half of the total population lived in small villages with fewer than 250 inhabitants—approximately 60 households. Few of these villages had stores. At least another 25 percent of the population in each country lived in larger villages, generally with fewer than 800 inhabitants but occasionally with as many as 1,000 to 2,000 residents. Stores were more common in larger villages, but farming families relied on periodic markets for most of their buying and selling. The line between rural and urban is more difficult to draw for level 7 central places. I treat them as villages because they were generally typical of rural settlements in population—mostly they contained between a few hundred and one thousand residents—and in the absence of large numbers of stores. Altogether in nineteenth century China about 25,000 villages were loci of primary marketing activities. The number for Japan was about 1,000. Anywhere between 1 and 100 ordinary villages clustered around a level 7 periodic market. G. William Skinner has suggested a fluctuating ratio gravitating around one standard marketing settlement for each eighteen villages in China.[46] Checking data in local gazetteers, I have found a somewhat higher ratio of villages to markets prevailing throughout the Ch'ing period. Variation was marked; some hsien contained one market for each 10 villages and other hsien contained a market for 50 or more villages. In Japan level 7 marketing settlements were comparatively scarce and a higher proportion of villagers relied directly on cities at level 6 or above for marketing. Moreover, the number of level 7 settlements may have been decreasing in late Tokugawa Japan in contrast to China where the figure continued to rise rapidly.

Level 6 central places are the smallest settlements I identify as cities, although I treat their populations as only half urban. They ranged from roughly 500 to 3,000 residents. One of these periodic markets could be found each five or ten miles in settled areas of China and Japan. More frequent marketing days and a wider variety of goods distinguished level 6 central places from the more widespread level 7 settlements. It was common for a level 6 market to act as an intermediate point for itinerant merchants journeying from one level 7 market to another. Skinner describes a pattern of six standard markets (SMT) in China forming a hexagon around a single intermediate market (IMT).[47] Since standard markets were also situated between intermediate ones, the actual ratio between the two was not 6:1 but more often 3:1 or 4:1. If it is accurate to substitute level 7 for SMTs and level 6 for IMTs, one could say that the level 6 city served simultaneously as a standard market for tens of nearby villages and as an intermediate market for more than 100 villages grouped in cellular fashion around level 7 central places. Of course, local conditions produced variations in the ratio of level 7 to level 6 settlements. There were small areas in China with nearly as many level 6 as level 7 central places and other areas with ratios between 5:1 and 10:1. In Japan level 6 cities frequently stood alone, bereft of supporting level 7 markets. I estimate an overall ratio of 5:2 for that country. Determining whether a marketing settlement is properly placed at level 6 or at level 7 is particularly difficult. I have based my decisions on population data, marketing frequencies and other scattered references, but the figures I propose must be considered highly tentative.

What kinds of cities were level 6 central places? Most nonadministrative cities, i.e., chen and zaikatachō, fit in at this lowest urban level. Many hsien cities and jōkamachi of han with less than 30,000 official koku also ranked at this level. Altogether more than 80 percent of all cities in China and about 55 percent of cities in Japan were at level 6.

Level 5 cities contained populations varying from 3,000 to 10,000. Included in this category are about half of the hsien and chou cities and a somewhat smaller number of chen. In Japan about 80 jōkamachi were joined by twice as many zaikatachō at this level. Comparable to Skinner's central marketing towns, level 5 cities stood at the pinnacle of marketing in areas totaling hundreds of square miles.

Altogether about 200 cities in China and 60 cities in Japan contained populations ranging between 10,000 and 30,000. A typical Chinese province was divided into the marketing spheres of about 10 cities at this level. Similarly the seven regions in Japan were divided between approximately 10 cities each. Level 4 cities were characteristically fu cities or jōkamachi of han with between 100,000 and 300,000 koku.

Level 3 might best be divided into 3a and 3b. The former were cities which had populations from 70,000 to 300,000 and the latter were smaller from 30,000 to 70,000. Included among the approximately 100 cities of China at 3a and 3b are most of the sheng capitals and many fu cities. At this level in Japan were 20 cities, nearly all of which were jōkamachi serving han in each of which at least 1 percent of the agricultural output of Japan was grown.

Levels 2 and 1 were regional cities and the national administrative centers respectively. Level 2 cities with populations over 300,000 were centers of interprovincial or interregional commerce. In Japan the two cities at this level were Osaka and Kyoto and in China the list likely included nine cities: Nanking, Soochow, Wuhan, Canton, Foochow, Hangchow, Chungking, Chengtu, and Sian. The administrative centers were Peking and Edo, probably the two largest cities in the world during the eighteenth century.

TABLE 5

Distribution of Early Nineteenth Century Central Places

	China		Japan	
Level	Number of Central Places	Population[b] (millions)	Number of Central Places	Population (millions)
1	1	1	1	1
2	9	5	2	.8
3	100	6	20	1
4	200	3	60	1
5	1,100	5.5	250	1.3
6	6,000	(3)[a]	400	(.2)[a]
7	24,000		1,000	

[a]Figures given for level 6 include only urban residents, i.e., one-half of the actual total.

[b]These figures for China refer to the years after 1820 when the total population of the country was rising to nearly 400 million. China's total urban population was as little as 18 or 19 million in 1800 if the percentage of the population in cities remained constant.

At a high level of generalization the cities of Ch'ing China and Tokugawa Japan would have to be classified together. Not many premodern societies had established all seven levels of central places. China and Japan had. Not many societies before 1800 had as many as 6-7 percent urban or as many as 5 million urban residents. China and Japan had. No other eighteenth century society had a city in which roughly 1 million people resided. China and Japan had. But closer examination of spatial patterns indicates substantial differences between the more than 1 million square miles of China's eighteen provinces and the more than 100,000 square miles of Japan's seven regions. Detailed examination of their urban networks provides a clue to basic differences between these societies.

What were the basic differences between the networks of cities in China and Japan? Japan was more than twice as urbanized. China contained an urban population 3-4 times and later 4-5 times that in Japan. Japan produced a city as large as Peking, yet had only 8-10 percent of the population of China. As the diagram on page xv illustrates, China's tower of central places had a much wider base; levels 7 and 6 were comparatively numerous in China while Japan's urban population was concentrated in larger cities.

Various factors mentioned in this chapter help to explain these urban differences. Japan's smaller scale, coupled with easier transportation, facilitated intensive urban growth. Possessing so large an area, Chinese officials required additional administrative levels, resulting in the dispersion of urban population. Power in Japan was especially centralized in three kinds of settlements: in the village at the expense of intravillage ties and of level 7 settlements; in the jōkamachi at the expense of other intra-han and inter-han ties; and in three central cities (which contained one-third of the urban residents in Japan) at the expense of other interregional ties. Being more concentrated and relatively more numerous than their Chinese counterparts, bushi could more effectively control the countryside for their lords. Japan was a more highly mobilized society. Its forms of centralization had been based on advanced premodern economic conditions. Despite divisions into han, the Tokugawa record of resource accumulation was remarkable. Ostensibly the Ch'ing bureaucracy had firmer central control, but the absence of feudal divisions did not ensure actual control. China's forms of social organization were far less adaptable for rapid growth even under premodern conditions.

F. W. Mote has found in China the rare example of a country without a rural-urban dichotomy. In the summary of Chapter 1 I have already given one explanation for this circumstance, contrasting it with the dichotomous conditions in Japan. In this chapter I have pointed out that central places at lower levels were relatively more numerous in China, while urban residents chose large cities in Japan. We might think of levels of central places as battlegrounds in which urban and rural life styles compete for predominance. If there is no substantial urban presence at higher levels, rural patterns set the tone. If populous urban areas are relatively numerous, then a distinct urban way of life prevails. The contrasts between China and Japan are apparent from Table 5: 76 percent of Chinese central places were at level 7, but only 58 percent of Japanese ones; 96 percent of Chinese central places were at levels 6 and 7, but only 81 percent of Japanese ones. Moreover, the much larger proportion of Japanese in cities contributed to the separation of urban from rural.

Two questions have served as the foundation for this chapter: (1) What were the factors underlying differences between cities in Ch'ing China and Tokugawa Japan? and (2) What were these differences? In the end we are left with the following additional questions: (1) Why was the proportion of city dwellers more than twice as high in Japan? (2) Why did so many central places at lower levels in China fail to produce a corresponding development of larger cities? (3) And how had Japanese established a network of cities so efficient that less than 5 percent as many central places at levels 6 and 7 supported 23 percent as many cities of over 3,000 population as in China? Examination of the geographical setting and administrative divisions, of land use and demographic structures, of stratification and transportation, and even of city plans provides some explanations of Tokugawa Japan's advantages in achieving a more efficient organization of space. If we also recall the temporal patterns detailed in Chapter 1, then we would find that Japan was developing faster, may have caught up with China during the seventeenth century and moved far ahead by 1800. The two dimensions of time (Chapter 1) and space (Chapter 2) are best represented by Table 2 and by the diagram on page xv.

⁂ 3 ⁂

PATTERNS OF MARKETING

The coexistence of intervillage exchange in minor periodic markets (levels 6 and 7) and interregional exchange in commercially prosperous centers, where were located daily markets and numerous stores (levels 1-4), lasted in China for about 1,200 years and in Japan for roughly 600 years. Marketing activities continually expanded during these centuries. Whereas at the beginning of these long periods administrative patterns were obviously the primary determinants of the urban network, by the seventeenth century marketing patterns were at least as important in determining the distribution of cities at various levels. Intensification of the marketing system was steadily transforming Chinese and Japanese rural and urban areas. Rural landscapes were altered by the closer proximity of central places. Higher level central places gained in prosperity and in population as expanded marketing networks pumped in greater volumes of goods. Generally, the higher the level of a central place as defined by population, the more active was its marketing. The only administrative centers which did not serve as loci of marketing were some jōkamachi of han with 10,000 to 20,000 koku, which will be treated as level 7 central places. With few exceptions, at the top levels were administrative centers with flourishing markets.

In China only during the final decades of this 1,200 year historical process did the effects of technology introduced from abroad begin to break down existing marketing conditions and not until the mid-twentieth century did the demise of traditional marketing relationships actually become widespread. The Ch'ing period was a time of continued maturation of previously established patterns of trade.

The Tokugawa period nearly coincided with the second half of the history of local periodic marketing in Japan. In contrast to China the number of periodic markets was already declining during the final century of Tokugawa rule. A small number of markets remained in the twentieth century, but these were insignificant atavisms and can be dismissed as regional aberrations. Although the rise of advanced premodern marketing had occurred 500 years later in Japan, during the nineteenth century Japan was 100 years ahead of China in superseding these patterns.

The two societies differed in the relationship of administrative divisions to marketing networks. On the one hand, han were potentially closed units in which the daimyo could impose highly restrictive barriers against inter-han trade. At the extreme, trade between nearby han would occur only by passing through distant cities of levels 1-3. Thus exchange was nearly bifurcated into intra-han and national markets. On the other hand, new administered areas had been established in Japan in response to local conditions during the fourteenth to sixteenth centuries. Japanese trade and administrative boundaries were more precisely adjusted to fit in with each other than were their Chinese equivalents.

The Development of Marketing

The history of redistribution might be divided into three stages. At first in relatively undeveloped premodern societies goods moved from local areas to distant consumers and from villages to cities chiefly through taxes in kind and rents. Recently in modernized societies stores have replaced markets for most exchange. In the interim, stores existed, but markets were the prevalent mechanism for bringing together supply and demand. Widespread commerce became possible when large numbers of periodic markets emerged in villages.

During the first stage of redistribution intracity markets existed mainly for those who received salaries or other payment originating in tax revenues. Receiving part of the surplus arriving in administrative cities, these wealthy urban residents were able to buy handicrafts finished within the chief administrative centers and small amounts of agricultural produce and luxury items sent commercially to cities.

In this stage a large capital city (level 1 or 2) and a number of small administrative centers (level 5) were generally the only cities. Gradually rising agricultural productivity and declining central control resulted in an increasing proportion of the harvest being taken not by officials, but by large landowners. This shift from taxes to rents as the foundation for urban expansion was much more pronounced in Japan than in China, but in both countries demands for commerce in areas outside cities were rising. New ties between local farmers and urban consumers were slowly forming through periodic marketing.

Early markets outside of administrative cities in China and Japan served local needs which had previously been met on a less regular basis without markets. Inhabitants of hilly areas and of fishing settlements had traditionally exchanged special products such as firewood and fish for grains grown on the plains. A market was not a necessity until areas became more diversified. By the T'ang dynasty and the Kamakura period reliance was increasingly being placed on markets for local exchange. Relatively prosperous rural dwellers, who accumulated more than enough agricultural goods to feed their families, sought not only the few outside necessities which somehow had always found their way into the village, but also a number of other products for which currency was needed. Marketing part of the harvest became a necessity to obtain currency for purchases and also for taxes, which were being converted into cash payments.

In China levels 6 and 7 were added onto a hierarchy of administrative centers which was already nearing completion. Eighth century China was divided into approximately 1,500 administrative cities corresponding to my levels 1, 3, 4, and 5. The addition of level 7 periodic markets had been taking place gradually, but by this century the widespread presence of local markets became apparent. How many of these small marketing centers had to exist before they were widely observed in China? For lack of any data, I choose the figure 500, or one level 7 settlement for every three administrative cities. In other words, if the total T'ang population was 80 million, living in 200,000 villages served by 1,500 administrative cities, then one-quarter of 1 percent of all villages had acquired marketing functions. Of course administrative cities contained markets which far exceeded these level 7 places in volume of trade.

In Table 5 I estimated that the number of central places during the early nineteenth century was about 31,500. Subtracting administrative centers from this figure, I arrive at a total number of 30,000 primarily marketing central places. During the previous 1,100-1,150 years the number of nonadministrative cities must have risen approximately sixty-fold. This rise averages 40-45 percent when reduced to periods of a century each. Assuming a constant rate of increase and an initial figure of 500 in A.D. 700, I have indicated in Table 6 roughly how many of these central places existed at intervals of a century.

TABLE 6

Nonadministrative Centers in China

Year	Nonadministrative Centers
750	600
850	900
950	1,300
1050	1,800
1150	2,600
1250	3,800
1350	5,500
1450	8,000
1550	11,500
1650	16,000
1750	23,000
1850	33,000

During the middle imperial period level 6 central places were added. It is difficult to determine an exact date for this transition. Certainly many of the late eleventh century tax collection points (described in Chapter One) were in level 6 cities. The chart indicates a total of about 1,500 marketing places outside of administrative cities in the year 1000. If these settlements were divided as in the Ch'ing period according to a ratio of four level 7 central places for one level 6 city (the fewer than twenty chen which were at levels 3-5 can be ignored), then already 300 level 6 cities would have come into existence. Since level 6 cities were commercially more active than level 7 locations, fewer would have been needed to establish their widespread presence.

One additional milestone in Chinese marketing history was reached around 1500, when there were about 10,000 marketing places. Level 2 regional marketing centers now were in evidence.

The history of marketing passed more quickly through similar changes in Japan. If in 1200 there were about 35 level 7 markets for 8-10 million Japanese living in 20,000-25,000 villages and in 1825 there were 1,600 nonadministrative cities, then the rate of increase was considerably faster than in China. However, evidence for the Tokugawa period indicates a decreasing rate of marketing settlement expansion. It is necessary to divide Japanese marketing history into varying rates. Tentatively I have chosen three rates: 1200-1700— 100 percent per century, 1700-1800—30 percent, and 1800-1868—0 percent. Table 7 below indicates my estimates of the growth in marketing settlements during the six and two-thirds centuries from 1200.

TABLE 7

Nonadministrative Centers in Japan

Year	Nonadministrative Centers
1200	35
1300	75
1400	150
1500	300
1600	600
1700	1,200
1800	1,600
1868	1,600

Approximately 7 percent as many central places as in China had to be present in order to signify that a given level had achieved a place in the urban network. It is likely that level 7 central places reached 7 percent of the figure for early T'ang China during the beginning of the thirteenth century. If the rate of increase in Japan was indeed 100 percent, then during the middle part of the fourteenth century there were 7 percent as many marketing settlements as in early Sung China; level 6 had joined level 7 in the Japanese urban network. During the first decades of the seventeenth century the number of nonadministrative central places in Japan reached approximately 700—7 percent of the total in China when levels 1 and 2 first existed together. At this time Osaka and Kyoto were developing as level 2 cities and Edo was emerging as the level 1 city. One difference between China and Japan was the absence of a continuous history of administrative cities in the latter. The sudden emergence of jōkamachi in the sixteenth century may have affected the rate of growth of nonadministrative cities. A steady rate of 100 percent each century is an unlikely pattern of growth under these changing circumstances. Moreover, the absence of administrative cities at levels 3, 4, and 5 meant that the appearance of these levels was related to the maturation of marketing central places. As the number of marketing places was rising from 150 to 600 during the fifteenth and sixteenth centuries, levels 5 and 4 emerged. Taking over local surpluses, bushi gained in local power as marketing settlements spread. Changes in Japanese society followed closely the developing urban network. In contrast, Chinese leaders succeeded in keeping expanded local exchange under central control, preventing convulsions in their remarkably resilient social structure.

In many respects the evolution of marketing in China and Japan followed similar courses. First level 7 markets and then level 6 markets were added. China was ahead. By the fourteenth and fifteenth centuries networks of markets were gradually forming in China, signifying growing differentiation of products within local areas.[1] Short-distance commerce prospered. The average number of marketing settlements per administrative city rose from three to six, and in advanced regions the average probably exceeded ten. These larger numbers made possible expanded links between central places at levels 6 and 7 and those at level 5. From the sixteenth to the nineteenth centuries the number of markets may have risen from 10,000 to 40,000. New periodic markets appeared as part of widespread marketing bonds, and old ones were absorbed in ever widening networks. Cities at high levels became the centers of tens and hundreds of central places. New markets served not only local exchange, but some became famed for specialty products which were in demand for hundreds of miles around. Long-distance commerce grew substantially during the Ming period and continued to expand after 1644. Regularized transport was added between distant cities at high levels. The rapid growth of hui-kuan in late Ming and Ch'ing China mirrored the development of a national market.[2]

The rise of daimyo in sixteenth century Japan should also be seen as a reflection of expanding marketing networks. Usually the emergence of daimyo is pointed out as a cause for substantial marketing growth. Certainly daimyo did promote widened commerce, but one ought not to ignore the commercial prerequisites for the appearance of daimyo. Opportunities to centralize control over local areas developed because marketing networks had already joined villages and central places in these areas. Since village self-sufficiency had previously broken down, daimyo were able to mobilize the resources of their han. Tokugawa centralized feudalism was based on advanced local marketing and national marketing.

Between 1500 and 1700 most of the central places in Japan were established. The building of new jōkamachi increased greatly the number of cities at levels 3-5. Smaller jōkamachi at levels 6 and 7 also appeared, but simultaneously other central places at these levels were eliminated through protectionist policies favoring jōkamachi commercial interests. Jōkamachi became nodes linking local flows of goods to national flows. At first great disparities in prices reflected the absence of regular trade routes and of stable commercial ties.[3] Areas distant from central cities had low prices, while the large cities were troubled by irregular and inadequate supplies at a time of rapidly increasing populations. As daimyo broke down old trade barriers and ended former guild monopolies within their han, they were able to concentrate the resources of the han at one location. The demands of Hideyoshi and later of Tokugawa Ieyasu spurred the flow of goods to Osaka. By the early seventeenth century separate han marketing networks as well as one unified national market were nearing realization.

Marketing in Local Areas

Grain was the basic commodity produced and exchanged in China and Japan. Especially common among commercial goods was rice, which joined such standards of exchange as copper, silver, and gold coins and banknotes as a means of reckoning the prices of other goods. Grain entered the commercial milieu in three ways: (1) through exchange on the market before taxes in order to pay taxes or rents in cash; (2) through exchange on the market after taxes using surplus not consumed at home; and (3) through exchange on the market of taxes to obtain cash for governmental operations or by those to whom stipends and salaries were paid in kind. Leaders in both China and Japan generally opposed either large increases or large decreases in grain prices. Hikes in rice prices stirred urban residents, whose way of life was furthest from self-sufficiency. Drops in rice prices were particularly feared in Japan since Bakufu, han, and bushi household finances were all dependent on obtaining cash for rice. Efforts to achieve price stability required the regulation of grain storage and, especially in Japan, of the production and shipment of grains. Of course, if famines were severe and widespread, granary reserves were quickly exhausted, prices rose rapidly, and thousands might die.

Early Ch'ing China and Tokugawa Japan differed in the extent the commercial economy penetrated into villages. In Japan most rice which was not needed to maintain the rural population was taken from farmers to be given to bushi. The fact that bushi and daimyo sold the rice in jōkamachi or in central cities meant that farmers could not sell it; consequently periodic markets outside of jōkamachi suffered while most jōkamachi became prosperous centers of han marketing. In China much of the surplus remained with farmers, who hiked periodically to nearby level 7 markets. Redistribution through taxes and rents was more often turned into commerce at lower level central places in China. The proportion of han commercial activities concentrated in administrative cities was greater than the proportion of hsien commercial activities concentrated in hsien cities.

Thanks to G. William Skinner's ground-breaking articles, we now have a model for understanding local marketing in China.[4] Levels 5-7 are roughly equivalent to his hierarchy of marketing places in local areas: level 7 = standard marketing towns (SMTs), level 6 = intermediate marketing towns (IMTs) and level 5 = central marketing towns (CMTs). Residents of ordinary villages periodically (in many areas of China twice every ten days, i.e., 2/10) visited a designated market. Usually about half of the people frequenting a level 7 market had to walk no more than two miles in each direction, while the remaining villagers followed paths between two and six miles in length. All benefited by the rotation of services between markets, which could not be supported by a single marketing area. Skinner has described the interdependence of SMTs, IMTs and CMTs, so there is no need for repetition here.

According to my calculations for the early nineteenth century, the average population of level 7 marketing areas was about 10,000 divided into 25-30 villages. One hundred and fifty years earlier at the beginning of the Ch'ing dynasty the average population per market would already have fallen to approximately 10,000 if my figures are correct that Chinese residents numbered about 150 million and marketing settlements numbered about 16,000. Moreover, if a rate of 40-45 percent is an accurate measure of the increase in marketing settlements, then between 1644 and 1911 the growth in population from less than 150 million to more than 400 million was closely paralleled by the expansion of nonadministrative cities. Unlike previous dynasties, the average population per market was not falling during the Ch'ing period.

The ordinary farmer in Ch'ing China lived in a village about two miles away from a level 7 market. Twice each ten days he had an opportunity to send someone from his household to the market. Most of the 2,000-3,000 families within the standard marketing area were represented frequently at the market. Itinerant merchants appeared to buy their grain, especially at harvest time, to buy various other local goods and to sell daily necessities. Level 6 periodic markets were about ten miles away from the ordinary villager. To journey so far required a special occasion or sufficient income and leisure to shop for the more varied goods available in level 6 central places. Tens of, or even as many as a hundred, merchants displayed their wares before a select fraction of the ten thousand families within the intermediate marketing area. Even more distant for most farmers were the central markets in level 5 cities. These were bustling communities serving about 250,000 people of whom 1-4 percent lived in the city, another 3-5 percent used the city as a standard market, and about 15 percent used the city as an intermediate market. Combining Skinner's terminology with my own, I would suggest that the following quantitative relationships prevailed: (1) the presence of a standard market contributed practically nothing to urban population; (2) the presence of an intermediate market contributed an average of 500 people to the urban population; (3) the presence of a central market contributed an average of 4,000-5,000 to the urban population. Thus a level 5 city, which contained all three types of markets, was likely to have an urban component many times larger than a level 6 city, which lacked a central market.

Marketing patterns did not strictly coincide with hsien boundaries. Villages near the border in one hsien frequently belonged to the marketing area of level 7 central places in neighboring hsien. Some level 7 and level 6 settlements were directly below cities in other hsien. But most late Ch'ing administrative cities were at level 5 and the majority of central places subordinate to them were located within the same administrative unit. The hundreds of level 5 cities which were not administrative centers more often stood above central places scattered in more than one hsien.

Markets can be compared by the quantity of goods handled.[5] Most transactions involved small quantities, e.g., purchases of grain often measured about one *tou* (approximately thirteen pounds). When harvests were collected, grain and other foodstuffs, and raw materials flowed in large quantities from markets at lower levels to ones at higher levels; many tributaries joined in a mighty flow to the highest level cities. Some goods made the journey back, channeling into trickles along the way. In general, the higher the level of the central place, the greater the quantity of goods traded. Some level 6 cities and many level 5 cities were centers of 4/10 markets in areas of China where level 7 settlements stayed open for marketing only two days in ten. Increased frequencies permitted more numerous transactions. If 20 million tons of grain were marketed annually in China and the total number of standard marketing areas was 31,000, then the average amount was about 660 tons. A market meeting seventy-two mornings each year would have had an average turnover of 9 to 10 tons per session. Of course, seasonal and regional variations were tremendous. Scattered references in gazetteers indicate that a small market's daily exchange was about 10 piculs of grain (one picul = 133 pounds), and a large market's exchange was 100 or even 100s of piculs.[6] Markets in Man-ch'eng hsien (Chihli) were divided into four levels according to quantities of grain traded: 200 piculs, 100 piculs, quite a lot (presumably tens of piculs) and 10-20 piculs.[7] Much of the grain that was not purchased for local consumption was forwarded to higher level markets in which occurred a larger volume of trade.

Markets differed in the variety of goods present and in the scale of exchange for each good. Occasionally a market was noted for only one specialty item traded in large quantity. Kato Shigeshi cites the example of one hsien in which a particular market was the center for livestock and another market was the center for silk.[8] Level 5 cities and level 6 cities with populations of 2,000 or more generally carried large quantities of nearly all categories of goods, but in level 7 central places not many categories of goods could be found and those that were present might only be traded in tiny amounts.

Second to periodic markets as centers of local commerce were fairs. Unlike markets which met a certain number of times every ten days (or every twelve days), fairs were annual events drawing large crowds from greater distances than standard marketing areas. Occurring most often in the spring and fall, fairs extended usually from one to five days. In Chihli province four-day fairs were prevalent.[9] They were held both in ordinary villages and in central places. The higher the level of a central place, the more likely it was that a fair was held there and especially level 5 cities were the sites of fairs which met during more than one season each year. Fairs supplemented periodic markets, providing a variety of annual needs, luxuries, and entertainment. Certain fairs were famous for one type of commodity, e.g., livestock or drugs, which attracted merchants from tens or hundreds of miles around.[10]

The system of markets and fairs in local areas of China was an efficient and durable way of bringing goods to those who demanded them. The size and distribution of cities was mainly a consequence of this unfettered flow. Merchants and craftsmen were free to move where business opportunities seemed best. Agricultural productivity, transportation costs, and population density were determining factors in the development of the urban network. Each city existed in a web of central places, dependent on settlements below and above.

Local marketing was in transition during the Tokugawa period. During the first decades of the seventeenth century periodic markets in many areas were weakened.[11] Those located near jōkamachi were likely to have their commercial activities absorbed there. Merchants were attracted by the rapid influx of population into administrative cities or were forced out of local centers by decisions to shut down their markets in order to protect jōkamachi commerce. Chōnin in abandoned castle cities lost their privileges to residents of the new jōkamachi. The decree that only one castle could exist in each han accelerated the concentration of privileges. Those periodic markets located near the perimeter of the han suffered the curtailment of trade with areas beyond the han border. Moreover, markets under the protection of local magnates faced possible collapse with the fall of these men or with their move to the jōkamachi. In many han nearly all division of labor associated with the commerce of central places became concentrated around the castle. Many kinds of commercial activities within the han were foreclosed to those outside of the jōkamachi. Farmers were expected to be highly self-sufficient, requiring few outside goods.[12] So much of the rural surplus was to be gathered in the castle city or exported on behalf of the daimyo that almost none would be left to market elsewhere. For all of these reasons a number of former central places at level 7 were reduced to ordinary villages with their urban activities absorbed in castle cities.

Whereas the hierarchy of local settlements in China formed a continuum, in Japan during these decades attempts were made to impose a dichotomous situation within the han. The underlying rationale was to improve han finances by increasing the agricultural produce under the daimyo's control and by reducing the amount of consumer goods that had to be diverted to villages or rival urban centers. Resources in Japan were mobilized as perhaps in no other country before collectivization spread through the Russian country-side in 1929-1930.

Yet, even in this period of suppression many periodic markets held on or even grew. Above all, prior to the Industrial Revolution the limitations on centralized control were considerable. In regions where the urban network was relatively undeveloped new markets were required to bring these poor areas under the control of the daimyo in the jōkamachi.[13] Advanced local commercial ties were a prerequisite for sustained jōkamachi expansion. Where inadequate transport prevented the jōkamachi from serving as the center of a united han, separate marketing centers facilitated control under one lord. There were also poor areas where daimyo were unsuccessful for a time in diminishing the control of bushi who were strongly entrenched in markets within the han. Small closed economic spheres remained a throwback to the previous period. Some markets persisted because they were valued by daimyo as points where special agricultural goods for export could readily be accumulated or where daikan, representing the daimyo, converted tax grains to cash. Particularly in rich areas of Japan, cities at levels 5 and 6 were considered necessary for han or Bakufu finances. Kinki zaikatachō were needed because national marketing could not yet be handled in the central cities alone.[14] For diverse reasons periodic markets remained important during the early seventeenth century.

Forced accumulation was on the rise in Japan. Daimyo needed large amounts of cash for bushi stipends, for living expenses in the urban environments of castle cities and Edo, and for the costly travel regularized under the sankin kōtai system.[15] Increasing numbers of bushi moved to jōkamachi and to Edo. Especially costly were the assessments imposed by the Bakufu, e.g., for the construction of Edo castle, for the reconstruction of Osaka castle and for rebuilding parts of Edo burned down in great conflagrations which swept through the city. To secure more income daimyo both encouraged rice production and devised improvements in the process of procuring rice. Policies were adopted to save currency by curtailing imports and to promote specialty products which earned export revenues. In areas suited to the production of certain special goods taxes in kind had to be paid with those goods. For example, farmers on each of the small Izu islands—tenryō land near the Kantō mainland—had to fulfill a quota in silkworms or salt to meet Bakufu demands.[16]

Daimyo were continually reorganizing for increased control of han resources. In the early decades makeshift measures to procure larger amounts in taxes sufficed. Local commerce was restricted for the benefit of daimyo, bushi, and those chōnin on whom they relied. If the farmer had marketed his surplus, he would have required some return for it. The burden of producing consumer goods for mass needs would have drained resources from the immediate tasks of building up han finances.

Further development of the sankin kōtai system from the 1630s increased the need for sending products to central cities in order to obtain currency for use in Edo. Problems of debts to merchants in central cities began to trouble many daimyo. While expenses remained fairly constant, revenues fluctuated from year to year. Rising costs incurred by daimyo prompted reorganization of han economies. Eager to stabilize the flow of goods to major han cities and to decrease the costs of collecting and shipping, daimyo lessened their reliance on a few merchants to whom they had earlier given monopolies. During the period when the jōkamachi were being built, these privileged chōnin had helped provide corvée labor for military needs and city construction. In return special rights were given them. These merchants depended on large price differences between cities, but when more regular trade reduced price differentials and more efficient large-scale shipping operations made self-owned ships obsolete, privileged merchants became a burden to the daimyo. Moreover, new groups of merchants within the han were challenging the predominance of a few. Recognition of these new groupings, called *toiya* or *tonya*, signaled a partial shift from procurement policies to incentives through marketing.[17]

By the second half of the seventeenth century the medium-sized independent farmer was increasingly able to market a part of his harvest.[18] His freedom was enhanced by rising agricultural productivity and by loosening obligations to villagers outside of his stem family. Taxes rose, but absorbed a reduced proportion of total production. Nevertheless, marketing did not acquire as much independence as in China. Daimyo succeeded in channeling expanded commerce into castle cities.

Jōkamachi benefited through the development of widened marketing networks within han. Whereas the selection of a few privileged merchants had reflected a situation of one castle imposed on a han, reliance on tonya reflected a marketing hierarchy within a unified han. As in China, the administrative head now loomed directly over farmers; there were no intervening bushi with private marketing controls. Small independent markets within the han were broken up. The prosperity of local markets became not only compatible with, but also indispensable for jōkamachi growth. Tonya centered in castle cities consisted of large numbers of merchants given control over the purchase and resale of such diverse goods as tea, lacquer, paper, and fish oil. Jōkamachi prospered as cities at levels 3 to 6, which were centers of blocks of markets.

The first spurt of urbanization during the seventeenth century relied on the concentration of tax wealth in the jōkamachi. Continued city growth rested on the growing commercial centrality of castle cities. Unification of the domain market preserved and even enhanced the central position of the jōkamachi. In Kaga han (Chūbu) the domain market prospered during the years 1649-1660, when twelve zaikatachō were established. Simultaneously the population of Kanazawa, the jōkamachi of the han, increased rapidly in the 1650s and 1660s.[19] During the second half of the seventeenth century the number of chōnin rose in cities at all levels. Table 6 indicates that if the estimated earlier growth rate was maintained, then the short span of the seventeenth century was the time when three-eighths of all nineteenth century Japanese marketing settlements were founded. The movement of commerce from farmers to residents of burgeoning castle cities required a hierarchy of cities and at the same time the continued maturation of local marketing made it possible for jōkamachi to prosper.

During the second half of the Tokugawa period urban activities formerly largely confined to jōkamachi developed in lower level central places. Most of these small central places fitted in neatly beneath jōkamachi in the local hierarchy, but a growing number did not. Some local cities were noted as centers for the collection and distribution of long-distance commerce. Inter-han and national marketing of raw materials and half-finished goods contributed especially to the prosperity of ports. Furthermore in the nineteenth century the processing of goods began to disperse to additional local cities, providing a new basis for prosperity. Vegetable oil was first processed mainly in Osaka, but during the nineteenth century Osaka's enterprises declined as windmills in nearby kuni were used to press this product locally. Similarly, dyeing techniques were dispersed from Kyoto to areas where textile raw materials were produced. Some large landowners hired village labor and used local harvests for such activities as sake-making and soy-sauce making. Urban activities in local areas began to break out of the 500-year-old pattern which had brought about a continuous doubling in each century of marketing settlements.

Why did the expansion of marketing settlements retard in Japan? One possible explanation is that this slowdown was a sign of economic stagnation. Other evidence lends itself to such a conclusion. After centuries of frequent social reorganization, the second half of the Tokugawa period was remarkably free of change; the process of innovation from above had ground nearly to a halt. Moreover, population growth stalled and large cities remained stable in their population. Yet, another more plausible explanation would postulate a new kind of social change. One might speculate that something akin to the development of incipient urban activities prior to the imperial period was once again under way, but the change in progress was partially hidden within the village. Evidence suggests that many central places declined in the face of competition from part-time village merchants.[20] The spread of processing and of more direct procedures for selling local products to distant areas made periodic markets in many places obsolete by the end of the Tokugawa period.

From the early eighteenth century policies to raise taxes, to reorganize commerce and to create han monopolies generally managed to maintain the position of the jōkamachi at the top of a pyramid of central places, but the foundation of the pyramid was crumbling. Central places at levels 6 and 7 could withstand local decentralization only if periodic markets acquired new functions, such as the accumulation of a special processed good for shipment to a large urban market. One sign that the existing urban network was cracking was the emergence of new chō areas along roads leading out of jōkamachi. During the early history of castle cities craft and merchant guilds had primarily located in one central area of the city, where they could readily serve the needs of bushi. By the end of the seventeenth century chōnin had spread out over wider areas of the city. Less concentrated by occupation, chōnin were no longer amenable to control by a few magnates with privileges and instead came under the leadership of the evolving tonya. During the eighteenth century while the total population of most jōkamachi remained steady, the pattern of chō dispersal continued. Chō located at the periphery of castle cities along roads to their hinterlands served merchants with strong local ties within the han. Commerce was undergoing further reorganization. Existing groupings of merchants recognized by daimyo were unable to control domain commerce, to stabilize prices, or to prevent outside merchants from diverting goods into inter-han trade.[21] For a time during the 1840s the Bakufu abolished all privileges of merchant groupings, but this only hastened the dispersal of urban activities. Changes in the form of the jōkamachi accompanied its decline as the center of a one-dimensional domain.

The hierarchy of local cities in Japan was more varied than in China. Jōkamachi were found at levels 3 to 7. Excluding castle cities at level 7—ones which lacked periodic markets—there were about 170 jōkamachi. Thus Japan contained slightly more than 10 percent as many administrative cities at levels 6 and above as China. Of these 170 jōkamachi 70-75 percent ranked at levels 5 and 6 as opposed to 80-85 percent of Chinese administrative cities. The remaining large jōkamachi were comparable to fu cities at levels 3 and 4, but they made up a greater proportion of all administrative cities than were at these levels in China. The prevailing distribution in China involved central places at levels 6 and 7 fitting below a hsien city at level 5 roughly in the following quantities: level 7—twenty; level

6—five; and level 5—one. Variations produced combinations such as 10:3:1 or 30:5:1, but in general central places at all three levels were present with far more at level 7 than at level 6 and more at level 6 than at level 5. The Japanese pattern, however, was not nearly as neat. Level 6 central places frequently existed without level 7 settlements or vice versa. A jōkamachi at level 5 or 6 might have a wide variety of settlement patterns in its han. Especially in the nineteenth century instances were common of level 5 cities existing without level 6 and 7 support. The overall ratio of level 7 to level 6 central places was between 2:1 and 3:1 in contrast to the Chinese figure of 4:1. Moreover the ratio of level 6 to level 5 cities was less than 2:1 as opposed to approximately 5:1 in China. The typical hsien city for an administered area with 200,000 people contained 4,000-5,000 residents, who shared the central place activities with residents of four cities at level 6 and fifteen settlements at level 7. A jōkamachi of a han holding only 40,000-50,000 people was as populous as the hsien city, but had an average of only two supporting level 6 or level 7 central places. The jōkamachi at level 5 or 6 rested on a narrower and more varied pyramid of central places than did its hsien counterpart.

Articles by Nakajima Giichi provide the basis for a model of local marketing in Tokugawa Japan.[22] Nakajima divides Echigo kuni (Chūbu) into seven kinds of areas. First there were areas with han which contained between 10,000 and 20,000 koku. Even in the jōkamachi of such han, markets were seldom present. The small number of bushi living in the jōkamachi did not have sufficient purchasing power to warrant a market. After subtracting bushi living in Edo and those stationed in villages within the han, the number remaining in the jōkamachi was generally considerably less than one hundred. They and their family members had to depend on central places in other han or in Bakufu-administered territory for marketing activities. Jōkamachi of these small han had populations of about one thousand, at least half of whom were farmers. The principal exceptions were castle cities which doubled as posts along major roads. The presence of this additional activity, together with the regular marketing needs of bushi and farmers, made a periodic market possible.

Second in Nakajima's list of areas were han of 20,000-30,000 official koku. Inside the jōkamachi was a periodic market, but elsewhere in the han, markets could not be sustained. If this model applied to all of the kuni in Japan, then the approximately two thousand villages in han of 10,000-20,000 koku were virtually without marketing representation, while the two thousand villages in han of 20,000-30,000 koku were represented by about forty markets in jōkamachi—a ratio of villages to central places of 50:1.

The third area in Echigo kuni, and by extension in all of Japan, was made up of han with 30,000-50,000 koku. Han of this size generally held a single market in the jōkamachi, but where sizable segments of the han were detached from the area around the jōkamachi additional markets might be found. Daimyo found it profitable to establish markets which attracted residents from neighboring han yet were far enough from the jōkamachi of their own han to prevent intra-han rivalry. Although jōkamachi in han of this size were level 5 cities—containing about 10 percent as many urban residents as koku—they commonly had no lower level central places below them.

The fourth and fifth areas distinguished by Nakajima were also characterized by what I label level 5 cities. The dividing line between han with simply one market and those with more was approximately 50,000 koku. Han of 50,000-70,000 koku generally had more than one market, and larger han with 70,000-100,000 koku could readily contain periodic markets and zaikatachō without hindering the prosperity of the jōkamachi. Unlike level 5 cities in han with 30,000-50,000 koku, these jōkamachi were at the top of a small network of central places at levels 6 and 7. While numbering only one quarter of all han under 100,000 koku, the han with 50,000-100,000 koku contained about one-half of the 15,000 villages in all of these han.

Forty-seven han enclosed at least 100,000 koku of agricultural capacity. Han of this size could support both daily trade in jōkamachi stores and markets and numerous central places scattered within the domain.

The seventh area consisted of tenryō and hatamoto land. These lands were not controlled by daimyo and did not have jōkamachi;

so officials representing the Bakufu were not concerned about protecting a privileged sanctuary for marketing, but were willing to honor petitions from village residents requesting new markets. In these areas markets were widespread.

TABLE 8

Number of Markets and Han Size

Koku of Han	Number of Han (approximate)	Number of Villages (approximate)	Number of Marketing Places[a] (approximate)
10–20,000	80	2,000	0–20
20–30,000	40	2,000	40
30–50,000	40	3,000	50–70
50–100,000	50	8,000	200–300
100,000 +	50	30,000	850–950
Tenryō and Hatamoto ryō	—	17,000	450–500

[a]Jōkamachi which were marketing places are included; therefore the only central places not included are level 7 jōkamachi.

Table 8 indicates the distribution of marketing settlements if Nakajima's classification for Echigo kuni—as I have interpreted it on the preceding pages—had applied throughout Japan. Assuming a total of 30 million koku and 1,700 central places (excluding level 7 jōkamachi), the average number of koku per marketing settlement was about 17,000-18,000. If han with less than 50,000 koku are set aside as possessing exceptional marketing patterns due to protectionist policies which favored their jōkamachi (these han contained 11-12 percent of all villages, but only 7 percent of all markets), then the average number of koku per market falls to 16,000-17,000. Using this average, I have divided the 15 million koku in han with more than 100,000 koku each into 850-950 marketing areas, and the 8 million koku in non-han lands into 450-500 marketing areas.

As in China marketing areas varied greatly. Some villages were located near high level cities and others were near level 7 central places. In general, Japanese marketing areas centered on larger settlements than those serving as marketing nodes for Chinese marketing areas. If the degree of "urbanness" of an entire marketing area is regarded as a function of the level of its central place, then the 1,700 marketing areas of Japan were far more urbanized than the more than 30,000 marketing areas of China.[23]

TABLE 9

Markets in Han with Fewer than 100,000 Koku

Level of Central Places	Number of Jōkamachi	Number of Nonadministrative Settlements
7	80	200
6	40	30
5	90	0

The basic division in Japan was between han with truncated networks of central places and those with potentially complete local urban networks. The former were found in han with fewer than 100,000 koku, which altogether contained 370-510 central places. Of this total approximately 210 were jōkamachi—roughly divided into 80 level 7 nonmarketing settlements, 40 level 6 central places, and 90 level 5 central places. It is unlikely that nonadministrative cities were distributed in han with fewer than 100,000 koku as they were in areas with more complete local urban networks. Level 7 periodic markets presumably predominated in han with less than 70,000 koku, which could support only one market in addition to their level 5 jōkamachi. Moreover, markets in detached areas of han were likely to be overwhelmingly at level 7. Thus only a small percentage of the 210 smallest han could maintain a level 6 market outside of the jōkamachi; I have estimated that approximately 30 out of the 230 (a number calculated by subtracting 210 from the average of 370 and 510, given above) nonadministrative places in such han were at level 6, as seen in Table 9.

Of course, in non-han areas there were no jōkamachi and in large han almost all jōkamachi ranked at levels 3 and 4. Consisting of only 3 to 4 percent of the 1,300-1,400 central places in these areas, jōkamachi of han with more than 100,000 koku did not interfere with the development of local marketing. In fact, large jōkamachi required a complete marketing hierarchy in order to receive commercial supplies essential for their growth. In these han the presence of jōkamachi did not prevent the development of marketing patterns typical of non-han areas. We can assume, as Skinner's model does for China, that complete urban networks uniformly prevailed in areas of large han and of Bakufu administration, i.e., in about 75 percent of Japan. Dividing the number of central places at each level typically present in local areas by 23 million koku, the approximate official number of koku in areas not carved up into small han, one can determine the number of koku per central place for each level as indicated in Table 10.

TABLE 10

Markets in Han with More than 100,000 Koku
and in Non-han Areas

Level of Central Place	Number of Central Places	Number of Koku (millions)	Number of Koku/ Central Place
7	720	23	32,000
6	330	23	70,000
5	210	23	110,000
5, 6, or 7	1,260	23	18,000

Local marketing patterns in China and Japan can be equated in terms of levels of central places. Level 7 markets correspond to SMTs and to some marketing places in han of more than 30,000 koku or in Bakufu administered areas. SMTs were subordinated to IMTs in China. Similarly the inability of level 7 markets to stand by themselves is seen in the absence of markets in the smallest han. There were about 1,700 SMT areas in Japan (including SMT areas served by cities at levels 1-6); therefore the average number of koku per market was 17,000-18,000. Han with up to 20,000 koku could not support a market, while the same number of koku in a large han was sufficient to produce a market. The explanation is that a single

SMT—whether in China or Japan—required other central places for support. In both countries groups of markets shared a ten-day cycle of marketing, permitting itinerant merchants to visit several places during the cycle. On the one hand, the frequency of 1/10 was more common in Japan and 2/10 was common in China and, on the other hand, Japanese villages frequently were part of the marketing systems of two or three central places, while Chinese villages invariably were associated with only one market. The average level 7 central place was supported by 11,000-13,000 people in China and 17,000-18,000 people (as many as there were official koku) in Japan.

IMTs can be equated with jōkamachi of 20,000-30,000 koku han and with some marketing places in han with at least 70,000 koku. Thus one level 6 city existed for every 75,000 people in Japan and for every 55,000-60,000 in China.

CMTs corresponded to jōkamachi of han with 30,000-100,000 koku and also to nonadministrative cities, mainly in large han containing at least 200,000 koku and in Bakufu administered lands. Altogether, one level 5 city was found for every 300,000 people in China and for every 100,000 people in Japan.

These two models of local marketing help us to understand the contrasting distributions of low level central places in China and Japan. Nakajima's model is applicable to a country with more concentrated local marketing activities than in Skinner's China. At levels 7 and 6 there were more Japanese per market, but at level 5—the highest level in local areas—the number of Chinese per market was larger. Marketing in Japan was relatively concentrated in more numerous level 5 cities at the expense of levels 6 and 7.

When population figures are available the number of central places at various levels can readily be determined and the applicability of these models can be checked. Also indicative of the scope of activities present in marketing places are the number of stores and the number of types of stores. If artisan stores are chosen as an example, then in both China and Japan five kinds of crafts were most widely represented: sawmills, carpentry stores, cooper stores, welder shops, and dyeing centers. All of these stores served the daily needs of consumers in central places. The larger the level of a city, the more stores of these types were likely to be present. In the level 5 city of Yamaguchi (Chūgoku) 263 of these five types of stores were located amidst the 1,500 households of the city.[24] Other craft stores which were present in cities at levels 5 and above included ones specializing in: oil, soy sauce, textiles, tile, rice-wine, and stonecutting. Where a large population could afford luxuries, such goods as elaborately woven textiles, raw silk, paper, lacquer, potteries, cosmetics, wax, ink, and vegetable oil would also be separated into private stores. The jōkamachi of Okazaki (Chūbu), which was a busy post in a han with 50,000 koku, had more than forty types of stores.[25]

National Markets

A national market exists when prices on items of mass consumption in principal cities of different regions are interrelated. Cities at levels 1 and 2 can be singled out as centers of regional branches within the national market, cities at level 3 served as funnels for goods from numerous local areas and cities at level 4 were collection points for goods from fewer than ten or even fewer than five level 5 centers. Goods flowed mainly in one direction. In China commerce moved from level 7 central places to cities at levels 1 and 2 in a step-by-step climb from one level to the next. Of course, many goods were diverted en route or were forwarded from levels 1 and 2 to other cities at lower levels, but most items moved from lower levels to higher levels. In Japan, except for the Kinki and Kantō areas where cities at levels 1 and 2 were drawing goods from their hinterlands and han boundaries were too close together to permit the trade barriers which existed elsewhere, jōkamachi linked local and national markets. Sea transportation made it possible for a single trip to connect cities at levels 1 and 2 to han collection and gathering centers. Moving by road or river from one city to the next, Chinese commerce was divided among a large number of cities. In contrast, the equivalent one-way flow in Japan was shipped primarily to three central cities. Correspondingly, the proportion of Japan's urban population living in the three cities of Edo, Osaka, and Kyoto matched the proportion of Chinese living in all cities at levels 1-4.

Long-distance shipments of goods had a long history in China. The old Grand Canal during the T'ang to Sung periods carried large shipments of rice from Kiangsu and Chekiang, areas so rich that they were said to be sufficient to feed the whole empire, i.e., to pay the salaries of the whole empire. The new canal as well as new sea routes during the Yuan and Ming periods carried even larger shipments of goods from the same areas to the northeast rather than to the northwest of China.

The birth of a national market can be traced to the Ming period. For instance, the contemporary Chinese historian Fu I-ling has described the development of commerce and the growing number of merchants in cities from the middle of the Ming period.[26] Information on the growth of hui-kuan and on rising specialization in products requiring a wide area for marketing, e.g., silk, hemp, ceramics, sugar, and cotton, indicates that the sixteenth century was a time of great advances.[27]

In some respects Ming long-distance trade resembled the lords' market in seventeenth century Japan. The system of supplying the vast needs of the officials and soldiers in northern China was similar to the early efforts to supply official needs in Edo and other central cities. Both tax revenues from various regions and commerce under licensed merchants moved to designated areas of consumption. The Ming system was characterized by the exchange of government-granted salt certificates for supplies brought by privileged merchants to soldiers stationed near the northern borders of China.[28] Salt was a government monopoly, but merchants given the right to sell large amounts of salt at fixed prices became some of the wealthiest men in China. Similar to the early privileged merchants in Japan, merchants from Hsin-an (Hui-chou fu in Anhwei) and from Shansi enriched themselves through the lucrative rewards from licensed commerce.[29]

In both Ch'ing China and Tokugawa Japan one economically advanced area in which the previous level 1 city had been located, stood out as the center of national marketing. Peking and, for a time, Edo were subsidiary marketing centers in poorer areas of their respective countries. The lower Yangtze and Kinki areas were favored by the intersection of major transport routes and by the abundance of rich agricultural lands. Three great arteries—the Yangtze river, the Grand Canal, and the Pacific Ocean converged in East-central China, where were located the three level 2 cities of

Nanking, Soochow, and Hangchow. The only other entrepôts in China which could rival Soochow alone were Wuhan (mainly the parts of the city known as Hankow and Wu-ch'ang), which dominated the center of China and joined routes to the northwest, west, and southwest to the lower Yangtze, and Canton, the principal city in the southeast. Kyoto, located on the shortest route across Honshū island, and Osaka, where this route connected to sea lanes linking East and West Japan, were the centers of the Kinki region. Holding the only level 2 cities in Japan, the Kinki region was a more concentrated locus of long-distance marketing than was the Yangtze delta, which held just three of the nine level 2 cities in China.

The national market of China can be divided into about fifteen primary trade routes for long-distance commerce. First the eighteen sheng should be regrouped into six regions: (1) North China: Chihli, Honan, Shantung, and Shansi; (2) East-central China: Kiangsu, Chekiang, and Anhwei; (3) Central China: Hupei, Hunan, and Kiangsi; (4) Southeast China: Fukien, Kwangtung, and Kwangsi; (5) Southwest China: Kweichow, Yunnan, and Szechwan; and (6) Northwest China: Shensi and Kansu.[30] Main arteries of intraregional trade within each of the six regions were sufficiently long to be listed as part of the long-distance network. In addition the principal ties between each region and its bordering regions formed about nine major flow patterns.

Of these fifteen trade routes, special attention should be paid to the routes between the East-central and the Central regions and between the East-central and the North regions. The Yangtze river joined many rich rice-producing provinces. By the Ch'ing period Kiangsu and Chekiang required rice imports from Anhwei, Kiangsi, and Hunan and at times from other sheng as well. When prices were exceptionally high in East-central China, even Szechwan rice was forwarded via Wuhan to these lower Yangtze sheng. Why did rice have to be imported into these fertile rice-growing provinces? There were three contributing conditions: population growth made parts of East-central China the most densely populated areas in the country; the imperial government forced rice exports as part of tax revenues to Peking; and a larger proportion of farmers in East-central China than elsewhere were engaged in commercial agricul-

TABLE 11

Major Long-distance Transportation Routes in China

Region	Point of Origin	Destination
1. North	Shantung, N. E. Honan, Chihli	Peking
2. East-central	S. Anhwei, N. Chekiang, S. Kiangsu	Soochow, Nanking Hangchow
3. Central	Hunan, Hupei	Wuhan
4. Southeast	Kwangsi, Kwangtung	Canton
5. Southwest	Szechwan	Chengtu, Chungking
6. Northwest	Kansu, Shensi	Sian
7. North & East-central	Chihli, Shantung, Kiangsu	Peking, Soochow
8. North & Central	Honan, Hupei	Wuhan
9. North & Northwest	Chihli, Shansi, Honan, Shensi	Peking, Sian
10. East-central & Central	Kiangsu, Anhwei, Hunan, Hupei, Kiangsi	Soochow, Nanking, Wuhan
11. East-central & Southeast	Kiangsu, Chekiang, Fukien, Kwangtung	Soochow, Hangchow, Foochow, Canton
12. Central & Southeast	Kiangsi, Fukien, Kwangtung	Foochow, Canton
13. Central & Southwest	Hupei, Szechwan	Wuhan, Chungking
14. Central & Northwest	Hupei, Shensi	Wuhan, Sian
15. Southwest & Northwest	Szechwan, Shensi	Chengtu, Sian

ture of products other than grain.[31] In addition to grain a wide variety of other goods floated down the Yangtze and many luxury items and processed goods sailed back in the opposite direction.[32]

Rice-marketing in nine sheng within three regions was notably interrelated. The three provinces of Central China sent rice to Chekiang and Kiangsu. Along the Yangtze the hsien city of Wu-hu in Anhwei sheng emerged as the number one rice market in China—the point at which rice bound for Chekiang and Kiangsu was concentrated. Taiwan (Fukien) and to a lesser extent south Chekiang and Kiangsi provided rice to mainland Fukien. And Kwangsi, with occasional support from Kiangsi and Hunan, supplied rice to Kwangtung. Within these three regions six sheng generally supplied rice and three sheng demanded it, but in years of unusual harvests patterns changed. Hunan and Kiangsi rice could be transferred to the southeast coast and Szechwan rice could be brought into the flow pattern.

Along the Grand Canal ships headed north carrying not only tax revenues in rice, but also smuggled goods. Sailors on vessels filled with government rice were frequently able to load illegal commerce during stops at bustling ports and to unload the goods further along where prices were higher.[33] Ceramics, drugs, paper, and tea made their way north in this way, at less cost to merchants than through regular commercial shipping. On the return trip south legal commercial cargoes such as fruits, beans, cotton, and wax were shipped, but some ships also carried salt illegally, a practice resulting in big financial losses to the government from the late eighteenth century.[34] The flow along the Grand Canal from south to north was mainly rice, certain luxury items, and processed goods; from north to south it was largely foodstuffs and nonprocessed goods.

The distribution of hui-kuan in Ch'ing China provides a clue to patterns of long-distance marketing. Groups of merchants living in cities generally outside of their own sheng organized hui-kuan. Altogether there were more than one thousand hui-kuan in Chinese cities. In general, the higher the level of a city, the more hui-kuan were present. Peking with the largest number was exceptional because of the noncommercial character of many of its hui-kuan.[35] Hankow (part of Wuhan) reached a total of 179 hui-kuan in 1920 and was probably second to Peking in the nineteenth century as well.[36] Other level 2 cities had tens of hui-kuan and level 3 cities usually had 1-7 hui-kuan during the nineteenth century.[37]

Merchants who founded hui-kuan were especially active in long-distance commerce. Typically the merchants from a particular administrative unit dominated traffic in a certain good within the city in which they built their hui-kuan. During the nineteenth century Kwangtung and Fukien merchants formed numerous hui-kuan in the Southeast, Anhwei merchants were declining from their former strength in the East-central region as merchants from the above two sheng and from Chekiang were extending their activities north along the coast, Shansi merchants were holding on while Shensi merchants were slipping in the North and Northwest and Kiangsi merchants were somewhat successful in Central, Southeast, and Southwest China. Of all the sheng, Kansu, Kwangsi, Yunnan and Kweichow were least represented in hui-kuan.[38] Shantung and Chihli also were not well known as sources for merchants who were active in outside provinces.

The growth of the national market in Japan can be seen from the fortunes of its three central cities. At the beginning of the Tokugawa period the total population of Edo, Osaka, and Kyoto probably did not reach 500,000. Kyoto stood out among the three in size. Three or four decades later the total population had climbed to 1 million, divided nearly evenly among the three cities. At the end of the seventeenth century the figure was about 1½ million. Half lived in Edo, but if only the chōnin population is considered, then the total of 1 million in the three cities was divided nearly evenly. By the beginning of the eighteenth century the state that was to remain essentially unchanged for 150 years was reached; the total population for the three cities was almost 2 million, with nearly 60 percent in Edo. When the populations of Kyoto and Osaka fell somewhat during the last third of the Tokugawa period, the proportion in Edo may have reached two-thirds. The growth of these three central cities required a continually increasing supply of goods from all over Japan. The extent of the national market was reflected in the population of these cities.

The national market in Japan can be divided into a lords' market and a farmers' market. Taxes generally brought in about 30 percent of the officially calculated agricultural production of a han—a figure which yielded the equivalent of approximately 6 million koku of rice. Of this total about one-third was received in cash and used locally and another one-third was received in rice and then distributed to bushi for consumption and sale within the han.[39] The remaining third was rice shipped out to be converted to money in the national marketing centers of Osaka and Edo or in ports en route to them. The conversion of government revenues into currency, whether in han, in intermediate ports or in central cities, constituted the lords' market, while goods which entered the commercial process after being sold directly by villagers formed the farmers' market. If the lords' and farmers' markets are combined, then the total flow moving into central places reached about 9 million koku, roughly divided into one-third to three central cities, one-third to jōkamachi, and one-third to other central places. In terms of consumption, Edo and Osaka (together with Kyoto and Sakai and other nearby Kinki central places) were each centers for approximately 1 million people. Among these consumers were some of the wealthiest people in Japan. Both the merchants—living chiefly in Osaka—who profited from commerce to the central cities and many of the daimyo and bushi—living chiefly in Edo—who relied on it were at the extreme of the income distribution. Similarly in China goods sent over long-distances were shipped and consumed largely by the wealthy. Private commerce made up a much larger part of long-distance transport in China; so for the Ch'ing period there is no need to refer to a separate lords' market.

The farmers' market in Japan filled gaps created by changes in the lords' market. The more the lords concentrated goods into jōkamachi, the more demand elsewhere in the han turned to new sources of supplies. Furthermore, the more daimyo sent goods to central cities, the more the residents of the jōkamachi had to seek commercial items as replacements. In central cities, too, supplies were generally inadequate; therefore commerce was encouraged by establishing or recognizing groups of merchants, who, it was expected, would increase the movement of goods at various levels of production and distribution. During the early seventeenth century merchants in other cities, especially within the Kinki region, were needed to supplement the flow coming into the central cities, but as more specialized merchant groupings developed in central cities from the mid-seventeenth century, many of the tasks previously undertaken in smaller cities were absorbed. During the second half of the seventeenth century a number of intermediate ports declined, e.g., Sakai fell from a population of about 90,000 in the mid-seventeenth century to about 50,000 a century later.[40] As the lords' market was becoming concentrated in Osaka and Edo, national marketing of all goods was switching to these cities.

Rice was commercialized mainly through the lords' market. Data for 1711 reveal that 1.4 million koku of rice arrived in Osaka, almost four-fifths of which was sent by daimyo or the Bakufu.[41] The remaining one-fifth was divided between 38 kuni; therefore the commercial export of rice to Osaka averaged less than 10,000 koku per kuni—an amount less than 2 percent of their rice output. The total supply of rice arriving in Edo was similar to the figure for Osaka, but larger amounts entered commercially while fewer daimyo sent their rice revenues to Edo.

Lists of nationally famous goods exist for late seventeenth century Japan and for fifty years earlier when the flow of specialized products was beginning to increase rapidly.[42] It is clear, especially from the earlier list, that high level crafts and specialty goods were concentrated in the Kinki area. Throughout the rest of Japan each large han was linked to the central market by a few special products such as a noted variety of cotton or oil sent to a Kinki area city. The number of goods which attracted sufficient acclaim to be mentioned on this list was usually fewer than thirty per kuni and even totals below ten were common. For instance, most of the Kantō kuni during the early seventeenth century had fewer than ten noteworthy items each. Edo was clearly a consumer city at this time; goods which were processed in the city attracted little notice. Kyoto, however, bedazzled the residents in other cities with its brilliant craftsmanship. Of the 287 items identified with this one city about 65 were related to clothing, 70 to artistic handicrafts, 17 to drugs, 14 to weapons, 4 to rice-wine, and 71 to daily-use goods. The city had the advantage of a long history as the center of traditional craft skills and of well-established patterns of imports and exports. In the production of textiles, weapons, and certain other goods more items were noted for Kyoto than for the rest of Japan combined. Second to Kyoto was Osaka, but unlike the older city in which luxury items prevailed, Osaka produced for a mass market. During the middle of the seventeenth century increased rice for consumption and raw materials for processing arrived in Osaka, and the city gained as the predominance of a small lords' market for luxury items in the first half of the century was giving way to large-scale production for the growing commercial needs in daily necessities of both bushi and chōnin. Not only Kyoto and Osaka, but other Kinki area jōka-machi and ports had nationwide reputations for large numbers of specialized goods.

From the time of the above list to 1692 commerce grew rapidly in Japan. Osaka was the real gainer, but Edo also improved its position markedly. By 1692 Kyoto and Edo were about equal in commercial importance, but Osaka had moved ahead with as many types of nationally famous items handled by merchants and artisans as could be found in the other two cities combined.[43] The list can be summarized as follows: (1) items for daily use: Osaka = 385; Kyoto = 251, and Edo = 163; (2) drugs: Osaka = 442, Edo = 126, and Kyoto = 70; (3) goods related to clothing and to rice: Osaka = 44, Edo = 15, and Kyoto = 15; (4) weapons: Osaka = 96, Edo = 83, and Kyoto = 76; (5) artistic crafts: Kyoto = 175, Edo = 154, and Osaka = 49; (6) publishing: Osaka = 50, Edo = 49, and Kyoto = 31; and (7) foodstuffs: Edo = 64, Kyoto = 40, and Osaka = 23. Each city had carved a niche in the national market. Osaka fared best in goods produced for mass needs. Supplying daily necessities to wide areas of Japan, Osaka was known as "the kitchen of Japan" and was particularly important in the supply of Edo. Kyoto was the principal source of high quality textiles and crafts, shipping to Edo, Osaka, and to other locations of scattered wealthy customers. Edo supplied little to the other two great cities, producing for its own residents.

If a similar list of notable products were available for the last century of the Tokugawa period, many of these patterns would likely have remained from 1692, but Edo's position would undoubtedly have risen relative to the other two cities. While the number of chōnin in Osaka and Kyoto increased a little and then declined, Edo's chōnin population rose substantially after the 1692 list appeared.

The usual view of Tokugawa cities is that Edo was a city of consumers who were dependent on the commercial entrepôt of Osaka for material support. Osaka is viewed as the collection and distribution center of both the nation's tax rice and its specialized commerce. To some extent this viewpoint is correct, though for at least the second half of Tokugawa rule Edo would deserve nearly equal billing as a center of the national market.[44] Osaka's situation was instrumental in its rise. Kyoto was located inland and could not serve as an intermediate point in the supply of Edo. Edo was located in the east and could not be a center for commerce between the more numerous western kuni. Five of the seven regions of Japan were more accessible to Osaka and a large part of the Tōhoku region was also more closely linked to Osaka than to Edo. The eclipse of Kyoto by Osaka in the mid-seventeenth century was accelerated by the emerging western mawari route carrying Tōhoku and Hokuriku and later Hokkaidō products all the way around the Chūgoku region to Osaka. Previously the overland route from Tsuruga (Chūbu) to Kyoto had carried heavy traffic, but Tsuruga declined rapidly after reaching its peak in the 1660s when more than 300,000 koku were sent annually across Lake Biwa toward Kyoto.

Osaka's supremacy was greatest during the early eighteenth century. In 1714 the value of imports to the city reached about 450,000 kan of silver, the equivalent of about 4 million koku of rice in that year.[45] Of this total more than 46 percent was rice, including noncommercial rice. Commercial items exceeding 10,000 kan in value were rice, dried sardines (fertilizer), paper, iron, vegetables, and vegetable oil. Many of these items were reexported to various han and to Edo. Shipments from Osaka to Edo, similar to traffic along the Grand Canal from Kiangsu sheng to Peking, were vital to the national administrative center. Concerned about high prices in Edo, the Bakufu recognized tonya to increase and control the supply from Osaka to Edo. At their height Osaka merchants stood at the zenith of a chain of credit extending to daimyo and to merchants throughout Japan. Han raw materials or partly finished goods were sent to tonya in Osaka, whose loans had cemented the relationships between merchants en route.

Other Bakufu policies were less beneficial to the commercial population of Osaka. For instance, to increase the supply of certain goods to Edo, production in Kinki and Kantō zaikatachō was encouraged. As a result, goods produced in Osaka faced stiff competition. From the late eighteenth century, the quantity of vegetable oil from Osaka was declining in Edo; nevertheless, of the 100,000 barrels of oil needed annually in Edo, Osaka continued to supply more than half.[46]

Chōnin from both Kyoto and Osaka were damaged by the dispersion of skills from their cities to smaller settlements. The growth of local textile processing especially affected Kyoto merchants. By the early nineteenth century old commercial monopolies had been broken, new han monopolies were appearing, zaikatachō in the Kantō region were flourishing, and decentralization was in full swing. Bakufu policies to lower the prices of commerce to Edo had first enhanced Osaka's rise and then contributed to its decline. Changes in marketing were reflected both in new Bakufu and han policies and in the redistribution of urban population and activities.

Summary

The development of marketing was accompanied by transformations in the countryside and the city, in the local area and the nation. For a time there were practically no local markets. Then a volatile period was reached when level 7 central places had become evident, but because level 6 cities had not yet appeared, they lacked regular ties to higher level cities. Free-floating resources in the countryside could be gathered by those who controlled these isolated centers of commerce. The late T'ang and Five Dynasties periods in China and the fourteenth century in Japan witnessed struggling efforts to reunite the two countries on a commercial foundation. Finally, in correspondence to the completion of the seven-level hierarchies and the expansion of national marketing another opportunity for substantial social change occurred. Although the basic forms of Chinese society until the twentieth century were established during these decisive decades of the mid to late Ming dynasty, the changes which resulted in patterns of social mobility, the system of hui-kuan, the transportation system, and other features of the society basically sustained rather than transformed preexisting patterns. In contrast, Japanese leaders responded to a rapidly changing network of marketing by creating an unprecedented centralized society. In both countries once the seven levels were firmly in existence few basic innovations were later introduced.

In this book I disregard the policies of leaders not because I regard all decisions as inevitable consequences of existing conditions, but because innovations are limited by the setting in which they occur. Prior to examining the innovations one ought to know the limiting conditions. Unfortunately, most students of history have concentrated on the innovators, not on their societies. We should remember that Toyotomi Hideyoshi and Tokugawa Ieyasu, renowned as the architects of the new society, appeared at the propitious moment when the seven-level hierarchy was nearing completion. In contrast, a more slowly changing network of marketing in China dulled the impact of steady development. China did not produce a Hideyoshi or an Ieyasu. Leaders failed to perceive new opportunities for dramatic innovations.

The three sections of Chapter 3 cast new light on the principal themes considered in Chapters 1 and 2. The section on the development of marketing should be viewed in connection with Table 2, which indicates the stages of premodern development as reflected in the number of urban levels in existence. As the number of nonadministrative central places steadily increased, the entire network was transformed. New levels of cities appeared at characteristic points in the growth of marketing settlements. Changes in the society accompanied expanding marketing.

All three sections of Chapter 3 should be viewed in connection with the diagram on page xv, which depicts advanced premodern societies in terms of their urban networks. As Tables 6 and 7 indicate, even after the completion of all seven levels considerable growth occurred in the number of nonadministrative cities. The section on marketing in local areas denotes the basic differences in patterns at one extreme of the hierarchy of urban levels and the section on national markets shows that activities concentrated in three Japanese cities were more dispersed in China.

The models devised by Skinner and Nakajima were based on a sample of the marketing data in both countries. One way to determine the applicability of these models is to examine selected areas in detail, as I do in Chapter 4. A second way is to compare regional variations, as I do in Chapter 5. The most fundamental approach, however, is to compare these models directly with each other, as I have done in this chapter. In this way, we can generalize about the entire urban network in China and Japan and about Chinese and Japanese societies as a whole. Further application of this spatial approach to societies would permit comparisons of all premodern countries in which marketing was the primary means of exchange.

PART

✻ *II* ✻

PART II: INTRODUCTION

Part II progresses from the more specific examination of local areas to the general presentation of national networks of central places. It begins with a closeup of cities in designated local areas, then shifts to an overview of urban patterns in all provinces and regions, and concludes with a focus on Peking and Edo as the pivotal points in the hierarchies of central places in China and Japan respectively. Chihli province and the Kantō region were chosen for special attention in Chapter 4 because they were the locations of the respective national administrative centers of Peking and Edo and are similarly regarded as neither advanced economic areas nor the poorest areas in their countries. Moving outward from these areas, we see in Chapter 5 the remaining areas of China and Japan and then conclude in Chapter 6 by observing the level 1 cities and by preparing to compare urban networks in China and Japan with those in other countries. This effort that begins with the close study of local areas will be completed only when generalized spatial patterns can be ascertained for many other premodern societies.

The greatest attention in these chapters is given to the presentation and analysis of data. Most statistics have been gathered with the aim of determining two essential figures: the number of central places in a given area and the number of urban residents in those central places. It is important to make clear where these numbers originated, how they were assembled and what error is likely to be present. I will make these clarifications separately for Chapters 4 and 5.

Data on hsien and chou in Chapter 4 are obtained by adding together all marketing towns mentioned in gazetteers and in other sources. The figures I have obtained for each Chinese administrative unit can be replicated by turning to the appropriate sections in the gazetteers in the special lists appended at the end of Chapter 4 and Chapter 5. The long lists of gazetteers for each of these two chapters are intended to be used as working bibliographies; only sources of information used in this book are included. Unfortunately the publication dates of these gazetteers vary widely. We may learn that one hsien had five markets in 1700 and that another had ten markets in 1875. This kind of information is a drawback in the effort to ascertain aggregate figures for a single date. Nonetheless, figures are noted for two or more dates in many hsien and chou, and they reveal a gradual rise in the number of central places. Approximate totals for the mid-nineteenth century can be obtained by assuming that central places were added at the same rate in areas for which only an earlier or a later figure is available. Despite the absence in most cases of sources that can be used to check the information in a single gazetteer, there is no reason to believe that the data on central places are inaccurate since these materials were written locally by men who could easily have counted the small numbers of markets in the area. The fact that gazetteers list the names, locations, frequencies, and sometimes other information about markets gives added credence to these figures.

The statistics on population and on numbers of villages in the administrative units of Chihli sheng also pertain to various points in time. Where possible the total is given for the mid-nineteenth century. Undoubtedly there are many cases where hsien and chou population totals are understated, even though I discard the notoriously unreliable low estimates given in late nineteenth century gazetteers whenever higher earlier enumerations are also available. Even more obvious are underestimations of the number of villages. However, these data are presented only for reference purposes. I am confident that the reader can quickly spot suspicious figures in the Tables by comparing the three columns showing area, population, and villages. A hsien with a large population and area is likely to have a correspondingly large total of villages. All of these figures provide background for evaluating the number of markets in an administrative unit, essential for determining the area's urban population.

The most difficult figures to determine are the number of central places at the seven levels as given in the summary at the end of this chapter. Although it is possible to calculate the total number of central places in Chihli province by adding the figures for each administrative unit and extrapolating for the few units for which no data are available, the task of distributing these central places among the various levels requires additional information. Throughout Chapter 4 I point to clues such as marketing frequencies and numbers of streets which can be used to estimate urban levels. Occasionally populations of cities are given in gazetteers. In addition, detailed accounts of some hsien and chou cities are found in the *Shina shōbetsu zenshi*, a Japanese publication written immediately after the fall of the Ch'ing dynasty. Fortunately the task is not to choose between two levels for a given city, but to divide the total number of hsien cities between levels 5 and 6, of nonadministrative periodic marketing centers between levels 5, 6, and 7, and of major chou cities between levels 4 and 5. Much of the information in Chapter 4 reveals how these choices were made. Yet, it should be remembered that the figures in the Tables are only approximations, an error of 10 percent or even 20 percent could conceivably be present.

The Japanese urban data in Chapter 4 also require some explanation. In contrast to the data for China, the population of large cities and even of many small jōkamachi and post stations is well documented. In addition, secondary sources referred to in footnotes describe many marketing centers and the late Tokugawa maps reprinted in the *DaiNihon koku saizu zen* [Complete detailed maps of Japan] show many central places. Especially useful is an article by Muto Tadashi, "Waga kuni kinsei makki ni okeru toshi seiritsu no kihon ni tsuite" [Concerning the foundations for the establishment of cities in late Tokugawa Japan]. Yet, it is usually difficult to determine the precise number of central places in a kuni and for many kuni the distribution of nonadministrative cities among levels 5, 6, and 7 is unclear. While the gaps in information and therefore the probable errors are smaller for the Kantō region than for Chihli, the reader should nonetheless be aware that the figures in the Japanese charts are also estimates, and for lower level central places the error may not be inconsiderable.

Data used in Chapter 5 as in Chapter 4 are from local gazetteers on China and from twentieth century secondary works on Japan.

Whereas I was able to refer to gazetteers for almost every administrative unit in Chihli province (116 in all), this would not have been possible for all of the more than 1,600 units in China. Instead I chose a sample of gazetteers for each sheng, obtaining useful information on at least 20 percent of the hsien and chou for all provinces except for Kansu and Yunnan, two provinces at the extreme northwest and southwest which are poorly represented by gazetteers. Provincial gazetteers from Shantung, Kweichow, and Kwangtung provide data on the number of central places in almost all hsien and chou, which added to the data on Chihli sheng accounts for more than one-fifth of all administrative units in China. Altogether information on central places in more than 600 Chinese hsien and chou forms the basis for most of the generalizations in Chapter 5.

Available data vary greatly from one Chinese province to another. For some provinces populations of large cities are determined without much difficulty. For other provinces the number of streets in major cities can be used for estimating population. However, in a few provinces accounts of large city populations are wildly at variance with each other. Although in Tables for each province I always choose a single figure for cities at a particular level, I also indicate in some cases that there is reason not to place confidence in these figures.

Populations given in the *Shina shōbetsu zenshi* for major cities in provinces which had experienced considerable change by the early twentieth century and figures given in the 1953 census, the most thorough compilation of the post-Ch'ing decades, are included for purposes of comparison. It is true that the definition of urban in 1953 was not precisely the same as mine, but the differences are not great. In 1953 all settlements were included which contained more than 1,000 people, in which more than half of those employed were engaged in nonagricultural occupations. Remember that the total urban population for the mid-nineteenth century is calculated by omitting level 7 central places and by dividing the population in level 6 central places in half.

Estimates of the total number of central places in most provinces are based on extrapolation from samples of roughly 25 percent of hsien and chou. This process was normally carried out by calculating the proportion of the total provincial population inhabiting the units sampled. The most difficult task was to divide central places between levels 7, 6, and 5. To the extent that information was not available, I have assumed that between 20 percent and 25 percent of periodic marketing settlements with fewer than 3,000 people ranked at level 6 and the rest ranked at level 7. Where level 6 centers appeared to be relatively numerous as in Kiangsu and Chekiang, I chose a figure close to 25 percent. The percentage ascertained through a more intensive survey of Chihli sheng fell just below 22 percent. In determining the number of central places at level 5, I sought some positive evidence, either from the sample of gazetteers chosen or from the *Shina shōbetsu zenshi*. Generally, the ratio of level 5 to level 6 settlements fell below 1:4, somewhat lower than the ratio of central market towns to intermediate market towns in Skinner's calculations for 1948 ("Marketing and Social Structure in Rural China," p. 228).

In any case, since the population figures assigned to all cities at each level are only estimates, they are rounded off to the nearest 100,000 or at times 50,000. Taking Honan province as an example, even if the 2,600 central places had consisted of 600 at level 6 and 90 at level 5 rather than 500 and 75 as recorded, the total urban population would only have been calculated as 100,000 greater, yielding 5.4 percent rather than 5.0 percent, urban. Percentages are calculated by using regional and provincial population data from Ho Ping-ti, *Studies in the Population of China, 1368-1953* and from Sekiyama Naotarō, *Nihon no jinko*, pp. 82-83. Owing to the inadequacy of data the reader should always be aware of the possibility of an error of this magnitude, which in any case would not substantially affect the conclusions of this book except for some of the comparisons of provinces and regions in China.

Japanese regional data are more abundant and detailed. Problems exist in calculating the total number of central places and in dividing central places between levels 5, 6, and 7, but some sources are especially useful such as *Shukueki* [Post stations], which lists the population of more than 200 settlements, and the above-mentioned *DaiNihon koku saizu zen*. Errors are likely to be less for the estimates given in the Tables on Japan, except for data on levels 6 and 7, which are not as important in calculating urban population totals.

✳ *4* ✳

CHIHLI SHENG AND THE KANTŌ REGION

The network of central places in a single area of each country is examined in this chapter. Chihli sheng with 1,500-2,000 central places was divided into nine fu and six chih-li chou. Tables 13-22 presented below for each fu (except Ta-ming for which data are not available) and chih-li chou give such information for hsien and chou as the number of central places, the number of villages, and the approximate area and population. The principal aim is to describe lower level central places, individually and in interrelationship. Level 7 periodic markets were so numerous and so little distinctive information is available that they are not considered separately. More attention is directed to level 6 intermediate markets, including some hsien cities. Most detailed descriptions are reserved for cities at levels 4 and 5, the centers for local areas of hundreds or thousands of square miles. Land use, population distribution, street patterns, and other factors relating to urban size are described, adding to our general knowledge about the urban network.

The second part of this chapter is devoted to the Kantō area, a region with 200-250 central places. The treatment of this region of Japan is much briefer because the number of central places was far fewer. The eight Kantō kuni are described separately, ranging from populous Musashino with roughly a third of the region's central places to tiny Awa with only a handful of central places. Han administrative boundaries and the overriding presence of Edo shaped the urban network in ways without any counterpart in China. Omitting any treatment of the historic development of this area, I will only focus in this short section on lower level central places as they existed during the early nineteenth century.

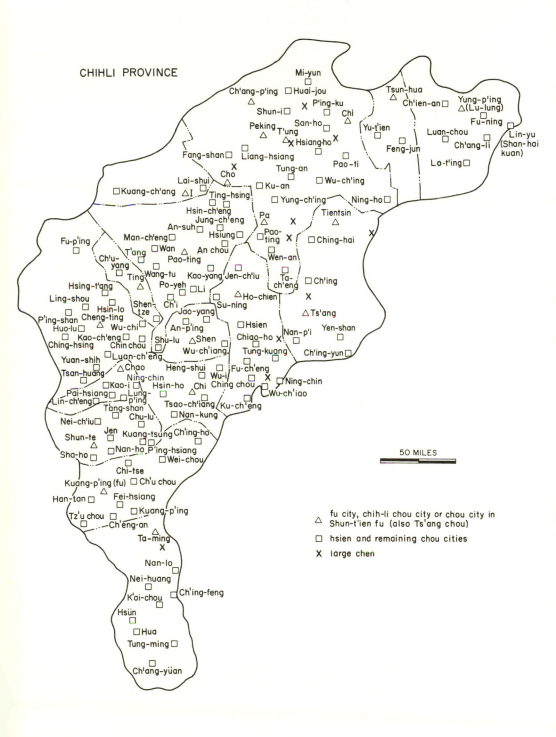

CHIHLI PROVINCE

Mi-yun
Ch'ang-p'ing Huai-jou
Shun-i X P'ing-ku
San-ho Chi
Peking T'ung
Fang-shan Hsiang-ho
Liang-hsiang
Cho
Lai-shui
Kuang-ch'ang I Ting-hsing
Hsin-ch'eng
Jung-ch'eng
An-suh
Man-ch'eng Hsiung
Fu-p'ing Wan An chou
Ch'u- T'ang
yang Pao-ting
Ting Wang-tu Kao-yang Jen-ch'iu
Hsing-t'ang Po-yeh Li Ta-
Ling-shou Shen- Ch'i ch'eng
Hsin-lo tze Jao-yang Su-ning
P'ing-shan Cheng-ting Ho-chien
Huo-lu Wu-chi An-p'ing Hsien
Kao-ch'eng Shen Nan-p'i
Ching-hsing Chin chou Shu-lu Chiao-ho
Yuan-shih Luan-ch'eng Wu-ch'iang Tung-kuang
Tsan-huang Chao Heng-shui Fu-ch'eng
Ning-chin Wu-i Ch'ing-yun
Pai-hsiang Kao-i Hsin-ho Chi Ching chou
Lin-ch'eng Lung- Ning-chin
T'ang-shan p'ing Tsao-ch'iang Ku-ch'eng Wu-ch'iao
Nei-ch'iu Chu-lu Nan-kung
Shun-te Jen Kuang-tsung Ch'ing-ho
Sha-ho Nan-ho P'ing-hsiang
Chi-tse Wei-chou
Kuang-p'ing (fu) Ch'u chou
Han-tan Fei-hsiang
Tz'u chou Kuang-p'ing
Ch'eng-an
Ta-ming
Nan-lo
Nei-huang
K'ai-chou Ch'ing-feng
Hsün
Hua
Tung-ming
Ch'ang-yüan

Mi-yun
Tsun-hua Ch'ien-an Yung-p'ing
(Lu-lung)
Yu-t'ien Fu-ning
Feng-jun Luan-chou Lin-yu
Ch'ang-li (Shan-hai
Pao-ti Lo-t'ing kuan)
Wu-ch'ing
Yung-ch'ing Ning-ho
Ku-an Tientsin
Pa
Pao- Ching-hai
ting Wen-an
Ch'ing
Ts'ang
Yen-shan

50 MILES

△ fu city, chih-li chou city or chou city in
   Shun-t'ien fu (also Ts'ang chou)

□ hsien and remaining chou cities

X large chen

Chihli—General

Since most of the information on Chihli sheng has been gathered from local gazetteers written for individual hsien, chou, chih-li chou, and fu, it will be useful to discuss briefly the constancy of administrative boundaries in Chihli during the Ch'ing period.[1] Omitting the period after 1880, we find that the first century of Ch'ing rule was the time of most frequent change in administrative units. In *Shun-t'ien fu* [the location of Peking] there were twenty-two hsien and five chou in 1644, but one hsien was transferred to a chih-li chou in 1659, another hsien was transferred out in 1676, and during the twelve-year reign of Yung-cheng (1723-35) as well as the first years of the Ch'ien-lung reign immediately following a number of other transfers occurred. By 1744 stability had at last been reached; the units in this fu numbered nineteen hsien and five chou. *Pao-ting fu* held seventeen hsien and three chou in 1644. During the Yung-cheng reign two hsien were transferred to chih-li chou and one chou was raised to become a chih-li chou. The only other change came in 1832 when Hsin-an hsien was incorporated into An chou, leaving fourteen hsien and two chou. The tendency for area to be taken away from large fu was also evident in *Cheng-ting fu*. From an initial state of twenty-seven hsien and five chou, the fu total fell to thirteen hsien and one chou after numerous changes during the Yung-cheng reign. Similarly *Ho-chien fu* dropped from sixteen hsien and two chou to ten hsien and one chou and *Ta-ming fu* dropped from ten hsien and one chou to six hsien and one chou. The three relatively small fu of *Yung-p'ing, Kuang-p'ing* and *Shun-te*, however, managed to hold constant or to add one unit to the seven to ten hsien and chou with which they began the Ch'ing period. *Tien-tsin fu*, after being established by Yung-cheng, remained at six hsien and one chou. From the above examples it is evident that the redistribution of hsien was mainly from large fu to chih-li chou. Chou were raised to chih-li chou and each received two to five hsien units.

Chihli sheng was the most northeasterly of the eighteen sheng, too dry for rice paddies and too far north for many of the famed crops of China. Concentrated on the large North China plain, the population was sparse in the generally mountainous and barren areas along the northern and western borders of the sheng. The southern and central parts of the sheng shared the farming conditions of northern Honan and western Shantung. Dry grains such as wheat, millet, and kaoliang, made up most of the harvest.

There were fewer than ten major transportation routes in Chihli sheng. First in importance was the Grand Canal uniting the eastern part of the sheng with the north central area, joining parts of Ho-chien fu, Tientsin fu, and Shun-t'ien fu. Along this route were many chen as well as the principal cities of Ts'ang chou, Tientsin, and T'ung chou. The presence of the Grand Canal in Shantung not far from the southern panhandle of Chihli was divisive. Cities in Ta-ming fu and in most of Kuang-p'ing fu were closely tied to Shan-tung and to northeastern Honan by various routes, including the Wei river. Unlike most of Chihli sheng, which was served by the three centers of the urban network in Peking, Tientsin, and Pao-ting, the far south was oriented to Lin-ch'ing, a level 3a chih-li chou city along the Grand Canal in Shantung. Next to these waterways in volume of transportation may have been two kuan-lu, forming north-south land routes intersecting in Peking. The eastern kuan-lu near the Grand Canal could not compete successfully for long-distance transport, but the western kuan-lu connected many of the major cities located in the west of Chihli sheng to Peking. The fu cities of Cheng-ting and Shun-te as well as the sheng city of Pao-ting were all stops on this western road. Moreover, a branch road veering west from Cheng-ting city provided the principal link between Chihli sheng and its neighbor Shansi. Other major roads in this province led to the northeast and northwest from Peking, joining inner areas of China to Manchuria and Mongolia. Both the north-eastern road from Peking and a road from Tientsin united Yung-p'ing fu to the remainder of the sheng. Even though the absence of large rivers in Chihli sheng necessitated exceptional dependence on land transport, rivers which did cross the province were readily used, especially for east-west trade joining areas of Pao-ting, Cheng-ting, and Shun-t'ien fu to Tientsin fu city.

There was no uniform standard for weighing grains in China. Each area adopted its own standard for measurement; yet similar standards were often used by areas with close marketing ties. By examining the distribution of standard weights used in a single hsien or even in an entire province, it is possible to identify marketing patterns. For instance, Momose Hiromu has used information on weights to divide Ch'ing hsien (Tientsin fu) into six areas, to which I will refer later.[2] Data on weights are also given in a gazetteer for Feng-jun hsien (Tsun-hua chih-li chou).[3] Unfortunately the only detailed listing of the weights used as grain standards in numerous areas of Chihli sheng dates from 1930. These figures given in a gazetteer for Pa chou (Shun-t'ien fu) may reflect the changed conditions after railroads had been constructed and Tientsin had quickly expanded, but they are still likely to provide clues to patterns of flow during the Ch'ing period, particularly since early efforts at modernization did not penetrate widely and most marketing areas remained little changed.[4] The standards were divided as follows: (1) more than fifty cities with standard weights ranging between 19 and 27 units, were located on or near straight lines from Pao-ting sheng city to Peking, from Peking to Tientsin and from Tientsin to Tsun-hua; (2) about twenty-five cities with weights of roughly 40 to 45, were located in areas either south or northeast of the above weights— one cluster was along river routes east of Pao-ting fu to the outskirts of Tientsin and a second cluster was found in Yung-p'ing fu; (3) another twenty cities with weights ranging between 192 and 420 units, were split along two paths—the lower scores followed the Grand Canal to Ts'ang chou (Tientsin fu) and the higher scores crossed the southern panhandle from Honan to Shantung. Since all of the above routes were widely used for Ch'ing transport, it is conceivable that clusters similar to the ones revealed in the 1930 data would have been indicated if earlier data had been available.

Momose has also brought to public attention extremely detailed late nineteenth century information on the population of settlements in certain areas of Chihli.[5] Figures for Ch'ing hsien, Shen chou (a pen chou, i.e., the part of a chih-li chou centering on the chih-li chou city rather than on a hsien city) and Cheng-ting hsien (Cheng-ting fu) indicate that villages with fewer than 100 households were most common. Settlements with more than 100 households numbered 15 percent in Ch'ing hsien, 33 percent in Shen chou, and 32 percent in Cheng-ting, and those with more than 200 households numbered

2 percent, 8 percent, and 7 percent respectively. Information on these administrative units reveals that markets were frequently, but not always, located in the largest settlements. For instance, the three most populous cities in Ch'ing hsien were marketing loci, but markets also could be found at three villages in which resided fewer than 100 households. While more than ten settlements with populations in excess of 200 households held markets in Shen chou, so too did several central places which had populations falling short of 100 households.

The relationship shown in these three areas between settlement size and marketing is substantiated by other information from North China.[6] The larger the population, the greater was the likelihood that a market was present. Although nearly all settlements counting fewer than 1,000 residents (four to five people per household) lacked markets, ones with as many as 2,000 people almost always possessed markets. In general, the more people in a marketing settlement, the more likely that it was at level 6 rather than at level 7. Roughly speaking, central places in Chihli sheng with fewer than 100 households were at level 7, those with 100-200 households were also predominantly at level 7 but occasionally at level 6, those with 200-700 households were likely to be sufficiently active to rank at level 6 and the rare nonadministrative city in which more than 700 households could be found ranked, by definition if the ratio of people to household was as expected, at level 5. Thus of the approximately 50,000 settlements in Chihli sheng, the estimated 12,000 which held more than 100 households may have been divided as in Table 12.

Figures from many administrative units indicate that approximately 20 percent of the settlements with more than 200 households

TABLE 12

Estimated Distribution of Chihli Settlements
with More than 100 Households

Number of Households	Without Market	Level 7	Level 6
100–200	8,500	600	100
200–700	2,250	300	250

were central places, that the percentage fell to less than 10 percent for settlements with 100-200 households and to only 1 percent for the three-fourths of all settlements in Chihli in which fewer than 100 households were found.

Chou

The five chou cities in *Shun-t'ien fu* were distinguished by their locations at the gateways to Peking. All except T'ung chou were

TABLE 13

Chihli—Shun-t'ien Fu

Administrative Unit[a]	Area[b]	Villages[c]	Population[d]	CFPN[e]	City Wall[f]	Markets[g]
Cho chou	A	400	A	CFN	9	11
T'ung chou	A	600	L	CFPN	21	10
Chi chou	L	900	L	CF	9	9
Pa chou	S	300	A	CN	6	9
Ch'ang-p'ing chou	L	400	A	CFN		5
Shun-i	VL	300	A	CN	6	5
Mi-yun	VL	300	A	CFN	9	2
P'ing-ku	VS	100	VS	J	3	2
Huai-jou	S	100	VS	CF	4	1
Ta-hsing	S	300	VL	CFPN	} 60–70	
Wan-p'ing	A	400	VL	CFPN		
Liang-hsiang	VS	100	VS	CFN	3	5
Fang-shan	L	200	A	FN	4	3
Ku-an	S	400	A	FN	5	14
Yung-ch'ing	S	400	A	Y	5	9
Tung-an	A	500	A	Y	7	10
Wen-an	A	400	L	FN	8	14
Ta-ch'eng	S	300	A	FN	4	8
Pao-ting	VS	100	VS	J	6	1
Hsiang-ho	VS	300	A	J	7	6
San-ho	A	500	L	CFN	6	10
Wu-ch'ing	L	400	VL	CFN	8	14
Pao-ti	L	900	L	FPN	6	13
Ning-ho	L	300	L	PN	10	4

[a]Administrative units unless otherwise designated are hsien.

near the boundaries of the fu about fifty miles from Peking: Cho chou to the southwest, Chi chou to the northeast, Pa chou to the south, and Ch'ang-p'ing chou to the north. T'ung chou city, to the east nearest the capital and the terminus of the Grand Canal, was the most populous of the five.

---

[b] Area refers to the percentage of the total sheng area occupied: VL = very large = 1.6%+; L = large = 1.0–1.59%; A = average = .65–.99%; S = small = .36–.64%; VS = very small = .35%–.

[c] Villages: the total is given, where possible, for the middle of the nineteenth century and is rounded off to the nearest 100. Figures are primarily from gazetteers, but where inconsistencies or gaps in data were evident twentieth century Chinese and Japanese compilations have been consulted in an effort to estimate earlier village totals.

[d] Population: the total is given, where possible, for the middle of the nineteenth century: VL = 350,000+, L = 175,000–349,999; A = 100,000–174,999; S = 70,000–99,999; VS = fewer than 70,000.

[e] CFPN: this is a system of rankings established for all administrative units in China during the Yung-cheng reign. See the *Ch'ien-lung fu t'ing chou hsien t'u-chih* (Peking, 1789). The rankings were used to match the ability of an official to the difficulty of an assignment.

C = *ch'ung* = a thoroughfare or an area with important communications leading in one or more directions; F = *fan* = full of complications or an area in which the pressure of business in government offices was great; P = *p'o* = fatiguing or an area in which the official would be exhausted with the complexity of legal cases; N = *nan* = difficult or an area in which it was not easy to govern the people; also used, though more sparingly over much of China, were Y = *yao* and J = *chun*, refering to strategic and to out-of-the-way areas. C indicates traffic; F indicates population; P indicates legal cases; and N indicates peace, but I have found no explanation of the standards used in deciding whether to award each of these letters to a given administrative unit. Therefore, these rankings can be used only as rough indications of differences between areas. While an area ranked CFPN had considerable traffic, a large population, a crowded docket, and an unruly population, one ranked J presumably displayed none of these characteristics. Generally the following division of these rankings corresponds to decreasingly developed urban networks (in terms of the level of the largest city and of the number of central places): (1) CFPN, (2) CFN, CFP and CF, (3) CN, CPN, CP, and (4) PN, N, P, J and Y. Not all of these rankings are found in Shun-t'ien fu, but all four of the groupings are represented. The two largest cities in the fu, Peking (Ta-hsing hsien and Wan-p'ing hsien) and T'ung chou, ranked in the first group and the tiny hsien of P'ing-ku and Pao-ting, which contained few marketing settlements, ranked in the fourth group. Exceptional cases of undeveloped hsien which ranked in the second or third groupings rather than in the fourth were particularly numerous in this fu because areas benefited by their proximity to Peking and to the defenses along the Great Wall; Shun-i and Mi-yun were not prosperous, but were located just north of Peking and south of the Great Wall. Notice that the chou all ranked in the first or second groupings, corresponding to the unusual attributes of these chou cities to which I will refer below.

[f] Walls: the figure indicates the number of *li* in circumference or perimeter for the administrative city's wall (3 li = ca. 1 mile, 1 li = 550 yards).

[g] Markets: the numbers given include all central places. The administrative city is listed only once although several marketing areas were frequently dispersed within its wall and kuan.

Cho chou was situated between a grain deficit area to the north and west and a grain surplus area to the east and south. Hsien in the deficit area held five or fewer markets, while hsien on the other sides of Cho chou held more than ten markets. Similarly, markets within the chou were concentrated in the south. The chou city, like many administrative centers in Chihli, was located ten to fifteen miles from the boundaries of the three neighboring hsien and about twenty miles from each of their hsien cities. Most markets were found near the borders between seven and thirteen miles from the chou city. Some of the markets served villagers in surrounding hsien as well as those in this chou and at least one market settlement straddled the boundary, being divided between two hsien. Evidence from other areas shows that it was common for two or even three hsien and chou to share a marketing settlement on or near their common border. When there were eleven central places in Cho chou, the chou city had a daily market, three markets met 4/10 and seven markets met 2/10. These three frequencies of marketing may correspond to three levels of central places: the administrative center was a level 4 or level 5 city, the three 4/10 markets were level 6 cities, and the seven 2/10 markets probably ranked at level 7.

The form of Cho chou city reflected its importance as a major post station. Both the southwest and northeast sections of the city, areas through which the kuan-lu from Pao-ting to Peking passed, were heavily settled. The relatively lively commerce within the southeastern part of the chou presumably contributed to the substantial buildup in the southeast section too.

T'ung chou was strategic, populous, and thriving. The military importance of the city lay not just in its position as the principal gateway to Peking, but also in its role as the storehouse for the capital. Large quantities of supplies filled vast granaries along the waterways cutting through the city. T'ung chou was divided into an old city and a new city, added during the Ming period to protect expanding granaries. By 1773, the new city wall enclosed twenty streets, the old city wall enclosed more than seventy, and an additional twenty or thirty streets were located in the kuan around the walls.[7] As will become evident in the following chapter, this large number of streets suggests a level 3 city.

By the late nineteenth century there were ten markets in T'ung chou, all of which, except for the chou city, met 4/10 or 5/10. The second city of the chou was Chang-chia wan, in which was found a 5/10 market as well as specialized markets for livestock, straw, and vegetables. In addition to the two garrisons of soldiers totaling more than 300 men in the chou city, there was a garrison stationed five miles south in Chang-chia wan. The large number of soldiers and the relatively frequent marketing set T'ung chou apart from other administrative units in the area; yet it was not so much the superior position of T'ung chou city vis-à-vis the central places subordinate to it, but its position at the receiving end of long-distance commerce on the Grand Canal which caused the city to prosper. Unlike central places at levels 5 to 7, T'ung chou city was dotted by specialized markets for a wide variety of goods.

Chi chou city contained approximately forty streets, a number suggestive of a city with roughly 10,000 inhabitants. Main streets were located within the walls and in the west and south kuan, the two kuan in which periodic markets met during the early Ch'ing period. Markets inside the walls were likewise situated on the west and south main streets until a chou magistrate announced new marketing days for the city, keeping the total number of open days at 4/10, but adding the east street and east kuan to make six locations each with a 2/30 market. In other words, at fifteen-day intervals in a thirty-day month a market was convened at six designated places in Chi chou city. Outside of the chou city three markets, which met 4/10 and were all located ten to twenty miles to the south and west are candidates for designation as level 6 central places.

Pa chou can be divided into three marketing zones according to data on weight standards used to measure a peck of grain. (This data is part of the information referred to above, p. 152.) The chou city and four other central places used 41 as the standard, as did markets in most nearby hsien. Pa chou city possessed a 4/10 market and, as was common, 2/10 was designated as the days for the big market, which served subordinate marketing areas outside of the local standard marketing area. Also in the first of the three marketing zones was Su-ch'iao chen, straddling the border with Wen-an hsien six miles southeast of the chou city. The second marketing zone consisted of two markets with standard weights of 23 and 25, figures which fell within the predominant range for northern Chihli sheng. Hsin-an chen was the sole occupant of the third zone. It shared the standard of 100 with markets at the gates of Peking and at the east entrance to Tientsin, cities to which Hsin-an chen was joined by Grand Canal commerce. As one of the few level 5 nonadministrative cities in Chihli cheng, Hsin-an was the most active market in the chou with the possible exception of the administrative city and may also have been the most active in Yung-ch'ing hsien, in which part of the chen was located. The 3-8 market (which met the third and eighth day of each ten-day period) in Hsin-an chen was open on the third day for residents of Yung-ch'ing and on the eighth day for those of Pa chou.

Ch'ang-p'ing chou was located in the barren area north of Peking, but was somewhat enriched by goods in transit passing between Peking and the outer areas of China beyond the Great Wall. During the mid-Ch'ing period there had been only two central places, but the total increased to five by the 1880s. Of these the chou city market can be singled out for its specialized areas dealing in firewood, old clothes, and fish.

The five chou cities of Shun-t'ien fu all ranked among the twenty-five most populous central places in Chihli sheng. Transportation was the function uniquely contributing to their prosperity. Located on the five principal routes to the capital of China, they were genuine gateways. Especially T'ung chou flourished owing to its location along a waterway on which large quantities of goods arrived bound for Peking. Yet even the other four chou cities, each of which had a population of approximately 10,000, appeared prosperous in comparison to the hsien cities in this fu.

North Lu

Shun-t'ien fu was divided into four *lu* (way). Four hsien were grouped with Ch'ang-p'ing chou in the poor northern lu. These administrative units barely achieved self-sufficiency in dry grains, required supplies for military outposts, and reaped commercial benefit only from transport passing through and from small-scale exports of such goods as fruit to Peking.

A gazetteer written during the early eighteenth century provides some information about marketing settlements in Shun-i hsien, roughly twenty miles northeast of Peking. The most prosperous center was Yang-ke chuang, ten miles northeast of the hsien city en route to San-ho hsien city. Second was Niu-lan shan, seven miles north of the hsien city, recorded as having hundreds of households in commercial activities and famed as the meeting place of five hsien. The hsien city was located on a well-traveled road from Peking to Jehol, a major retreat across the Great Wall where the Manchus frequently traveled. While the northern kuan of Shun-i hsien city was as populous as the area inside the wall, the southern and western kuan, which were not on the main road, contained few households.

Further northeast along the Peking-Jehol road was Mi-yun hsien, a large and partly mountainous area reaching to the Great Wall, just beyond which was a well-known trading center Ku-pei k'ou. Mi-yun hsien city in the southwestern corner of its administered area had a 5/10 market in the old city and a 5/10 market in the new city, walled for bannermen residents. In 1910, Mi-yun city held 6,800 of the 93,000 residents counted in the hsien. The other market in Mi-yun hsien was Shih-hsia, a post between the hsien city and Ku-pei k'ou along the commercial route to Jehol. Evidently commerce in Mi-yun was concentrated along one road.

The two remaining hsien in this lu were small and mountainous. Both were encircled by unusually tiny walls despite their locations in this strategic area of walled fortresses. During the late seventeenth century P'ing-ku hsien had four markets, each meeting 2/30. This infrequent scheduling was replaced by a more common pattern when a 4/10 market was established in the hsien city and a 2/10 market was founded in one other settlement. A switch from extremely infrequent or irregular marketing days, as occurred in backward P'ing-ku hsien at the beginning of the Ch'ing period, is indicative of an early stage in the regularization of marketing. Under these circumstances a reduction in the number of settlements in which marketing occurred could signify a more advanced commercial state. In my calculations, I omit, where possible, markets with frequencies of less than 1/10 (3/30).

West Lu

The western lu of Shun-t'ien fu also consisted of four hsien and one chou. Agriculture was unusually poor in this lu too; the meager local commerce centered on dry grains and livestock. Ta-hsing and Wan-p'ing hsien included Peking and no other markets of note, except perhaps for Ch'ing-ho chen, a 4/10 market northwest of the capital. Of the other two hsien, Liang-hsiang was the smallest in the fu. Like other cities near Peking, this hsien city had its most built-up area away from the capital, in the southwest. Presumably goods moved into the city en route to Peking. All three of the 4/10 markets outside of the hsien city were located in the southwest, contributing to the southwestern orientation of the hsien city. Liang-hsiang was a typical example of hsien cities; it had four gates, four main streets which intersected in the center of the walled city, twenty or more minor streets, and, for the most part, built-up areas near the main streets but not in the corners near the wall.

South Lu

Compared to the two lu described above, the southern lu was a prosperous agricultural region with many intersecting waterways. Its six hsien plus Pa chou contained some prominent chen, including Hsin-an mentioned above. Ku-an and Yung-ch'ing hsien were both about forty miles from Peking. In the mid-nineteenth century Ku-an hsien city had roughly twenty streets. While the hsien city market met 4/10, rotating between five streets, all of the other markets met only 2/10. Fairs and markets each occurred at fourteen settlements within the hsien. In general, the more annual fairs in a given settlement, the higher its urban level. Some of the places with one fair annually were not marketing settlements, but both locations with two fairs each year were the sites of 2/10 markets and the hsien city was the only place with three fairs per year.

Central places in Yung-ch'ing hsien can be compared by the number of licensed operators who owed fees for various kinds of goods. Data from the late nineteenth century are available for every central place except Hsin-an. First was the south kuan of the hsien city, whose 1,200 residents included nineteen operators owing taxes on the following six kinds of goods: pigs, asses, hemp, grain, lumber, and cotton. Second was Han ts'un, ten miles northeast with 1,300 residents, a 4/10 market, and operators dealing in five kinds of goods. One of the remaining central places had 1,000 residents and three kinds of operators, but the other five had smaller populations, and all but one counted only one licensed operator, invariably a dealer in grains. We can conclude that in this hsien, level 7 central places held primarily grain markets which met 2/10, level 6 central places were more diversified and possessed either a 2/10 or 4/10 market, and level 5 central places were the most diversified with the hsien city possessing a 4/10 market.

It is possible to trace the development of Tung-an hsien back through the Ch'ing period. From the mid-Ch'ing period to the 1910s the number of villages in Tung-an hsien rose from 326 to 468. During the late seventeenth century there were ten central places and somewhat later in the mid-eighteenth century all of these ten markets except the hsien city met 2/10. Subsequently, of the fourteen markets in Tung-an hsien, the hsien city met 4/10 as did two others, while the remaining eleven met 2/10.

The most prosperous marketing settlements in Wen-an hsien outside of the hsien city were located along rivers. A large port, Sheng-fang chen, had once been designated one of the six principal chen of Chihli sheng. In contrast, level 7 settlements in this hsien generally lacked water transport and their markets were operated almost solely for the exchange in neighboring villages of such goods as grains and cloth.

The southernmost hsien in Shun-t'ien fu was Ta-ch'eng, 130 miles southeast of Peking. During the late nineteenth century the hsien city contained a 180-man garrison and a 5/10 market. All other hsien markets met 2/10.

Pao-ting, later known as Hsin-chen hsien, was also in the southern lu. Its extremely small area, E-W five miles and N-S eight miles, apparently contained only one market, i.e., the hsien city.

East Lu

The eastern lu of Shun-t'ien fu contained five hsien as well as two chou described above. This area varied in terrain and commerce.

The fact that the administrative units were located between Peking and Tientsin helps to explain the relative prosperity of some of the cities in the lu. Hsiang-ho hsien was small in area, but grew in population during the Ch'ing period as its total number of villages rose from 157 to 356. The hsien city was famous for its fall horse and cattle fair. San-ho hsien was mountainous in the north, but flat in the south. Correspondingly, the built-up areas of the hsien city were mainly in the south. A fee was paid by fourteen grain operators, nine livestock operators, and one cloth operator, a fact suggestive of the relative amounts of trade carried out in the hsien in these activities.

Wu-ch'ing and Pao-ti hsien were the only large administrative units in this fu to contain as many as ten periodic markets. Unlike the other large hsien and chou, these two were distant from the mountains along the Great Wall. In 1730 Wu-ch'ing lost 123 villages to Tientsin fu, a rare example of the transfer of villages from one administrative unit to another. Both the 4/10 market in Wu-ch'ing hsien city and the 5/10 market in Pao-ti hsien city met on streets entirely within the walled area, indicating that the kuan were not heavily settled. About thirteen miles north of Pao-ti hsien city was Hsin-chi chen, famed as the most prosperous nonadministrative city in the entire fu, as the commercial center of Pao-ti hsien and as a market serving areas in San-ho hsien, Hsiang-ho hsien, and Chi chou.

In the far east of Shun-t'ien fu was Ning-ho hsien, in which all four markets met 2/10. These low frequencies suggest that there was no level 5 city and correspond to the "PN" classification noted on Table 14 for this hsien.

In summary, Shun-t'ien fu was exceptionally large, with twenty-four administrative units. Its 9,000-10,000 villages and 3-4 million people (excluding Peking) made the fu a microcosm of slightly more than 1 percent of China. Yet, its total of approximately 170 central places numbered only half of the national average for these quantities of villages and people. Of the seven administrative units which ranked VL or L in area, six averaged no more than one central place for every sixty-six villages and only in a minority of hsien and chou did the pattern prevail of many level 7 central places around two or more level 6 central places with perhaps a single level 5 central place. Throughout most of the fu, agriculture was poor and trade was scanty. It was not so much the network of local marketing as it was long-distance commerce bound for Peking which made possible the largest cities—the five chou. It is likely that the presence of a level 1 city prompted level 4 cities to appear out of proportion to the number of smaller central places.

TABLE 14

Chihli—Pao-ting Fu

Administrative Unit	Area	Villages	Population	CFPN	City Wall	Markets
Ch'ing-yuan	A	400	VL	CFPN	12	31/62
Man-ch'eng	VS	200	S	C	4	10/20
An-su	A	300	A	C	4	6/14/30
Ting-hsing	S	200	A	CF	5	9
Hsin-ch'eng	S	500	L	CF	3	25/19
T'ang	A	400	A	J	4	12/29
Po-yeh	VS	100	S	P	4	11
Wang-tu	VS	100	VS	CN	4	1
Jung-ch'eng	VS	100	VS	J	3	1
Wan	S	—	A	J	9	14/24
Li	S	200	A	FN	8	20/22
Hsiung	S	200	A	CFN	9	9/ 7
Ch'i	VS	300	A	J	4	14
Shu-lu	A	400	L	FN	6	12
An chou	S	100	A	J	5	11
Kao-yang	VS	100	A	J	4	—

Note: See notes to Table 13 above for explanation of abbreviations.

Pao-ting sheng city (Ch'ing-yuan hsien) was one of the smallest walled provincial administrative centers in China, but its four-mile perimeter contained little vacant land. Moreover the north kuan remained a developed area about one mile in length with more than 1,000 households, although it was described in the late seventeenth century as having emptied in comparison to fifty years earlier.[8] Altogether Pao-ting city in the late nineteenth century held more than 20 percent of the over 300,000 people in the hsien, making it the third largest city in Chihli.[9] At an earlier date marketing had been complex in Pao-ting city. Many locations inside the walls and in the south and north kuan shared a daily market, and marketing days were irregular. For instance, the south kuan market met 3, 8, and 28 and the north kuan market met 4, 14, 19, 24, and 29; the former was a 1/10 market and the latter a 5/30 market. However, by the early eighteenth century order prevailed as the four kuan shared a regular 4/10 market and daily commerce in stores replaced periodic street markets within the walls. Like T'ung chou, the sheng city was distinguished by numerous specialized shopping areas for such goods as silver, salt, vegetables, mats, cows and sheep, asses and horses, fuels (separated by type), fruit, fish, grains, and cloth.

The development of marketing can be observed in Man-ch'eng hsien, northwest of Pao-ting. On the north and south main streets of the hsien city there had been a 3-6-9 market until the late Ming period when a 5/10 market was established in the north and south kuan. The north-south buildup corresponded to the presence of only two gates in the walled city and it was manifested in the widespread existence of fields inside the wall in the east and west. Many of the other nine markets recorded for mid-eighteenth century Man-ch'eng hsien had been established during the Ming period: (1) one was founded between 1567 and 1573; (2) four were founded during the reign period from 1573 to 1620; (3) one was founded between 1621 and 1628. Of these early markets two eventually failed, one switched from 2/10 to 3/10, one switched days but kept a 2/10 schedule, and the others maintained a constant schedule. It was strikingly typical in China for periodic markets to open on the same days of the month at the same location serving the same villages for hundreds of years in succession.

Three small but not sparsely populated hsien in the northeast of the fu were An-su, Ting-hsing, and Hsin-ch'eng. The number of markets in An-su was rising quickly from six to fourteen in the early nineteenth century and eventually to thirty by the 1930s. As in Ch'ing-yuan hsien, the turn of the twentieth century was a time of increasing periodic markets. An-su hsien city held a 4/10 market and five of the twenty-three fairs in the hsien. The population of Ting-hsing hsien rose from 94,000 in the late eighteenth century to 166,-000 in the early nineteenth century, but its market total rose over 100 years to the late nineteenth century only from eight to nine. Further study of local areas is needed to determine why the number of markets in some hsien rose rapidly while in other hsien there was little change.

Hsin-ch'eng hsien contained 495 villages with 166,000 people in 1838. Population data for the 1930s indicates that the hsien city included 670 households; four central places followed with 400-600; six others with 200-400; and the remaining eight central places had fewer than 200 households.

T'ang hsien was described as poor, even to the point that the moat surrounding its walled administrative city was shallow, narrow, and contained no water. During the K'ang-hsi reign (1662-1722) the three street marketing locations in the hsien city were abandoned in favor of the three kuan; the new 4/10 market met 2/10 in the south kuan and 1/10 each in the east and west kuan. This is just one of many examples during the late Ming and early Ch'ing periods of city markets being moved from streets within the administrative center to the kuan. Population data are unusually complete for late nineteenth century T'ang hsien. Inside the walled city were approximately ten streets, on which were registered 45 shopkeeper households (*p'u-hu*) and 141 other households with a total population of 965. In the south kuan were five more streets (three *chieh* or large streets and two *hsiang* or small streets), on which resided more than 200 people, including 14 shopkeeper households. There were 283 people, but no shopkeeper households, on the three chieh and one hsiang in the west kuan and the 121 people residing in the east kuan also did not belong to shopkeeper households. Thus the population of this level 6 hsien city numbered somewhat more than 1,500, including 59 shopkeeper households.

Information on the other central places in this hsien has also been left for posterity. Almost all of the eleven markets outside the hsien city in the seventeenth century persisted for the following two centuries as the total number of markets was more than doubling; only one of the eleven had ceased to exist and another was reduced to a 2/10 market of such minor significance that it was not counted in the listing of the late nineteenth century. T'ang hsien was divided into seven lu. Each lu contained 20-57 villages and 7,000-20,000 people. Chün-ch'eng chen thirty miles from the hsien city in the northwest lu held a 4/10 market and approximately 1,000 people. A second central place seventeen miles out from the hsien city in the same direction held 700-800 people. In the west lu one 5/10 market held more than 1,200 residents, while a 2/10 market held 1,800. In the north lu a 4/10 market held 385 people and another held 640. Although these late nineteenth century examples indicate that marketing frequencies were not necessarily a function of settlement populations, they also reveal the range of populations in level 6 cities. Definitions of central place levels 6 and 7 cannot be strictly in terms of population. There were central places with only a standard market, i.e., at level 7, with as many as 2,000 people and others at level 6 having intermediate marketing activities but only several hundred residents. Nevertheless, the pattern in this hsien and elsewhere was that 4/10 markets were more populous than 2/10 ones.

Two very small hsien in Pao-ting fu were Po-yeh and Wang-tu. They provide a contrasting picture of marketing. Po-yeh hsien city contained a 4/10 market shared by its three kuan and elsewhere in the hsien were ten additional markets, but Wang-tu hsien seems to have contained only one market, the one in the hsien city. Wang-tu was described as having few wealthy men, a population which engaged in almost no occupations besides farming and much barren and mountainous land. Moreover, part of the commerce serving this hsien was carried on just beyond its borders at two markets about ten miles from Wang-tu hsien city in Ting chou chih-li chou and in Man-ch'eng hsien. The hsien city market met only 2/10 and transactions were confined to grains, fruits, and cloth. This was certainly one of the least populous administrative cities. In 1906 the total population inside the wall was listed at only 130 households, numbering somewhat more than 600 people. Approximately 40 of these households were shopkeeper households. The kuan were also sparsely populated, with only nine shopkeeper households in all.

Wan hsien had a large walled area, but much open land inside the wall. During the early eighteenth century the city market met 4/10 at the three kuan and at one location inside the wall. There were three main streets: East street with few merchants, South street with more commerce, and North street with the city's main commercial area. In the 1930s the hsien city held more than 5,000 residents, about 40 percent of whom lived in the north kuan.

Li hsien once held a city market which met 5/30, 1/30 at both the north and south streets, and 3/30 (or 1/10) at the north kuan. During the Ming period marketing was regularized with the establishment of a 3/10 market. By the late nineteenth century the city market met 7/10, 5/10 at the north kuan, and 2/10 at the south kuan. The number of markets in the hsien rose slightly from 20 during the Ming period to 22 by 1876. All but the hsien city met 2/10, but three of these central places were designated as big markets, suggesting that there were eighteen level 7 settlements, three level 6 settlements, and the hsien city at level 5.

In the far northeast of Pao-ting fu was Hsiung hsien, in which a bustling street stretched for nearly one mile along the kuan-lu from Peking to Te chou in Shantung. Two unusual features marked the hsien city: there was a hui-kuan of Shansi merchants and a residential area with approximately 100 households of Manchu bannermen. In the late seventeenth century the hsien city market met 6/10 at five locations within the wall and in one kuan. The number of markets inside the hsien declined from nine in the late seventeenth century to seven in the 1920s. The earlier total, however, included two places which had only 1/10 markets as well as six which met 2/10.

Two other administrative units are Shu-lu hsien and An chou. The latter was exceptional in having eleven markets for 114 villages in the mid-nineteenth century. The former was more typical of the rest of the fu, possessing twelve markets for 280 villages in the late seventeenth century, but the number of markets remained constant as the number of villages was rising to nearly 360. Shu-lu hsien had an old and a new administrative city, twelve miles apart. Administrative functions had been transferred because of frequent floods, one of which in 1622 was said to have totally inundated the old hsien city. At first the old city kept a 5/10 market, while the new city resembled other markets with only a 2/10 frequency, but by the mid-eighteenth century the new city's frequency had almost caught up at 4/10. Like many hsien in south and central Chihli sheng, Shu-lu was ravaged in the late 1860s during the Nien rebellion, regaining population in the following decade. During the last years of the dynasty an enumeration of the adult male population listed approximately 100,000 peasants, 6,000 artisans, 9,000 merchants, and 5,000 gentry.

In summary, Pao-ting fu with 200 to 250 central places consisted of many small hsien, which in comparison to hsien elsewhere in Chihli were densely settled. Although the figures in the chart for villages include some probable underestimations, it is possible to estimate from the population of 2 to 3 million people in the fu that the number of villages was about 5,000. Therefore, the ratio of central places to villages was 1:20 or 1:25, much lower than in Shunt'ien fu; yet, central places at levels 4 and 5 were less common in Pao-ting fu, and there were not many notable chen. A distribution of central places typical of China as a whole seems to have prevailed in this fu; there were approximately 170 level 7 markets, 40-45 level 6 cities, 6-10 level 5 cities, and at least one city at higher levels. As a sheng city Pao-ting reached a population of roughly 70,000 or level 3a and it is possible that one or two hsien cities reached 10,000. Most of the large administrative cities in this fu were at level 5 and many others were only at level 6. Except for the presence of a sheng city there were no unusual conditions to alter the usual urban network.

Following Table 15, *Cheng-ting fu* can be divided into areas at four levels of development: (1) Chin chou, Cheng-ting hsien, Huo-lu hsien, and Kao-ch'eng hsien at the most developed level; (2) the five hsien from Ching-hsing to Hsing-t'ang; (3) Hsin-lo, P'ing-shan, and Ling-shou hsien; and (4) Fu-p'ing and Tsan-huang hsien at the least developed level. Although the evidence is not conclusive, the populations of the administrative cities in this fu may well have reflected these divisions: for the top group, urban levels 4 and 5 predominated, for the second group, only level 5 was present, for the third group, levels 5 and 6 could be found, and both hsien in the bottom group belonged to level 6.

Cheng-ting fu city declined during the Ch'ing period. In the mid-seventeenth century it was thriving, but by the late nineteenth century much of the huge area enclosed by eight miles of wall was empty. The population had fallen to 2,600 or 2,700 households within the wall and an additional 200 households in the four kuan. How can the decline be explained? In the late seventeenth century Chenting (its name later was changed to Cheng-ting) lost the functions of sheng administrative center to Pao-ting, relinquishing as a consequence some of the large population and prosperous trade it had enjoyed during the early Ch'ing period. A second loss occurred by the early eighteenth century as four big areas from the fu were released to become separate chih-li chou; therefore the number of administrative units fell from 32 to 14. Finally Cheng-ting city suffered from the redeployment of troops during the early nineteenth century. Despite all of these setbacks, this fu city continued as a level

TABLE 15

Chihli—Cheng-ting Fu

Administrative Unit	Area	Villages	Population	CFPN	Markets	A	B	C	D	E
Cheng-ting	—	200	A	CFN	17	13	65	212		VL
Chin chou	S	—	L	J	19	12	60	170	VL	VL
Huo-lu	A	—	L	C	8/19	16	80	112	VL	
Kao-ch'eng	A	—	L	J	12/8/7	23	115	214	VL	VL
Ching-hsing	L	200	L	C	8	—	—	—	—	—
Yuan-shih	A	100	A	—	8/20	—	—	—	—	—
Wu-chi	VL	100	A	J	4	—	—	—	—	—
Luan-ch'eng	VS	200	S	C	4/3	—	—	—	—	—
Hsing-t'ang	A	200	A	J	—	8		183		
Hsin-lo	S	100	VS	C	—	6	30	37		
Ling-shou	A	200	L	C	8	6	30	24		
P'ing-shan	VL	700	L	J	8/13	6	30	12		
Fu-p'ing	VL	300	S	J	2/6	2	10	20	VS	VS
Tsan-huang	S	200	A	J	7	3	10	14	VS	VS

Notes:

A = the number of pawnshops

B = the pawnshop tax paid in taels of silver

C = the number of brokers involved in commercial transactions

D = the mid-eighteenth century ranking of able-bodied males; only the administrative units with very large or very small totals are indicated

E = the number of mou of land; again only units at the extremes are indicated

4 city above cities in its own hsien and in many nearby hsien and as a commercial center of western Chihli sheng.

The 120,000 people living in Cheng-ting hsien were divided between 214 settlements, a number which had risen from 130 at the beginning of the Ch'ing period. The sixteen markets outside of the administrative city all met 2/10 or 3/10. The most populous of these central places were located fifteen miles northeast and seven miles southwest of the fu city and contained more than 400 households each. Of the remaining fourteen markets, three exceeded 1,000 in population, eight held 100-200 households, two held fewer than 100 households, and the population of one is unknown.

The other three chou and hsien in the most developed category for this fu were, like Cheng-ting hsien, prosperous relative to the remainder of this fu, but not in comparison to the rest of China. In fact, the Chin chou gazetteer described it as a poor area with poor people who engaged in simple agricultural trade only to meet their daily needs. Marketing days in the chou city had gradually shifted from 4-9 to 3-6-9 and then to 2-7-4-9. In the 1920s the chou city contained 1,200 households, but only one other central place inside the chou reached as many as 300 households.

A second relatively developed hsien was Huo-lu. The four main streets in the city extended beyond the gates to all four directions in the hsien, uniting the hsien city with the rest of the hsien and beyond. Especially built-up was the east-west axis since this formed the kuan-lu from Shansi sheng to Cheng-ting fu city and beyond. In the west kuan were five streets and in the east kuan were three more.

The second group of administrative units includes five hsien. Yuan-shih hsien was located south along the mountains dividing Chihli and Shansi. In the late nineteenth century the hsien city population totaled 3,800, of whom 1,200 were quite evenly divided between the three kuan. Inside the city wall were four main streets, but unlike the usual pattern there was a center street rather than a north street, corresponding to the fact there was no gate in the northern part of the wall. Inhabitants of the hsien city were grouped for administrative purposes by the main streets; the number of residents listed for each street was 600-700. In the late nineteenth century the city held a 4/10 market and the other nineteen markets all met 2/10. Three markets outside the hsien city were labeled big in the gazetteer: Sung-ts'ao, a settlement seven miles southeast with 900 people; Yin-ts'un, a settlement seven miles northwest with 1,400 people; and Nan-tsuo ts'un, a settlement thirteen miles northwest with 3,200 people. We can estimate that there were two level 5 central places and at least two level 6 central places in this hsien.

The gazetteer for Luan-ch'eng hsien is unusually informative. In the early eighteenth century there were four markets in the hsien, but the number fell to only three for 150 settlements during the late nineteenth century, and residents of one part of this hsien used a handy market just across the border. The hsien was divided into four lu: (1) the east lu with thirty-five villages and 10,000 people; (2) the south lu with forty-seven villages and 16,000 people; (3) the west lu with fifty villages and 31,000 people; and (4) the north lu with eighteen villages and 16,000 people. An additional 3,400 of the 77,000 hsien residents lived in the hsien city. City residents were divided according to six locations as in Table 16.

TABLE 16

Sections of Luan-ch'eng Hsien City

Division of City	Number of Streets	Total Population	Shopkeeper Households
East main street	5	894	49
West main street	7	1,001	33
East kuan	—	390	12
West kuan	1	371	0
South kuan	3	220	31
North kuan	2	522	1

Three hsien belong to the third classification of hsien in Cheng-ting fu. Ling-shou hsien held six markets in the late seventeeth century, including the 4/10 market which had recently moved out of the walled portion of the hsien city to the four kuan. Hsin-lo hsien had grown from a population of 20,000-25,000 in the 1650s to 70,000 in the late nineteenth century. The hsien city market had been 2/10 inside the wall and 1/10 in the kuan, but by 1900 it had become

5/10 in the two main kuan. P'ing-shan hsien was a large but mountainous area near the Shansi border. The number of markets rose from ten in the late seventeenth century to thirteen in the mid-nineteenth century. A gazetteer of 1876 provides information on some of the marketing settlements. One settlement had a 2/10 market and was walled with two gates during the Ming period, but it was burned down in 1644, flooded in the 1660s and then rebuilt in the 1670s with three gates. A second marketing settlement experienced the same disasters, but maintained its two gates. Two other markets were walled for the first time in the 1770s, while the remaining markets appear not to have been enclosed by walls. Thus marketing settlements differed in such respects as the presence of a wall, the number of years the wall had been standing, and the length of the perimeter of the wall. For the most part nonadministrative cities had smaller walls than the sizes noted on the tables for hsien and chou cities, e.g., the perimeters given in this hsien were two li and one li (if the walls were rectangular, then they measured less than 300 yards on each side). Also these walls were more cheaply constructed. Although most central places did not have actual walls, those which did can be compared by the condition of their walls.

The two least-developed hsien were both in the mountains near the Shansi border. In the mid-eighteenth century Tsan-huang hsien contained seven markets, all of which met 2/10. Fu-p'ing also was near the bottom of the fu in total markets, but the number had risen to six by the late nineteenth century.

Tientsin fu city was the second largest city of Chihli sheng, ranking at level 3a until its dramatic growth in the late nineteenth century. Tientsin was the outer port of Peking, the arrival point for canal and sea traffic. Inside the city various hui-kuan had been established during the Ch'ing period and merchants brought commerce from nearly all areas of China to warehouses and docks.

Momose Hiromu has divided Tientsin hsien into eight areas on the basis of data from 1846 (see p. 91).[10] By this date the number of villages had risen from 314 at the beginning of the Ch'ing dynasty to nearly 400. Area one—the fu city—can be separated into three parts: (1) inside the wall where the population was listed as 53 percent commercial and 29 percent agricultural; (2) the east and north kuan along the Grand Canal which was even more populous and contained 62 percent commercial and 26 percent agricultural households; and (3) elsewhere in the kuan where the population was 45 percent commercial and 43 percent agricultural. Actually this classification of the city population is deceptive since most of the households considered to be agricultural must have been engaged in nonfarming activities. There was a tendency in both China and Japan to label hired laborers and others not as merchants and artisans but as part of the residual agricultural category. Altogether these

TABLE 17

Chihli—Tientsin Fu

Administrative Unit	Area	Villages	Population	Markets
Tientsin	L	400	VL	—
Ch'ing	A	400	L	6/7
Ch'ing-yun	S	—	A	8
Ching-hai	S	—	—	8
Nan-p'i	S	400	A	7/9
Yen-shan	VL	700	L	14/24/39
Ts'ang chou	VL	—	VL	14/30/43

Note: See notes to Table 13 above for explanation of abbreviations.

areas contained about 33,000 households. Area two was in the poor, often flooded, eastern part of the hsien. Villages there yielded grains to be consumed by troops stationed near the coast. One walled garrison city had a population which was 19 percent commercial, but in the other twenty villages only 8 percent of the population was registered as commercial. Area three in the southeast, along the sea route to Manchuria and to the East-central part of China, can be divided into two sections: the level 5 city of T'ai-chih and other nearby settlements with a total of 7,600 households, 34 percent of which were commercial; and the remaining 135 settlements which had a population 13 percent commercial. There were many marketing settlements in this area of the hsien, corresponding to the large proportion of commercial residents. Area four in the northwest contained the major shipping route to Peking and can also be divided into two sections: the level 6 central place of Hsi-chih and nine nearby settlements, which together contained 2,700 households, 39 percent of which were commercial; and the remaining 46 settlements in which 18 percent of the households were commercial. Areas five, six, and seven were located in the north, northeast, and southwest of the hsien. Except for one cluster of three settlements with 32 percent of the households commercial, the commercial population was small, varying from 11 percent in one group of settlements to 2 percent in eleven villages in the southwest. Finally area 8 was in the southwest along the Grand Canal, but this part of the Canal did not have much commerce with the exception of one chen, Yang-liu ch'ing. In addition to the commercial and agricultural households in these areas, there was an exceptional number of transportation households. In areas three, four, and eight 17-26 percent of the household heads were employed in the transportation sector. Tientsin certainly was an atypical hsien, but the conditions in some of its least commercialized areas were probably indicative of most clusters of hundreds of villages in Chihli hsien in which only central places at levels 6 and 7 could be found.

Southwest fifty-five miles from Tientsin was Ch'ing hsien city. The number of markets in this hsien rose slowly from six in the early Ch'ing period to seven at the beginning of the nineteenth century. Momose Hiromu has also examined detailed figures for this hsien dating from between 1875 and 1880.[11] The original information gives: the distance from the hsien city of each village; the number of households in each village and the population of males and females divided according to age groups; where markets met, on what days they met, and which villages belonged to the marketing areas; and where and when fairs occurred. There were then ten markets in Ch'ing hsien. The largest were Hsing-chi chen, a former hsien city which had been absorbed into Ch'ing hsien in 1649 and by 1880 was the marketing center for 92 villages with 36,000 residents, and the hsien city, ten miles north on the Grand Canal, serving 98 villages with 31,000 residents. Also noteworthy was Liu-ho chen, a level 6 central place farther north on the Grand Canal with a standard marketing area radius of four miles which encompassed 26 villages holding 8,000 people.

There were many prominent nonadministrative cities in Tientsin fu. Of the eight markets in Ching-hai hsien during the mid-nineteenth century, at least four served large areas. Chung-wang chen was a marketing center for fourteen villages in Ch'ing hsien, for villages in Ts'ang chou, and of course for villages in Ching-hai hsien. Similarly Tzu-ya was a marketing center for Ta-ch'eng, Ch'ing, and Ching-hai hsien. T'ang-kuan tun on the east bank of the Grand Canal was the next major chen north of Liu-ho and served a marketing area including twenty-nine villages inside Ch'ing hsien. Finally Tu-liu should be mentioned as a large market on a major river route to Tientsin.

Nan-p'i hsien south of Ts'ang chou held nine markets for 370 villages and 150,000 people in the late nineteenth century. Population data from 1930 show that the hsien city's figure was 4,000, the largest nonadministrative city's figure was 2,000, and smaller markets generally were located in settlements with fewer than 1,000 people.

Yen-shan hsien along the coast contained three kinds of markets: small ones with few varieties of goods; middle ones with meat, rice-wine, and vegetables in addition to the staples also present in small markets; and large markets which were distinguished by trade in livestock. Yen-shan hsien city had a population of 3,000 in the mid-nineteenth century and of 6,000 in 1915.

The second city of the fu was Ts'ang chou city, eighty miles south of Tientsin on the Grand Canal. This thriving commercial center contained 380 shops and 15,000-20,000 people by the end of the Ch'ing period. As in Yen-shan hsien, the number of central places was increasing rapidly in Ts'ang chou. This administrative unit contained more markets than in any other unit of the fu, including Tientsin hsien for which no figure is given in Table 17 due to a lack of precise data.

Since the walled area of *Ho-chien fu* city contained six of the seventy-four administrative divisions within its hsien (and in addition its kuan included part of three other administrative divisions), it would be expected according to the pao-chia system which divided areas according to population that the city held approximately 10 percent of the more than 200,000 residents in its hsien. This is, in fact, a plausible figure for a fu city. Although the other thirty-four markets in Ho-chien all met 2/10, seven were labeled big markets and presumably ranked at level 6.

During the late seventeenth century the only market in Chiao-ho hsien which met 4/10 was in Po-t'ou chen on the Grand Canal. By the early nineteenth century a second market was also labeled big, which together with the hsien city and the thriving Grand Canal

TABLE 18

Chihli—Ho-chien Fu

Administrative Units	Area	Villages	Population	Markets
Ho-chien	L	700	L	35
Chiao-ho	A	700	L	9/26
Ching chou	A	900	L	23/38
Wu-ch'iao	S	(800)	A	32
Ku-ch'eng	S	300	L	8/11
Hsien	L	800	VL	20/59
Fu-ch'eng	VS	400	S	12
Su-ning	VS	—	A	21
Jen-ch'iu	A	300	L	10
Tung-kuang	S	700	L	12/27
Ning-tsin	S	900	L	11/32

Note: See notes to Table 13 above for explanation of abbreviations.

chen gave the hsien three level 5 or large level 6 cities out of twenty-five central places.

Of Ching chou's thirty-eight markets in 1931 four stood out in their large numbers of licensed commercial operators. The chou city had eighty and the other three cities had fifteen-twenty-one, contrasting with middle-size markets with nine-eleven, and with small markets with fewer than nine licensed operators. The chou city grain operators numbered fifteen, while middle-size markets had three-four, and small markets had one-two.

All markets in Wu-ch'iao hsien met only 2/10 except Lien chen, a commercial center on the Grand Canal. The hsien city held what was termed the biggest fair of the spring in Chihli province. Called the Po-i hui, the fair lasted for two months and attracted great numbers of merchants from outside the hsien.

In the early eighteenth century there were eight marketing settlements in Ku-ch'eng hsien. The hsien city market met 5/10, the market in Cheng-chia k'ou on the Grand Canal met 3/10, and the others met 2/10. There were twenty markets in mid-eighteenth century Hsien hsien. The hsien city market met 5/10, two others met 4/10, one met 3/10, and the rest met only 2/10. The fact that the hsien city contained only one of forty-eight pao-chia divisions within the wall and shared two others in its kuan suggests that the urban population in the administrative center numbered not much more than 2 percent of the hsien total. The post-Ch'ing population inside the wall was 495 households and in the two kuan, 148 households.

In summary, Ho-chien fu was a densely settled area with numerous markets. While the total number of markets in Table 18 includes some added after the middle of the nineteenth century, there were probably about 250 central places in the fu, resulting in an average number of markets per administrative unit higher than elsewhere in the province. Next to the fu city the largest cities were administrative centers such as Ching chou and chen located on the Grand Canal.

Shun-te fu city (Hsing-t'ai hsien) was one of the largest cities in Chihli sheng, remaining a level 3b city although it declined from a temporary peak reached around 1600. Development was centered in the south kuan on the road from Honan sheng to Peking.

Figures in Table 19 show that the number of markets in Chu-lu hsien rose from nine in the late seventeenth century to twenty-nine in the late nineteenth century. Of the total of twenty-nine, two met 2/10, ten met 4/10, and seventeen met 5/10. In this southern part of Chihli sheng markets met with greater frequency and, unlike areas further north, level 7 central places commonly had 4/10 and even 5/10 markets.

Population data are available for late nineteenth century T'ang-shan hsien city. Inside the wall 2,000 people were accredited to the north-south streets and 600 to the east-west streets. Correspondingly the north-south road was described as quite crowded with many merchants and the only two gates were in the north and south. The south kuan held 800 people and the north and southeast kuan (not directly outside a gate) held 200 people each. Thus this small hsien held a city population of nearly 4,000.

TABLE 19

Chihli—Shun-te Fu

Administrative Units	Size	Villages	Population	Markets
Hsing-t'ai	L	700	L	6/8/9/16
Chu-lu	S	900	A	9/12/29
P'ing-hsiang	VS	200	–	12
Sha-ho	A	300	A	5/14
Kuang-tsung	VS	100	A	6/8
T'ang-shan	VS	100	VS	6
Nei-ch'iu	A	100	S	3
Nan-ho	VS	200	S	3/5/7
Jen	VS	100	S	3

Note: See notes to Table 13 above for explanation of abbreviations.

Nei-ch'iu hsien and Jen hsien each were divided into the marketing areas of three central places. The former in the mid-nineteenth century contained 146 villages. Four brokers were licensed in Nei-ch'iu, two of whom were in the hsien city. Likewise, one of the two livestock licenses went to the hsien city. Similarly, the administrative city was the principal mart in early twentieth century Jen hsien. The population in the hsien city of 3,800 was twice that in the prosperous chen, Hsin-tien.

In *Kuang-p'ing fu* the ratio of markets to population and to villages was substantially higher than in northern Chihli. During the late nineteenth century Yung-nien hsien (the fu city was in this hsien) held 21 markets for 336 villages and 232,000 people. In late seventeenth century Kuang-p'ing hsien there were 4 markets for 128 villages and two centuries later there were 5 markets for 68,000 people. Chi-tse hsien was similar to Kuang-p'ing hsien; an early enumeration listed 137 villages, while by the late nineteenth century there were 6 markets for 64,000 people. The corresponding figures for Han-tan hsien were 173 villages, 11 markets, and 100,000 people. It is likely that by the late nineteenth century the more than 150 marketing settlements shown in Table 20 for this fu served approximately 2,500 villages and fewer than 1½ million people.

TABLE 20

Chihli—Kuang-p'ing Fu

Administrative Unit	Area	Villages	Population	Markets
Yung-nien	A	300	L	11/21
Ch'u chou	A	–	A	15/18
Fei-hsiang	S	200	S	11/11
Chi-tse	VS	100	VS	6
Kuang-p'ing	VS	100	VS	4/5
Ch'eng-an	VS	200	S	4/9
Tz'u chou	L	400	L	9/22
Han-tan	S	200	S	5/11
Wei	S	300	A	8/21/35
Ch'ing-ho	A	300	A	9/24

Note: See notes to Table 13 above for explanation of abbreviations.

Kuang-p'ing fu was divided into relatively small administrative units, most of which could probably not give rise to level 5 administrative cities. Although in 1911 the population of Ch'eng-an hsien city was given as 6,000, it is unlikely that most hsien with populations of less than 70,000 gave rise to cities any larger than level 6. Moreover except for a few chen in the east along the Grand Canal, there were probably no chen above level 6. Although no figures are available for the fu city, it was undoubtedly one of the least populous fu cities in the province. In short, Kuang-p'ing fu corresponded closely to the ratio of five cities at levels 5 and above for every 100 central places—the ratio indicated for all of China in Table 5.

Yung-p'ing fu in the northeast of Chihli sheng consisted of large hsien and chou, many of which extended north of the Great Wall. Ch'ien-an hsien, the largest in the sheng, together with four other very large hsien in this fu occupied more than 10 percent of the entire area of Chihli sheng. The population of the seven units in Yung-p'ing fu was only 1.4 million in the late eighteenth century, but was increasing rapidly in the following century. Note in Table 21 the exceptionally high ratio of villages to markets. Although this ratio in part reflects the fact that villages were sparsely populated in barren areas of these large administrative units, the ratio of population to markets was also high in this fu.

TABLE 21

Chihli—Yung-p'ing Fu

Administrative Units	Area	Villages	Population	Markets
Lu-lung	—	1,300	VL	6/26
Ch'ien-an	VL	1,200	L	7/15
Fu-ning	VL	600	L	10/13
Ch'ang-li	VL	500	L	12
Luan chou	VL	1,300	VL	23
Lo-t'ing	—	800	L	8/10
Lin-yü	—	900	VL	6/8/12

Note: See Table 13 above for explanation of abbreviations.

Luan chou city had a 6/10 market, while three other central places in the chou met 4/10. In the late nineteenth century the population of the chou city totaled 4,200. One of the 4/10 markets was K'ai-p'ing which was located on an important road into the fu and was known as the northern gateway to Tientsin. The second 4/10 market was Pang-tzy, which was famed as a large chen of eastern Chihli. Its population lined the main road for nearly two miles.

During the late nineteenth century Fu-ning hsien held 280,000 people, of whom approximately 10,000 lived in the hsien city. Outside the administrative city three markets were labeled big in the gazetteer, indicating that there were nine level 7 central places and three at level 6. Ch'ang-li hsien with similar totals of population and markets had a hsien city market which met 6/10 and one other market which met 4/10.

The most populous city in Yung-p'ing fu was Lin-yü hsien city, a combination of four walled areas known as Shan-hai kuan. This city had been the entry to China used by the Manchus and remained a Great Wall crossing between Peking and Manchuria. Merchants were numerous and profits large in the city's daily market. There were at least sixty streets in the various walled areas and more than 20,000 residents. Also noteworthy in Lin-yü hsien was the city of Hai-yang, known as one of the six principal chen in the province.

Chihli—Ta-ming Fu

I do not have enough information to be able to construct a table for Ta-ming fu, the southernmost area in Chihli nearly 400 miles from Peking. During the 1930s the fu city contained a population of approximately 17,000 and its hsien held 801 villages with 533,000 residents who were served by twenty-four central places. Yuan-ch'eng hsien in this fu had only seven central places for 436 villages. Perhaps the largest chen in the fu was Hsiao-tan, twelve miles north-east of the fu city. From the Yuan dynasty this chen at a narrow point on the Wei river to Lin-ch'ing chih-li chou city in Shantung had been a busy and strategic place, but in the early eighteenth century when Honan taxes in grain began to be gathered upriver in Ch'u-wang chen within Honan sheng this city lost much of its prosperity. A second prosperous chen on the same river was Lung-wang miao.

Ting chou

During the middle eighteenth century the pen chou was divided into thirty-six subadministrative areas called li, two of which were in the pen chou city. If the distribution of population had corresponded to the distribution of li, then 1/18 of the 178,000 residents of the pen chou would have lived in the chou city. In fact, the city population of slightly more than 5,000 in 1848 was divided as shown in Table 23.

Table 24 includes information on the eleven markets in the pen chou. If we compare the number of shopkeeper households per

TABLE 22

Chihli—Chih-li Chou

Administrative Units	Area	Villages	Population	Markets
Ting chou				
pen chou	A	–	L	11
Shen-tze	VS	100	–	5
Ch'u-yang	A	400	–	8
I chou				
pen chou	VL	300	L	5
Lai-shui	L	300	A	3/4
Kuang-ch'ang	–	–	VS	–
Tsun-hua chou				
pen chou	VL	500	–	8
Feng-jun	L	900	VL	20
Yü-t'ien	A	800	L	8
Chao chou				
pen chou	S	–	L	–
Pai-hsiang	VS	100	VS	2/5
Lung-p'ing	VS	–	–	–
Kao-i	VS	100	VS	9
Lin-ch'eng	L	–	A	9
Ning-chin	L	–	L	16
Shen chou				
pen chou	A	500	L	16
Wu-ch'iang	VS	300	–	7
Jao-yang	S	200	A	23
An-p'ing	S	200	A	12
Chi chou				
pen chou	A	500	L	17/23
Heng-shui	S	300	A	6/13
Hsin-ho	VS	200	S	6/8
Tsao-ch'iang	A	600	VL	10
Nan-kung	A	–	L	10/16/41
Wu-i	S	500	L	12

Note: See Table 13 above for explanation of abbreviations.

settlement to the ratio of population to mou (unit of cultivated land; see p. 74) we find that the more shopkeeper households, the higher the ratio. Presumably the more urban the settlement, the larger was the population in comparison to the amount of land farmed, and the more shopkeeper households, the more urban was the settlement. Ch'ing-feng chen with seventy-six such households had the highest ratio of almost 1:1. Ming-yueh chen, second in shopkeeper households with sixty-four, had a ratio of slightly more than 1:2. Most

TABLE 23

Sections of Ting chou City

Street Name	Number of Minor Streets	Population	Shopkeeper Households
East	4	1,100	71
South	6	710	45
West	3	1,299	—
North	3	583	38
East kuan	1	396	—
West kuan	4	1,151	42

other central places with fewer shopkeeper households had ratios of less than 1:2 and even less than 1:3. Villages which were not central places had ratios between 1:4 and 1:7. In contrast, West street in the chou city had a ratio of 13:9 and it also was the only location of a 4/10 market within the city. North, East, and South streets together had a ratio of greater than 1:2, higher than in most central places.

I chou

There may have been only two markets with frequencies as high as 4/10 in this chou. I chou city's market met 4/10 as opposed to the four 2/10 markets in its pen chou and Lai-shui hsien city's market also met 4/10.

Tsun-hua chou

In this chou, administrative city markets also met with the greatest frequency. Tsun-hua chou city with roughly forty streets already had a daily market during the late eighteenth century. The market in Feng-jun hsien city met 5/10 while the rest of the numerous markets in this hsien met 2/10. And Yü-t'ien hsien city was the only one of eight markets in its hsien to meet 4/10.

Chao chou

Almost all central places in this chih-li chou met 2/10. The exceptions were Kao-i hsien, where the administrative city was the

TABLE 24

Ting Chou Central Places

Central Place	Distance to Chou City (miles)	Population	Shopkeeper Households	Mou
Tung-t'ing chen	7	1,113	22	3,600
Wu-nu chi	13	547	15	1,200
Ta-hsin chuang	13	930	30	2,000
Han-i chen	17	2,160	—	6,100
Li-kuan ku chen	17	1,630	14	700
Shih-chuang chen	20	753	11	3,700
Tzy-wei	23	—	9	—
Ming-yueh chen	10	842	64	1,600
Po-lu chen	12	1,842	—	3,800
Ch'ing-feng chen	—	1,139	76	1,200

only one of nine markets which met 4/10, Lin-ch'eng hsien city and two cities in Ning-chin hsien, where at the beginning of the Ch'ing period all markets met 2/10 except the hsien city and one other, both of which met 3/10.

Shen chou

Ratios of markets to villages varied greatly from one hsien to another. In Wu-ch'ing hsien there were seven markets for 251 villages in the early nineteenth century and in Jao-yang hsien there were twenty-three markets for 189 villages and 120,000 people in the mid-eighteenth century.

Chi chou

For mid-eighteenth century Heng-shui hsien an unusual amount of information is available. The hsien city's population was approximately 1,800 households, making it a large level 5 city. Other central places varied from 69 households to 700 households. They served a total of 310 villages, half of which were located in the western lu. Correspondingly the western part of the city was heavily built-up, especially in the kuan.

Hsin-ho hsien was also described in detail. During the late nineteenth century the city's three kuan contained populations ranging from 400 to 800, while inside the wall lived fewer than 500 people. The seven central places outside the hsien city ranged in population from 300 to 1,300. Altogether 7,000 of the approximately 80,000 residents of Hsin-ho hsien lived in central places spaced among the 172 villages. Since I count only one-half of those in level 6 settlements as urban, the percentage of Hsin-ho's population that was urban measured at most 3 percent.

Kantō—General

The Kantō region was much more the hinterland for Edo than was Chihli the hinterland for Peking because the Kantō region was similar in size and population to Shun-t'ien fu, not to Chihli sheng. Concern over the economic conditions in the Kantō region was especially keen in Edo for various reasons. First the military situation in Japan was a balance of independent forces under daimyo who were viewed as potential threats to the Bakufu in Edo. Where Chinese defenses were concentrated against external coalitions and rural insurgents, Bakufu defenses were directed against urban-based daimyo. During the Sengoku period the fortunes of war had been tied to the daimyo's ability to mobilize the resources of his base area. Concern for the distribution of land and of markets remained during the Tokugawa period. Bakufu attention to the distribution of loyal daimyo forces in the Kantō region reflected this military preoccupation. Second, whereas Peking had a long history of receiving supplies from long-distance commerce, Edo and its vicinity at the

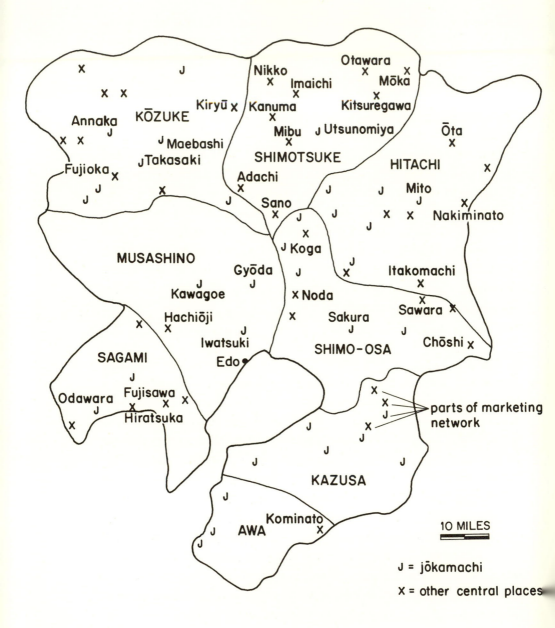

KANTŌ

KŌZUKE

X   J   Nikko   Otawara
                              X   Mōka
X X   Imaichi   X
            Kiryū X Kanuma   Kitsuregawa
Annaka   X
     J   Mibu
                          X   Ōta
J Maebashi   X
X X   SHIMOTSUKE
J Takasaki   HITACHI
Fujioka   Adachi
       X   X   Mito
  J   Sano   J   X
    J   J   X   J   J X Nakiminato
              X   X X
                        X
                       J Koga
       MUSASHINO   X   J   Itakomachi
            Gyōda   J   X
                 J   J   X
       J   Kawagoe   J X Noda   Sawara X
  Hachiōji   X Sakura   X
       X   J   J   Chōshi X
SAGAMI   J   Iwatsuki   SHIMO-OSA
            X   Edo●
Odawara   Fujisawa
     J   X   X X   X
  X   Hiratsuka   X
                              J   parts of marketing
                              X   network
                              J
                    J   J
                    J   KAZUSA
              J
  AWA   Kominato   10 MILES
       J   X
    J   J = jōkamachi
                              X = other central places

beginning of the Tokugawa period were far removed from the major routes of transport in Japan. Forced accumulation of goods in the Kantō region (through taxes in kind) to supply rapidly growing Edo lasted until the late seventeenth century, by which time inter-regional commerce was increasingly centered on Edo as well as on Osaka. Third, the financial importance of the Kantō region to hatamoto, gokenin, and daimyo who were the political figures closest to the Bakufu necessitated close scrutiny and intensive efforts to insure that this area was meeting growing financial needs.

What policies were adopted to strengthen the economic conditions in the Kantō region? During the seventeenth century the amount of land was rapidly expanded. The early eighteenth century Kyōhō reforms were directed at lowering and stabilizing prices in Edo, partially by expanding Kantō production. Policies of Tanuma Okitsugu in the eighteenth century strengthened monopolies of Edo merchants who were expected to promote commerce in the Kantō region while absorbing the commercial profits of the area. Clearly, the Bakufu was unwilling to receive as income only the land (*nengu*) tax when commerce to the city was rising. Later in that same century the Tenmei reforms aimed at preserving the rural population by denying them the opportunity to migrate to urban areas. Finally, the Tempō reforms were enacted in the nineteenth century in response to the breakdown of the monopoly system as crafts were spreading outside of the big cities. While antiluxury laws at this time hurt such enterprises as the silk industries in north-west Kantō, freer commerce generally helped Kantō merchants. Throughout the Tokugawa period reforms were directed, at least partly, at increasing local production in the Kantō area and at ex-panding Edo's supplies.

During the fifteenth and sixteenth centuries castles abounded in the Kantō region. The lords of these castles, as elsewhere in Japan, struggled for supremacy and for secure alliances. Markets became established in castle cities and in nearby villages under men loyal to the daimyo, but unlike Tokugawa daimyo, these lords could com-mand little control over the commercial pursuits of their loosely affiliated bushi. Links between marketing areas were hindered by the absence of stability and large networks did not form. Prior to

Tokugawa Ieyasu's arrival in 1590 the consolidation of local branch castles and periodic markets, which met either 1/10 or 2/10, was under way, but not yet complete.

After Tokugawa Ieyasu entered Edo he permitted thirty-four daimyo in the Kantō region, who held a total of 870,000 koku.[12] The small scale of jōkamachi in the Kantō region contrasted with conditions in other areas of Japan. Lords of most Kantō han could not take measures to make the jōkamachi the center of marketing because their domains were too small to be self-sufficient.

Small han of 20,000 people could not easily remain independent marketing units during the Tokugawa period. Moreover, the incentive of high prices in Edo undermined local self-sufficiency. Specialization in such primary goods as fish, lumber, and vegetables developed for the Edo market. In han and Bakufu-administered areas alike Edo exerted a strong pull. A second influence on the Kantō area was the early practice of stationing daikan outside of Edo. These officials were sent to large villages, in which storage facilities were placed to collect grain taxes. In many of these daikan encampments markets were established. When the control of daikan in the Kantō region ended around 1700, some of these markets collapsed, but others were able to continue.

Rising commercial agriculture characterized the Kantō region and elsewhere in Japan during the late seventeenth and early eighteenth centuries. Many markets which began as 1/10 increased their frequencies to 2/10. Markets previously dominated by a small number of men generally came under the control of a large number of merchants or of many homeowners whose land fronted on the marketing street. This transformation paralleled the move from a few merchants to broadly based tonya as the principal beneficiaries within the jōkamachi. The peak of Kantō periodic marketing was being reached.

Mid-Tokugawa Kantō markets filled local and regional needs for commercial distribution. Daily necessities in one area were exchanged for those in a nearby area, e.g., hillsmen brought charcoal to market and returned with grains. Many markets existed at points of intersection such as where mountain ranges met plains. Yet, while these markets served as centers of local exchange, underlying their presence in the eighteenth century was a factor absent in the six-teenth century: within three days' walk was Edo, a city with 1 million consumers. Charcoal and wood brought from the moun-tains were mostly bound for Edo, with only a fraction of the grain produced diverted to mountain dwellers. For the Kantō plain Edo was not only the level 1 city, but it was the only city above level 4 and for most of the region it replaced level 5 cities too. Level 6 cities sent their commerce directly to Edo. At first Kantō farmers were expected to supply those of Edo's needs not available through national exchange, but by the late eighteenth century emphasis was increasingly on replacing costly items shipped from afar. Prac-tically all of the Kantō region was viewed as a vast supply area for Edo.[13]

In the last century of the Tokugawa period the number of Kantō periodic markets was not increasing and may even have been declining. Some markets which disappeared left behind fairs in their central places, but fairs were not sufficient to sustain much com-merce. While some markets were declining, others were flourishing as new kinds of commercial centers. In place of primary dependence on local merchants gathered to further exchange in nearby villages, these cities were converted into centers for the accumulation of special goods destined for Edo. Part-time merchants and artisans proliferated within villages, replacing the periodic market as a source for daily purchases. Store commerce replaced market commerce both in ordinary villages and in the now prospering zaikatachō. Merchants in marketing settlements competed to secure the position of their localities as centers of accumulation for Edo. The central places that became processing and accumulation centers for special goods gained in population while other periodic markets declined.[14]

During the late Tokugawa period Kantō villages were brought more closely into economic ties with Edo. Nothing similar occurred in Chihli province, where the small economic spheres which formed the foundation for the hierarchy of cities remained intact. Appro-priately, the term used to describe the growing commerce from Kantō to Edo in the second half of the Tokugawa period was Edo *chimawari* [literally, to go by way of local areas to Edo].

The Kantō region was divided into eight kuni, as shown in Table

25. Although these were not units of administration, they can be divided according to many of the same characteristics as noted on Tables 13-22 for Chihli sheng. One table will suffice for this region. Figures are rounded off, but are still probably more precise than those for Chihli sheng.

TABLE 25

The Eight Kantō Kuni

Kuni	Villages (1834)	Population (1834)	Koku[b] (1598)	Koku[b] (1721)	Oil Stores[c] (1864)
Musashino	3,000	1,300,000[a]	700,000	1,200,000	163
Shimo-osa	1,600	400,000	400,000	600,000	213
Shimotsuke	1,400	400,000	–	700,000	116
Hitachi	1,700	500,000	500,000	900,000	167
Kozuke	1,200	500,000	500,000	600,000	31
Kazusa	1,200	400,000	–	400,000	21
Sagami	700	300,000	–	300,000	–
Awa	300	100,000	–	100,000	8

[a]This figure for the population of Musashino excludes Edo.

[b]The koku numbers indicate official koku totals, not the higher unofficial figures.

[c]The number of oil stores outside of Edo is included here as one indication of the state of economic development in each kuni. The cleavage is sharp between the number of stores in the top four kuni and in the rest of the region. Although the figure is not available for Sagami, it must be considered one of the four kuni in the poor category.

Kantō—Musashino Kuni

Musashino, the largest and most populous Kantō kuni, can be compared to Chihli sheng—both contained 7-8 percent of the population of their country and the national administrative center. Of course, Edo made up 40 percent of the total population of its kuni while Peking made up only 4 percent of the Chihli total.

Although in 1596 there were nine han in Musashino, by the mid-seventeenth century the number had been reduced to three. The largest of these han was Kawagoe, rising from 113,500 koku to approximately 170,000 official koku plus 25-30 percent more unrecorded koku. The second han was Gyōda (Shinōbu), which in 1869 held 100,000 official koku and 42 percent more unrecorded koku. Third was the much smaller han Iwatsuki. Some of the lands belonging to the daimyo of these han were scattered in other kuni, both nearby and distant, e.g., Kawagoe han lands were located in four kuni. Moreover, lands of han with jōkamachi in other kuni were scattered in Musashino. At least 800,000 koku of the total in Musashino kuni belonged not to daimyo, but to temples and shrines (ca. 3 percent), to hatamoto (ca. 37 percent), and to the Bakufu as tenryō (ca. 60 percent). The complexity of this land arrangement was such that most of the twenty-two gun in Musashino kuni were divided up between many overlords and even villages were under joint outside control.

In most kuni, the jōkamachi of the largest han was the most populous city. If we exclude Edo, this principle applied in Musashino. The city of Kawagoe was located near the center of Musashino, in an area where the first markets were mentioned in 1361. Marketing at the site of Kawagoe began in 1415 and continued for most of the following centuries. As the center of a relatively rich agricultural area and as an important transport point, Kawagoe long served as one of the principal castles. During the early Tokugawa period the population of the jōkamachi increased until, by 1698 it reached 9,000, of whom one-third were buke.[15]

For most han with as many koku as in Kawagoe, a population of 9,000 in the jōkamachi would have indicated that commerce was relatively slight; yet, this han was only about twenty miles from Edo and, given the complex land distribution, was not as closed a unit as were most han of its koku level. The city functioned as a central market for about five periodic markets to the north and west and goods bound for Edo passed through from further west in Musashino and beyond. During the mid-seventeenth century Kawagoe city had a 3/10 market in contrast to other markets in the area which met 2/10. By the following century stores had increased within the jōkamachi, reaching a level of commerce comparable to that taking place in the periodic market. Later the city was successful in making the transition crucial to markets in the late Tokugawa period, becoming a major source of exports to Edo. Silk became the number one special product in the han, charcoal was gathered at a special 2/10 market in a south chō within the city, and soy sauce also was sent to Edo. Imports received in return included various kinds of oil, clothes, sugar, rice-wine, paper, and salted fish. Kawagoe was clearly an important distribution center in the vicinity of Edo.

The other two Musashino jōkamachi were located north of Edo between the Arakawa and Edogawa rivers. Gyōda did not lie on any major transport route nor were there many nearby markets grouped under the city. Bushi predominated in the city's population: in the early 1800s there were only 555 chō households, but 1,030 bushi ones. Iwatsuki's situation was the reverse. As a post on a road from Edo to Nikko, the shrine city in north Kantō where Tokugawa Ieyasu was buried, this city contained as many as 3,000 chōnin, but only 251 bushi households.

There were more post stations in central places within Musashino than in any other kuni. The five main roads of Japan all began at Nihonbashi in Edo. These roads left Musashino kuni in the southeast, northeast, northwest, and southwest, passing through nearly all areas within the kuni. Along the routes of these five roads were most of the level 5 and level 6 central places of Musashino. Altogether there were 225 posts on these five roads within Japan.[16] Of this total, 8 percent exceeded 5,000 in population. Three of these large posts were Senju, Shinagawa, and Hachiōji, all in Musashino. Senju and Shinagawa were the first posts to the north and south of Edo and should be regarded for our purposes as part of Edo. Hachiōji, however, was usually the first place at some distance outside Edo on the Ōshūkaidō where travelers stopped to sleep.

Hachiōji had been a jōkamachi prior to the ascent of the Tokugawa and it retained its position as the premier city for the southwestern gun of Musashino even after 1600. The city served for a time as a military and administrative post of the Bakufu, continued as a periodic market, and later prospered as a center of textile production. The city's population rose from 3,400 in 1702 to 3,900 in 1715 to 5,500 in 1837 and to as high as 7,400 in 1854. In 1702 among the 95 artisans were 20 makers of rice-wine, and 11 carpenters, and among the 194 merchants were 56 grain dealers.[17]

Approximately twenty post station settlements in Musashino kuni had populations between 1,000 and 4,000 and two posts had populations of 4,000-5,000. These central places (almost all of them had markets) were spaced about five miles apart along two sides of the main road and extended for hundreds of yards. Honjō, the most populous post on the Nakasendō which was not a jōkamachi, extended for almost one-half mile or seventeen chō near the north-western corner of Musashino. Seven other posts in the east of the kuni ranged from ten to fifteen chō in length, unusual in comparison to many posts in other kuni which reached only three to ten chō in length. Normal width was about two chō.

At least twenty markets in this kuni were located in river ports. Traffic to Edo was heavy. Especially the Arakawa and Edogawa rivers flowing in the vicinity of Edo brought goods from the north.

Musashino kuni contained twenty-two gun. For thirteen of these, mainly in the north of the kuni, Muto Tadashi has listed the number of settlements in which markets were found in the 1870s and the population of each.[18] The population per gun ranged from 6,000 to 36,000 and the number of marketing settlements ranged between 0 and 12. Three of the gun had no marketing settlements and five had only one or two markets. Kodama gun in the northwest contained four markets, two with fewer than 200 households, one with 400-500 households and Honjō with more than 1,000 households. Kori gun in the west-central had four markets, all with fewer than 200 households. Iruma gun contained nine markets, six with fewer than 200 households, two at the 400-500 level, and Kawagoe. Saitama gun in the north-central was the site of eleven markets, including six with 200-400 households, two with 400-1,000 households, Gyōda and Iwatsuki jōkamachi, both of which exceeded 1,000 households in the 1870s, and Koshigaya, a post on the Nikko road with nearly 5,000 residents. The largest number of central places was in Adachi gun with thirteen: three held fewer than 200 households, three held 200-400, three held 400-500, and four held between 500 and 1,000 households. Altogether these thirteen gun contained forty-eight marketing settlements. The rest of Musashino may have contained as many as thirty central places at one time, but its numerous markets on the boundaries between mountains and plains were particularly affected by the late Tokugawa decline in periodic markets and may have been reduced to as few as twenty in number. In short, by the early nineteenth century Musashino kuni likely contained 70-80 central places or approximately one market for forty villages. Of the total perhaps fifteen were level 5 cities and the rest ranked at levels 6 and 7.

Kantō—Sagami Kuni

This kuni southwest of Edo was the site of Kamakura and Odawara, formerly the largest cities in the Kantō region. While Kamakura had declined sharply, Odawara remained the largest city in Sagami with about 10,000 people and was the jōkamachi of a han in which there were more than 100,000 koku.

The urban population of Sagami was concentrated along the coast. Six posts on the Tōkaidō road, including Odawara, contained a total of 20-25,000 people, more than two-thirds of the urban residents in the kuni. The second city of Sagami was Fujisawa, which held about 4,000 people at a point where a river from inland Sagami flowed across the Tōkaidō into Tokyo Bay. Hiratsuka, the next stop after Fujisawa on the Tōkaidō, also doubled as a port where an inland river entered the sea. This city had more than 2,000 residents. Inland Sagami was poor, supplying little but wood, charcoal, silkworms, and fruit by river or land to the six Tōkaidō posts and from there to Edo. Most cities at levels 5 and 6 were located along the coast while some level 7 periodic markets were found inland.

Kantō—Awa Kuni

Awa is one of the least significant kuni for the study of urban development. This small kuni was divided into even smaller han in which tiny jōkamachi formed the principal central places. There were some fishing settlements, but no active ports since little transport stopped in this kuni. In the northeast of the kuni was Kominato, a famous religious center which held a monzenmachi from 1276.

Kantō—Kazusa Kuni

Across Tokyo Bay from Edo, Kazusa was a rice-growing area with more commerce than Awa to the south, but less than Shimo-osa to the north. Small han and Bakufu-administered land shared this peninsula, but central places at levels 5 to 7 formed marketing networks irrespective of these administrative units. Five locations in the east of Kazusa kuni formed a complete circuit, each holding a 2/10 market with no overlapping days; therefore every day of the month a market in the area was open. One market in this circuit was likewise part of a second circuit formed with four other central places. There were no level 4 cities and few level 5 cities in Kazusa.

Kantō—Shimo-osa Kuni

This kuni just east and northeast of Edo was an area of rice production and river transport. Most land was under direct Bakufu rule. The nengu tax in rice was brought to storage spots on specified days and then sent on to Edo by river or if necessary by horse to the nearest river and then by boat. Five of the seven daimyo in Shimo-osa administered only 10,000-20,000 koku. The two principal jōkamachi were Sakura in the center and Koga in the northwest. Koga with a 4/10 market prospered as a point in the accumulation of rice and soybeans for Edo.

Rivers in north and west Shimo-osa formed part of a route for long-distance commercial shipments and tax revenue shipments from the Tōhoku region and from northern Kantō areas to Edo. To avoid the lengthy land route from Mito in Hitachi to Edo and the sea route around the Chiba peninsula the Tonegawa river through Shimo-osa underwent improvements during the seventeenth century. The city of Choshi developed rapidly as a port at the mouth of the river and in 1781, 180,000 koku of rice arrived in the city, mostly for transshipment. Salt, marine products, rice-wine, beans, lumber, and charcoal were all popular items on the Tonegawa and the Edogawa rivers from this kuni to Edo. Large quantities of soy sauce produced in Choshi and in the post of Noda, which had a 2/10 market, were sent to Edo. Sawara, another 2/10 market on the Tonegawa river, was a rice-wine manufacturing center. More similar to Musashino than to Sagami, Awa and Kazusa, Shimo-osa was a prosperous kuni from which diverse goods flowed to Edo.

Kantō—Kozuke Kuni

Located in the northwest of the Kantō region, this kuni contained two main cities, Takasaki and Maebashi, both about sixty miles from

Edo on rivers connecting to the Tonegawa. Like the chou in Shun-t'ien fu which served as gateways about fifty miles from Peking, these cities together with Odawara, Mito in Hitachi kuni, and Utsunomiya in Shimotsuke kuni were gateways to Edo.

Urban development centered in the south-central and southeast of Kōzuke kuni. By the late eighteenth century there were nearly twenty marketing settlements with commerce in silk.[19] The most flourishing silk center was the 4/10 market of Fujioka, in which approximately 10 percent of the total turnover of bolts of silk in Musashino and Kozuke—the two Kantō silk centers—occurred. Kiryu further northeast also was an important weaving center. In the south of Kozuke kuni there were two examples of jōkamachi which could not maintain markets in the face of competition from nearby central places. One of these was in a han of 10,000-20,000 koku and the other was in a han of 20,000-30,000 koku. Further to the northwest was Annaka, a post on the Nakasendō, and a jōkamachi in a 30,000 koku han, where a 2/10 market flourished.

Kantō—Shimotsuke Kuni

Ten main cities can be identified in Shimotsuke kuni. In the southwest corner nearest Edo stood the markets and river ports of Adachi and Sano. Four cities not far from each other in west-central Shimotsuke were Nikko, Imaichi, Kanuma, and Mibu. Kanuma, having a population which rose from 1,000 to more than 3,000 during the Tokugawa period, became one of the largest posts on the road from Edo to the Nikko shrine. Lumber, charcoal, salt, and hemp were all traded at its 2/10 market. Mibu (Tochigi) functioned as a jōkamachi, a post, and a marketing settlement. Further east in separate river valleys were Otawara, a small castle city, and a post on the Okushu road with 1,400 people excluding bushi, Kitsuregawa with 1,200 residents, and Mōka, a castle city and cotton-producing center.

The first city of Shimotsuke kuni was the jōkamachi Utsunomiya. Transport from as far away as the Tōhoku region was gathered here to be shipped by water to Edo. Rice, lumber, and varnish passed through Utsunomiya. The number of koku in this han was changing during the Tokugawa period as the total fell from more than

100,000 official koku in the seventeenth century to a stable figure of 78,000 koku during the last century. When the han contained 110,000 koku, it was divided into four main gun with 223 villages: one gun with 63,000 koku and 104 villages, one gun with 23,000 koku and 65 villages, one gun with 15,000 koku and 34 villages, and one gun with 7,500 koku and 20 villages. These divisions into gun approximated the divisions of Chinese administrative units into lu.

In 1720 the population of Utsunomiya han was about 80,000. Bushi with their families made up 3,000 of this total, other jōkamachi residents added 9,000, and almost all the rest were farmers, except for 444 Buddhist priests, 92 people attached to Shinto shrines, 150 eta, and 20 beggars.[20] For the early nineteenth century a listing of the occupations for non-bushi households in Utsunomiya reads as follows: merchants—497, artisans—254, innkeepers—39, operators of eating places—58, and farmers—305. An additional 200 households in areas separately governed as monzenmachi were not included.[21]

Kantō—Hitachi Kuni

Hitachi kuni, bordering the sea in northeast Kantō, contained the largest han in the region, Mito han. Altogether in this kuni were 1,677 villages in the late seventeenth century and 1,729 in 1868. Four gun with 462 villages were completely outside Mito han, but the other seven gun all were at least partially occupied by the land of this han. The core areas of the han were gun in which all villages belonged to the han while fringe areas ranged to one gun in which only 6 of 127 villages were part of this han. As the number of villages was rising slowly, the population of Mito han, after increasing in the seventeenth century, declined from 277,000 to 230,000.

Han commerce was organized around the jōkamachi. Within approximately twelve miles of Mito jōkamachi markets were largely abolished. Farther out, marketing days were revised in order not to conflict with the periodic market inside the castle city. There were ten regular 2/10 markets, seven temporary markets, and the castle city market in Mito han, making an average of 15,000-20,000 koku per central place.[22] The jōkamachi served as the center for imports and exports, while most han markets served for local needs or, perhaps, for the accumulation of a specialty product such as paper, a mineral, firewood, charcoal, or fish. A few han cities can be singled out as level 6 or even level 5 central places: Nakaminato was the port for Mito city, Ota was a former jōkamachi at a river juncture in the north, and Itakomachi was located on a detached area of the han at the southern boundary of Hitachi along the Tonegawa river.

The northeast area of Mito han was exceptionally rural in character. A section in this area in 1868 contained 3,142 farm households, 46 merchant households, 10 artisan households, and 35 others.[23] Urban activities were largely confined to marketing settlements outside of this area and to Mito.

As a jōkamachi of a poor han in which the number of koku was rising unusually slowly, Mito was not in a favorable economic position. Correspondingly periodic marketing waned slowly in this level 4 city. Population in the chō of the city dropped from 13,000 to 8,000 and in the temple and shrine areas from 6,000 to 4,000.[24] Since many of the 21,000 buke in the han lived in Edo, the jōkamachi fell far short of the customary 10 percent as many people as the 350,000 registered koku in the han.

SUMMARY

Holding respectively 5-6 percent of the central places in China and 12-13 percent of the central places in Japan, Chihli sheng and the Kantō region approached the average for provinces and regions in their countries. Yet, in some respects these areas were atypical. Above all, the presence of national administrative centers influenced patterns of land-holding and prompted special efforts to speed the flow of goods to the residents of these great population centers. As Table 26 below indicates, both areas, but especially the Kantō region, were dominated by a single city.

So far in this chapter, we have observed marketing patterns in single hsien and chou and in separate fu and chih-li chou. Now we will try to put together the pieces in the puzzle which forms Chihli sheng by examining the urban network of the province as a whole. Of overriding importance is the fact that roughly half of all urban residents lived in Peking. Tens of thousands of shopkeeper households resided along the more than 1,000 streets of Peking. All main roads led to the city. The Grand Canal, the sea route to Tientsin, the kuan-lu through neighboring provinces, and the strategic routes through passes in the Great Wall all were predicated on the existence of a tremendous center of civilian and military consumption at Peking. To the extent that local areas could support exports which could be transported without excessive cost, these goods were sent to Peking.

TABLE 26

Distribution of Central Places in Chihli and Kantō

Level of Central Place	Number of Settlements	Total Population (millions)
Chihli		
1	1	1.0
2	0	–
3a	2	.2
3b	2	.1
4	15	.2
5	80	.4
6	350	.35[a]
7	1,250	–
Totals	1,700	2.1
Kantō		
1	1	1.0
2	0	–
3a	0	–
3b	0	–
4	5	.1
5	30	.15
6	70	.07[a]
7	125	–
Totals	230[b]	1.3

[a]Remember that only one-half the totals given for level six population are counted as urban.

[b]Figures are approximate; therefore population and settlement totals in excess of twenty are rounded off to multiples of ten or occasionally of five.

Level 2 cities were not found in Chihli sheng, but there were two level 3a cities—Tientsin and Pao-ting. The former served the east and southeast of the province, while the latter served the west and southwest. Three other level 3a cities—T'ai-yuan (Shansi), K'ai-feng (Honan), and Lin-ch'ing (Shantung)—were located close enough to parts of Chihli to exert an impact on the province's urban network. Espccially Lin-ch'ing succeeded in casting a centripetal force on southern Chihli. Nevertheless, most of the province remained oriented to cities within Chihli.

Pao-ting and Tientsin owed some of their prosperity to their importance as funnels for goods bound for Peking. Tientsin was much the larger city, with nearly 200,000 people in 1846 (the ratio of population to households was given as almost six; so the total population was unexpectedly high for a city with 33,000 households). In addition to the 11,000-12,000 shopkeeper households in the city, there were 5,000-6,000 peddlers, including many with families. We should assume that in other cities the number of shopkeeper households also ought to be supplemented by a figure for peddlers. Altogether Pao-ting and Tientsin contained roughly 13 percent of Chihli's urban inhabitants.

Ranging between 30,000 and 70,000 in population were Shun-te fu city and T'ung chou city. Shun-te, located between K'ai-feng in Honan and Pao-ting, was a major transportation point on the north-south kuan-lu through western Chihli and served a hinterland that was not readily accessible to the level 3a cities further north and to Lin-ch'ing to the east. In contrast, T'ung chou lacked a large hinterland, but was dependent for its thriving commerce on Grand Canal traffic bound for Peking. When the Grand Canal fell into disuse in the late Ch'ing period, T'ung chou also declined. The evidence indicates that cities at this level contained about 100 streets and 1,000-2,000 store households.

Ranking at level 4 were four distinguishable types of cities in Chihli sheng: fu cities such as Cheng-ting and Ta-ming; chih-li chou cities such as Tsun-hua; chou cities at the gateways to Peking; and a small proportion of hsien and chou cities located at transportation nexuses along principal routes through the province, e.g., Shan-hai kuan (Lin-yü hsien city) at the northeast pass and Ts'ang chou with its 380 shopkeeper households along the Grand Canal. Scattered about the province, these cities with 10,000 to 30,000 residents doubled as administrative and commercial centers for many administrative units or benefited mainly from commerce bound for Peking.

Of the approximately 120 hsien and chou in Chihli sheng the smallest resembled intermediate marketing areas, with the administrative city serving as the level 6 city and the most populous appeared as one or even two central marketing areas in which the administrative city and, perhaps, one other city ranked at level 5. Particularly along the Grand Canal chen surpassed administrative cities as prosperous commercial centers. Of course, marketing areas frequently did not coincide with administrative boundaries. Examples have been cited of level 5 chen which were advantageously situated to serve commerce from three or more hsien. Whether an administrative center or a chen, the typical level 5 city contained 100 to 300 shopkeeper households and more than twenty streets.

More than 70 percent of the urban residents of Chihli sheng lived in cities at levels 4 and above. Most of the remaining city dwellers were found in administrative centers at level 5. All of the first twenty cities in this sheng had administrative functions and most of the next eighty cities at level 5 were likewise administrative centers. Thus the population of nonadministrative cities probably contributed less than 5 percent of the nearly two million people who lived in cities with 3,000 or more residents in Chihli sheng.

Most level 6 central places were nonadministrative cities, but at least thirty hsien cities fell short of 3,000 people. The examples of T'ang hsien and Wang-tu hsien indicate that such small administrative cities contained fewer than 100 shopkeeper households. Most cities at this level also contained fewer than twenty streets. Although differences in area, population, and number of villages make it difficult to speak of an average administrative unit, the figures in Table 26 indicate that such a unit would have contained three cities at level 6 and ten or eleven level 7 settlements.

The Kantō region was exceptionally bifurcated. There were no cities at levels 2 or 3. Cities at levels 4 served as jōkamachi at the fringe of the region, forming a ring around Edo resembling the circle of chou cities surrounding Peking. Intermediate-sized han of

30,000 to 100,000 koku and major roads gave rise to level 5 cities doubling as marketing centers. Level 6 cities also were particularly numerous among jōkamachi and post stations.

The primary difference between the Kantō and Chihli areas was reflected in the relative proportions of their total populations subsumed by the level 1 cities. One of six people in the Kantō region lived in Edo while one of twenty to twenty-five people in Chihli sheng lived in Peking. Edo's impact spread across the Kantō plain, permeating all eight kuni. No level 2 or level 3 city was necessary for the marketing networks of the region or for the supply of long-distance commerce mainly by sea. Edo required no T'ung chou or Tientsin as outer ports. Levels 4 and 5, however, were essential as funnels for local commerce. The Kantō region was better represented at these levels because marketing had become more advanced. One-tenth as many level 7 markets sustained one-fifth as many level 6 markets which in turn sustained almost two-fifths as many level 5 markets as in Chihli. Even in the Kantō region with its atypically small jōkamachi, the urban network appeared compact and concentrated as contrasted to China.

✵ 5 ✵

REGIONAL VARIATIONS IN CITIES

The initial response of many of us to gross statistics about large-scale premodern countries is skepticism that the sum of the data for the various areas of the country is an accurate reflection of all areas. Each of us who has singled out one area such as Chihli or the Kantō region for detailed study is likely either brazenly to extrapolate his findings to the nation as a whole or cautiously to find exceptions to prevalent generalizations about the nation as a whole. To date comparisons of regions are so rare that we usually have no way of determining to what extent our knowledge of a given area can be applied beyond that area.

The underlying assumption in this work is that the degree of a premodern society's urbanization was relevant to other critical characteristics of the society. Presumably the same assumption can be applied to regions within a single society. If regions were all urbanized to the same degree, then the initial conclusion would be that the social structure of these regions was similar in relevant respects. However, we would want to specify not only whether the proportion in cities was identical, but also whether the distribution among the various levels was the same. Two areas which were 10 percent urban may have differed because in the first area half the population lived in a single level 1 or 2 city and in the second area less than 30 percent of urban residents were in cities at levels 1-3. Comparisons of urbanization in the various regions of a country should prove to be a first step to more detailed study of regional variations in social structure.

Another reason for treating regions separately in Japan and especially in China is the vast scale of the countries. In this chapter

I have divided Japan into two regions and China into six. The smallest region in these countries during the mid-nineteenth century contained roughly 15 million people. Three of the regions of China exceeded 80 million in population. Such heavily populated areas, some exceeding 5 percent of the world's population, deserve separate attention.

Finally, many of the large cities of China and Japan are identified and briefly described in this chapter. Central places at levels 4-7 were emphasized in Chapter 4 since in Chihli province and the Kantō region there were not many cities at levels 2 and 3. Now by scanning all areas of China and Japan, we can observe many of these larger cities with 30,000 or more residents as well as the lesser cities with which they were connected.

North China

The three sheng listed in Table 27 together with Chihli sheng comprised North China, an area with roughly 95 million people, approximately 5 million of whom were urban. One-fifth of the urban population of the region resided in Peking, about five times as many as in the second city K'ai-feng, the capital of Honan sheng. Neither Peking nor K'ai-feng was located on a navigable river nor did many people in either city live in areas beyond the city wall, truly unusual characteristics for the largest cities of a Chinese region. In contrast the next three largest cities in North China, Tsi-ning, Lin-ch'ing and Tientsin, were all located along the Grand Canal and consisted of populations which in a large part resided outside the main city wall. The sixth, seventh, and eighth cities were T'ai-yuan, Tsi-nan, and Pao-ting, sheng capitals served mainly by land transportation. We should have an impression then of a region in which 10-15 million people and almost 1,000 central places were required to sustain a city with more than 70,000 people and in which major cities depended on land transportation with the exception of a single water route on which large amounts of long-distance trade threaded their way between Peking and East-central China.

We can add to the information already presented for Chihli sheng on the factors contributing to urban development and the ways of measuring it by reviewing some Japanese articles and a sample of

TABLE 27

North China

Level	Shantung						Shansi				Honan			
	Mid-19th		1910s		1953		Mid-19th		1953		Mid-19th		1953	
	No.	Pop.	No.	Pop.	No.	Pop.	No.	Pop.	No.	Pop.	No.	Pop.	No.	Pop.
1	0		0		0		0		0		0		0	
2	0		0		2	1.6	0		1	.7	0		1	.6
3a	3	.4	5	.7	4	.5	1	.1	3	.5	1	.2	6	1.0
3b	7	.3	7	.3	10	.4	1	.2	5	.2	4	.3	12	.5
4	13	.2					10	.2			10	.3		
5	90	.45					45	.2			75	.4		
6	400	.4					200	.2			500	.5		
7	1500						750				2000			
Total Pop.	35				49		15		14		23		44	
Urban Pop.	1.55				3.4		.6		1.8		1.15		2.9	
Urban %	4–5%				7%		4%		13%		5%		6.5%	
Urban % in levels 1–3	45%				74%		22%		78%		30%		72%	

gazetteers from the other three provinces of North China. Two articles by Yamane Yukio examine the history of fairs and periodic markets in Shantung sheng.[1] Yamane shows that although many fairs originated as religious festivals, they acquired increased economic significance during the late Ming and the Ch'ing periods. Yamane cites four signs of the substantial economic significance of fairs in Shantung: (1) fairs were often located in marketing settlements; (2) the more developed the area, the more successful were scholar-officials in establishing new fairs; (3) where demand for commerce was rising, fairs were extended by lengthening the existing sessions by a day or two or by meeting more than once each year; and (4) there were practically no fairs in the busy summer months. Of course, the number of periodic markets is an even better indication of an area's economic development than the number of annual fairs. Yamane has shown that new periodic markets appeared in rapid succession in Shantung from the early sixteenth century. In short, the Ch'ing period was a time of continued growth in the number of periodic markets and fairs in Shantung as elsewhere in North China.

An article by Kono Michihiro demonstrates a way of measuring one form of land transportation by analyzing the pattern of post stations in Shantung.[2] Dividing post stations into three classes, Kono defines "A" class posts as those with fifty or more horses, "B" class posts as those with ten to forty-nine horses, and "C" class posts as those with nine or fewer horses. A total of 139 posts, more than 25 percent of the central places in this province at levels 3-6, were spread over all 108 administrative units, with most posts located in hsien and chou cities. The following spatial pattern prevailed: (1) all "A" class posts were located along the two kuan-lu (national highways) with the exception of the post in Tsi-nan, the sheng city a single stop away from a kuan-lu; (2) most "B" class posts were located along ta-lu (the second highest designation for a road), which formed radials between the kuan-lu serving intraprovince commerce; and (3) "C" class posts were dispersed throughout Shantung. If the number of animals was indeed suggestive of the quantity of traffic through the city, then Kono has given us a clue to the importance of numerous cities in land transport.

One factor influencing the size of an administrative city was the number of people within the area of its jurisdiction. Gazetteers from Shansi sheng help us to understand this factor. The 101 administrative units (85 hsien, 6 chou, and 10 pen chou) of Shansi held an average population of 150,000, lower than in most provinces. In order to demonstrate the substantial variations obscured by this average, we unfortunately must rely on data from the 1880s, which, at 10.7 million, apparently underestimate the total sheng population by about 4 million. These data reveal that the 36 units within chih-li chou (26 hsien and 10 pen chou) were with few exceptions sparsely settled: 9 of the units were below 50,000; 15 more were between 50,000 and 100,000; and no more than 3 units exceeded 180,000 in population. In contrast, 180,000 was the average population during the eighteenth century for the 19 chou and hsien in T'ai-yuan fu and Fen-chou fu. T'ai-yuan, the sheng city, and Fen-chou fu city were administrative centers of densely populated areas as opposed to chih-li chou cities near the borders of the province. Variations in the populations of hsien and chou within a single fu are striking too. For instance, Ta-t'ung hsien (in which was located Ta-t'ung fu city) held 420,000 people and Ying chou held 141,000, while the rest of the hsien and chou in the fu according to these data ranged in population only between 28,000 and 78,000.

Obviously a hsien with 50,000 people was less likely to produce a hsien city of at least 5,000 people than a hsien with 200,000 people. After subtracting from the total sheng urban population of 600,000, the population in the sheng city, in the 9 fu cities, in 10 chih-li chou cities and in nearly 150 nonadministrative cities, the population remaining in the 82 hsien and chou cities in Shansi probably amounted to 300,000—an average of 3,000 to 4,000 per city. Approximately 2½ percent of the population resided in hsien and chou cities. If the proportion of an area's population in the administrative city had not varied, then units with fewer than 130,000 residents would have yielded level 6 cities, those with 130,000-400,000 would have yielded level 5 cities, and those with more than 400,000 residents would have yielded level 4 cities. Although other factors such as density of settlement, convenience of transportation, and marketing prosperity all affected this proportion, in general, the larger the population of the administrative unit, the more people were apt to live in its designated city.

In fact, during the nineteenth century there were five hsien in Shansi in which at least 300,000 people lived: Yang-ch'u (T'ai-yuan sheng city), Ta-t'ung (a fu city), Fen-yang (Fen-chou fu city), P'ing-yao (within Fen-chou fu), and Chieh-hsiu (also within Fen-chou fu). T'ai-yuan city with an estimated 100,000 people and Ta-t'ung, which in 1830 was recorded as having 35,000 residents, were probably the two most populous cities in the province. The other three populous hsien are among nineteen hsien and chou for which I have obtained figures of a broker tax—the *ya* tax—a possible indication of the quantity of commerce within the hsien. While the taxes of twelve of these nineteen hsien and chou were between 13 and 74 taels and of four hsien and chou between 100 and 200 taels; these three hsien stood out with ya tax figures of 200, 217, and 325. Fen-chou fu city, having a hsien tax of 325 taels of silver, was clearly at least a large level 4 city. Chieh-hsiu and P'ing-yao hsien were transport centers located thirty miles apart on the kuan-lu between T'ai-yuan and P'ing-yang fu cities. During the early nineteenth century Chieh-hsiu city had more than fifty streets and P'ing-yao city had approximately fifty streets. In this part of China as many as fifty streets were rare in cities with fewer than 10,000 people. Thus, by combining information on the population of administrative areas, on broker taxes, and on the number of streets in various cities, we emerge with a composite view of Shansi urban populations.

Nakamura Jihei in two articles divides hsien and chou cities in Shansi and Shantung into those with populations of 3,000 to 5,000 and those with populations of 6,000 to 7,000.[3] Most of his examples held 5 percent or less of the total administrative area's population. For instance, Jui-ch'eng hsien city on the southern border held 4,900 of 96,000 hsien residents in 1764. Since his sample is small and his hsien population data are often questionable, Nakamura's findings are necessarily tentative, but they do show, except for the omission of level 6 cities, the range of population in the lowest administrative seats of these provinces.

Gazetteers of Honan sheng provide data on the number of streets in several large cities. According to one nineteenth century gazetteer,

K'ai-feng was divided into nine yü, seven of which contained between 31 and 43 streets each. Altogether there were 290 streets. Among the several level 3b cities was Lo-yang, the second former imperial capital in Honan about 140 miles west of K'ai-feng, which contained four yü and about 49 streets within the wall and another 41 streets in the four kuan. In the opposite direction from the sheng city, Kuei-te fu city also contained approximately 90 streets. Cities at levels 4 and 5 normally contained fewer streets than level 3b cities. Wei-hui fu city during the mid-eighteenth century was crossed by 25 streets within the wall and 40 more in the four kuan. Other level 4 cities probably held fewer than 50 streets and level 5 cities such as Kuang chou chih-li chou contained roughly 25 streets. Sometimes not only the total number of streets, but also the number of chieh or main streets provide an index of city prosperity. For instance, Shen chou chih-li chou city contained as many as 24 streets, but was poorly represented with only six chieh. In this case the number of households in the city is given, divided for convenience between the four main chieh and three other streets. Tallies associated with each street show between 75 and 107 households, adding up to a total of 641 households.

Three of the eight largest cities in this region were located in Shantung sheng. Tsi-nan, the sheng city, held only 6,100 households within its wall, and 6,400 more in its kuan as late as 1772, but later as Shantung's population grew, this city swelled to more than 100,000 people. Tsi-ning chih-li chou city dominated the commerce of southwest Shantung. Its rising prosperity from the eighteenth century reflected a successful rivalry with the third level 3a city, Lin-ch'ing chih-li chou, for preeminence among Grand Canal entrepôts north of the Yangtze river. During the late eighteenth century Tsi-ning contained about 90 streets (half in the kuan) and 14,500 households. Subsequent growth centered in the south kuan, where goods arrived along the Grand Canal. As the city population climbed to 100,000 in 1840, the number of streets in the city reached 290, including 183 in the kuan, of which 100 were in the south kuan. Correspondingly, 17,000 of 22,000 households were outside the city wall. The third level 3a city Lin-ch'ing, was previously mentioned in Chapter 4. From the Ming period to the early Ch'ing period,

Lin-ch'ing reigned as the major city of Shantung, but by 1749 a gazetteer was vividly portraying the declining prosperity of the city. Nonetheless, Lin-ch'ing remained until the late 19th century one of the three large cities of Shantung.

Frequently it is possible to discover the number of official units into which an administrative area was divided and the proportion of these which were in the administrative city. Is it correct to estimate the administrative city's population from the proportion of official units assigned to it? In the case of Tsi-ning it is. Before 1800, 22 of 107 *ti-fang* (the official unit of that area) in the pen chou belonged to the pen chou city, corresponding to the 20 percent of 71,000 pen chou households in Tsi-ning city. Later Tsi-ning's total population climbed above 100,000 as the pen chou total rose from 380,000 to 500,000. Similarly during the late eighteenth century, T'ai-an fu city in Shantung contained 13 of its hsien's 110 ti-fang; which likely corresponded to roughly 35,000-40,000 of the 310,000 residents of the hsien. A mid-nineteenth century description of the west kuan of T'ai-an mentioned thousands of households. Although we must be careful in relying on the proportion of official units as a measure of city population, some evidence indicates that these units are often a reliable measure.

Yamane Yukio has supplied the most complete description for a level 4 city in Shantung.[4] Relying on a detailed enumeration from about 1880, Yamane identifies the occupations present in one-fifth of Yen-chou fu city. Among 572 households for which occupations were noted, 319 were engaged in merchant activities (183 of these can be further divided into 85 dealing with foodstuffs, 27 with clothing, 33 with eating places, 34 with sundries, and 4 with metals), 64 were active as artisans, 49 were absentee landlords and farmers and the rest fit into such categories as degree-holders, subofficials, soldiers, priests and hired labor. The wealth of information on this fraction of Yen-chou fu city could be used in many ways, but here I will only cite four facts which appear typical of cities throughout China: (1) crafts were small-scale enterprises with few employees; (2) stores were concentrated on particular streets according to product, e.g., there was a district known for second-hand clothes; (3) tea houses, rice-wine houses, noodle shops, fried cake shops, and tobacco and opium stores (a temporary phenomenon) were some of the most common stores; and (4) many merchants were in fact peddlers. While items 1, 3, and 4 applied to cities at all levels, item 2 was apparent only in high-level cities, especially in level 3 and above.

Information concerning the concentration of stores on particular streets is also presented in a nineteenth century gazetteer of K'aifeng. Stores for certain types of goods were grouped in one or two areas of the city. Areas were known for such specialties as hats, drugs, shoes, stationery, old books, second-hand clothing, and pottery. Scattered throughout the city were tea houses. Next most widespread were rice-wine houses, fruit stores, oil stores, and fragrance shops located on each of the main streets.

Among the four provinces of North China, central places were most numerous in Honan. In fact, Honan was the only sheng in this region in which the ratio of population to markets was below 10,000:1. Moreover, marketing frequencies in Honan were generally 5/10, while 2/10 and 3/10 frequencies prevailed elsewhere. Yet, abundant opportunities to market goods were not reflected in large urban populations. Indeed, Honan resembled Chihli minus Peking, since in both the total population was roughly 23 million and the urban population 1.1 million.

Using the data in Table 27 we can also compare the provinces of this region in other respects. An unusually large number of level 3b cities is indicated in Shantung. Analogous to the argument above that hsien and chou administrative areas with greater populations were likely to produce larger cities, it can be argued that the fact that fu in Shantung tended to be more populous boosted more fu cities from level 4, common in these provinces, to level 3. With most fu cities containing more than 30,000 residents, Shantung was left relatively poorly represented at level 4. Since administrative units in Shantung were on the average more than twice as populous as those in Shansi, we would expect that administrative cities in the former were large, i.e., most were higher in the population range of level 5 between 3,000 and 10,000, but it was still unusual for hsien and chou cities to contain as many as 10,000 inhabitants.

Probably the most revealing differences between these four provinces can be found in the data showing the proportion of the urban population in cities at levels 1-3. The range extended from Chihli with 65 percent, to Shantung with 45 percent, to Honan with 30 percent, and finally to Shansi with 22 percent. The explanation may be that the greater the amount of long-distance commerce imported into a province, the higher the proportion of urban residents in large cities. In Chihli both Peking and Tientsin were heavily dependent on long-distance shipments. The presence of the Grand Canal in Shantung also enabled trade to be concentrated, but apart from the Canal, Shantung sheng was highly self-contained with few outside merchants.

Where exports far exceed imports, urban residents at levels 1-3 may have been relatively few. Honan sheng was bisected by the principal north-south land route from Peking to Wuhan through K'ai-feng, but lacked many waterways that could carry long-distance commerce. Exports were substantial since there were several level 3a and 3b cities in neighboring provinces just across the borders. Shansi merchants thrived by transporting goods from lower level cities in Honan to cities on major water routes in Hupei, Shantung, and Anhwei. Ringed by mountains and the unnavigable Yellow river, Shansi was one of the most isolated provinces of China, yet, merchants originating from Shansi engaged in commerce in many provinces, and goods from Shansi contributed to the growth of such large cities as Peking, Lin-ch'ing, K'ai-feng, and Sian. The imbalance favoring exports in Shansi and Honan is evident from the fact that unlike Chihli and Shantung, the two provinces farther west held only one city each with more than 70,000 residents and in both cases that city was dependent on land transport for shipments of long-distance goods.

It may be worth speculating what the consequences would have been if North China had not been the seat of the imperial capital and no special system of long-distance supply to Peking had been developed. The apparent answer is that instead of 5-6 percent of the population in these four sheng living in cities, 4-5 percent would have been urban. Sheng cities would still have ranked at level 3a. Major fu cities would have continued at level 3b and most fu cities together with some chih-li chou at level 4. More than half of all hsien and chou cities plus some large chen, small fu cities and chih-li chou cities would have composed the level 5 category and levels 6 and 7 would likewise have remained virtually unchanged. Peking's impact extended along the Grand Canal and outward to some nearby chou cities, but apparently no further.

Northwest China

Shensi and Kansu, the two provinces listed in Table 28, were located in the northwest corner of the inner provinces of China. The small region which they formed contained only two cities with more than 70,000 residents and both were sheng administrative seats. As in North China, about one-fifth of the urban population of the

TABLE 28

Northwest China

	Shensi				Kansu			
	Mid-19th		1953		Mid-19th		1953	
Level	No.	Pop.	No.	Pop.	No.	Pop.	No.	Pop.
1	0		0		0		0	
2	1	.3	1	.8	0		1	.4
3a	0		3	.3	1	.1	1	.1
3b	3	.1	4	.1	4	.15	6	.3
4	6	.1			–	.1		
5	40	.2			–	.2		
6	175	.2			–	.2		
7	750				–			
Total Pop.	11		16		15		13	
Urban Pop.	.8		1.6		.65		1.1	
Urban %	7%		9.9%		4–5%		8.6%	
Urban % in levels 1–3	50%		75%		38%		73%	

region lived in a single city, in this case Sian, the only city in the two northerly regions with the exception of Peking, which was divided into two hsien. The immense walled perimeter of Sian, formerly the capital called Ch'ang-an, was exceeded only by the walls of Nanking and Peking.

The second sheng city was Lan-chou, located near the center of

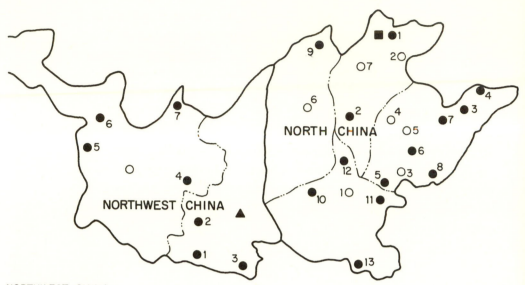

NORTHWEST CHINA

▲ LEVEL 2   Sian

○   3a Lan-chou

●   3b 1, Han-chung fu; 2, Feng-hsiang fu; 3, Hsing-an fu; 4, P'ing-liang fu; 5, Hsi-ning fu;
               6, Liang-chou fu; 7, Ning-hsia fu

NORTH CHINA

■ LEVEL 1   Peking

▲   2   –

○   3a 1, K'ai-feng; 2, Tientsin; 3, Tsi-ning; 4, Lin-ch'ing; 5, Tsi-nan; 6, T'ai-yuan; 7, Pao-ting

●   3b 1, T'ung chou; 2, Shun-te fu; 3, Lai-chou fu; 4, Teng-chou fu; 5, Ts'ao-chou fu; 6, T'ai-an fu;
               7, Ch'ing-chou fu; 8, I-chou fu; 9, Ta-t'ung fu; 10, Honan fu (Lo-yang); 11, Kuei-te fu;
               12, Chang-te fu; 13, Hsin-yang chou

Kansu province. Dependent on Sian for most contacts with other areas of China, Lan-chou could not rival the Shensi city, but still was able to achieve a large population through its administrative, military, and commercial importance in the strategic province of Kansu.

In 1778, nearly a quarter of the total population of Shensi, about 2.8 million people, lived in the fourteen hsien and chou of Sian fu. The average administrative unit in this area was twice as populous as units in the remainder of this generally sparsely settled province. Not only was Sian the principal urban center, other cities in its fu were also comparatively large. For instance, Ching-yang hsien city, twenty-five miles northwest of the sheng city, was a flourishing commercial center (probably level 4) before the Moslem rebellion of the 1860s. In 1841, the total hsien population reached 161,000 of whom 32,500 were registered as members of merchant families. The nearby hsien city of San-yuan also prospered, holding as many as four hui-kuan, and was more successful than Ching-yuan in maintaining its position as a commercial gateway north of Sian.

Cities at levels 3 and 4 in Shensi were mostly fu administrative centers. Han-chung fu city had a big walled area with at least 50,000 residents. Feng-hsiang fu city, the center of west Shensi on the Wei river, was nearly as populous. The third level 3b fu city was Hsing-an on the Han river. An example of a smaller fu city was T'ung-chou, which in the early nineteenth century contained some forty streets. Ch'iang-po chen in the same hsien achieved fame as a 5/10 market where during the spring and summer numerous merchants came to purchase sheepskin for export to cities as far away as Peking; however, when the prosperity of the fur trade suddenly fell, the number of merchants in this chen decreased by 70 to 80 percent.

Kansu sheng was large in area, but was divided into just fifty-nine hsien, chou, and t'ing. Especially in the west and long northwest corridor huge areas were administered from widely separated cities. Yet, with two-thirds as many administrative units as Shensi, Kansu held a larger population, roughly 15 million. The average population per administrative unit was 250,000—twice the figure for Shensi. The contrast was striking between large fu cities located in relatively settled areas and small frontier hsien cities. In Kansu fu cities made up a greater proportion of all administrative cities than in other sheng; for every four hsien or other equivalent administrative city, there was one fu city. Presumably this ratio reflected the vast areas of many hsien within the province. It would have been difficult to govern from fu cities any further apart.

Lan-chou was located on the Yellow river near the center of the sheng area if the northwest corridor is excluded. Its hsien population rose from 401,000 in 1772 to 468,000 in 1830. The sheng city contained approximately 20 percent of this total. The fact that two chou within Lan-chou fu also were densely settled—one held 517,000 and the other 698,000 people in 1830—contributed to the potential for concentrating nearly 100,000 people in the sheng city.

Merchants from Shensi and Shansi monopolized long-distance trade within Kansu. Their hui-kuan were present even in some level 5 cities. For instance, in Ti-tao chou about seventy miles south of Lan-chou a hui-kuan was established in the southwest kuan despite the fact that the city was listed as having only 3,000 residents. The main stores in P'ing-liang fu city, in which approximately 35,000 people resided, also were in the hands of Shansi and Shensi merchants engaged in shipping such goods as wool, drugs, wood and minerals from Lan-chou to Sian.

Although the data for Kansu are deficient, it is likely that this province was about 4 to 5 percent urban. Lan-chou and the several large fu cities totaled nearly 2 percent of the province's population and if patterns prevalent elsewhere were typical in Kansu as well, then 2 to 3 percent of the population were in lower-level central places.

Kansu was less urbanized and had a less concentrated urban population than Shensi. Yet, since Kansu was strategically located as the gateway to outer areas in the west and southwest of China, it was a heavily garrisoned area in which cities probably contained an exceptional proportion of soldiers and military transport filled the roads.

Shensi appears to have been an exceptionally urbanized province of North and Northwest China. Although it was poor in the north, its rich river valleys in the south, the kuan-lu to Peking and Kansu and the Han river transport link with Hupei all supported a high concentration of urban residents. As the communications center for parts of six sheng including Shensi and Kansu, Sian, combining administrative and commercial centrality, prospered.

Joining the figures for Shensi and Kansu in Table 28, we find that the proportion of the region's population living in cities was 5.6 percent, about the same as the figure for North China. Roughly 43 percent of the region's urban dwellers lived in cities at levels 1-3, also remarkably similar to North China, in which transportation conditions were comparable. Resembling the region to the east, Northwest China was connected to areas farther south and central by one major waterway, in this case the Han river. In many respects the regions dominated by Sian and by Peking were alike.

East-central China

The population of the three provinces of East-central China listed in Table 29, was 105 million, 25-30 percent of the total population of China during the mid-nineteenth century. Roughly 6 million people were urban, the highest total for any region. Moreover, this was the only region with as many as three cities at levels 1-2 and with as many as twelve cities at levels 1-3. East-central China became noted as the area in which Chinese urbanization was most conspicuous.

During the early Ch'ing period Anhwei and Kiangsu were grouped together as Kiangnan sheng. It is likely that this provincial unit was twice as populous as any other. Even after the split into Anhwei and Kiangsu, each of these sheng contained approximately 10 percent of the population of China. While the population of these sheng continued to be exceptionally large, the number of administrative units was unusually few. Consequently, the average population per hsien or chou reached more than 500,000 and examples of units in which there were populations in excess of 1 million were not rare. An average administrative unit in Anhwei or Kiangsu held three or four times the population of one in Shansi or Shensi.

Kiangsu was both the smallest sheng in area and the largest in population. Administrative centrality was concentrated in fewer cities than elsewhere. Unlike Anhwei, many cases existed where more than one hsien shared a fu city; therefore, fu cities typically

TABLE 29

East-central China

Level	Anhwei Mid-19th No.	Pop.	1953 No.	Pop.	Kiangsu Mid-19th No.	Pop.	1910s No.	Pop.	1953 No.	Pop.	Chekiang Mid-19th No.	Pop.	1910s No.	Pop.	1953 No.	Pop.
1	0		0		0		1	2.0	2	7.1	0		0		0	
2	0		0		2	1.5	2	1.0	3	1.4	1	.6	1	.3	1	.7
3a	3	.25	7	1.2	3	.3			8	1.5	3	.3	3	.5	4	.6
3b	4	.2	8	.3	7	.3			12	.4	3	.2	3	.1	8	.3
4	13	.2			18	.3					12	.2				
5	90	.45			100	.5					70	.35				
6	550	.55			600	.6					400	.4				
7	2,000				2,000						1,300					
Total Pop.	35		31		43				47		27				23	
Urban Pop.	1.4		2.0		3.2				13.7		1.65				2.2	
Urban %	4%		6.7%		7%				29.1%		6%				7.7%	
Urban % in levels 1–3	33%		75%		68%				73%		55%				73%	

served as the fu seats for populations of roughly 4 million and, simultaneously, as the administrative centers for two hsien totaling more than 1 million people. Nanking and Soochow, the two level 2 cities in Kiangsu, were easily the two largest cities to be found in any single province.

All three provinces of this region can be conveniently divided into two zones. While the northern plain of Anhwei was an extension of conditions prevalent in North China, but with a denser population and more numerous marketing settlements, mountain ranges in the south were typical of parts of Southeast and Central China. Similarly dry-grain producing areas in north Kiangsu contrasted with the highly commercialized agricultural areas of the south. The convergence of long-distance trade routes in the central and southern parts of Kiangsu contributed to the concentration of large cities there. The third province Chekiang was divided into a fertile north and a larger more mountainous south. Differences between these areas were reflected in administrative divisions: while all of the fu cities in the four northern fu were split into two hsien, the other seven fu of Chekiang contained only one city with two hsien.

Typical variations in hsien populations occurred in Chekiang. While most hsien ranged from 150,000 to 400,000, at least ten large hsien and ten small hsien ranked at opposite extremes outside of this range. Fu cities were usually centers of hsien with large populations. Other cities at level 4 and above also were administrative centers of the most populous hsien. Even if these cities had merely held the same proportion of hsien residents as in other hsien cities, they would have been up to four or five times more populous. In contrast, many cities at level 6 were centers of sparsely populated hsien.

Of course, to the extent that marketing activities were the primary determinant of urban populations, then a larger hsien population might merely have been reflected in the addition of a nonadministrative level 5 city, which divided control over the level 6 central places with the existing hsien city. Indeed, a single hsien would not have had to support completely both cities since marketing was not confined by administrative boundaries and it was customary for large chen to be located near or at the hsien border. Despite these qualifications, it was still common for large cities to contain exceptionally large populations in their administrative hinterlands.

The division of hsien cities, as opposed to sheng or fu cities, into two administrative units was unique to Kiangsu. One example is Wu-chiang hsien city. This city had held fewer than 1,000 households until the Yuan period, then prospered to the point where it exceeded 2,000 households and acquired a daily market in the Ming period. But with the growth of commerce in local marketing settlements, the hsien city's portion of hsien commerce fell from a peak of 40-50 percent during the early Ming period. The city remained at about 10,000 in population while nonadministrative cities were expanding. Then during the early Ch'ing period the city was split into two hsien, Wu-chiang and Chen-tze. Certainly the split was not due to the growth of the hsien city. A gazetteer of Ch'ang chou hsien explains such divisions as follows: "Although the population is dense in large cities and chen of Kiangsu and there are many bodies of water, between [the urban areas] are also fields. If [the fields] were taken for building city walls and moats, the form could not be regular and moreover they would have to encroach on paddy land and dry land. [Therefore there is a tendency for two hsien to share a city and save the expense of a new wall]."[5]

East-central China was not only the area with the greatest concentration of large cities, it was also the location of many of the most populous nonadministrative cities in China. An exceptional example of flourishing nonadministrative cities was the above-mentioned Wu-chiang hsien on the Grand Canal south of Soochow near the Chekiang border. After the settlements in Chen-tze hsien were split off from this hsien during the Yung-cheng reign, Wu-chiang was left with four chen, five *shih* (interchangeable with *chi* meaning market) and 175 villages for a population of 247,000. P'ing-wang chen, sixteen miles southeast on the Grand Canal and divided between the two hsien, held more than 1,000 households in the early Ming period and was described as being similar to a small hsien city. Also southeast in Wu-chiang hsien was Sheng-tze chen, formerly a village of 50 to 60 households in the early Ming period, which first became a shih owing to trade in silk thread and later was reputed to have increased its population a hundred times, becoming the largest chen in the hsien. The other two chen in this hsien were level 5 cities: Li-li chen reached a population of about 5,000 during the late Ming period and T'ung-li chen was recorded as holding 1,000 households during the K'ang-hsi reign of the early Ch'ing period.

In Chekiang Wu-ch'ing chen consisted of two built-up areas on opposite sides of a river which separated Hu-chou fu and Chia-hsing fu near Kiangsu. Although the two parts of the city were in separate fu, they should be treated as a single urban area. Together they had more than 5,000 households and about 87 streets. Resembling other nonadministrative cities, Wu-ch'ing chen was built along a river without an enclosing wall. A few long streets paralleled the river, while many short streets intersected them.

An unusually complete description of nonadministrative cities in Kuei-an hsien of fertile Hu-chou fu is available for 1884. The two largest chen were Shuang-lin and Ling-hu, which held 9,200 and 6,700 residents respectively. Other big marketing settlements ranged in population from 1,500 to 3,000 and small marketing settlements dipped to far fewer than 1,000 people. For each central place the number of shopkeeper households was listed: more than 100 households = eight central places; 10-88 households = fifteen central places and fewer than 10 households = one central place. One could hypothesize that level 6 central places held at least 100 shopkeeper households and that level 5 central places held several hundreds in this commercially prosperous area.

Anhwei

Although Anhwei sheng was the least urbanized part of this region, plentiful information enables me to describe in some detail the cities that did exist in this province. In the north of Anhwei a cluster of urban areas was formed by Feng-yang fu city, its hsien city one mile away and Lin-huai kuan six miles distant. Feng-yang city may have been the only example in all of China where the walled area containing the fu city did not also contain at least one hsien city. While the hsien administrative seat was an old city, the separate fu city had first been built only in the eighteenth century. Lin-huai kuan and its counterpart Cheng-yang kuan, further west on the

Huai river, were level 3b cities, but not administrative centers. Stores lined the wharves along the river in both chen. Much of the traffic stopping in Lin-huai kuan was headed for Chen-chiang (Kiangsu), and the guilds in the two cities were closely associated.

Another sizable city in northern Anhwei was Shou chou, located along the Huai river between Lin-huai and Cheng-yang kuan. Approximately fifty streets were visible on the gazetteer city map; however, since the city wall measured an enormous thirteen li in circumference, the four corners inside the wall were nearly empty. Even with a population of 20,000 this city would have contained only 2 to 3 percent of the 733,000 chou population.

Po chou in the northwest corner of Anhwei was located on a river which joined the Huai river near Feng-yang fu city. Po chou city contained four pao inside the wall and three more plus part of a fourth in its kuan. Thus of the seventy-two pao in this chou of 1,345,000 people (1823) approximately 10 percent belonged to the chou city. The street count gives further evidence of the scale of this city. During the Ch'ing period the number of streets more than tripled with most of the increase occurring in the kuan along the river. Data from this city is one indication that cities which gained population during the second half of the Ch'ing dynasty expanded mainly in their kuan.

TABLE 30

Streets in Po chou, Anhwei

City area	1740	1774	1825	1894
Walled area	21	48	54	54
North kuan	33	51		112
Other kuan				14

Another large city near the north border of Anhwei was Su chou. Its administrative area may have held more markets than any other chou or hsien in China. The number of markets was listed as 176 in 1889, but during the 1860s the total may have been higher since nineteen central places were redistricted out of this chou into Kuo-yang hsien.

While cities in the north of Anhwei were agricultural collection and distribution points and stops in transit for the lively trade between the 20 to 30 million inhabitants of northern Anhwei, eastern Honan, and parts of Kiangsu, central Anhwei between the Huai and Yangtze rivers was not as accessible. Primarily inside the commercial sphere of Wu-hu hsien city to the south on the Yangtze river, the area was poorly served by rivers. In the east near Nanking and Yang-chou in Kiangsu were some levels 4 and 5 cities such as Ch'u chou chih-li chou, from which hemp, peanuts, drugs, and foodstuffs were gathered for Kiangsu consumers. But the fact that much of this eastern area exported rice to Wu-hu instead of to Kiangsu cities testifies to the importance of the rice market in Wu-hu. At this city rice from Anhwei joined rice from Central China moving east along the Yangtze river.

Directly in the center of Anhwei was Lu-chou fu city (Ho-fei hsien) from which exports were sent by river to Wu-hu and imports were collected in return for redistribution in central Anhwei. As Table 31 indicates, the fu city was the largest in the area.

TABLE 31

Markets and Streets in Lu-chou Fu, Anhwei

Administrative Unit	Population	Markets	Streets in Administrative City
Lu-chou (Ho-fei hsien)	1,598,000	42	105
Wu-wei chou		35	49
Ch'ao hsien		17	45
Shu-ch'eng hsien		13	31
Lu-chiang hsien		36	16

The southern part of this province can be divided into the two hinterlands of Wu-hu and An-ch'ing plus some areas distant from these cities, but connected in the southeast to the level 2 city of Hangchow in Chekiang and in the southwest to Chiu-chiang in Kiangsi and Wuhan in Hupei, cities at levels 3a and 2 respectively. Roughly 100 miles apart along the Yangtze river from Hupei to

Kiangsu were cities at levels 2 or 3a. The length of the river in this province permitted two such cities: Wu-hu and An-ch'ing, the sheng city at the opposite end of the sheng. Moreover, in Anhwei, as elsewhere along the Yangtze river there was a city of about 10,000 people—Ch'ih-chou fu city—approximately midway between the two higher level cities.

Wu-hu hsien city in the east of Anhwei was well situated just upstream from the great consuming areas of the lower Yangtze delta. Not only was Wu-hu probably the most populous city in Anhwei with more than 100,000 people, it also was one of the two largest hsien cities in China. In the early nineteenth century there were thirty-nine streets within the wall and eighty-six more outside, mainly along the Yangtze river south of the city. Moreover, there were twenty hui-kuan in Wu-hu, a number indicative of the great influx of merchants into the city.

The third largest city in south Anhwei had been Hui-chou fu, famous as the source of Hsin-an merchants who were active throughout large areas of China. This city was both a collection point for specialty products from southeast Anhwei and a stop for goods in transit between northeastern Kiangsi, including its level 3a city of Ching-te chen, and Chekiang and Kiangsu. But in the late Ch'ing period Hui-chou city was losing prosperity to T'un-ch'i, a level 4 chen seventeen miles to the southwest.

Kiangsu

Table 32 shows data for hsien and chou in two areas of Kiangsu sheng. Such information as the population of the administrative unit and the number of streets is clear and I have previously compared cities using the number of chieh (main streets) and the broker tax, but two other categories in the table require explanation. In Kiangsu many nonadministrative cities were customarily called chen. Sometimes they contained markets and thus qualified as central places, but not always. A separate listing of markets not treated as chen was given as chi. Although it is difficult to determine the actual number of central places, by adding the number of chen and the number of chi plus the administrative city, we are not likely to overestimate the total by much.

TABLE 32

North and South Kiangsu

Administrative Unit	Population	Chen	Chi	Chieh	All Streets	Broker Tax
			North Kiangsu			
Shan-yang hsien (Huai-an fu city)		44	10	34	74	
T'ung-shan hsien (Hsu-chou fu city)	396,000		58			
Hai chou chih-li	505,000	48				
Fu-ning hsien	540,000	12	22		77	
An-tung hsien		9	22	15	40	
Pao-ying hsien	565,000			13	33	
P'i chou			38	6	18	
Yen-ch'eng hsien	330,000	9		17	28	
Kan-yu hsien	210,000	30	3	7		
Shu-yang hsien	434,000	26	94		9	
			South Kiangsu			
Tan-t'u hsien (Chen-chiang fu city)				31	153	
Chiang-tu hsien (Yang-chou fu city)	658,000	6			{ 200	487
Kan-ch'uan hsien (Yang-chou fu city)				28		394
Hua-t'ing hsien (Sung-chiang fu city)	303,000			22	82	65
Lou hsien (Sung-chiang fu city)	276,000					133
I-cheng hsien	238,000				{ 55	121
Ching-ch'i hsien	165,000					
Chiang-yin hsien	978,000	40		13	68	227
Kao-cheng hsien	278,000	10	12	10		
Chia-ting hsien	436,000	16	5	5	44	84
Nan-hui hsien		50			23	
Wu-hsi hsien	650,000				{ 112	66
Chin-kuei hsien	500,000					

North Kiangsu probably contained one level 5a city (Huai-an fu), one level 5b city (Hsü-chou fu) and at least four level 4 cities (Fu-ning hsien, Hai chou chih-li chou, An-tung, and Pao-ying). All were located on or near the Grand Canal except Hai chou and Fu-ning in the east and Hsü-chou on a river in the northwest corner. Huai-an fu city was the largest city along the Grand Canal between Yang-chou fu city and Tsi-ning in Shantung.

Containing only 3 percent of the administrative units of China, south Kiangsu had 10 to 15 percent of the population which lived in cities with more than 10,000 people. Approximately 2 million residents of more than twenty cities at levels 4 and above made this area the most urbanized part of China. After 1842 Shanghai rapidly developed to become the largest city in the country in the twentieth century, maintaining the predominance of this area. Since the growth of Shanghai must be regarded as part of the transformation from the premodern urban network, it will not be considered in this study. Moreover, nineteenth century Kiangsu, like many other sheng, was ravaged by civil war, from which some of China's largest cities never recovered. Both the effects of the T'ai-p'ing rebellion and later wars and those of emerging treaty ports should be ignored where possible in order to focus on the urban network as it was before these transformations.

Unfortunately, many of the large cities in southern Kiangsu are omitted from Table 32. The two largest cities for which I was able to find the number of streets were Chen-chiang and Yang-chou, located about thirty miles apart on the Grand Canal between Nanking and Soochow. Chen-chiang, at the intersection of the Yangtze river and the Grand Canal, was the gathering point for goods bound for North China, but after the Grand Canal fell into disuse and the city was destroyed during the T'ai-p'ing rebellion, it never fully recovered. By 1880 the number of streets had fallen to approximately 100. Yang-chou was divided into two hsien in 1731. Historically this city had been a great shipping center and during the Ch'ing period its total of 200 streets and a combined broker tax of nearly 900 taels indicate that the old prosperity remained. Furthermore Yang-chou was famed as the residence of many of China's wealthiest salt merchants.

Soochow was the only city with three hsien in China. Within its fifteen-mile walled circumference and in the kuan along the two sides of the wall bordered by the Grand Canal lived at least 500,000 and possibly as many as 1 million people. In contrast to Peking, which was surrounded by low-level central places with infrequent periodic markets, within fifty miles of Soochow were at least forty locations with daily markets or with commerce mainly in stores. Canals within the city were connected by water gates to river transport and sea transport leading to every one of China's level 1 and 2 cities. As the hsien city for three hsien, the fu city for nine hsien (more than in any other fu in Kiangsu), the sheng city for China's most populous province and the main marketing center for the richest area of China and an area with transportation ties as excellent as those in Osaka, Soochow ranked as one of the two or three most populous cities in China.

The relationship between Nanking and Soochow resembled that between Kyoto and Osaka. Nanking was inland, the old capital, a place with special administrative functions, a center of textiles and arts and may have been the fourth or fifth most populous city in early nineteenth century China. It had not so much declined as it had receded into the background, while maintaining its reputation as the cultural center. Serving as the principal market for southwest Kiangsu and east Anhwei, Nanking was more central than Soochow for the administration of both sheng. It kept the offices of the governor-general of the two sheng and served as the secondary capital after Peking. Moreover, Nanking was a fu city, a city divided into two hsien and a port on the Yangtze river.

Chekiang

Chekiang was intermediate in urbanization between Anhwei and Kiangsu. Its principal city, Hangchow, probably held more than 500,000 people before the T'ai-p'ing war and even after the destruction of the war years remained a level 2 city. In 1893, one of the two hsien within the city contained approximately 200 streets and 39,000 households. There were eighteen hui-kuan in the city and while other administrative cities in Chekiang contained two to twenty *fang* [wards], in Hangchow there were eighty-nine.

Three other cities in Chekiang were probably level 3a cities. Ning-po was more dependent on sea transport than any large city further north in China. Especially during the nineteenth century when the city was opened as a treaty port long before Hangchow, it gained rapidly in population, but even before foreign trade developed Ning-po had been well situated to connect Southeast China to Hangchow and the Grand Canal. Shao-hsing fu city in the rich northern plain between Hangchow and Ning-po was also a large city. The third level 3a center was Wen-chou fu city at the southeastern juncture of inland rivers near the ocean. In 1882 the city held about 190 streets. The total number of *t'u* (official unit) inside the hsien was 216, of which 19 were in the walled city and 6 more in the kuan. This official division of Wen-chou city corresponds closely to the distribution of streets—150 were inside the wall and 40 were in the kuan. If 25/216 of the 951,000 hsien residents had inhabited the fu city, then its population would have been 110,000.

In addition to Ning-po and Shao-hsing fu cities there were two level 3 fu cities in the north of Chekiang. Chia-hsing fu city was located near the Grand Canal in the rich agricultural area north-east of Hangchow and Hu-chou fu city further to the west held 97 streets as well as 10 t'u inside the city wall. The remaining level 3b city was Lan-ch'i hsien, which was located at a river juncture serving transport from Chin-hua, Yen-chou and Chu-chou fu cities bound for Hangchow. Lan-ch'i hsien city held 103 streets and ten fang.

While the East-central region's urban population, its number of cities at levels 1 to 3 and other characteristics stand out, they are not so distinctive when viewed in a per capita perspective. If the figures presented are essentially correct, then this region was only a fraction of 1 percent more urban than North and Northwest China. Its twenty-six cities at levels 1 to 3 are fewer than would be expected from its population since there were more than 100 cities at these levels in China. And the 7,000 central places in this region further indicate that national averages were not exceeded. Yet, one comparison does distinguish East-central China from other regions. The ratio of urban population to central places (6 million: 7,000, i.e., 860) was highest in this region. The urban network was, therefore, different from that of Northwest China with a ratio of 520 and from that of North China with a ratio of 710. I shall return to these ratios later in this chapter.

Kiangsu sheng, China's commercial center, can be usefully compared with all of Japan. Its population, which was rising above 40 million, was somewhat larger and more densely settled than that of Japan. And with more than 2,500 central places Kiangsu also was somewhat ahead of Japan. Nevertheless at nearly all levels Japan held a larger urban population. While Kiangsu had about 1½ million people in cities at levels 1 and 2, Japan was closer to 1.8 million. Kiangsu held 300,000 people in three level 3a cities, but Japan held 300,000 to 400,000 in four cities at that level. Turning to lower levels, we find Japan's urban total much further ahead. At level 3b Japan contained three times as many cities as the seven in Kiangsu and at level 4 the ratio was even higher. Kiangsu's total population was about 30 to 40 percent greater than Japan's, but its urban total was less than 60 percent of the figure for Japan. Yet, one interesting comparison which should not be overlooked is that the proportion of urban dwellers in large cities was higher in Kiangsu than in Japan, while the percentages were about even for all of China and Japan. Long-distance commerce from wide areas of China contributed to the concentration of city residents in large cities in this sheng. Presumably if the rest of China had not supported this province (though it is also true that rice from Kiangsu helped support Peking), its large cities would have been substantially reduced in size and more easily dwarfed by the large cities of Japan.

It was mentioned previously that the sheng in this region were sharply divided into at least two zones. In each of the less-developed zones (north and central Anhwei, north Kiangsu and south Chekiang) there was one city at level 3a, but in the more developed zones there were two to four cities at level 3a or higher. Of the twelve cities with more than 70,000 residents, all except Shao-hsing and Po chou were located along the Yangtze river, the Pacific Ocean, or the Grand Canal. Nearly every one of these twelve cities was a center of long-distance transport.

In conclusion, I should reiterate that a hsien in this region did not mean the same thing in terms of population as a hsien elsewhere. Administrative units were much more populous than in other areas of China. One would expect that the average administrative city was larger and that there were more large marketing places in an administrative unit. Whereas in other regions there was little need for additional level 5 cities because the administrative unit could support just one city at that level, in the populous hsien of Anhwei, Kiangsu, and to a lesser extent, Chekiang, two level 5 cities could easily develop. The widespread presence of relatively large chen, the larger average population in administrative cities and the proximity of three level 2 cities closer together than in any other area of China all give the impression of an exceptionally urbanized area in East-central China.

Central China

Hupei, Hunan, and Kiangsi are generally regarded as areas intermediate in development as in location between the advanced Yangtze delta and the backward southwestern sheng of Kweichow and Yunnan. As is noted in Table 33, these three provinces ranged in total population from 24 to 30 million and in urban population from 1.3 to 1.8 million. As in North China and Northwest China, more than one-fifth of the urban population lived in a single urban area Wuhan, including the sheng city of Hupei. The second and third largest cities in the region were also sheng cities, Ch'ang-sha in Hunan and Nan-ch'ang in Kiangsi. Each was advantageously located along the main river of its province flowing north to a large lake just below the Yangtze river. Other level 3a cities, with the exception of Ching-te chen, a center in Kiangsi for the manufacture of pottery, were also located on the principal rivers in this region.

Although I am treating Wuhan as a single city, during the Ch'ing period it was in fact regarded as a complex of three separate cities. One of the three was Wu-ch'ang, the sheng city, in which a population of more than 100,000 lived. A second urban component was Han-yang, a fu city shielded by mountains which provided protection against military incursions. Its built-up areas reached outside the city wall along the Yangtze river and were extensive enough to encompass a population comparable to that in the sheng city. Largest of the three segments of Wuhan was Hankow, which extended

TABLE 33

Central China

Level	Hupei						Hunan				Kiangsi			
	Mid-19th		1910s		1953		Mid-19th		1953		Mid-19th		1953	
	No.	Pop.	No.	Pop.	No.	Pop.	No.	Pop.	No.	Pop.	No.	Pop.	No.	Pop.
1	0		1	1.0	1	1.4	0		0		0		0	
2	1	.8	0		0		0		1	.65	0		1	.4
3a	2	.15	2	.15	3	.3	3	.4	6	.75	3	.5	2	.2
3b	3	.1	3	.1	3	.1	2	.1	8	.3	4	.2	7	.3
4	11	.15					11	.2			14	.2		
5	75	.4					75	.35			75	.35		
6	450	.45					450	.45			450	.45		
7	1,600						1,600				1,600			
Total Pop. (millions)	30				28		25		33		24		17	
Urban Pop. (millions)	1.8				2.4		1.3		2.3		1.5		1.3	
Urban %	6%				8.6%		5%		7%		6%		7.6%	
Urban % in levels 1–3	58%				75%		39%		74%		48%		69%	

CENTRAL CHINA

▲ LEVEL 2 Wuhan

○　　　　3a 1, Ching-chou (includes Sha-shih); 2, Hsiang-yang; 3, Ch'ang-sha; 4, Hsiang-t'an; 5, Heng-chou; 6, Nan-ch'ang; 7, Ching-te chen; 8, Chiu-chiang

●　　　　3b 1, Lao-ho k'ou; 2, I-ch'ang fu; 3, Ching-men chih-li chou; 4, Ch'ang-te fu; 5, Yueh-chou fu; 6, Kan-chou fu; 7, Jao-chou fu; 8, Fu-chou fu; 9, Chi-an fu

EAST-CENTRAL CHINA

▲ LEVEL 2 1, Soochow; 2, Nanking; 3, Hangchow

○　　　　3a 1, Yang-chou; 2, Chen-chiang; 3, Huai-an; 4, Ning-po; 5, Shao-hsing; 6, Wen-chou; 7, Wu-hu; 8, An-ch'ing; 9, Po chou

●　　　　3b 1, Hsü-chou fu; 2, T'ung chou chih-li chou; 3, Ch'ang-chou fu; 4, Wu-hsi and Chin-kuei hsien; 5, Sung-chiang fu; 6, Shang-hai hsien; 7, Hu-chou fu; 8, Chia-hsing fu; 9, Lan-ch'i hsien; 10, Lu-chou fu; 11, Lin-huai kuan; 12, Cheng-yang kuan

along both the Yangtze and the Han rivers. By far the biggest of the three Chinese chen in which more than 100,000 people resided, Han-kow was the major locus of commercial exchange from South-west and Northwest China to East-central China and from South-east and East-central China to much of inland China. The three parts of Wuhan combined the administrative, military and com-mercial functions which contributed to a large urban concentration. This city could have been equaled only by Soochow as the greatest market and by Peking or Soochow as the most populous city in China.

Ch'ang-sha and Nan-ch'ang each had populations of 200,000 to 300,000. Ch'ang-sha benefited as the site of two hsien in which re-sided a total of 1.1 million people, as the fu city for 6 million more people, as the sheng city for an additional 20 to 25 million and as a great collection and distribution point, stretching along the major river which linked densely settled east Hunan with the Yangtze river. Hui-kuan from all areas of China were found in Ch'ang-sha. Inside the wall in one of the two hsien were 84 streets and, if the number of streets in the second hsien and along the wharves outside the wall are added, the total may well have surpassed 200. Nan-ch'ang was the only city in Kiangsi sheng which was divided into two hsien. Information on one of its hsien also reveals a total of roughly 100 streets. Resembling other cities along rivers, Ch'ang-sha and Nan-ch'ang were long and narrow in form.

Level 3 cities in Hupei were located along the two principal rivers west of Wuhan. Sha-shih chen and nearby Ching-chou fu city can be considered one city on the north bank of the Yangtze river. Their hinterland extended north into Hupei and south to the lake area of Chang-te fu in Hunan. Trade from Szechwan stopped in Sha-shih en route to Wuhan and, hui-kuan in the chen represented most areas of the country except the far north and the far southwest. Competing with Sha-shih for commerce along the Yangtze river between Central China and Szechwan was I-ch'ang fu city, located midway between Wuhan and Chungking. The more mountainous vicinity of I-ch'ang provided neither major access to consumers nor as plentiful a supply of products for export.

Northwest about 300 miles by river from Wuhan was Hsiang-yang fu city and opposite it on the north bank of the Han river Fan-ch'eng chen. Together they formed the third city of this sheng after Sha-shih prospered during the nineteenth century. Rivers joined the Han at Hsiang-yang, forming a large hinterland from north Hupei to south Honan. Farther up the Han river other tributaries from west Hupei carried transport to Lao-ho k'ou, a level 3b city. Both Fan-ch'eng and this chen were built up for one to two miles along the river. Major east-west streets paralleling the river were cut by tens of short north-south streets. The contrast between unplanned cities such as these and the regular walled-off forms of administrative centers was evident throughout China.

The second and third cities of Hunan were ports upstream from Ch'ang-sha along the Hsiang river. Hsiang-t'an, south in Ch'ang-sha fu, was similar to Anhwei's Wu-hu; both were hsien cities with populations in excess of 100,000 renowned for rice markets. Miles of wharves bordered the Hsiang river and ships from more than twenty hsien and chou docked with grains and other goods. Heng-chou fu city was further upstream in the south of Hunan. It was the only city besides Ch'ang-sha which was divided into two hsien. Altogether there were at least 125 streets in this fu city.

The three level 3a cities in Kiangsi were all located in the north near Po-yang lake. Nan-ch'ang's location to the southwest of the lake provided the most access to areas in Kiangsi. Less centrally situated were Ching-te chen, northeast of the lake, and Chiu-chiang fu city, northwest of the lake. Together with Hankow and Fo-shan (Kwangtung), Ching-te chen was one of the three great chen of Ch'ing China. The city was unique in China, having up to 200,000 residents whose activities were focused around the manufacture of a single product—ceramics—destined not for any particular urban market, but for customers throughout China. Exports of pottery did not have far to go to reach the Yangtze river or smaller rivers lead-ing to Anhwei and Chekiang. While the chen was unusually de-pendent on timber from nearby mountainous areas to heat its many kilns, it was not supplied by as large a hinterland as was Nan-ch'ang because imports were not destined for further distribution outside the city. In other words, this was an unusual example of a city which was not a point for redistribution of goods accumulated from nearby areas. In contrast, Chiu-chiang served primarily as an accumulation point for Kiangsi rice and as a stop for commercial transport on the Yangtze river between Wuhan and An-ch'ing. During the late eighteenth century there were 221 *chia* (official divisions within the pao-chia system, which reflected population) inside the city and approximately 1,900 chia in the remainder of the hsien, indicating that 10 percent of the hsien population resided in Chiu-chiang city.

The four level 3b cities in Kiangsi were dispersed over a wide area. Jao-chou fu city, just east of Po-yang lake, contained 106 streets in 1871. Prior to that date there had been approximately eighteen fang in the city. Since the gazetteer described one fang as equal to 500 households, the population of the city must have been 9,000 households. The city was also divided into t'u; inside the wall were 22 t'u and 69 streets (the number of streets per t'u varied from two to five) and in the kuan were 18 t'u and 37 streets. Fu-chou fu city was located on a river southeast of Nan-ch'ang. The city was divided into 23 t'u inside the wall and 23 more in the kuan. Altogether the hsien area held 492 t'u for a population of 400,000. Near the center of Kiangsi sheng on the river system to Nan-ch'ang was Chi-an fu city. Two facts about Chi-an suggest a large city: the city held twenty-one li (the equivalent of twenty-one fang), which indicated a population of 10,500 households in 1781; and there were 48 streets inside the wall and another 100 streets in the kuan. The other city with more than 30,000 residents was Kan-chou fu.

Data on a number of level 4 cities is available in Kiangsi gazetteers. The contrast between large level 4 cities with more than 20,000 residents and small ones with only 10,000 to 15,000 residents can be seen in the descriptions of Kuang-hsin fu city and Yü-shan hsien city, thirty miles apart near the Chekiang border. Kuang-hsin was the larger. There were four t'u within its wall and nine more outside the gates along a river. Yü-shan did not have such flourishing river transport, but also was built-up in its kuan. It held 780 households inside the wall and 2,400 more outside. Another city with slightly more than 10,000 inhabitants was Wan-an hsien located between Chi-an and Kan-chou fu cities on the Kan river. The area within the wall was divided into four pao (official divisions within the pao-chia system) which may be compared with the 39 pao in Chiu-chiang fu city or with the 134 pao in all of Wan-an hsien, for which a total population of 318,000 was given. Farther up the Kan river, Kiangsi's counterpart for the Hsiang river in Hunan, was Lin-chiang fu city with its 61 streets. Only ten miles away in the same hsien sprawled Chang-shu chen, one of the four big chen of Kiangsi together with Ching-te, Ho-k'ou and Wu-ch'eng. Presumably these three cities smaller than Ching-te chen each totaled about 10,000 in population. Much larger was Jui-chou fu city in the northwest of Kiangsi. Containing 10 of the 145 t'u in its hsien of 655,000 people, Jui-chou may have been a large level 4 or a small level 3b city.

A few examples of smaller cities in Kiangsi will add to the picture of this particularly well-documented sheng. Chi-shui hsien consisted of ten chieh and twelve hsiang, a total of 22 streets. The population was divided according to the four main chieh: the east gate chieh and west main street each extended for one li (one li = 1,800 Chinese feet) on which lived more than 200 households, a third one-li street in the east was the location of tens of households, and a two-li street was noted on the registrations of more than 200 households. Thus Chi-shui city held at least 600 to 800 households. Data on An-i hsien is most complete concerning street lengths. This four t'u city held nine chieh, the shortest of which was 500 feet (one Chinese foot = 14.1 English inches) and the longest of which was 2,850 feet. Most streets measured between one-half and one li in length.

Detailed information is available for two cities in Hupei during the 1880s. Huang-chou fu city, east of Wuhan on the Yangtze river, was a level 4 or, perhaps, even a level 3b, city since it contained approximately 100 streets. Yet, just two of the seventy-six *li* (official units) in its hsien of 662,000 people were within the fu city. The number of households was given for Ching-shan hsien city in the central part of Hupei. Inside the wall were 402 households, in the two east kuan were 254, and in the west kuan were 221. Altogether there were 32 streets on which these 877 households were located. A breakdown by streets indicates that the average number of households per street was 21 within the wall and 40 in the east kuan.

An example of a level 5 city in Hunan was Pao-ching hsien in the northwest near Szechwan and Kweichow. In 1871, the hsien contained fourteen 2/10 markets for a population rising from 97,000 in 1816 to 159,000 in 1914. The hsien city consisted of 30 streets, in-cluding twelve chieh.

Along the Yangtze and other rivers in southeast Hupei were many large chen. Seventeen miles from Huang-chou fu city along the Yangtze river was Tuan-feng chen in which there were more than 30 streets. Wu-ch'ang hsien held approximately twenty-three mar-keting settlements, including one with more than 400 households in marketing pursuits and two others with more than 200 households so engaged. Chien-li hsien was also a fertile area for chen since it was located by the Yangtze river in an area crossed by numerous rivers and contained a population of 883,000. One chen in this hsien served villages in four administrative units and was a center of merchants represented by hui-kuan from Fukien, Kiangsi, and Hui-chou fu in Anhwei.

Shu-p'u hsien, also in west Hunan, held only twelve marketing settlements for a population rising from 248,000 in 1816 to 397,000 in 1914. All were 2/10, but they varied in the number of people going to market as discussed in an article by Morita Akira.[6] The smallest were frequented by fewer than 100 people, three others had at most a few hundred visitors, two had nearly 1,000 visitors, at two markets the number reached a few thousand, and at the largest market there were 10,000 or more people on marketing days. Although the fre-quency of all of these markets was the same, their scale differed greatly.

The provinces of the Central region of China ranged from 39 percent to 58 percent in what has previously been identified as the critical figure of the percentage of the urban population in cities with 30,000 or more residents. At one extreme was Hupei sheng with 58 percent of its urban inhabitants in large cities. This province was a crossroads. A map of Hupei is dominated by two rivers flowing from west to east, the Yangtze river from Szechwan and the Han river from Shensi. Gradually descending, the rivers finally inter-sect at Wuhan. Wuhan was also the center of north-south traffic through Central China. By water and land this urban area had rela-tively good connections with every region in China and was the closest thing that existed to a central market for all of China.

At the other extreme was Hunan sheng with 39 percent of its

urban population in cities at levels 2-3. The urban network in Hunan was exceptionally interdependent with that of Hupei. Cities in Hunan emerged as centers for the collection of grain bound for Wuhan. A comparison of ratios of urban population to central places also reveals a sharp discrepancy between Hunan and Hupei. While Hupei's ratio of 840 (1.8 million people in 2,140 central places) ranked near the top in China, Hunan's ratio of 610 ranked much lower. Clearly the explanation is that smaller central places in Hunan supported Wuhan's enormous population.

Kiangsi was intermediate between Hupei and Hunan in total urban population and in the percent of the urban total in cities at levels 2-3. Kiangsi resembled Hunan in many respects, but an important difference was the fact that Kiangsi was less dependent on large cities outside its sheng. Whereas Hunan's surplus flowed primarily to the large Yangtze port of Wuhan, Kiangsi's surplus joined the Yangtze at a port within its own boundaries—at Chiu-chiang. Furthermore, in addition to the rice which both of these provinces shipped to cities in East-central China via Yangtze ports, each province contributed to the support of one of China's three great chen. In the case of Hunan this support moved out of the province to Hankow chen, part of Wuhan, but in Kiangsi consumption took place within the province at Ching-te-chen.

Two facts stand out concerning cities in Central China. First the three largest cities in the region were all sheng cities. Indeed, more than 25 percent of the urban residents in the region were found in the urban areas of the three sheng cities. As in Northwest and East-central China where the proportion of urban residents living in sheng cities was similar, sheng cities were located on major water routes. Second, unlike many provinces, these three sheng were each natural units formed by one or two river systems. The sheng city could effectively serve as the single provincial center.

Southeast China

The region consisting of the two provinces along the southeastern coast and of inland Kwangsi was probably the most urbanized part of China with more than 7 percent of the population in cities as shown in Table 34. Most of the largest cities were seaports. Canton

TABLE 34

Southeast China

Level	Fukien				Kwangtung				Kwangsi			
	Mid-19th		1953		Mid-19th		1953		Mid-19th		1953	
	No.	Pop.	No.	Pop.	No.	Pop.	No.	Pop.	No.	Pop.	No.	Pop.
1	0		0		0		1	1.6	0		0	
2	1	} .6	1	.55	1	.8	0		0		0	
3a	2		3	.4	2	.3	8	1.0	2	} .2	4	.6
3b	3	.1	6	.2	6	.2	15	.6	2		1	
4	14	.2			12	.2			10	.1		
5	65	.3			65	.3			30	.15		
6	350	.35			350	.35			200	.2		
7	1,200				1,300				1,300			
Total Pop.	17		13		30		37		9		18	
Urban Pop.	1.4		1.6		2.0		4.5		.55		.85	
Urban %	8%		12.0%		7%		12.2%		6%		4.8%	
Urban % in levels 1–3	51%		72%		66%		77%		36%		71%	

served as both the center of sea transportation along a huge coastal area and as the outlet for a vast network of inland waterways. As the sheng city of Kwangtung and as the recipient of practically all of China's foreign maritime trade during the middle part of the Ch'ing period, Canton flourished along with Soochow, Wuhan, and Nanking as a city that could have surpassed 800,000 in population. Foochow, the sheng city of Fukien, was well established as the second city of the region. The two hsien within the city contained at least 250 streets, and an estimate of 400,000 to 500,000 for the city population is unlikely to be too high. Carrying goods to these and other seaports were numerous rivers within this region. Ch'uan-chou and Chang-chou fu cities in Fukien and Ch'ao-chou fu city (modern Swatow) in northeast Kwangtung were all situated near the mouths of rivers which connected to hinterlands of several million people.

All six of the coastal cities with more than 70,000 inhabitants from Wen-chou fu in Chekiang to Canton should be viewed as having had a stake in a small wedge into inland China. Resources moved outward primarily by water to these six cities by the sea. The most extensive hinterlands supported Canton and Foochow. The great river systems that flowed by these two cities brought products from most of Kwangtung and Fukien as well as from much of Kwangsi and from a small part of Kiangsi. Chang-chou fu city in southeast Fukien declined somewhat during the nineteenth century, in response to the rise of Amoy (Hsia-men t'ing) as a seaport, but Chang-chou continued to hold roughly 100,000 people. Ch'uan-chou fu city, which was located between Foochow and Chang-chou, was crossed by more than 100 streets as well as an unspecified number of lesser roads which were not tallied. The only other comparable strings of cities at levels 2 and 3a were along the Yangtze river and the Grand Canal.

Fukien is a small and mountainous sheng cut by rivers which flow to the sea. Approximately twenty cities in this province contained more than 10,000 people. These cities can be visualized in terms of three semicircles. The innermost arc followed the coast between Foochow and Chang-chou, joining the most populous cities in Fukien. A second arc midway through the province connected the level 3b cities of Yen-p'ing fu and Chien-ning fu as well as other smaller cities. The longest semicircle followed the borders of the province, linking mainly cities of 10,000 to 30,000 people. One large level 4 city near the Kiangsi border was Shao-wu fu, which before the destruction of the T'ai-p'ing rebellion contained nearly 100 streets.

Kwangtung sheng is exceptional in its water resources. Not only did its mainland area have the longest coastline in China, but the nearby island of Hainan, which together with Taiwan (Fukien) is one of the two largest Chinese islands, formed an entire fu. G. William Skinner has divided Kwangtung province into nine regions according to the density of rural population.[7] Using data on the number of markets and villages in every hsien, he determined the average village-to-market ratios for each region. Except in the central region around Canton, there is a direct correlation between the number of persons per square kilometer and the average village-to-market ratios. Skinner explains the data in terms of an intensification cycle: village-to-market ratios begin low, increase steadily until a certain point and then new markets begin to form. The various regions of Kwangtung were arrayed along the intensification cycle with the most highly developed central region at the point where new markets had already begun to form.

Another way of using the plentiful data for Kwangtung is by comparing the levels of administrative cities according to the number of markets and people in the hsien or chou. Although I have designated only the estimated levels of the largest cities in the province, it can be assumed that most of the cities in Table 35 that are not identified with any level were, in fact, at level 5.

Next to Yunnan and Kweichow, Kwangsi was the least populated province. Among its 9 million people were a large number who belonged to ethnic minorities. Few of the non-Chinese in the province lived in cities. They mostly lived in mountainous areas away from the main rivers on which were located the four level 3 cities.

In 1932 Kwangsi consisted of ninety-eight hsien and their corresponding hsien cities: (1) twelve hsien cities held more than 10,000 residents; (2) thirteen hsien cities held 5,000 to 10,000 residents; (3) thirteen hsien cities held 3,000 to 5,000 residents; (4) fourteen hsien cities held 2,000 to 3,000 residents; (5) twenty-five hsien cities held 1,000 to 2,000 residents; and (5) twenty-one hsien cities held

TABLE 35

Markets, Populations, and Urban Levels for Some Hsien and Chou of Kwangtung

| City | Level | Administrative Unit | |
		Population (millions)	Number of Markets
Canton	2	2.1 (2 hsien)	209 (2 hsien)
Ch'ao-chou fu	3a	.9	10
Ch'iung-chou fu	3b	.4	36
Hsiang-shan hsien	3b	1.2	—
Hsin-hui hsien	3b	.8	—
Chao-ch'ing fu	3b	.5	—
Mei hsien	3b	.5	—
Lien-chou fu	3b	.3	—
Shun-te hsien	4	.8	73
Tung-kuan hsien	4	1.3	79
Lei-chou fu	4	.3	35
Chin-ning hsien	4	.5	13
Kao-chou fu	4	.6	—
Te-ch'ing fu	4	.2	—
Nan-shing chou	4	.3	23
Ch'ing-yuan hsien	4	.7	—
Hui-lai hsien	4	.4	99
Hui-chou fu	4	—	—
Chao-chou fu	4	.2	25
Hsing-ning hsien	4	.5	—
Lo-ch'ang hsien	—	.1	8
Jen-hua hsien	—	.1	9
Ju-yuan hsien	—	.1	18
Ying-te hsien	—	.3	47
Lin-kao hsien	—	.2	15
Ch'ao-yang hsien	—	.9	18
Sui-ch'i hsien	—	.2	25
Feng-shun hsien	—	.2	7
Ling-shui hsien	—	.1	2
Wen-ch'ang hsien	—	.4	42
Chieh-yang hsien	—	.7	15
Jao-p'ing hsien	—	.5	15
Teng-hai hsien	—	.5	9
Totals: 33 cities	—	17 million	—

Level	Ave. Pop. of Admin. Unit	Ave. No. of Markets[a]
2	1.1	105
3a	.9	—
3b	.6	—
4	.5	37
5	.3	18

[a]Figures for the number of markets associated with cities at levels 3a and 3b are omitted because I obtained data for only a single hsien in each case.

fewer than 1,000 residents.[8] By this date fu and chou cities had been eliminated; so all administrative cities are listed as hsien cities. In terms of population, the twelve largest cities contained 260,000 and the twenty-six cities at level 5 contained 130,000. The remaining sixty administrative centers ranked at level 6, but were generally larger than other level 6 cities. While I have estimated that the average level 6 city had a population of 1,000, these sixty cities totaled 80,000 to 90,000 in population. Although minor redistribution of urban residents had occurred during the preceding decades with the rapid growth of population in Kwangsi, the number of cities and of people at these various levels may not have changed substantially after the mid-nineteenth century. In this remote sheng the effects of growing foreign trade and treaty ports must have been slight.

Since most of the cities at levels 3 to 5 were located on a small number of rivers, it is possible to describe the city system of Kwangsi just by following these rivers through the province. In the northeast of Kwangsi flowed a short stretch of the Hsiang river—the major river of Hunan. Along this river was Ch'üan-chou, a commercial center with more than 10,000 residents near the Hunan border. Hui-kuan from several provinces of East-central, Central, and Southeast China were located in Ch'üan-chou. The only level 5 city between Ch'üan-chou and Kuei-lin, the sheng city, was Hsing-an hsien, at a point where the trading spheres of Hankow and Canton met. All of Hunan and a small corner of Kwangsi belonged to the Hankow level 2 hinterland and all of Kwangtung and most of Kwangsi belonged to the Canton level 2 hinterland. Kuei-lin to the southwest of the dividing line was part of Canton's sphere of dominance.

Kuei-lin is located near the source of the Kuei river, which flows to what was the second city of Kwangsi, Wu-chou fu. The contrast between Kuei-lin, a city of 70,000 to 100,000 population with the diverse administrative functions of a sheng center, and Wu-chou, having a similar population but different principal functions, can be seen in their built-up areas. Kuei-lin's population was almost entirely concentrated within its city wall, while Wu-chou's development centered along rivers in the south and west kuan. In other provinces a contrast also could be drawn between the two largest cities, one a sheng administrative center and the other a fu commercial center. Typically the fu city was most built-up in its kuan and the sheng city filled a large walled area.

Between the two 3a cities on the Kuei river was the level 4 fu city of P'ing-lo. Merchants in P'ing-lo were most often from Kwangtung, second from Hunan, and third from Kiangsi. Sharing the position of an intermediate stop on this river with P'ing-lo was Chao-p'ing hsien, a level 5 city.

An even longer river which flowed through Wu-chou to Canton was the Pearl. One level 3b city, Nan-ning fu, and two level 4 cities, Hsün-chou fu and Kuei hsien, served as ports en route to Wu-chou. The other level 3b city, Liu-chou fu, was located on a tributary of the Pearl river in an area from which lumber was sent to Kwangtung. Together with rice from Hsün-chou fu and Nan-ning fu, lumber and other products from the mountains sailed downriver to Wu-chou.

Kwangsi sheng resembled Hunan as an area which contributed heavily to the support of a level 2 city in another province. Having a population far smaller than that of Hunan, Kwangsi could be more affected by the tremendous demand generated in Canton. One could argue that this explains why a slightly larger proportion of the total population in Kwangsi was urban. But in both cases the percent of urban residents who lived in level 3 cities and above was low because some of the surplus was shipped to outside consumers and because products from Canton and Wuhan competed favorably with local items which were typically produced in high-level cities.

An interesting parallel can be shown between Southeast China and East-central China. The proportion of the urban population in level 3 cities and above in Kwangtung resembled that in Kiangsu, in Fukien resembled that in Chekiang and in Kwangsi resembled that in Anhwei. These were the two regions most advantageously located for sea transport. Almost all principal cities in both regions bordered rivers. And the ratio of urban population to central places was highest in these two regions. Five of China's ten cities in which more than 300,000 people lived flourished in Southeast and East-central China.

High agricultural productivity also contributed to the 7 percent who lived in cities in Southeast China. Double-cropping of rice was possible in many parts of this fertile, warm region; therefore, higher yields could be obtained than elsewhere in China. Although population densities were great in rural areas, urban consumers did compete successfully for an increasing share of this vast grain crop.

Southeast China was roughly 7 percent urban, higher than any other region in the country. The explanation probably lies in better river and sea transportation. Since Hangchow port could be used only with difficulty, the only level 2 seaports in China were located in this region. Probably more of the people of Fukien and Kwangtung lived within a short river journey of the sea than the people of any other province. The fact that 55 percent of all urban residents in this region lived in cities with more than 30,000 people, a figure that was not matched in any other region of China, also indicates the relative ease of concentrating resources.

Southwest China

The three provinces of Southwest China shown in Table 36 together contained about the same number of rural inhabitants as the provinces in the Southeast, but they trailed by nearly 1 million in urban population. These inland areas did not achieve the concentration of resources that was possible along the waterways of the Southeast. Nonetheless, Szechwan sheng, which contained more than three of every four city dwellers in the Southwest region, was second only to Kiangsu in total urban population. While Kweichow sheng and Yunnan sheng produced just one city each of more than 70,000

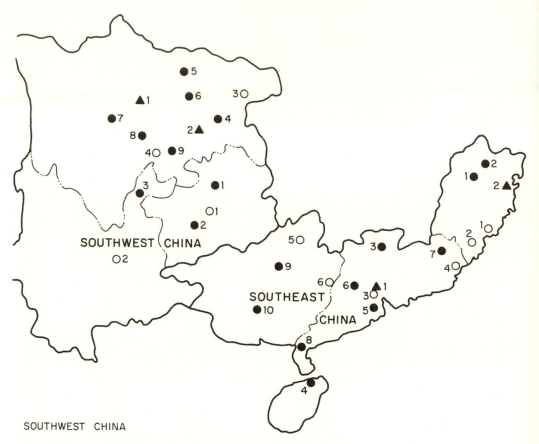

SOUTHWEST CHINA

▲   LEVEL 2   1, Chengtu;   2, Chungking

○   3a   1, Kuei-yang;   2, K'un-ming; 3, Wan hsien; 4, Chia-ting fu

●   3b   1, Tsun-i fu; 2, An-shun fu; 3, Chao-t'ung fu; 4, Fu chou; 5, Pao-ning fu; 6, Shun-ch'ing fu; 7, Ya-an fu; 8, Lo chou; 9, Lu-chou fu

SOUTHEAST CHINA

▲   LEVEL 2   1, Canton;   2, Foochow

○   3a   1, Ch'üan-chou; 2, Chang-chou; 3, Fo-shan chen; 4, Ch'ao-chou; 5, Kuei-lin; 6, Wu-chou fu;

●   3b   1, Yen-p'ing fu; 2, Chien-ning fu; 3, Ch'iung-chou fu; 4, Hsiang-shan hsien; 5, Hsin-hui hsien; 6, Chao-ch'ing fu; 7, Mei hsien; 8, Lien-chou fu; 9, Liu-chou fu; 10, Nan-ning fu

TABLE 36

Southwest China

Level	Kweichow Mid-19th No.	Pop.	1953 No.	Pop.	Yunnan Mid-19th No.	Pop.	1953 No.	Pop.	Szechwan Mid-19th No.	Pop.	1953 No.	Pop.
1	0		0		0		0		0		1	1.8
2	0		0		0		1	.7	2	.8	1	.9
3a	1	.1	2	.3	1	.1	1	.15	2	.15	8	1.4
3b	2	{.1	2	.1	1	{.1	3	.1	8	.3	16	.7
4	4				5				14	.2		
5	20	.1			20	.1			120	.6		
6	100	.1			100	.1			700	.7		
7	500				400				2,800			
Total Pop.	6		15		8		17		40		66	
Urban Pop.		.35		.6		.35		1.3		2.4		6.4
Urban %	6%		4%		4%		7.4%		6%		9.7%	
Urban % in levels 1–3	43%		67%		38%		73%		52%		75%	

people, Szechwan supported two level 3a cities and two level 2 cities. Chengtu, the sheng city of Szechwan, and Chungking, a fu city on the Yangtze river, were not as populous as Nanking and Soochow and lacked the considerable interprovincial trade of the Kiangsu cities, but together they consisted of nearly 2 percent of the residents of their region, a higher proportion than in the first two cities of any other region except the Southeast.

Chengtu is usually regarded as primarily an administrative city and Chungking as primarily a commercial city. In fact, each city was the administrative center for a large fu. There were sixteen chou and hsien in Chengtu fu and thirteen in Chungking fu, more administrative units than were served by any other fu city in Szechwan. Chengtu protruded from the fertile central part of the province, an extensively irrigated large plain in which cities at levels 4 to 6 were nearly as dense as in the Yangtze delta. Numerous rivers joined areas in all directions. One of the two hsien sharing the sheng city contained 115 streets plus 41 additional streets in the Manchu city with its 14,000 privileged residents. Chungking city was located farther east at a point where traffic along the Yangtze river was heavy. Long-distance transport moved between here and Wuhan. Moreover, this fu city was situated just north of Kweichow and Yunnan, making it the terminus of the routes from Kuei-yang to Tsun-i and from K'un-ming to Chao-t'ung. While Chengtu dominated the central and northern areas of Szechwan, Chungking dominated the southeast of the province and the two neighboring provinces in Southwest China. Chungking city held a total of approximately 250 streets inside and outside its wall.

The level 3a and 3b cities of Szechwan were located on the Yangtze river and its main tributaries through eastern and central areas of the province. Wan hsien, the first port west of Hupei at a point where the Yangtze river turns south, was a city of approximately 70,000 people, most of whom lived outside the five city gates near the river. Further upriver was Fu chou, the second city of eastern Szechwan. Of its 42 streets, 33 were located in the kuan. Urban development in these cities was concentrated along the river.

Kuramochi Tokuichirō has accumulated data on the number of markets per administrative unit in Szechwan.[9] For all periods during the Ch'ing dynasty he found an average of thirty markets per hsien or chou. During the late nineteenth century the average was even higher reaching thirty-nine per unit. Kuramochi notes that Katō Shigeshi had found smaller averages in other provinces, reaching as low as nine markets per unit in Shansi. Of course, the average hsien in Shansi held only a third of the population in its Szechwan counterpart.

The mountainous inland province of Kweichow was the least populated area of the eighteen inner provinces of China. The thirteen fu cities provided administrative services for populations smaller than those in the average hsien of some provinces. Indeed, in one fu gazetteer it was asserted that the whole province of Kweichow did not compare with one large chou or hsien of the lower Yangtze. Of course, this was an exaggeration, but it may have referred to the difficulty of raising tax revenues in this poor province. Indeed, Kweichow was subsidized from other provinces to supply the troops stationed there especially to quell uprisings of ethnic minorities.

Kweichow sheng consisted of approximately 10,000 villages and 600 central places. More than 1 of every 50 central places—a ratio far higher than in other sheng—was a fu city. Consequently fu cities were smaller than elsewhere; most were level 5 central places. As in Kwangsi, hsien cities ranked primarily at level 6. The only level 3a city was Kuei-yang, the sheng capital. Located in the center of the province, this sheng city reflected the inward-looking character of Kweichow. The two level 3b cities were Tsun-i fu and An-shun fu. The former benefited both from a location in the most fertile area of Kweichow and from traffic passing through on the main route between Kweichow and the Yangtze river in Szechwan. At least two of the level 4 cities did not have fu administrative activities, but prospered as centers of border exchange near Yunnan. Tung-jen fu city in the northeast near Hunan ranked at level 5, not having a single hsien city in the fu and containing only sixteen streets—all within the city wall. Similarly Li-p'ing fu city in the southeast held only about fifteen streets.

A common pattern in Kweichow was for Chinese to live in cities and in nearby lowlands, which they farmed, and for minority peoples to live in more mountainous areas. The Chinese were depicted as officials, soldiers, farmers, and students, while the others were portrayed as weavers and simple mountain folk. More than in other areas of the empire, cities loomed as garrisoned enclaves.

Yunnan was the most distant sheng from Peking. Its capital city K'un-ming was erected almost 2,000 miles from the imperial center. Together with Kweichow, Yunnan remained the least developed area of the inner provinces. Yet, during the nineteenth century both Kweichow and Yunnan increased substantially in population. The total in Yunnan may have risen from about 4 million to near 10 million. It is likely that the number of central places was increasing rapidly during the same time span. Suddenly the southwestern wilderness was being conquered by migrants from other areas of China.

Although the population of Yunnan was sparse, its area was exceptionally large. The fourteen fu cities were separated by great distances. Half of these cities merited only a "Y" or a "J" on the CFPN system discussed in Chapter Four. Such a low rating put them in the class of mountainous level 6 administrative cities of other provinces. Furthermore, fu city walls tended to measure just four to seven li in circumference, the size of hsien city walls in some sheng. And hsien city walls in Yunnan often failed to reach three li or one mile in circumference.

Only a single city in Yunnan ranked as high as level 3a. Moreover, Yunnan may have been the only province apart from Shansi in which just two cities contained a minimum of 30,000 residents. The larger of these cities was K'un-ming, the sheng capital. Located on trade routes to Kweichow and Szechwan, K'un-ming served as both the commercial center and the administrative center of Yunnan. Hui-kuan from Southwest, Southeast, and Central China were all present in the sheng city. An enumeration of the population of K'un-ming during the last years of the Ch'ing dynasty reveals that the city contained some 95,000 people. The second city of Yunnan, Chao-t'ung fu, commanded the northeastern trade route between K'un-ming and the large cities along the Yangtze river in southern Szechwan.

Population growth in the Southwest region was more rapid than in most other regions of China. Not only were Kweichow and

Yunnan becoming quickly settled during the nineteenth century, but Szechwan was also gaining substantially. After being ravaged in the fighting at the end of the Ming dynasty, Szechwan did not completely recover until the eighteenth century. Afterwards the province kept growing in population and in the number of central places, more than doubling by the end of the Ch'ing dynasty to totals of 50 million and 4,000 to 5,000 respectively. The figures given in this section are estimates for the final decades of the first half of the nineteenth century. They are undoubtedly too high to apply to most of the eighteenth century and too low for the turn of the twentieth century.

Although Szechwan sheng contained many more central places than Kiangsu sheng, it was less urbanized. The difference was particularly apparent in cities at levels 3a and 2. Nearly twice as many Kiangsu residents lived in such large cities. Long-distance trade arrived in Kiangsu cities from a much more densely populated region and from nearby regions which relied on level 2 cities in East-central China. Approximately 150 million people lived in areas dependent on level 2 cities in East-central China, but less than 40 percent of that figure could conceivably have relied on the two great cities of Szechwan.

Why was the population of Kweichow as urban as or even more urban than the population in other provinces which are widely recognized as more developed? A possible explanation is that this province was favored by grain imports and military garrisons for purposes of maintaining order. Having such a small population, Kweichow required little to raise its proportion of urban dwellers.

Why was Yunnan one of the least urbanized provinces in China? First, its location at the far corner of China eliminated commerce in transit except for some luxury items transported from foreign countries in Southeast Asia. Second, intraprovincial trade was difficult in such a vast area. Finally, part of the surplus gravitated toward Szechwan.

The contrast between Southwest and Southeast China is revealing since the two regions were similar in population. Southwest China was much greater in area, but had only three-quarters the number of city dwellers as in the region to the east. Longer distances between cities and less accessible transportation routes hindered the development of cities in the Southwest region. The six largest cities were either on the Yangtze river or were sheng centers, but the Yangtze intraregional and interregional link could not match the long seacoast of the Southeast region along which most of its cities stretched. Another contrast is between the effects of population growth in the two regions. The Southeast was one of the most densely populated areas and the Southwest one of the least. Especially during the nineteenth century the three sheng in the Southwest absorbed a rapidly expanding population without the pressure on resources that fostered considerable emigration from the Southeast.

TABLE 37

East Japan

Level	Tōhoku		Chūbu	
	No.	Pop.	No.	Pop.
1	0		0	
2	0		0	
3a	1	.07	2	.24
3b	3	.12	1	.04
4	6	.08	19	.28
5	30	.15	60	.30
6	40	.04	120	.12
7	120		300	
Total Pop.	3.5		7	
Urban Pop.	.44		.92	
Urban %	12–13%		13%	
Urban % in levels 1–3	43%		30%	

East Japan

The Tōhoku, Chūbu, and Kantō areas formed the three regions of East Japan shown in Table 37. Together they were slightly more than 16 percent urban. Edo was easily the largest city in East Japan, containing 35-40 percent of all urban inhabitants. The three level 3a cities, Kanazawa, Nagoya, and Sendai each held only one-eighth to one-fifteenth the population of Edo. Other jōkamachi of large han and seaports ranked at levels 3b and 4.

Tōhoku

The Tōhoku region, located on the northeast of Honshū island was surrounded on three sides by water. Although much of the region was far from the commercial centers of Tokugawa Japan, by the eighteenth century the development of sea transportation was bringing this region increasingly into contact with the advanced commercial economy of Osaka and Edo. With a population equal to that of a large fu in China, the Tōhoku region achieved exceptional urban growth by Chinese standards.

Four cities in the Tōhoku region had populations in excess of 30,000. The largest city was Sendai, the jōkamachi for a han of approximately 1 million actual koku. An unusually high proportion of the more than 500,000 inhabitants of Sendai han were buke; therefore, the fact that only half of the buke lived in the castle city did not result in a small han center. On the contrary, almost 50,000 of the 70,000 city dwellers were buke. The second city in the region was Aizu-Wakamatsu, an inland jōkamachi for the second largest han in the region. Third was Akita, a jōkamachi located on the Japan Sea. At the end of the Tokugawa period Akita han's population of 335,000 included approximately 30,000 buke and 28,000 chōnin.[10] Half of the buke lived in the jōkamachi and nearly 20,000 of the chōnin resided there, a figure much larger than the city's chōnin population of only 8,000 in 1663. Hirosaki, near the northern tip of Honshū island, was probably the fourth city of the region. The han population of 225,000 included 9 percent who were considered buke, most of whom lived in the jōkamachi. These first four cities of the Tōhoku region were all jōkamachi of large han. Together their han contained more than 60 percent of the koku in the region. An unusually large number of bushi and their families absorbed much of the surplus produced in these han. Almost 3 percent of all Tōhoku inhabitants were buke living in these four level 3 jōkamachi.

Sakata, the only level 4 city that was not a jōkamachi, served as a prosperous port south of Akita. The city received rice from many inland han and from tenryō areas (under the Bakufu) for reshipment to Hokuriku ports and to Osaka. The only city with 20,000 to 30,000 residents was Morioka. Its han resembled Hirosaki in actual koku total, and the jōkamachi was only slightly smaller in nineteenth century population. An example of a smaller level 4 jōkamachi was Nakamura, located in a han consisting of 225 villages. Although in 1681 the jōkamachi had contained approximately 11,000 bushi and 991 households of chōnin and temple area residents, the population fell in the eighteenth century until less than half the earlier total of bushi remained.[11]

Data on smaller central places exists for Morioka han. The number of periodic markets was first fourteen and later rose to seventeen. Markets differed in frequency—some met 2/10, others 1/10, and a few even 1/30. They differed also in the variety of goods traded—one market serving fifteen villages had tens of kinds of goods and another serving only two villages had just two kinds. Most settlements with periodic markets remained below 3,000 in population.

Central places in the Tōhoku region can be divided into twenty-three jōkamachi, ten settlements in which tenryō rice was collected and in which a periodic market presumably met, about twenty seaports which were not jōkamachi, many inland zaikatachō and numerous small periodic markets. All six han in which more than 100,000 koku were officially registered held jōkamachi with at least 10,000 residents. In addition, more than half of those in cities with more than 3,000 residents who did not live in these six administrative centers of large han lived in other castle cities. This region was exceptional in the great proportion of urban dwellers who lived in jōkamachi. Approximately 75 percent of those in all cities and 90 percent of those in cities at level 4 and above resided in castle cities. Within these administrative centers the many buke claimants to the local surplus were vulnerable to the sharp fluctuations in harvests identified with this relatively poor region.

Chūbu

Second in number to the Kinki region with sixteen kuni was the Chūbu region with fourteen, as shown in Table 38. These fourteen kuni were divided into 108 gun, averaging 60,000-70,000 people. Most kuni were located along the Japan Sea or the Pacific Ocean, but kuni

TABLE 38

Kuni and Cities in the Chūbu Region

Kuni	Population[a] (thousands)	Koku (thousands)	Area[b]	Gun	Han[c]	Cities at levels 3 & 4
Echigo	932	816	L	7	10	Niigata, Takada, Nagaoka
Shinano	694	615	L	10	8	Matsumoto, Matsushiro
Owari	555	521	S	7	1	Nagoya, Atsuta
Mino	546	645	A	16	6	Ogaki, Gifu
Echizen	368	634	A	10	6	Fukui, Tsuruga
Etchu	314	611	A	4	1	Toyama
Mikawa	416	383	A	8	7	Okazaki, Yoshida
Mie	343	328	S	13	4	Hamamatsu
Kaga	207	438	S	4	2	Kanazawa
Kai	291	253	A	4	0	Kofu
Suruga	246	237	A	7	2	Sumpu, Numatsu
Noto	152	239	S	4	0	—
Sado	96	130	VS	3	0	—
Izu	97	83	S	4	0	—
Wakasa	87	88	VS	3	1	Obama
Hida	67	44	A	4	1	Takayama

[a]Population and koku figures are official values for 1721.

[b]Area is classified as follows: L = large = more than 750 square *ri* (1 ri = 2.44 miles); A = average = 200–405 square ri; S = small = 100–199 square ri; VS = very small = fewer than 100 square ri.

[c]The number of han refers to the number of castle cities located in the kuni.

with average or large areas tended to be landlocked and tiny Sado kuni resembled small kuni elsewhere in Japan in occupying an island. Han were dispersed through all kuni except Sado and Izu, which was located on a strategic peninsula.

Two level 3a cities, Kanazawa and Nagoya, were located in this region. The former served as the jōkamachi of the largest han in Japan, a unit which sprawled into Noto and Etchu kuni as well as Kaga kuni. The latter was the jōkamachi of another of Japan's largest han, but one primarily confined to one kuni Owari. Together Kanazawa and Nagoya han contained over 2 million actual koku and about 6 percent of the villages in Japan. Approximately 15 percent of the population in these two han lived in the castle cities. Of the more than 100,000 residents in each city 60 to 70 percent were chōnin.

During the seventeenth century both Kanazawa and Nagoya grew rapidly. By the 1660s the daimyo of Kanazawa sought to slow rampant city growth, fearing a fall in the farming force which remained in the villages. One effort was directed against the widespread practice of farmers on the outskirts of the jōkamachi renting land or lodgings to recent migrants such as buke servants, peddlers, and hired laborers who were eager to find cheap housing. Laws promulgated to prevent such encroachment on valued farm lands were unsuccessful since at intervals new areas were incorporated as chō under the city administration. For instance in 1665, 995 houses were brought into Kanazawa city; in 1687, 191 houses were switched to chō status; and as late as 1821 the final major reorganization occurred which brought former farmland into the city. While at the beginning of the Tokugawa period Kanazawa consisted of 27 *honmachi* (original chō) and 7 additional chō, by the nineteenth century there were 40 honmachi and 129 outside chō.[12]

Differences between urban areas within Kanazawa city can be seen by comparing honmachi, outside chō, and the non-chō vicinity which had already become partially built-up but had not yet been incorporated into the city. Omitted is the majority of the city which was set aside for bushi residences. In 1811 honmachi areas were populated as follows: (1) merchants—55 percent, (2) artisans—24 percent, (3) bushi—7 percent, and (4) miscellaneous—14 percent.

Outside chō had the following composition: (1) merchants—24 percent, (2) artisans—12 percent, (3) bushi—33 percent, and (4) miscellaneous—31 percent. The non-chō areas contained: (1) merchants—20 percent, (2) artisans—9 percent, (3) bushi—37 percent and (4) miscellaneous—34 percent.[13] The miscellaneous category includes farmers, servants, hired laborers, unemployed, and others. These figures indicate that merchants and artisans were most concentrated in the honmachi and least in evidence at the urban fringe. By the nineteenth century lower bushi had dispersed considerably from the main bushi areas to the outer chō and the city perimeter. Other large cities also could be divided into three similar zones.

The data for Kanazawa may be compared to data for the level 4 city of Okazaki. In that Chūbu city the population of chō areas was divided as follows: (1) merchants—39 percent, (2) artisans—18 percent, (3) farmers—21 percent, (4) hired laborers—17 percent, and (5) servants—4 percent.[14] It should be remembered that those classified as farmers were not necessarily engaged in agricultural occupations.

The Chūbu region contained at least 20 percent of the Japanese cities at levels 5 and above. The single level 3b city was Fukui jōkamachi. Level 4 cities were mostly jōkamachi, but the four seaports of Niigata, Tsuruga, and Obama on the Japan Sea and Atsuta on the Pacific Ocean did not have han administrative functions. Moreover, some jōkamachi which doubled as ports active in long-distance commerce or as posts on the busy Tōkaidō road held populations considerably larger than one-tenth of their han koku figures, indicative of the significance of nonadministrative activities. At level 5 approximately one-third of the cities were jōkamachi. Most nonadministrative cities served as ports and as posts on the Tōkaidō and Nakasendō roads, the two main roads of Japan, which followed the length of the Chūbu region from the Kantō area to the Kinki area.

Most central places ranked at levels 6 and 7. For instance, in one gun of Etchu kuni (part of Kanazawa han) there were eight central places. The four smallest each held about 100 households, two others probably ranked at level 6, and Jōhana with 726 households and Oyabe with 1,162 households were level 5 cities.[15] In Owari kuni there had apparently been about 108 markets in existence during the centuries before the late Tokugawa period.[16] Many were short-lived, especially in the turbulent decades of the Sengoku period, but others remained as small periodic markets. In one area of Owari approximately ten central places three to five miles apart formed an unusually dense pattern of marketing.

The proportion of Chūbu area residents who lived in cities was 13 percent, not much higher than in the Tōhoku region; yet, there were two major differences. First, Chūbu jōkamachi had more thriving commerce, reflected in the smaller proportion of buke residents. Second, the percent of the urban total in cities at levels 3 and above was considerably lower in the Chūbu regions. Large quantities of goods flowed out of the region to support consumers in Edo, Osaka, and Kyoto. Areas along the Pacific coast (the Tōkai) were divided between three spheres of influence emanating from Edo in the east, Osaka in the west, and Nagoya in between. Along the Japan Sea (the Hokuriku area) goods were shipped by sea to Osaka, by land to Kyoto, or were consumed in Kanazawa jōkamachi, a city which was the equal of Nagoya. Moreover, some transport from Echigo and nearby kuni moved through mountainous trails to Edo. Thus the Chūbu region contributed substantially to urban consumption in outside areas.

The three regions of East Japan differed greatly in the proportion of their urban residents in cities with 30,000 or more people. While 77 percent of the city dwellers in the Kantō area lived in large cities, only 43 percent of those in the Tōhoku area and 30 percent of those in the Chūbu area lived in such cities. The figure for the Tōhoku area corresponds to our knowledge that this area was relatively inaccessible and that the high proportion of bushi in the area consumed most of the local surplus. More than any other area of Japan, the Tōhoku region was self-contained, neither exporting nor importing large quantities of goods. The low figure of 30 percent in the Chūbu area should be considered as a mark of the great significance of this area in supplying the highly urbanized areas on both sides of it. In East Japan as a whole 48 percent of the urban population lived in cities at levels 1-3. Presumably this figure would have been larger if none of the Chūbu surplus had flowed into Kinki area cities, but we should not overlook that at least as much of the surplus of West Japan was flowing in the reverse direction from Osaka to Edo.

West Japan

The four regions of West Japan shown in Table 39 varied markedly in number of kuni as in number of people. At one extreme was the highly urbanized Kinki region with sixteen kuni and 5½ million inhabitants. At the other extreme was Shikoku island with four kuni and 2 million inhabitants. Intermediate in these figures were Kyūshū island with nine kuni and 4 million people and the Chūgoku region, at the southeast tip of Honshū island, with twelve kuni and 3½ million people. Approximately 30 percent of West Japan's urban population were found in the two cities of Osaka and Kyoto. Next most populous were Hiroshima in the Chūgoku region and Kagoshima in the Kyūshū area. Another ten cities ranged from 30,000 to 70,000 in population.

The *Kinki* region stood out as the most urbanized area in Japan except for the Kantō region. Moreover, it ranked second only to the

TABLE 39

West Japan

Level	Kinki		Chūgoku		Shikoku		Kyūshū	
	No.	Pop.	No.	Pop.	No.	Pop.	No.	Pop.
1	0		0		0		0	
2	2	.75	0		0		0	
3a	0		1	.07	0		1	.07
3b	3	.13	3	.11	2	.07	3	.15
4	12	.17	7	.09	5	.07	4	.06
5	40	.20	30	.15	20	.10	40	.20
6	80	.08	60	.06	40	.04	80	.08
7	150		140		100		200	
Total Pop.	5.5		3.5		2.0		4.0	
Urban Pop.	1.3		.45		.26		.52	
Urban %	24%		13%		13%		13%	
Urban % in levels 1–3	68%		40%		27%		42%	

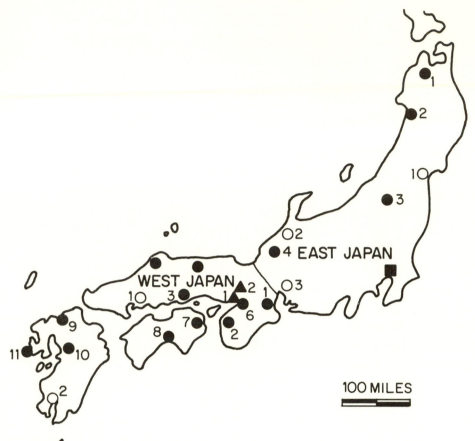

WEST JAPAN

▲ LEVEL 2   1, Osaka; 2, Kyoto

○   3a 1, Hiroshima; 2, Kagoshima

●   3b 1, Tsu; 2, Wakayama; 3, Okayama; 4, Tottori; 5, Matsue;
                   6, Sakai; 7, Tokushima; 8, Kochi; 9, Fukuoka; 10, Kumamoto;
                   11, Nagasaki

EAST JAPAN

■ LEVEL 1   Edo

○   3a 1, Sendai; 2, Kanazawa; 3, Nagoya

●   3b 1, Hirosaki; 2, Akita; 3, Aizu-Wakamatsu; 4, Fukui

Kantō region in the percentage of urban residents in cities at levels 1-3. As in the area around Edo, small han predominated in the Kinki region. Of the more than fifty han, half belonged to the smallest classification with only 10,000-20,000 koku. The scarcity of large han meant that there were few large jōkamachi to fill the gap between Osaka and Kyoto and the nearly 300 central places at levels 4-7. There were no cities at level 3a and just three cities at level 3b. Not only were han small, but kuni were also small in this region. There were no kuni with more than 500 square ri, while seven of the sixteen kuni contained fewer than 100 square ri. Yet, the land was rich and the population was dense. Four of the five Kinai kuni (the five kuni around Osaka and Kyoto) together with Owari in the Chūbu region were the most densely settled kuni of Japan. As in the southern part of Kiangsu, these fertile rice-producing areas helped support the urban needs of two level 2 cities.

An unusual proportion of cities at levels 3 to 5 in the Kinki region were not jōkamachi. For a time the fourth largest city in Japan was Sakai. During the first century of the Tokugawa period this seaport within ten miles of Osaka flourished with roughly 100,000 residents, complementing its large neighbor during the period of Osaka's rapid expansion. After the rate of commercial growth in Osaka had slowed, however, Sakai declined to about 50,000 people, losing out to the competition in a relatively stagnant market. Hyōgo, Nara, Otsu, and Yokkaichi were all level 4 cities, but not jōkamachi. Hyōgo and Nara were located in the Kinai area, the center for large nonadministrative cities. In 1878, of ninety-nine cities in Japan with 10,000 or more residents just thirty-six were not former jōkamachi.[17] More than half of these cities in each area of Japan were jōkamachi except in the Kinai kuni where nine of twelve cities of this size were not jōkamachi.

Level 5 nonadministrative cities also were widespread in the Kinai kuni. Approximately twenty zaikatachō, mostly at level 5, were spaced three to six miles apart within fifteen miles of Osaka.[18] Some of these cities were seaports, e.g., Nishinomiya, which by the early eighteenth century had achieved a population of 7,000. Some were former jōkamachi, e.g., Itami, which prospered as a rice-wine pro-ducing center and as a collection point for rice and reached a peak of 27 chō. Many of these cities in the vicinity of Osaka passed from periodic markets to daily markets with shops during the late seventeenth century, at about the same time as this change was occurring in chen of the Yangtze delta. Nearly all of these cities prospered in the seventeenth century when newly expanding jōkamachi scattered over Japan required processed goods which local residents were not yet able to make for themselves.

The changing nature of the national market in Japan corresponded to the transformation of nonadministrative cities in the Osaka vicinity. During the seventeenth century areas throughout Japan were dependent on Kinki cities for a tremendous variety of goods. The list of 1,807 specialty products of Japan referred to in Chapter 3 consisted of nearly 60 percent from the Kinki region and 39 percent from the five Kinai kuni. Zaikatachō such as Ikeda, Itami, Nishinomiya, and Hyōgo all were represented by at least ten nationally famous items. Gradually these cities narrowed in their specialties as jōkamachi became more self-sufficient in certain kinds of needs and as mass production increased in Osaka. By the second half of the Tokugawa period the zaikatachō were losing direct ties to long-distance commerce and were being transformed into local agricultural centers under Osaka merchants.

Zaikatachō in the Kinai area differed from those in many areas of Japan since most were not located in han and even when they were inside han their ties with outside areas were extensive. In many han throughout Japan zaikatachō were regarded as rivals for the commercial activities which gathered in the jōkamachi. Unless a nonadministrative city was a port or a post station which attracted transport from outside the han, city growth was normally approved by han lords only if it contributed to the flow of commerce to the jōkamachi and from the han to Osaka and Edo. Not many cities could meet these standards. One exception in the Kinki region was Hikone han's Nakahama, which was a large level 5 marketing center.

The size of cities was influenced by the variety of activities present. In most jōkamachi the number of activities can be seen as largely a function of the number of koku in the han. For most periodic markets the number of activities was a function of the quantity of goods exchanged. Although a majority of central places can be characterized as either jōkamachi or simple periodic markets at levels 7 or 6, some multifunctional cities require a breakdown of activities in order to determine the relative contributions of various components of city size.

For evidence on the variety of urban activities, witness the seven posts on the Tōkaidō road within Ise kuni between Nagoya and Kyoto.[19] At one extreme was a post station settlement located on a mountain pass. The majority of households were either engaged in operating inns or were employed in such service-related facilities as eating places and barber shops. This tiny settlement typified the many posts throughout Japan which were located near mountain crossings. Lacking periodic markets, such settlements were not central places.

Two posts in Ise kuni had a high proportion of households which were active in agriculture, including some farmers who doubled as part-time innkeepers. Located on plains, these central places resembled ordinary villages. In 1840 these two level 7 post settlements numbered only 210 and 241 households.

An example of a third type of post in Ise kuni was Seki, a city with 632 households. Since merchants and artisans were numerous in this economic center, households which directly served travelers consisted of only a small fraction of the total population. In such level 6 central places, marketing was brisk.

Most posts with as many as 3,000 inhabitants were simultaneously jōkamachi and/or seaports. In Ise kuni a 60,000 koku jōkamachi, Kameyama, stretched along the Tōkaidō road. The usual jōkamachi form was modified because of the city's position on this road; the commercial population lined the main road, while buke resided in estates away from the road.

The two largest post cities in Ise were Kuwana and Yokkaichi. Together they held more than 4,000 households. Most chō in these cities were either strung out along the main road, or formed along the waterfronts at which sea-going vessels docked. Kuwana also served as a jōkamachi for a 110,000 koku han.

Jōkamachi can be characterized not only by the number of koku in their han and by the presence or absence of unusual features such as a large seaport or a Tōkaidō post station, but also by the compactness of their han. The more compact the han, the easier it was to concentrate commerce inside the jōkamachi. Kinai han were relatively dispersed. For example, Yodo jōkamachi on the river between Osaka and Kyoto was in a han of more than 100,000 koku, but han lands were distributed in six kuni, including 26 percent of the land area located in the distant Kantō region. Another example was Tsu jōkamachi in Ise kuni. Although the city contained 20,000 to 25,000 people, one would have expected more from the over 300,000 koku in the han if it were not for the fact that han land was dispersed in four other kuni.

An example of a compact han was Takatsuki, near the Yodo river.[20] Bypassed by transport along the river and along a nearby road and lacking any noteworthy product, the jōkamachi in this small han of 36,000 koku still ranked at level 5 because buke were gathered there and intra-han commerce was centered there. The city population totaled about 3,000 to 3,500, consisting of 1,700 to 2,500 chōnin plus more than one-half of the buke of the han. Most of the remaining buke lived in Edo. At the end of the seventeenth century it was noted that about 29 percent of the chōnin belonged to families which rented houses. This figure was lower than in large jōkamachi of West Japan, suggesting that opportunities for migrants were few. Without much transportation or exceptional economic vitality, this compact han was still able to maintain nearly 10 percent of its residents in the jōkamachi.

In short, the Kinki region was a highly urbanized area in which 15 percent of the total population lived in two level 2 cities. Residents of jōkamachi at levels 3 and 4 comprised less than 2 percent of the region's population. In contrast to other regions, ports and other zaikatachō were prosperous and the proportion of buke in the urban population was low. Long-distance commerce from other regions clearly helped to support Kinki urban dwellers.

Chūgoku

The Chūgoku region was customarily divided into two. Along the Japan Sea was the Sanin area, consisting of five kuni, each of which held about 200,000 people. Bordering the Inland Sea were the more populous kuni of the Sanyō area. In both the Sanin and Sanyō areas mountainous inland gun were less settled. Just one of the eleven cities at levels 3 and 4 was located far inland, i.e., Tsuyama, a jōka-machi for a 100,000 koku han in inland Mimasaka kuni. Central places at low levels also clustered in the well settled lowlands, especially in the Sanyō area.

The five Sanin kuni contained about 100 central places. Two of these exceeded 30,000 in population: Tottori, the jōkamachi for a han of 330,000 koku, and Matsue, the jōkamachi for a han of 190,000 koku. Yonago, a 60,000 koku han's jōkamachi and a seaport was probably the only level 4 city. An example of a han which gave rise to a level 5 city is Tsuwano. The 70,000 to 80,000 inhabitants of the han were divided as follows: (1) buke—7 percent, (2) farmers—87 percent, (3) artisans—2 percent, (4) merchants—3 percent, and (5) miscellaneous—1 percent. Of the nearly 10,000 residents who were not farmers it is likely that 60 to 80 percent lived in the jōkamachi.

The two largest cities in the Chūgoku region, Hiroshima and Okayama, were both located near the Inland Sea. Okayama han consisted of 670 villages and more than 400,000 actual koku. Oka-yama jōkamachi was conveniently connected by rivers to much of its domain. The chōnin population of the city included about 8 per-cent of the non-buke han dwellers, indicating that the commercial activities of the han were concentrated mainly in this one city. The pattern of consolidation in Okayama was similar to that which oc-curred elsewhere. During the early seventeenth century zaikatachō in the han declined as many commercial activities were prohibited outside of the jōkamachi. Merchants who gathered in chō within the city were grouped according to the zaikatachō from which they came. However, by the middle seventeenth century the nonadminis-trative cities were being restored. Altogether 13 zaikatachō were recognized, thereby enhancing the position of Okayama as the high-est level city. Continued growth brought the jōkamachi's chōnin population to 34,000, which included 4,900 servants plus 29,000 others divided as follows: (1) merchants—29 percent, (2) artisans—19 per-cent, (3) day laborers—28 percent, and (4) miscellaneous—24 per-cent.[21] Later the chōnin total decreased as new commercial activities sprouted in villages and rerouted commerce undercut the position of Okayama as the uni-dimensional center of its han.

Hiroshima was the only city with as many as 70,000 residents in this region. Records reveal the sizes of estates in the buke areas of the city.[22] The 8 large estates in the area of the castle termed San-no-maru averaged 2,550 *tsubo* (one tsubo = 3.95 square yards). Also near the daimyo's residence were 47 estates which averaged 1,485 tsubo, 123 estates which averaged 565 tsubo, and 29 estates which averaged 468 tsubo. In contrast, lower bushi were more crowded; the 354 estates in which they resided averaged only 72 tsubo in area. The principle of the higher the bushi rank, the more space allotted prevailed in Hiroshima as elsewhere.

Three other cities in Hiroshima han also merited separate urban administrations. Foremost among them was Onomichi, a seaport on the Inland Sea at the opposite end of the han from the jōkamachi. The others were Miyajima, an island port near Hiroshima city, and Miyoshi, a zaikatachō on an inland river which was used to cross between Sanin and Sanyō.

At the tip of Honshū island were Nagato and Suwo kuni. The principal han in these kuni was Hagi (Chōshū) with 370,000 official koku and more than 700,000 actual koku. In 1610 the jōkamachi at Hagi was just beginning to develop, but there were other central places which divided up more than 6,000 commercial households.[23] Nearly half of these households were located in Yamaguchi city and an additional 20 percent were found in the neighboring settlements of Shimonoseki, a thriving seaport later in the Tokugawa period, and Chōfu. Five other official zaikatachō were mining settlements, which enjoyed a temporary boom and then declined during the seventeenth century. There were forty to fifty additional central places in these two kuni. Central places at levels 6 and 7 stood only two or three miles apart along the main road of the Sanyō plain, but were five or more miles apart in other areas and as many as ten miles apart in mountainous areas.

Marketing settlements can be divided as more urban or more rural not only by total population but also by the number of tsubo per household. Presumably the more urbanized the settlement, the less area per household. The range in the Hagi area was between 23.7 tsubo per household in Shimonoseki and 558 tsubo per household in predominantly farming settlements where some part-time commercial activities occurred. An article by Kobayashi Kentarō divides the central places in Hagi han according to size and tsubo per household.[24] In the top group were settlements with more than ninety-nine households and fewer than 105.3 tsubo per average household. Included were central places famed for specialized commerce and crafts, among which were all the settlements recognized as zaikatachō by the daimyo. Fifteen settlements met these standards for the top group, and were probably level 6 central places. The remaining thirty-five central places, which held between 11 and 115 households, mostly ranked at level 7.

Another way of classifying settlements is according to the tax assessment in number of koku per commercial household.[25] At one extreme in Nagato and Suwo kuni were Yamaguchi, Shimonoseki, Fuchu, and Hagi cities, all of which had more than two registered koku per household for tax purposes. At the other extreme were level 7 central places, which owed far fewer koku and generally bore the same obligations as ordinary villages. Combining this criterion with the two above, the following four groups of Hagi han urban areas can be distinguished: (1) relatively large cities mostly at levels 5 and above—their streets were lined with rectangular lots which had narrow street frontage and they were occupied by merchants and artisans who served several gun or even the whole han; (2) level 6 zaikatachō with 100 to 200 households—these were along main roads, but households occupied a larger area than those in the first since larger lots were needed by families engaging at least part-time in agriculture; (3) central places with fewer than 100 households but having the same activities and basically the same form as those in the second group; and (4) the smallest marketing settlements— their houses had as wide frontage as those in ordinary villages and commercial pursuits were almost entirely restricted to marketing days.

Like the provinces in Central China, the Chūgoku region is commonly regarded as an intermediate area between the advanced Kinki region and such less developed areas as parts of Kyūshū and the Tōhoku regions. In fact, there was great diversity within the Chūgoku region. Yet, the overall proportion of residents who were urban is remarkably consistent with figures for all but the two highly urbanized regions in Japan. The fact that 40 percent of urban dwellers lived in cities with 30,000 or more residents may indicate that, as a whole, this region contributed less of its surplus for outside consumption than the Chūbu region. No doubt Osaka's prosperity to some extent depended on trade with the Chūgoku region, but this was just one of several regions contributing to that urban center.

Shikoku

Across the Inland Sea from the Chūgoku and Kinki areas was the island of Shikoku. The major han on the island were Tokushima, officially with 260,000 koku, and Kōchi, officially with 240,000 koku and actually climbing to more than 600,000 koku in 1,060 villages. The jōkamachi of these han were the level 3b cities in Shikoku. The three han with official koku totals of 100,000 to 150,000 all had level 4 jōkamachi. One of these level 4 castle cities was Matsuyama situated in large Iyo kuni. Of the total han population, which reached 160,000 to 170,000 in 1691, 17,000 were chōnin in the jōkamachi, but in 1789 that figure had dropped to 12,000. In addition, there were more than 10,000 buke in Matsuyama city.

Tokushima in Awa kuni consisted of six small islands in the delta of three rivers.[26] Located on one of these islands, the castle formed the core area around which the city developed. For Hiroshima city we observed the varying areas of bushi estates. In this han we can specify the designated number of koku per bushi during the early nineteenth century: (1) 30 bushi with more than 1,000 koku; (2) 32 bushi with 500-1,000 koku; (3) 91 bushi with 300-500 koku; (4) 342 bushi with 100-300 koku; and (5) 720 bushi with fewer than 100 koku. The closer the bushi lived to the castle, the more koku he was likely to have accredited to him. Half of the bushi on the island with the castle held at least 500 koku and all but one held more than 100 koku. On a second nearby island 16 percent were in the over-500 category, 60 percent in the 100-500 category, and 24 percent belonged to the sub-100 category. A third island also sheltered some wealthy bushi: 9 percent were in the over-500 category, 56 percent in the 100-500 category, and 35 percent in the sub-100 category. The remaining islands can be divided into two groups: the intermediate areas in which half of 329 bushi households held more than 100 koku and areas at the periphery of the city in which 314 of 405 bushi households had fewer than 100 koku. In Tokushima as in other jōkamachi there was clear residential segregation among bushi based on income.

Groups of chō can also be distinguished within Tokushima. On one island with many wealthy bushi lived privileged chōnin, many of whom could trace their families' contributions to the city back to the time of the establishment of the han. The 450 households in these eight chō controlled monopolies over special products such as fish. Artisans whose crafts were of military importance were prominent in these chō. A second set of chō was conveniently connected by a bridge to the above chō and was located at the juncture of two of the major roads in the han. The population in these sixteen chō was rising more rapidly during the seventeenth century, which was typical of the pattern whereby chōnin outside of the originally designated special chō gained in numbers and successfully challenged the established families at about the same time as tonya and zaikatachō were recognized as desirable for improved intra-han commerce. Other chō could also be found either wedged inside bushi areas or along major roads. Especially from the eighteenth century chō proliferated along roads at the perimeter of the city. These were more loosely controlled areas reflecting the breakdown in commercial concentration within the city as within the han from the eighteenth century.

Some areas in Tokushima as in other jōkamachi were set aside for temples and shrines. When the jōkamachi was established many of these religious structures were moved from locations inside the domain to the new city and others were built anew by the daimyo. Important shrines were placed at entrances to the city.

Tokushima had two centers—the administrative and military center at the castle and the economic center in the oldest chō. From the building of the castle to the mid-seventeenth century the oldest chō prospered, aided by prohibitions on local commerce. From about the 1660s the growing power of the daimyo over the whole han was reflected in the expansion of the jōkamachi. New bushi areas were founded and new chō were incorporated under the city administration. The growth of the city from its core to the urban fringes related to the development of the urban network inside the han. For instance, in Tokushima han eight zaikatachō were established at about the time the preeminence of the inner chō was being challenged. Subsequently stores spread in villages and central control over merchants inside the han weakened, corresponding to further changes inside the jōkamachi. Noteworthy in Tokushima were the breakdown in the division between buke and chō areas, the expansion of buke estates at the city's perimeter, the fragmentation of the estates of inner-city bushi, and the general decline of the city's military activities in favor of its commercial ones. Although the two centers of the city remained focal points, they were beginning to become superfluous for the daily activities of the jōkamachi. I have used Tokushima as an example of a large jōkamachi with every expectation that similar remarks could be made about other cities in this region and throughout Japan.

A fact which should not escape attention is the low proportion of urban residents in the Shikoku region who lived in level 3 cities and above. As an island, this region enjoyed particularly convenient transportation to nearby Osaka. More than in any other region of Japan local urban growth was stymied by reliance on large cities outside the region. Yet, in the percent of its population which was urban, Shikoku was at the same level as most regions in Japan.

Kyūshū

Four of the fifteen largest cities in Japan were located in the Kyūshū region. Three of the four were jōkamachi, all in han in which at least 500,000 koku had been officially registered. Together these three han held approximately 2½ million actual koku and more than 40 percent of the population of their region. Kagoshima, the largest of the three, had an enormous buke population of at least 40,000. Kumamoto jōkamachi was also more than 50 percent buke in population and more than two-thirds buke in area. The third large jōkamachi was Fukuoka, which should be considered together with its commercial port Hakata as one level 3b city. The fourth large Kyūshū city, the port of Nagasaki, remained under Bakufu control during the Tokugawa period.

For some purposes we can usefully divide Kyūshū into northern and southern parts. In the north were traditional centers of foreign trade and a commercially developed hinterland. This area was more accessible both to the major Kinki cities and to the historic partners in foreign trade, Korea and China. It was the city of Nagasaki in the north which was proclaimed the authorized location for most foreign trade. South Kyūshū resembled parts of the Tōhoku region in its inaccessibility. Yet, this area benefited from growing trade with the Ryūkyū Islands and from access to pirated goods originating in China. Most urban development was concentrated in north Kyūshū, but the largest city in the region was Kagoshima, located in huge Satsuma han at the southern tip of the island.

In most respects Kyūshū island's urban network resembled that of other regions in Japan. The region was 13 percent urban, roughly the same as all regions except the Kantō and Kinki areas. Approximately 10 percent of han residents lived in jōkamachi as in other regions. However, one unusual characteristic was the small number of cities at level 4. If the figure of four cities in the 10,000-30,000 range is not a result of faulty data, then we must assume that the distribution of han in this region was such that not many jōkamachi of this size appeared. Moreover, transport gravitated to Nagasaki and Hakata; so that nonadministrative cities of 10,000-30,000 did not appear in large number.

The urban population in Kyūshū numbered roughly 520,000. Approximately 42 percent of them lived in cities with more than 30,000 residents. Being an island, the Kyūshū region had convenient transportation ties to the Chūgoku and Kinki areas. Nonetheless, the region was sufficiently distant from Osaka so as not to be as well integrated into Osaka's trading sphere as Shikoku. In addition, many parts of Kyūshū were far enough inland to resemble inaccessible Tōhoku areas rather than easily reached Shikoku areas. The figure of 42 percent in cities at levels 1-3 reveals a region primarily supplying its own major cities, but also partially supporting distant Osaka.

West Japan was highly centralized commercially, but loosely integrated administratively. Two central cities at level 2 enclosed 5 percent of the population of West Japan. Another 4 percent of the population were scattered in thirteen cities at level 3. Roughly 1,000 lower level central places with more than 1 million urban residents

(8 percent of West Japan's population) comprised the base of the urban pyramid. The three outlying regions all were 13 percent urban, while the Kinki region sheltering Osaka and Kyoto was 24 percent urban. The Chūgoku, the Kyūshū, and especially the Shikoku regions aided the Kinki area inhabitants in supporting these central cities.

Summary

Data have been presented in this and the previous chapter for eighteen provinces of China grouped into six regions and for seven regions of Japan combined as East and West Japan. The provinces of China were each no less than 4 percent and no more than 9 percent urban. Falling within an even narrower range, the regions of China varied from 5.6 percent to 7.1 percent urban. The range of urbanization was much broader in Japan, extending from 12.6 percent in the Tōhoku region to 23.6 percent in the Kinki region. Yet, East and West Japan were quite similar with 16.4 and 16.9 percent respectively in cities. Through these figures in Table 40 we can begin to explore regional variations in the two countries.

The findings in this chapter lend support to the conclusions in Part I. In Chapters 1 and 2 it was argued that a rural-urban dichotomy was more characteristic of Japan than of China. We have ob-

TABLE 40

Regions in China and Japan

Region	Total Population (millions)	Urban Population (millions)	Urban (percent)	Urban Percent in Levels 1–3
North China	96	5.40	5.7	42
Northwest China	26	1.45	5.6	43
East-central China	105	6.25	6.0	53
Central China	80	4.60	5.8	49
Southeast China	55	3.95	7.1	55
Southwest China	55	3.10	5.7	49
East Japan	16.5	2.70	16.4	55
West Japan	15.0	2.50	16.9	54

served in this chapter that urbanization in the Kantō and Kinki regions was 21.7 and 23.6 percent respectively, in sharp contrast to the range of 12.6-13.1 percent in Japan's other five regions. Sharply opposed to this bipolarized distribution was the continuum in China, in which no more than 0.7 percent separated the level of urbanization of one province from the level of the province most similar to it. At one end of the spectrum were Chihli at 8.8 percent, Fukien at 8.2 percent, and Kiangsu at 7.5 percent and at the other end were Shansi and Anhwei at 4.0 percent and Kansu at 4.2 percent. Many provinces were bunched in the middle. There was no big gap between relatively urbanized and less urbanized areas of the country as in Japan.

Some of the general conclusions of Part I would have required qualification if the data had revealed that these conclusions did not apply to all large areas of China and Japan. However, the data are so consistent that no qualifications are needed. For instance, it was shown in Chapter 2 that the distribution of central places formed a much narrower pyramid in Japan than in China. The evidence presented in this chapter affirms that this pattern prevailed for all provinces of China and for all regions in both countries. Provinces in China typically contained as many as 1,500 level 7 settlements, but fewer than 100 level 5 cities and no more than 15 level 4 cities, while regions in Japan with just 100-150 level 7 settlements supported 25-50 level 5 cities and 5 or more cities at level 4. It is also now apparent that the most urbanized province of China was considerably less urban than the least urbanized region of Japan. Chihli sheng was 8.8 percent urban while the Tōhoku region was 12.6 percent urban. Clearly general comparisons of the two countries are supported by the data on individual provinces and regions.

In Chapter 3 it was argued that the national market was more completely integrated in Tokugawa Japan. A measure of the degree of market and administrative integration that has been used in this chapter is the proportion of the urban population in cities at levels 1-3. It is likely that nearby provinces and, in the case of Japan, regions varied markedly in this measure because goods being accumulated at lower level cities in one province were destined for the support of people in large cities in another province. The provinces of China varied greatly in this measure, a sign of flourishing regional markets, but the regions of China varied much less. At the two extremes, Southeast China was only 13 percent above North China. Moreover, differences between regions in China corresponded closely to variations in transportation capability, with the Southeast and East-central regions ahead of the 'North and Northwest, which were much more dependent on inefficient land transportation. Movement of goods from region to region does not seem to have made much impact on the urban network; regions were essentially self-contained. In contrast, Japanese regions ranged from 27 percent to 77 percent of urban residents in cities of 30,000 or more people. This great diversity indicates that vast shipments of goods from most regions contributed to the support of the central cities in the Kantō and Kinki regions. A national market with two centers thrived in Japan.

Using this vital index of urban concentration, we can classify Chinese provinces and Japanese regions: (1) national or regional centers—Kiangsu, Kwangtung, Chihli, and the Kantō and Kinki regions; (2) subsidiary centers—Hupei, Chekiang, Szechwan, Fukien, and Shensi; (3) self-centered—Kiangsi, Shantung, Kweichow, and the Tōhoku region; (4) other-centered—Hunan, Kansu, Yunnan, Kwangsi, Anhwei, and the Kyūshū and Chūgoku regions; and (5) other-dominated—Shansi, Honan and the Chūbu and Shikoku regions. Japan stood out at the two extremes while China was better represented among subsidiary centers and self-centered provinces. Single Chinese provinces or two provinces together formed trading units, while only East Japan and West Japan existed as separate marketing entities in Japan.

The three provinces of Kiangsu, Kwangtung, and Chihli and the Kinki and Kantō regions all were far above national averages, each counting over 60 percent of its urban residents in large cities. Kiangsu and Kwangtung benefited from low rates of 33 and 36 percent in Anhwei and Kwangsi, respectively, in achieving their high levels. The Kinki region also relied on neighboring areas with low rates to boost its standing. Among the areas with more than 60 percent in large cities, the major difference appears between the Kantō region at 77 percent and Chihli at 62 percent. As the locations of the national administrative centers, these areas were supported in part by distant regions. The Kantō region was more accessible, enabling it to reach 77 percent. It is likely that the Kantō region was well above the Kinki region in this index since the Kinki area had numerous local centers, helping to support its central cities.

While not a single Japanese region counted between 50 percent and 60 percent of its population in cities of more than 30,000 people, five Chinese provinces belonged to this range. All of these provinces boasted level 2 cities. Wuhan in Hupei (58 percent) was supported by Hunan (39 percent), Sian in Shensi (50 percent) was supported by Kansu (38 percent), and Chungking and Chengtu in Szechwan (52 percent) were supported by Yunnan (38 percent) and to a lesser extent by Kweichow (43 percent). Foochow in Fukien (51 percent) and Hangchow in Chekiang (55 percent) do not seem to have received large-scale support from outside, but did receive some shipments from inland provinces and enjoyed active coastal trade.

The ratio between the proportion of the Chinese population in cities in the most urbanized province and in the least urbanized province was slightly more than 2:1. The same ratio for Japanese regions was just less than 2:1. Thus internal variations in both countries in the range of urbanization were approximately the same. In Table 41 below I have grouped Chinese provinces into four groups and Japanese regions into two groups according to the percentage of their population in cities. The order from top to bottom and from left to right indicates ascending urban percentages.

Another way of dividing China is into north, south, and central areas. The north, consisting of the North and Northwest regions, contained roughly 120 million people, 9,000 central places, and slightly less than 7 million city residents. Southwest China resembled the northern regions: 5.7 percent urban and 4,500 central places for 55 million people. Southeast China was markedly different: 7.1 percent urban and 5,000 central places for 55 million people (a ratio of 0.91), both figures the highest in China. The East-central and Central regions joined to form central China. Holding about 185 million people, 13,500 central places, and 11 million city inhabitants, central China was slightly less than 6 percent urban. In short, China's urban population was distributed roughly as follows: (1) north—7 million; (2) south—7 million; (3) central—11 million.

The comparisons of provinces and regions in this chapter are based for the most part on a sample of urban data. We can expect that the accumulation of more data will require some modifications of the figures presented and also of the provincial and regional rank-

TABLE 41

Urbanization of Provinces and Regions

China			
4% (4.0–4.4%)	5% (4.8–5.2%)	6% (5.9–6.3%)	7–9% (6.7–8.8%)
Shansi	Honan	Kweichow	Kwangtung
Anhwei	Hunan	Hupei	Shensi
Kansu	—	Szechwan	Kiangsu
Yunnan	—	Chekiang	Fukien
Shantung	—	Kwangsi	Chihli
		Kiangsi	

Japan	
13% (12.6–13.0%)	22–24% (21.7–23.6%)
Tōhoku	Kantō
Chūgoku	—
Shikoku	Kinki
Kyūshū	—
Chūbu	—

ings. Not only should we direct our efforts toward finding more data on the network of central places, but we should also be seeking to better account for the variations between areas. Study of demographic characteristics, of land use, of the distribution of social classes, of transportation capabilities, and of other topics introduced in Chapter 2 as they pertain to regional and provincial variations is essential to make more meaningful the initial (sweeping strokes) of this chapter.

✳ *6* ✳

PEKING, EDO, AND
THE HIERARCHY OF CITIES

Each of the first five chapters offers a perspective from which to examine Ch'ing Peking and Tokugawa Edo. Chapter 1 provides a history of cities before these two national centers reached their final premodern forms. As the last in a long tradition of great capital cities, Peking is best considered in continuity with earlier Chinese urban development. Edo, of course, was an upstart, emerging in the two centuries of unparalleled urbanization from the late Sengoku period to the mid-Tokugawa period. Stages in Edo's rapid growth mirrored the dynamism of Japanese society. Chapter 2 outlines relationships between systems of cities and various aspects of social structure. Since Edo contained 3 percent of the Japanese population in contrast to Peking's 0.3 percent of China's total, the former necessarily had a different place within the larger context of its society. Comparisons of stratification, administration, transportation, and other subjects reveal how Edo stood at the top of a more centralized city system than did Peking. Similarly differences in marketing patterns, discussed in Chapter 3, underlay the relative concentrations of urban residents in the two cities. Situated in an accessible bay, Edo prospered as a center of a highly integrated national market. The intensive examination in Chapter 4 of the areas immediately surrounding the two level 1 cities permits a clearer perspective of the local support which sustained the two cities. Yet, it is only as national centers that such huge concentrations of population can be adequately understood. Bringing together the areas treated separately in Chapter 5, we should think of all China and all Japan as two separate urban networks. Standing at the head of the urban networks of these two advanced premodern societies were Peking and

Edo, the premier cities of the world. For more than a century until about 1800, these two were the most populous of all the millions of settlements on the globe.

While in Chapter 6 I conclude this study of Chinese and Japanese cities, I also begin another study of even wider scope. The techniques developed for comparing two East Asian societies are presumably applicable to other large-scale premodern societies. It seems proper to ask at this time what questions based on these comparisons of China and Japan should form the starting points of further research, including research already begun on Russian cities. Can the seven levels of cities be identified in other countries? If so, did cities at these levels appear approximately as rapidly as in China? As in Japan? Did they emerge in an order similar to the path followed in China? In Japan? Can other advanced premodern societies be characterized in terms of the distribution of cities among these seven levels? Do the approaches used for comparing marketing in China and Japan apply elsewhere? In other words, is this approach to urban networks a useful tool for comparing other premodern societies? Eventually, I expect that we shall find that we can learn more about individual countries through comparisons than through single country studies.

The Development of Peking and Edo

For most of the past two thousand years the largest city in the world has probably been the capital of China. At least five sites were the locations of capital cities reputed to have reached populations in excess of 1 million and Lo-yang was a sixth capital of impressive proportions. Thus Peking's position as the largest city in the world from the fifteenth century to the beginning of the Industrial Revolution in England (with the possible exceptions of Nanking until the late sixteenth century and of Edo from the late seventeenth century) was the culmination of a long history of great cities.[1]

The progression of level 1 cities from Han Ch'ang-an to Ch'ing Peking can be described in terms of three stages as indicated in Chapter 1: the early imperial city, the middle imperial city, and the late imperial city. The first 900 or 1,000 years of imperial history produced imposing capital cities. Such early imperial centers as

Ch'ang-an and Lo-yang were carefully planned and highly ordered. Walls delimited the built-up areas of cities. Rectangular wards formed easily controlled administrative units. Markets were enclosed and supervised. The form of these impressive urban centers reflected the concentration of power and of resources which were not consumed locally under the imperial bureaucracy.

What was the urban network like during the early imperial period? Although the data are meager in comparison to what is available for the Ch'ing period, I think it is useful to attempt an initial reconstruction of the distribution of urban residents in T'ang China. Note that Table 42 and subsequent tables use definitions of the seven levels given for Chapters 2 to 5 and not those for Chapter 1.

TABLE 42

Tang China

Level	Number	Population (millions)
1	1	1.0
2	1	.5
3a	6	.5
3b	12	.5
4	30	.5
5	200	.8
6	1,600	1.8
7	600	

Total population: 100 million
Urban population: 4.3 million
Percent urban: 4–5%
Urban percent 58%
in levels 1–3:

Ch'ang-an and Lo-yang (the secondary capital and level 2 city) were the centers of a highly centralized urban network. However, unlike Tokugawa Japan, this centralized network was characterized by a low proportion of the total population in cities. Moreover, the ratio of central places to total population was considerably less than half of the figure for Tokugawa Japan.

The above table of T'ang China refers to the time of transition when the old patterns of early imperial China were beginning to give way to the new patterns of middle imperial China. During the approximately six centuries of the middle imperial period Ch'ang-an, K'ai-feng and Hangchow in succession remained at the peak population of premodern cities, but were gradually losing significance as loci of administrative controls on commerce. As this tentative chart for mid-Sung China indicates, the urban network was changing.

TABLE 43

Sung China

Level	Number	Population
1	1	1.0
2	0	
3a	10	.9
3b	20	.8
4	60	1.0
5	400	1.8
6	1,800	1.4
7	2,000	

Total population: 120 million
Urban population: 6.2 million
Percent urban: 5%
Urban percent 44%
in levels 1–3

As the proportion of the population which was urban rose, the percent living in large cities declined. The early imperial capital city rested on a narrower urban network, consisting almost entirely of administrative cities. By the Sung period marketing had expanded, the number of central places had increased in proportion to the total population, and there were perhaps, twice as many cities at levels 3 to 5. As capital cities in this middle imperial period became more dependent on private commerce to supplement tax shipments, they became less orderly.

Peking first emerged as the capital of a united China in the thirteenth century. The fact that it was the smallest capital city in approximately a thousand years might be considered a reversion to the patterns of the Han period, but the continued expansion of the network of cities to more than 6,000 central places reveals that Han patterns could not be reimposed. From the standpoint of traditional intercity relationships it is likely that Yuan Peking did not meet the old standards of a capital city. During the Yuan period the city lacked the multitude of commercial ties to other cities which would have been needed to take advantage of the growing urban network. During the T'ang period when the ties between administrative and nonadministrative cities were negligible, Ch'ang-an at the outskirts of the empire could serve as an effective capital. Subsequently the capital was moved successively closer to the economic heartland and the transportation center, corresponding to the rising importance of commerce. This trend was reversed with Yuan Peking. Once again the capital was moved to the outskirts. With their interest in mulcting the countryside, the Mongols imposed an administrative center which relied more on tax revenues. Relinquishing the efforts to combine administrative and commercial centrality, the Yuan leaders set the pattern for following capitals except Ming Nanking. Strategic factors were given precedence in determining the location of the capital. Unlike other capitals in Chinese history, Peking from the Yuan to the Ch'ing periods was the product of a choice between a strategic and a commercial center. In making that choice, the leaders of China may have gained security at the expense of expanded control over resources.

During the Ming period Peking regained the population level of previous large capital cities. Yet, its population represented a declining proportion of Chinese urban residents. Table 44 is an attempt to reconstruct the hierarchy of cities of the mid-Ming dynasty during the late imperial period.

While the proportion of urban residents who lived in one capital city was falling, the proportion in cities at levels 1 to 3 had stabilized. Long-distance commerce was making it possible for other large cities to prosper outside of the national capital. The late imperial administrative center not only did not represent a reordered society, it increasingly reflected a decentralized society.

While Peking remained the level 1 city during the Ch'ing period,

TABLE 44

Ming China

Level	Number	Population
1	1	1.0
2	1	.8
3a	10	.9
3b	25	1.0
4	75	1.2
5	500	2.5
6	2,000	2.0
7	7,500	

Total population: 130 million
Urban population: 8.4 million
Percent urban: 6–7%
Urban percent   44%
in levels 1–3

the urban network continued to expand. Since in previous chapters I have considered in any detail only the nineteenth century city system, it would be appropriate at this point to attempt to describe the early Ch'ing pattern of cities. Table 45 refers to the middle seventeenth century after recovery from a decade or more of wars.

If these tables are at all accurate, then the rapid increase of central places at levels 7 and 6 was not accompanied by substantial urban growth. Local commerce was not efficiently accumulated for movement to high level cities.

During the first two centuries of the Ch'ing dynasty the population of China increased by approximately 150 percent. At no time during the previous 2,000 years is there evidence of a similar increase. What changes in the urban network accompanied these two centuries of rapid population growth? For the first time since before the T'ang dynasty the total number of central places was not increasing in proportion to population. Despite the fact that the number rose from about 15,000 to more than 30,000, population was increasing faster. The proportion of the total population in cities probably remained almost constant at roughly 6 percent. Long-dis-

TABLE 45

Early Ch'ing China

Level	Number	Population
1	1	1.0
2	3	1.4
3a	12	1.0
3b	30	1.2
4	90	1.4
5	600	3.0
6	2,500	2.5
7	12,000	

Total population: 150 million
Urban population: 10.2 million
Percent urban: 6–7%
Urban percent 45%
in levels 1–3

tance commerce expanded, permitting a somewhat greater percentage of the urban total in cities at levels 3 and above. At the level of national percentages there does not seem to have been much change during the Ch'ing period; so it is necessary to examine what was happening at regional, provincial, and lower levels.

A comparison of Table 45 and Table 5 indicates that the number of level 2 cities tripled during the 200 years. Whereas in 1660 Peking may have contained 40 percent of all residents in cities of 300,000 or more people, in 1830 Peking's percentage had dropped below 20. It was during the Ch'ing dynasty that the commercial centrality of other cities enabled them as a group to dwarf the capital in total population.

Similarly the number of level 3 cities and the population in these rose sharply from the seventeenth century. In the early Ch'ing period there were an average of two or three cities at this level per sheng. By the nineteenth century this average had risen to five or six cities despite the addition of three sheng. When cities corresponding to the sheng level were introduced during the T'ang period, there was an average of one city of 30,000 or more residents per sheng. As late as the Ming period the average stood at two. It seems possible that the sudden rise to five or six large cities per sheng may have strained the capacity to govern with existing organizations.

The near doubling of cities at levels 4 and 5 must be seen in the context of great stability in the number of administrative units. During the early Ch'ing decades the fu city was just beginning to make the transition from a level 5 city to a level 4 city. In 1660 most fu cities still ranked at level 5. By 1830 almost all fu cities ranked at level 4 or higher. Simultaneously the balance of hsien cities was shifting from level 6 to level 5. Probably no more than 400 of the hsien and chou cities in the seventeenth century ranked at level 5, but by 1830 as fu cities climbed to level 4, hsien and chou cities not only filled the vacancies, they scrambled to add new positions at level 5 as well. Unless Ming China was substantially more urban than the following dynasty, its hsien cities remained at level 6. Only in the eighteenth century did the pivotal period arrive when fu, chou, and hsien cities rose a rank in the hierarchy of cities.

Finally, it should be pointed out that at the beginning of the Ch'ing period there were approximately eight level 7 markets per administrative unit and one to two level 6 markets per unit. Less than 200 years later these averages had risen to sixteen and four respectively. This meant that the hsien city which had originally been chosen to serve as the sole marketing center of its unit had become the center of a swelling network of markets. Not only were as many as four cities at level 6 common, but in at least 10 percent of the administrative units a second level 5 city had emerged and in the more than 20 percent of administrative units in which the official city ranked only at level 6 there was considerable possibility that a second city ranked as high. The development of periodic markets reflected the increasing complexity of local administration. Particularly during the Ch'ing period the urban network was undergoing unprecedented changes.

Despite these many changes, the Chinese administrative system and administrative units remained as before. The seeming constancy in Peking's population reflects this stability in the face of change.

Like Peking, Edo served as the administrative center of its country from the time when the seven-level hierarchy was completed. But unlike Peking, Edo was not the heir to a uniform tradition of large cities. Nara, Kyoto, and Kamakura had all held populations of more than 100,000; yet these cities had varied substantially as the extent of administrative centralization had fluctuated. No city in Japan had approached the size which Edo was to reach. Moreover, whereas the model for Ch'ing Peking had undergone a long history, there was no model for Tokugawa Edo. Reflecting the novelty of a new society, Edo was unprecedented in Japanese history. Yet, one continuity with Japan's past was the presence in cities at levels 1 and 2 of at least one-third of all urban residents. The tradition of concentrated populations in a small number of cities was carried on almost single-handedly by Edo, in which almost 20 percent of urban dwellers lived.

The contrast between early Tokugawa cities and late Tokugawa cities reveals tremendous changes in the urban network. Note that in Table 46 levels are defined in terms of populations, as in the historical charts for China presented in this chapter.

In the course of two centuries Japan's urban population increased by almost 400 percent. During this same period the total population of Japan rose by only 70 percent. Therefore, by the nineteenth century the percentage urban had risen about two and one-half times.

TABLE 46

Early Tokugawa Japan

Level	Number	Population
1	0	
2	0	
3a	3	.4
3b	3	.1
4	25	.3
5	100	.5
6	200	.2
7	500	
Total population:	18 million	
Urban population:	1.4 million	
Percent urban:	7–8%	
Urban percent in levels 1–3	36%	

Edo began its reign with an urban network in some respects similar to the one in early Ch'ing China, but by the nineteenth century both Edo and its urban network had changed drastically. We can divide these changes into four stages.[2]

From the time it was chosen as a castle site in 1456 until the arrival of Tokugawa Ieyasu in 1590 Edo rose and fell with the tides of war. For most of the time Edo was a branch castle of the lord in Odawara. As a level 6 central place, it was one of more than 100 Sengoku cities. Only after Hideyoshi captured Odawara and enfeoffed Tokugawa Ieyasu in the Kantō plain did Edo rise to prominence among the cities of Japan.

Edo's first stage of continuous development can be dated from 1590. As the jōkamachi of one of Japan's largest han, Edo quickly grew from a tiny settlement to a level 4 and, perhaps, even a level 3 city. An early decision was necessary on the location of the castle, important in legitimating the Tokugawa family's position as well as in providing a center for the han's military and administrative activities. The advantageous location of one of the city's five bluffs, which overlooked the lowlands adjoining the bay, was chosen for the castle. High ground in the vicinity served as the spacious residential areas for buke estates. Canals were dug linking the castle to the bay. Used to transport materials, to provide soil for reclamation, for drainage and defense, the canals became the centers of commercial activity. Tax exemptions, free markets, and monopolies for the entire han market enticed merchants and artisans to the lowlands along the canals. With a moderately large castle, a large concentration of buke, a skeleton system of canals, and a growing merchant and artisan population, Edo joined tens of cities as one of the principle secondary centers after Kyoto and Osaka. Yet, unlike the other large jōkamachi which appeared at the end of the sixteenth or the beginning of the seventeenth centuries, Edo continued to expand rapidly after this initial spurt.

In the second stage of its growth Edo was no longer one of many castle cities, but had become instead the seat of the Bakufu administration. One of the first steps heralding the existence of the Tokugawa central government was the decision to construct a castle superior to the one in Osaka, displaying to the country the unrivaled authority of Edo's lord. The castle was surrounded by an inner moat, and farther out a broadened system of canals was emerging. During the first decades of Tokugawa preeminence daimyo began to build residences in the vicinity of the castle as a partial sankin kōtai system was put into operation. Accompanying the arrival of increasing numbers of daimyo and their dependents came rising shipments of goods from outside the Kantō region. Merchants and artisans who handled the increased flow of goods gathered around the commercial center of Nihonbashi, where the five roads merged which connected Edo to areas throughout the country. Many of the approximately 300 chō which had been established by the second decade of Bakufu rule stretched along these roads or along the nearby bodies of water. By this time the city's population was climbing above 100,000.

Edo continued to expand rapidly after initial efforts to construct the administrative and commercial centers. After Tokugawa Ieyasu's death in Sumpu to which he had retired, his large retinue was resettled in Edo. At about the same time victory in the battle of Osaka secured the paramount position of Edo's rulers. Gradually they completed the establishment of the sankin kōtai system, which brought tens of thousands and later hundreds of thousands of buke into the city. Merchants and artisans followed, though forming a smaller part of Edo's total population than at a later date. During the seventeenth century the population of the city was rising at a rate of almost 10,000 a year.

Few cities have had to overcome the adversity that has shadowed the short history of Edo, later renamed Tokyo. In our century the city has twice suffered more than 50 percent destruction at the hands of an earthquake and wartime bombing. In both cases winds swept fires through densely populated areas, producing most of the damage. Vulnerability to fires was characteristic too of the city's earlier history. During the Tokugawa period at least ten fires swept across hundreds of chō, destroying up to two-thirds of Edo. One of the most damaging blazes was the Meireki fire of 1657. In the aftermath of the destruction of most of Edo in that fire the city took on a new shape which was to remain in its general features until 1868.

The third stage of Edo's development lasted from 1657 to 1716.

Previously, planning had focused on defensive needs, but after the Meireki tragedy, renewed emphasis on fire prevention captivated city planners. In rebuilding the city open spaces were cleared in the castle area, daimyo estates and temples were relocated far from the castle, main roads were widened, and new bridges were constructed. As many of the less built-up areas enclosed by the new expanded perimeters became densely settled at the end of the seventeenth century, Edo approached its peak population. Whereas in the second stage of its continuous growth Edo had risen to a population numbering in the hundreds of thousands and to a place as one of the three largest cities of Japan, in its third stage after 1657 Edo became the first city of the land, more than doubling its population to nearly 1 million.

The final stage in Edo's development dates from 1716. I have chosen this date, following Naitō Akira, because it marks the beginning of the first of three major reform periods at intervals of about sixty years. All of the reforms were directed against the influx of migrants into Edo and the changing modes of urban life. Especially during the later reform periods drastic measures were initiated to halt the growth in Edo's population. If a recent migrant had no permanent job or had left his wife behind, then he was subject to deportation. Although these policies were adopted to halt the sudden influx of refugees in times of famine, in fact, the long-run population of Edo had stabilized. During the second half of the Tokugawa period Edo continued to hold about 1 million people.

The more underlying need for reform was based on the changing distribution of the nation's wealth. A rising proportion of the national income was being redistributed through commerce rather than through tax payments. The plight of the bushi in the cities was worsening. Indicative of the changes in the second half of the Tokugawa period was the appearance of sprawl; chō spread in a linear fashion along roads leading from the city. Moreover, buke residences were more scattered than earlier in the Tokugawa period. The declining order of Edo should not be overestimated, but to the extent it occurred it should be regarded as a sign of decentralizing tendencies in Tokugawa society.

In contrasting the development of Peking and Edo, we should not fail to note the critical seventeenth century. While there were no clear stages in the growth of Chinese cities, Edo and other Japanese cities passed through at least three stages: the time of founding and initial expansion, the time of growth based on rising control of tax revenues and accumulation of goods bound for central cities, and the time of recognition of zaikatachō as indicative of a growing commerce funneled into jōkamachi. The Ch'ing rulers reaffirmed Peking as the capital, adopted no new strategies for controlling resources, and permitted a steady rate of commercial expansion concentrated around rising regional cities. They provided stability, but little direction. The Tokugawa rulers provided both stability and direction. By the end of the seventeenth century their policies and the corresponding policies of daimyo had substantially transformed the urban network with which they began.

Structure of Peking and Edo

The establishment of a city at the site of Peking predates imperial China. For centuries this location was the administrative center of a preimperial state and later a chou. From the late T'ang period Peking gained prominence as the seat of a governor-general, as the Liao dynasty capital known as Yen-ching, as the twelfth century Chin dynasty capital, as a Mongol center and finally from 1264 as the capital of the empire established by Kubla Khan. Although in the early Ming period the walls of the former Yuan national capital were reduced to dimensions appropriate for a sheng city, they were quickly rebuilt with an imposing perimeter of roughly fifteen miles when Emperor Yung-lo decided to return the capital to Peking. More than a century later a three-sided wall was added, adjoining the south side of the existing rectangular city. The earlier and larger north city became known as the Inner City and the newly built walled area was called the Outer City. By the mid-sixteenth century the form which was to persist through the Ch'ing period was clear.

In contrast to cities in the south of China where city plans were often irregular, the outline of Peking was symmetrical. The Inner City formed a rectangle with nine gates. Bounded by a wall of about two-thirds the perimeter of the Inner City's wall, the Outer City stretched somewhat longer from east to west, but was much shorter

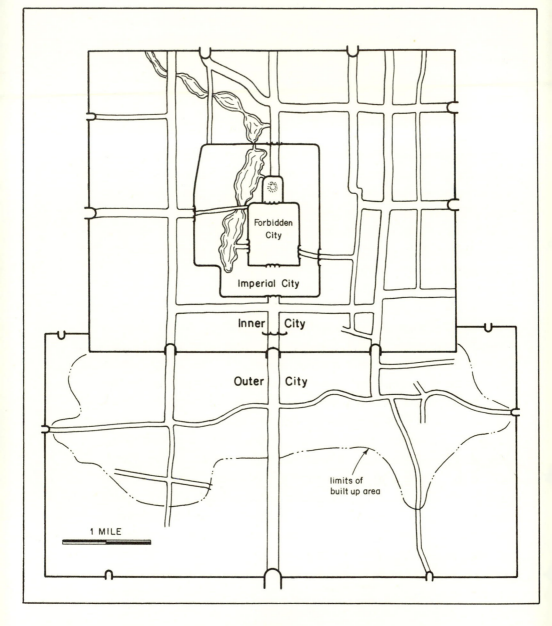

Forbidden City

Imperial City

Inner City

Outer City

limits of
built up area

1 MILE

PEKING

from north to south. Seven gates cut the wall of the Outer City in addition to the three gates leading through the wall shared with the Inner City. Inside the Inner City were two additional rectangular walled "cities." Measuring about six miles in perimeter with six gates was the Imperial City and located within it was the two-mile wall with four gates of the Forbidden City.

The four walled areas of Peking were further divided for administrative purposes. According to the T'ien fu kuang chi, written about 1670, Peking was divided into five ch'eng (cities), four of which were found in the Inner City and only one of which stood beyond the south gates in the Outer City.[3] The south ch'eng contained six of the thirty-four fang (wards) of the city. Similarly an early nineteenth century Russian translation of a 1788 Chinese description of Peking refers to five ch'eng, but places all of them in the Inner City and counts a total of thirty-six fang.[4] These were divisions for the purpose of maintaining order in the city, resembling those given for other cities in Chapter 5.

Next to walls, streets were the most prominent boundaries within Chinese cities. The main streets of Peking were straight and wide, many leading to the more than twenty gates of the four walled "cities." More than 1,000 dusty lanes, most called *hu-t'ung*, crisscrossed the areas between the tens of main streets.

Slightly less than 10 percent of the area within the Inner and Outer Cities was located inside the Imperial and Forbidden Cities. Subdivided into symmetrical districts which made up the central palace grounds, the Forbidden City included an eastern area of temples and the palace of the heir and a western area with administrative offices for the affairs of court and with palaces for the ladies of the court. Many open spaces were preserved within this walled city for the few, privileged inhabitants. Three times the size of the Forbidden City, the Imperial City contained many administrative offices and the residences of officials. Figures from 1851 list the population within the Imperial City as 8,966 regular households plus 1,081 households of p'u-hu or shopkeepers.[5] An additional 72 people were cited as dwelling in temples. Assuming a high ratio of population to households (more than 5:1 due to exceptional numbers of concubines and servants) and that some residents remained uncounted, I would estimate that the total residing in the Imperial City may have reached as high as 60,000.

The same source for 1851 gives the population for the rest of the Inner City as 67,477 regular households, 14,252 p'u-hu, and 794 temple dwellers. The ratio of residential households to p'u-hu was 19:4 in this area in contrast to 33:4 inside the Imperial City; stores were more widespread in the Inner City. The Inner City was divided into twenty-four residential zones, one for each of the banners. Most densely populated were the eight locales of Manchu bannermen, containing about 36,000 of the residential households and half of the p'u-hu. Mongol bannermen also lived in locales which were more populous than the areas designated for the eight Chinese banners. Although the p'u-hu consisted overwhelmingly of Chinese (bannermen could not switch into merchant or artisan activities), the Chinese were clearly in the minority in the Inner City. Probably no more than 40 percent of the 400,000 to 500,000 residents were Chinese. Figures from 1911 reveal that in the entire city of Peking 55 to 60 percent of residents were Chinese (the Han ethnic majority), 25 percent were Manchus and the remainder were mostly Moslems and Mongols.[6]

The Inner City, known as the Tartar city, was the location from 1644 of all Manchus and nearly all Mongols in Peking. These ethnic groups were divided according to their banner registrations, designated by colors. Chinese, Manchu, and Mongol bannermen whose standard was yellow were grouped in the north of the Inner City, while those with a blue standard resided in the south. Men in the same company resided together within the area designated for their banner. Altogether, fewer than two-thirds but probably more than one-half the 116,000 bannermen in China resided in Peking's Inner City. Together with their families, they formed a majority of the population in the Inner City and approximately 30 percent of the population in nineteenth century Peking.

The Outer City was known as the Chinese city. Land in the southeast and southwest portions was not built up, but the north-central area along the wall shared with the Inner City was undoubtedly the most densely populated area in Peking. This was the commercial center where thousands of small shops lined countless intersecting streets. Merchant and artisan households lived in the back of their stores and many peddlers and hired laborers rented lodgings in the crowded courtyards. Although I know of no enumeration of the Outer City's population before the last decade of the Ch'ing period, it is possible that its three to four square miles of densely settled commercial areas were as crowded as the chō in Edo, in which approximately 150,000 people snuggled into a square mile. In both Peking and Edo primitive means of transportation required a densely settled urban population. At the very least, the Outer City contained 300,000 inhabitants and it is likely that the actual total reached in excess of 450,000 or 500,000 if densities in built-up areas were comparable to those in Edo.

An enumeration of lattice gates in eighteenth century Peking is suggestive about the distribution of streets within the city. Of 1,735 railings which were used to close streets at night, 1,099 were located in the Inner City, 196 in the Imperial City, and 440 in the Outer City.[7] Since Hsü-chou fu city in Kiangsu held 63 railings and its population was correspondingly about one-thirtieth of the total in Peking and Hung-ya hsien city in Szechwan held 14 railings with a much smaller population than in Hsü-chou, we can surmise that the number of railings as well as the number of streets provides a rough indication of population.[8] Correspondingly the Shun-t'ien fu chih of 1885 listed about 1,350 streets in Peking, of which 25 to 30 percent were situated in the Outer City.[9]

From another perspective Peking can be seen as a complex of 60,000 to 70,000 courtyards. A map of the city published around 1750, the *Ch'ien-lung Ching-ch'eng t'u*, shows every street in exceptional detail.[10] The 187 full pages of the map capture the shape of individual blocks and courtyards, together providing a panorama of Peking at a scale of 650:1. Approximately 50,000 courtyards are visible in the Inner City and 16,000 in the Outer City. The number of households in each courtyard varied, making it difficult to estimate the city's residents from the map. Yet, a clue is given in the following description of Chinese cities in an eighteenth century collection of accounts by Western travelers. "The city buildings are of brick, neat and well adorned, but the houses low, chiefly one, at most two stories high, but commonly of such length and depth as to contain

3, 4, 5 or 6 families."[11] If the mean number of households per court-yard had been four and the mean number of household members had also been four, then the population of Peking would have num-bered about 1 million. More likely, courtyards in the Inner City had fewer households than those in the Outer City. The large num-ber of temporary male migrants was concentrated in the Outer City.

Data on two kinds of commercial activities suggest the great wealth consumed in Peking. In 1744 there were about 700 pawn-brokers in the city, a figure more than five times the total for all of Cheng-ting fu, as indicated in Table 15.[12] Also Peking held almost 400 hui-kuan, nearly all of which were located in the Outer City. These numerous organizations provided a form of self-government on the basis of common places of origin and common occupations as well. In the *Ching-shih fang-hsiang chih*, dating from about 1900, the hui-kuan meeting halls were listed by street.[13] Dividing the Outer City into five areas, the authors showed that there were few hui-kuan in the northern and eastern areas, about 100 in the western and central areas together, and more than 200 in the built-up portion of the southern part of the Outer City. Hui-kuan tended to be lo-cated in relatively sparsely populated areas of Peking. Although many of the hui-kuan in Peking joined officials from a single area, others resembled those elsewhere with predominantly commercial activities centering on the long-distance movement of certain goods. Hui-kuan served as an important means of integrating outsiders, whether officials or merchants and artisans, into the life of a distant and often foreign city.

Edo was divided into three administrative jurisdictions. The ap-proximately two-thirds of the city reserved for residences of buke can for the most part be encompassed by drawing a semicircle with a radius of two and one-half miles in a westwardly direction from south of the castle to north of it.[14] Another large area of buke resi-dences developed across the Sumidagawa river to the northeast. Similar to Peking's Inner City in population and in size, the buke areas of Edo were even more predominantly residential. Although in the early Ch'ing period efforts to segregate bannermen were some-what successful, by the eighteenth century Chinese merchants and artisans had entered the Inner City in increasing numbers. By con-

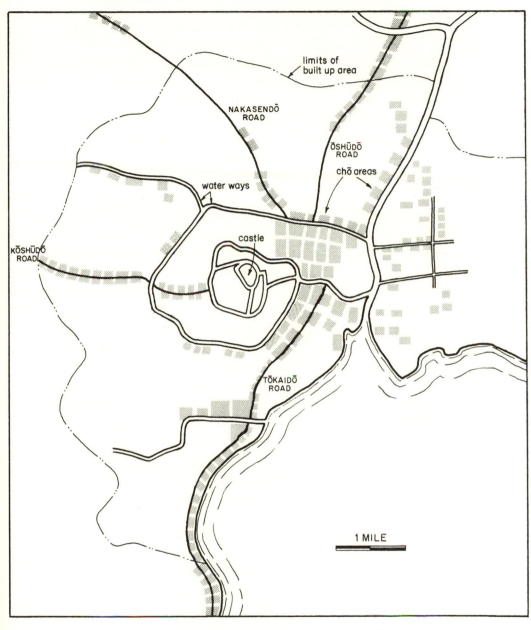

EDO

trast, the principle of segregated classes was applied more strictly and maintained longer in Edo. As in the Inner City, most of the population in buke areas lived under military discipline with ascribed statuses supported by stipends and salaries. The more than 1,000 estates of daimyo and buke directly under the Tokugawa shogun resembled the companies of 100 bannermen clustered together in Peking. In both cities the density of these large residential neighborhoods was approximately 40,000 per square mile.

Containing fewer than five square miles, the approximately 1,700 chō of Edo were densely packed. Not only was the density of residence four times that of the buke areas and ten times that of the 20 percent of Edo allocated to temple lands, but land use in the chō was highly mixed. Shops and residences were combined in a single dwelling. Within a chō it was prestigious to occupy a street front, resulting in the back alleyways being left for poor servants, peddlers, and hired labor.

Enumerations of chōnin begun in 1721 fluctuated within 10 percent of the initial figure of 501,000.[15] The average number of residents per chō was about 300. Altogether there were 5,000 to 10,000 blocks into which chō were divided. They were separated only by narrow, dusty roads as in Peking. Some wider main streets formed radials through the city. As in Peking's Outer City, migration in and out of the chō was frequent.

The 1 million residents of Edo can be roughly divided into about 35-40 percent buke, 50-55 percent chōnin, 5 percent servants, 2-3 percent temple and shrine personnel, and fewer than 2 percent eta and hinin. These last lowly classes had a form of self-administration and residential segregation independent of the three main administrative divisions of Edo. The temple and shrine areas contained other inhabitants beside those who served these religious institutions, but compared to other parts of the city they were sparsely populated and were mostly located near the perimeter of the city.

In some respects Edo and Peking were remarkably similar. Built-up areas in both cities covered about twenty square miles, of which less than one-fourth was a combination of commercial and residential with up to 150,000 inhabitants per square mile. More than 60 percent of each city was less densely settled, predominantly residential in land use. Temples in Peking and Edo enclosed much of the cities' open spaces. Some of the more than 1,000 religious dwellings in Peking contained within their walls considerable green belts. Both cities had many residents who identified with their places of origin and were organized accordingly. Moreover, both cities maintained the administrative and economic centers and most other characteristics of the city plan which existed in the seventeenth century. As renowned centers of military and administrative forces, Peking and Edo were distinguished for high levels of consumption, but not for items exported to other cities. In population, land use, and distribution of social classes as well as in the principal urban activities Peking and Edo resembled each other.

Since Peking and Edo were exceptionally dependent on supplies from distant areas of their respective countries and on migration from all areas of their respective countries, it is imperative to view these cities not just as separate entities, but also as part of the city systems of China and Japan.

Peking, Edo, and Systems of Cities

Peking and Edo were similar in total population and in other respects, but they differed in the ways in which the various parts of the city were brought together. Contributing to the great size of Peking were four principal ingredients: the banner system; the examination system; the bureaucracy; and the movement in and out of commercial population. Contributing to the great size of Edo were at least three basic ingredients: the system requiring that nearly all who received stipends from lands directly administered by the Bakufu must live in Edo; the sankin kōtai system; and the movement in and out of commercial population. Comparing the permanent residents, the bannermen in Peking and the hatamoto and gokenin in Edo, we find that the former numbered about three times the latter. Yet, the sankin kōtai system of alternate residences raised the population in Edo's primarily residential areas to the total in the Inner City, which included officials and examination candidates in temporary residence as well as shopkeepers' families. Temporary residence played a more substantial role in Edo, an indication of the closer ties between the city and its country.

Japan with only about 8 percent as many settlements and 10 percent as many people as China in 1800 produced a city as large as Peking. The explanation lies in the fact that Edo had a different part in the total city system of its country and that the city system in Japan was more centralized than the one in China. The sankin kōtai system brought Edo not only large numbers of representatives from each area of Japan, but also—in part through Osaka—resources from the entire country. Whereas nearly all hsien cities were located inland and Chinese marketing areas are best described as concentric circles focusing inward, at least those centered on central places from levels 4 to 7, many han cities faced toward the sea as windows to Osaka and Edo. A comparison of level 4 cities reveals that Japanese cities were more outward looking, favored by more advantageous situations.

The stability of Tokugawa society rested on a distribution of men and resources in which the role of the cities was explicitly planned. The three principal cities differed in the clear separation of their primary activities. In Edo were located the organs of the Bakufu government, directly administering one-fifth of the country and overseeing the daimyo lords of the remainder. Effective control against usurpation was maintained through the sankin kōtai system. In Osaka occurred the major financial transactions of Japan. Here more than 20 percent of the rice taxes of the various han were converted into cash. Kyoto was a craft center best known as the seat of the emperor and the small band of aristocrats who served him. The principal administrative, commercial, and court functions were divided among these three great cities.

At the local level the efficient accumulation of resources was facilitated by removing the elite from villages, requiring about 80 percent of bushi to live with their families in the han jōkamachi or in Edo. Moreover in a given han the requirement that there could be only one jōkamachi provided a clear seat of authority. Denied unauthorized sources of revenue, bushi were restricted to fixed stipends, often in return for administrative services. By mobilizing their rural elite and converting them into an urban elite, the Japanese gained effective control of resources both through taxes in kind and through commerce. The sankin kōtai insured Edo's position at the center of resource accumulation as opposed to the examination system, which only insured Peking's centrality in a loosely controlled hierarchy of hsien and sheng.

Peking and Edo in Regional and National Context

Peking and Edo were both located in the northeast of their countries at a time when advanced premodern marketing had already appeared. Their locations were removed from the centers of marketing. Particularly in northern Chihli periodic markets were not numerous. Moreover, Peking lacked water transportation ties in all directions except southeast through T'ung chou and Tientsin. The limits of areas substantially dependent on Peking can be identified as the outer fringes of the hinterlands of the three closest level 3a cities, excluding Tientsin which was closely tied by water to the capital. To the west T'ai-yuan extended its commercial influence to the Chihli border. To the south, K'ai-feng dominated almost all of northern Honan. And to the southeast, Lin-ch'ing's sphere of marketing importance reached across the south of Chihli. Peking was confined to an area including most of Chihli, with a population below 20 million, perhaps as low as 15 million. Peking's base for local support included only about 5 percent of the population of China and the base was difficult to tap.

Edo also was flanked by three level 3a cities: Sendai, Nagoya, and Kanazawa. Since the trading influence of these cities did not extend far beyond their han boundaries, a vacuum existed in the Tōhoku and Chūbu regions which was filled by the extension of Edo's commercial sphere. The han system made inter-han ties fragile, promoting the dependence of cities at levels 3b and 4 directly on Edo. Good transportation ties enhanced Edo's centrality. Altogether at least 7 million and, perhaps, as many as 10 million people provided direct local support to Edo. Thus, approximately 25 percent of Japan served as a relatively easy base to tap for supplies to Edo.

Cities were distributed quite evenly over the Inner Provinces of China and over the three main islands of Japan. Every region of China had at least one level 2 city and every region of Japan except the small island of Shikoku had at least one level 3a city. The proportion of urban residents living in levels 1 to 3b in North China was close to the average for all of China. The number of Japanese in levels 1 to 3b in East Japan was about the same as in West Japan, much higher than in most regions of China. Distant areas of Japan were contributing more to the support of Edo's huge population than were comparable areas of China contributing to the support of Peking. Whether we compare the immediate hinterlands of Kantō and Chihli, the regions of East Japan and North China or the nations as a whole, the differences always point to the greater support given to Edo than to Peking. The combination of these three advantageous situations enabled Edo to reach a population equal to that of Peking despite the fact that the Kantō area was only one-fourth of Chihli in population, that East Japan was only one-sixth of North China in population and that all of Japan was only one-tenth to one-twelfth of China in population.

From the Far East to the World

Population data, however inadequate, are one of our best clues to comparing societies. Generally speaking, the world human population has risen consistently from at least the last millennia B.C. From a likely total of fewer than 20 million at the time when cities originated, the world population had climbed to more than 900 million by A.D. 1800. Several hundred million of the increase apparently occurred in the last two or three centuries before 1800.

During the centuries after premodern cities were first formed and before the upswing in the Industrial Revolution around 1800, at least 20 percent and, perhaps, as many as 25 percent of the cumulative world population had lived in China during its 3,600 years of urban history. Japan contributed an additional 1 percent of the world's total during its 1,100 year urban history. As the total population in China and Japan had increased, the proportion urban-to-rural had also risen. Roughly speaking, in the ancient stage 1-2 percent were urban, in the early imperial stage 3-4 percent were urban, in the middle imperial and feudal stage 5 percent were urban, and in the late imperial and Sengoku stage 6-7 percent were urban. Then in the Ch'ing and Tokugawa period a striking gap opened up between China and Japan; the former remained at the 6-7 percent level, while the latter climbed above 16 percent.

Preliminary estimates of urban development elsewhere might begin with data for 1800. According to Kingsley Davis, of the world's 900 million inhabitants, 2.4 percent lived in cities of 20,000 or more and 1.7 percent lived in cities of 100,000 or more.[16] In other words, 22 million and 15 million lived in cities at these respective sizes. Yet, in China and Japan alone 13-14 million probably lived in cities meeting the 20,000 criterion and 9 million in cities meeting the 100,000 minimum. Undoubtedly Kingsley Davis' totals are too low, but even so they suggest that China and Japan together approached or exceeded half of the world's urban totals at these levels. Using my definition of urban (levels 1-5 plus ½ of level 6), I would tentatively estimate that world urban inhabitants in 1800 totaled 55 to 65 million, of whom nearly 25 million lived in China and Japan.

It is interesting to note that in 1800 nearly two-thirds of the world's population lived in Asia and an additional 20 percent lived in Europe. Half of the Asian population lived in China, 5 percent lived in Japan and about 30 percent lived in India. Of the European total the Russian Empire held over 15 percent and France was second with 12 percent. If we add the tens of millions in the Ottoman Empire, these six countries together contained roughly two-thirds of the world's inhabitants. Any comparison of late premodern societies should begin with an awareness of the concentration of people in a small number of large-scale countries.

Moving back in time, we find that the world population in 1650 is estimated at 550 million. Of these 60 percent were Asians and 18 percent were Europeans. Although China and Japan contributed somewhat less proportionately than in 1800, they still encompassed approximately 30 percent of the world figure. If the world's urban total already had reached the same proportion of the total as in 1800, an unlikely assumption given the changes in such European countries as Russia and France in the interim, then about 35 million would have lived in cities. Presumably the actual figure was closer to 30 million, in which case China and Japan again would have stood out with two-fifths of the total.

As the world population rose from tens to hundreds of millions, the number of urban dwellers rose from less than one million to tens of millions. Most likely the proportion urban was rising gradually over 3,000 years from less than 1 percent to 6-7 percent in 1800. By identifying the percentage urban in any society and changes in the figure over time, we should be able to compare these figures with the world average and with the specific situations in China and Japan. Did other countries gain steadily from 1 percent to 6 percent in city inhabitants as new levels of cities were added? Obviously most countries did not, if the world figures for 1800 are correct. If some countries did, can their rates of change be compared with the cases studied here? Or in countries which did not have as many as 6 percent of their people in cities was there still an observable process of adding new levels? Perhaps, in nonrice growing areas lower percentages characterized the same processes of adding new levels.

In China and Japan at least 40 percent of all city inhabitants prior to 1850 lived after 1600. Did this pattern prevail elsewhere? If so, can a stage in development similar to the Ch'ing and Tokugawa periods be singled out in other societies? If graphs similar to those on p. xv can be drawn to spatially represent other advanced premodern societies, then we should be able to determine whether they are similar to the figure for China or to the one for Japan. Similarly observations of administrative divisions, marketing patterns, and regional variations should provide a context for comparing one society with another. It is time to refine the techniques developed for comparing China and Japan by carrying out more detailed work on local areas in these two countries and by extending the comparisons to other premodern societies.

GLOSSARY

Frequently used terms referring to China (C) or Japan (J)
(Chinese and Japanese terms can signify either singular or plural)

Bakufu (J)	Government under a shogun; the central authorities
Bannermen (C)	Privileged warrior elite, including many Manchus and Mongols
Buke (J)	Samurai family; members of warrior households
Bushi (J)	Samurai; a warrior
Chen (C)	Nonadministrative city
Ch'eng (C)	City or the wall of a city
Chieh (C)	Main street
Chih-li chou (C)	Administrative unit; a directly administered department
Chō (J)	Commercial area of a city
Chōbu (J)	Unit of land measurement; 1 chōbu = 2.5 acres
Chōnin (J)	Resident in a chō; usually merchants and artisans
Chou (C)	Administrative unit; a department
Chün (C)	Administrative unit prior to the Ch'ing period
Daikan (J)	Official directly administering local areas
Daimyo (J)	Lord; the ruler of a domain or han
Eta (J)	Pariah or outcaste
Fang (C)	Ward; a subdivision of a city
Fu (C)	Administrative unit; a prefecture
Gokenin (J)	Bushi, an inferior personal retainer of the shogun
Gun (J)	Subadministrative unit; a territorial division
Han (J)	Domain or fief
Hatamoto (J)	Bushi, a superior personal retainer of the shogun
Hinin (J)	Outcaste, pariah

Hsiang (C)	1. Section of a city
	2. Local area as t'ung-hsiang, from the same hsien
	3. Alley or a minor street
Hsien (C)	Administrative unit; district or county
Hui-kuan (C)	*Landsmannschaften*; an organization of men from the same local area
I (C)	Post station; a stop along a major road
Jōkamachi (J)	Castle city or castle town; a domain administrative center
Koku (J)	Measure of rice harvest; unit of account
Kokufu (J)	Pre-Tokugawa local administrative center
Kuan (C)	1. A unit of currency
	2. A built-up area just outside the city wall
Kuan-lu (C)	National highway; the highest classification of roads
Kuge (J)	Aristocrat; court noble
Kuni (J)	Territorial division; originally an administrative unit
Li (C)	1. Unit of measurement, roughly 550 yards
	2. Official division of a hsien or chou
Lu (C)	1. Pre-Ch'ing administrative unit; a province
	2. Division of a fu, a chou or a hsien; a way
Mawari (J) (Chimawari)	Route, way; such as eastern route, western route
Monzenmachi (J)	Town associated with a temple; literally in front of a temple gate
Mou (C)	Unit of land measurement; 16 mou = 2.5 acres
Pao-chia (C)	System of enumerating households; pao and chia are official divisions of local areas
Pen chou (C)	Administrative unit; the non-hsien area of a chih-li chou
P'u (C)	Road-side station; minor in comparison to "I" above
P'u-hu (C)	Shopkeeper household
Sankin kōtai (J)	System of alternate residence in Edo
Sheng (C)	Administrative unit; a province
Shōen (J)	Manor; estate often consisting of many villages
Shogun (J)	The commander or principal official of the central government
Tao (C)	Pre-Ch'ing administrative unit; province
Tenryō (J)	Land under direct control of the central government

Tonya (J)	Organization of merchants
Uji (J)	Union of people through kinship or fictive kinship ties
Ya tax (C)	Broker tax
Yü (C)	Section of a city
Zaikatachō (J)	Nonadministrative city

NOTES

NOTES TO GENERAL INTRODUCTION

1. Subfields such as sociological theory, comparative sociology, historical sociology, and social change are sweepingly broad in name and frequently overlapping in content. Here I have in mind a body of studies concerned with identifying stages of societal development in the tradition of Karl Marx and Max Weber.

2. The area of urban research known as "central place" studies is primarily concerned with networks of cities. The central place approach has been extensively applied to 20th century societies, but rarely to earlier ones. G. William Skinner's application of this approach to China (see Chapter 3 below) is one of the few treatments of an earlier society thus far undertaken.

3. Kingsley Davis estimates that in the year 1800, 2.4 percent of the world's population lived in cities of 20,000 or more. See "The Origin and Growth of Urbanization in the World," *American Journal of Sociology* 60 (March 1955), 133. His estimate is undoubtedly too low.

NOTES TO CHAPTER 1

1. See Chang Kwang-chih, *The Archaeology of Ancient China* (Yale University Press, New Haven, 1968), 256-351, for an account of archaeological and textual information concerning the development of ancient Chinese cities. Also see Paul Wheatley, *The Pivot of the Four Quarters: A Preliminary Enquiry into the Origins and Character of the Ancient Chinese City* (Aldine Press, Chicago, 1971), a work which explores the view that the ceremonial center which evolved in Shang China and elsewhere was a necessary stage in the evolution of cities in general.

2. Chang Kwang-chih, "Towns and Cities in Ancient China," 19; an unpublished paper prepared for the 1968 conference on Urban Society in Traditional China, Wentworth-by-the-Sea, New Hampshire.

3. At the same conference Arthur F. Wright discussed the centrality of Chinese cities in forming an orderly empire, emphasizing the nature and significance of the ritualized layout of Chinese cities. His paper entitled, "The Cosmology of the Chinese City," will appear in *The City in Late Imperial China*, ed., G. William Skinner (Stanford University Press, Stanford, forthcoming).

4. Chang Kwang-chih, *Towns and Cities in Ancient China*, 5-8.

5. For discussions of the changing form of the city in ancient China see the various articles by Miyazaki Ichisada: "Chūgoku jōkaku no kigen isetsu" [Hypothesis on the origin of the inner and outer cities in China], *Ajiashi Kenkyū* 1 (Kyoto University, Tōyōshi Kenkyūkai, 1957), 50-65: "Chūgoku Jōdai wa hokensei ka toshi kokka ka?" [Was the Shang Period in China a feudal system or a time of city-states] *Ajiashi Kenkyū* 3 (1963), 63-86; and "Sengoku jidai no toshi" [Cities of the Warring States period], *Tōhōgaku Ronshū* (Tōhōgakkai, Tokyo, 1962), 342-57.

6. See Hsü Cho-yun, *Ancient China in Transition: An Analysis of Social Mobility, 722-222 B.C.* (Stanford University Press, Stanford, 1965).

7. Chang Sen-dou examines the development of hsien cities in "The Chinese Hsien Capital: A Study in Historical Urban Geography," a dissertation at the University of Washington in 1961, and in his article "Historical Trend of Chinese Urbanization," *Annals of the Association of American Geographers* 53:2 (June 1963), 109-43.

8. Cities of the Warring States period are discussed by Gotō Kimpei, "Wang Ts'ai Ch'eng chou k'ao" [On Ch'eng Chou, the metropolis of the Chou dynasty], *Tōyōgakuhō* 44:3 (December 1961), 36-60.

9. See F. W. Mote, *Intellectual Foundations of China* (Alfred A. Knopf, New York, 1971), 29-52.

10. Arthur F. Wright describes all of these activities in "The Cosmology of the Chinese City."

11. Yazaki Takeo, *Social Change and the City in Japan: From Earliest Times Through the Industrial Revolution* (Japan Publications, Inc., Tokyo, 1968), 3-10. This book was originally published in Japanese as *Nihon toshi no hatten katei* (Marubundō, Tokyo, 1962). The ancient period is also described by Kawahara Tairō and Kikuura Sugeo in *Nihon shōgyō hatten-shi* [History of the development of Japanese commerce] (Tokyo, 1960), 1-24.

12. Yazaki Takeo, *Social Change and the City in Japan*, 32-33.

13. See Watanabe Eisaburō, "Kodai Nihon ni okeru toshi no hattatsu" [The development of cities in ancient Japan], *Toshi Mondai* 48:8 (August 1957), 944-52, and 49:5 (May 1958), 546-54. Early planned cities are also described in *Shūraku chiri kōsa II: hattatsu to kōsō* [Examination of settlement geography: development and plan] (Chōsō shoten, Tokyo, 1957), jointly edited by Kiuchi Shinzo, Fujioka Kenjirō, and Yajima Ninkichi.

14. Chang Sen-dou discusses when hsien capitals were founded in "Some Aspects of the Urban Geography of the Chinese Hsien Capital," *Annals of the Association of American Geographers*, 51:1 (March 1961), 23-45.

15. For a discussion of Han Ch'ang-an and other cities in early imperial China see Miyazaki Ichisada, "Les Villes en Chine a l'époque des Han," *T'oung Pao* 48 (1960), 376-92 and "Rokucho jidai Kahoku no toshi" [Cities of Six Dynasties North China], *Tōyōshi Kenkyū* 20:2 (March 1962), 53-74. The population figure of 250,000 is also given in Fujimoto Eijirō, *Chūgoku keizaishi* [Chinese economic history] (Hōritsu Bunkasha, Kyoto, 1967), 38.

16. See Utsunomiya Kiyoyoshi, *Kandai shakai keizaishi kenkyū* [Study of the social and economic history of the Han period] (Marubundō, Tokyo, 1955), especially 107-40. Although Utsunomiya's estimate that 30 percent of

the Chinese lived in cities seems far too high, his statement on 116-17 that the 11 largest cities of Han China contained about 2 percent of the total population is credible.

17. Descriptions of Han period city plans are included in Arthur F. Wright's "The Cosmology of the Chinese City."

18. See John W. Hall, "The Traditional Japanese City," an unpublished paper presented at the conference on Urban Society in Traditional China.

19. Kuramochi Tokuichirō, "Shina toshi hattatsu no gaikan: kenkyū seika o chūshin to shite" [A general view of the development of Chinese cities: centering on the results of studies], Rekishigaku Kenkyū 7:11 (November 1937), 213-28. After reviewing conflicting Japanese viewpoints about ancient Chinese cities, Kuramochi discusses urban development during the centuries prior to the reunification of China in 583. He notes that early capital cities were quickly reduced to villages when abandoned by rulers, an indication of their enormous dependence on administrative activities; however, rising commercial exchange between the Han and T'ang periods was finally permitting prosperity even in places without the advantages of a capital city. Another description of Chinese urban history between the fourth and seventh centuries can be found in Shida Fudōmaro, "Shina toshi hattatsu shi no hito shaku" [A sketch of the history of Chinese city development], Rekishigaku Kenkyū 1:1 (1933), 10-18.

20. Two writings of the mid-1960s relate exceptional details on Lo-yang: Ho Ping-ti, "Lo-yang, A.D. 495-534," Harvard Journal of Asiatic Studies (1966), 52-101, and Hattori Katsuhiko, Hokugi Rakuyō no shakai to bunka [The society and culture of Northern Wei Lo-yang] (Mineruva, Tokyo, 1965).

21. See Tada Kenkai, "Kandai no chihō shōgyō ni tsuite: gozoku to konomin no kankei o chūshin ni" [Han period local commerce: centering on the relations of wealthy families and small farmers], Shichō 92 (July 1965), 36-49.

22. Divisions within T'ang cities are described by Hino Kaisaburō, "Tōdai jōyo no 'fang, shih no chiao, yü'" (Fang, shih, chiao, and yü in the cities of the T'ang period), Tōyōgakuhō 47:3 (December 1964), 1-34.

23. See Arthur F. Wright, "Symbolism and Function: Reflections on Ch'ang-an and Other Great Cities," Journal of Asian Studies 24 (August 1965), 667-79.

24. Yazaki Takeo, Social Change and the City in Japan, 34.

25. Figures for Ch'ang-an, as for most large cities in Chinese history, vary markedly. Figures substantially in excess of 1 million may include people living at some distance from the city.

26. John W. Hall, "The Traditional Japanese City," 17.

27. Descriptions of cities in the Ritsuryō period can be found in Fujioka Kenjirō, Toshi to kōtsūro no rekishi chirigakuteki kenkyū [An historical geographical study of cities and traffic routes] (Ōmeido, Tokyo, 1960), and in Asaka Yukio, ed., Nihon no rekishi chiri [Historical geography of Japan] (Ōmeido, Tokyo, 1966), 34-42.

28. John W. Hall, "The Traditional Japanese City," 19.

29. Kawahara Tairō and Kikuura Sugeo, *Nihon shōgyō hattenshi*, 36.

30. My interest in the declining ability of Chinese leaders to order cities was aroused by F. W. Mote, who discussed this topic in "The Transformation of Nanking, 1350-1400," a paper presented at the conference on Urban Society in Traditional China, and to appear in *The City in Late Imperial China*.

31. This trend has been mentioned by Katō Shigeshi in a number of articles, including three in his collection, *Shina keizaishi kōshō* [Studies in the economic history of China] (Tōyōbunko, Tokyo, 1952-53): "Sōdai ni okeru toshi no hattatsu ni tsuite" [Concerning the development of cities in the Sung period], I, 299-346; "Tō Sō jidai no ichi" [Markets of the T'ang and Sung periods], I, 347-86; and "Tō Sō jidai no soshi oyobi sono hatten" [Ts'ao markets of the T'ang and Sung periods and their development], I, 387-421. More recently Denis Twitchett has written on the same topic, "The T'ang Market System," *Asia Major* (1966), 202-48.

32. Information on the city in the tenth century can be found in T'ao Hsi-sheng, "Wu-tai ti tu-shih yü shang-yeh" [Cities and commerce in the Five Dynasties period], *Shih Hua* 1:10 (1935), 31-35.

33. See Aoyama Sadao, *Tō Sō jidai no kōtsū to chishi chizu no kenkyū* [Study of the communications systems and local maps of the T'ang and Sung periods] (Yoshikawa kōbunkan, Tokyo, 1963). An older book in Chinese on historic communications is Po Shou-i, *Chung-kuo chiao-t'ung shih* [History of Chinese communications] (Chung-kuo wen-hua tseng-shu, Shang wu-yin shu-kuan, 1937).

34. Discussion of Sung commercial taxes can be found in the following sources: (1) Étienne Balazs, "Une Carte Économique de la Chine au XIᵉ Siècle," *Annales Économies, Sociétés, Civilisations* 12:4 (October-December 1957), 587-93 (2) Katō Shigeshi, "Tō Sō jidai no soshi oyobi sono hatten"; (3) Kawakami Kōichi, *Sōdai no keizai seikatsu* [Economic life of the Sung period] (Yurasha bunkashi senshū: Yoshikawa kōbunkan, Tokyo, 1966), especially Chapter 6, 235-90, "The development of commerce and city life"; (4) Lawrence J. C. Ma, *Commercial Development and Urban Change in Sung China (960-1279)* (Michigan Geographical Publications, Ann Arbor, 1971); (5) Meng Wen-t'ung, "Ts'ung Sung-tai ti shang-shui ho ch'eng-shih k'an Chung-kuo feng-chien she-hui ti tzu-jan ching-chi" [To observe the natural economy of Chinese feudal society from commercial taxes and cities of the Sung period], *Li-shih Yen-chiu* 4 (1961), 45-52; and (6) E. P. Stuzhina, "Problems of the economic and social structure of the city and of craft production in China during the xıth-xıııth centuries in contemporary historiography," *Istoriographiia Stran Vostoka* (Moscow University Press, Moscow, 1969), 343-76.

35. Lawrence J. C. Ma, *Commercial Development and Urban Change in Sung China (960-1279)*, 67-69.

36. Kawakami Kōichi, *Sōdai no keizai seikatsu*, 242-43.

37. Katō Shigeshi, "Tō Sō jidai no soshi oyobi sono hatten," 399-404.

38. *Ibid.*

39. Meng Wen-t'ung, "Ts'ung Sung-tai ti shang-shui ho ch'eng-shih k'an Chung-kuo feng-chien she-hui ti tzu-jan ching-chi," 47.

40. See Robert Hartwell, "A Cycle of Economic Change in Imperial China: Coal and Iron in Northeast China, 750-1350," *Journal of the Social and Economic History of the Orient* 10:1 (July 1967), 102-55.

41. On the structure of cities during the Five Dynasties and Sung periods see Kuramochi Tokuichirō, "Shina toshi hattatsu no gaikan: kenkyū seika o chūshin to shite," 229-33.

42. See another article by Kuramochi Tokuichirō, "Min Shin jidai toshi kukaku ko (1) 'yü' no kōzō to bunpu: Min Shin jidai chiishi yori mitaru" [A treatise on urban divisions in the Ming and Ch'ing periods (1) the structure and distribution of "yü": as seen from Ming and Ch'ing period gazetteers], *Nihon Daigaku Shigakkai Kenkyū Ihō* 4 (December 1960), 1-18.

43. Shiba Yoshinobu, *Sōdai shōgyōshi kenkyū* [Commercial activities during the Sung dynasty] (Kazama shobō, Tokyo, 1968). Shiba's main chapter on cities was also published as "10-13 seiki ni okeru Chūgoku toshi no tenkan" [Conversion of Chinese cities in the tenth to thirteenth centuries], *Sekaishi Kenkyū* 14 (January 1966), 22-37.

44. Again see Shiba Yoshinobu, *Sōdai shōgyōshi kenkyū*, chapter 3, "Sōdai ni okeru zenkokuteki shijō no keisei" [The situation of the national market in the Sung period] for a discussion of the various items involved in commerce and see later chapters for descriptions of specialized craft goods.

45. Umehara Kaoru, "Sōdai chihō kotoshi no ichimen" [One feature of small local cities in the Sung period], *Shirin* 41:6 (November 1958), 43.

46. K'ai-feng was also briefly restored as a capital during the territorial shifts of the thirteenth century.

47. Yazaki Takeo, *Social Change and the City in Japan*, 69.

48. John W. Hall, "The Traditional Japanese City," 35, referring to Watanabe Tamotsu, *Kamakura* (Tokyo, 1963), 82-83.

49. See Sasaki Ginya, "Kamakura jidai ni okeru ryōshūsei to shōgyō no kankei" [Relationship of the domain ownership system and commerce during the Kamakura period], *Rekishi Kyōiku* 7:7 (July 1959), 61-67.

50. Local exchange is discussed by Sasaki Ginya in his book, *Chūsei no shōgyō* [Commerce of the Kamakura to Sengoku periods] (Shibundō, Tokyo, 1966).

51. Self-government has been examined by Harada Tomohiko and Toyoda Takeshi. An example of the former's work is "Hōken toshi no jichi soshiki" [Self-government organizations of feudal cities], *Toshi Mondai* 48:8 (August 1957), 55-61. One of Toyoda's articles is "Higashi to Nishi hōken toshi" [Feudal cities of East and West], *Rekishi Kyōiku* 14:11 (November 1966), 1-11.

52. Nakabe Yoshiko, *Kinsei toshi no seiritsu to kōzō* [Establishment and plan of Tokugawa cities] (Shinseisha, Toyko, 1967), 15-78. Nakabe describes the relationship between the central position of Kyoto in the flow of goods during the Muromachi period and efforts by the Bakufu to strengthen its control in Kyoto.

53. Dwight H. Perkins, *Agricultural Development in China 1368-1968* (Aldine Press, Chicago, 1969).

54. Charles O. Hucker, "Governmental Organization of the Ming Dynasty,"

Harvard Journal of Asiatic Studies 21 (1958), 12-20. On Ming administration also see Charles Hucker, ed., *Chinese Government in Ming Times* (Columbia University Press, New York, 1969).

55. See Ho Ping-ti, *The Ladder of Success in Imperial China: Aspects of Mobility, 1368-1911* (Columbia University Press, Science Editions, New York, 1964).

56. I have benefited from comments by F. W. Mote and Mark Elvin on the criteria for choosing a capital in conjunction with a discussion of Mote's article, "The Transformation of Nanking, 1350-1400," at the conference on Urban Society in Traditional China.

57. The economic spurt of the late Ming is described by Fu I-ling, *Ming Ch'ing shih-tai shang-jen chi shang-yeh tzu-pen* [Merchants and commercial capital of the Ming and Ch'ing periods] (Jen-min ch'u-pan she, Peking, 1956) and by Fujii Hiroshi, "Shin-an shōnin no kenkyū" [A study of Shin-an merchants], *Tōyōgakuhō* 36 (parts 1-4, 1953-54).

58. Saeki Yuichi points to a quote from a late Ming gazetteer, which lists many of the large cities of the time. See "Mindai shōekisei no hōkai to tō kinu orimonogyō ryūtsū shijō no tenkan" [Collapse of the artisan corvée system of the Ming period and development of market circulation of the urban silk goods industry], *Tōyōbunka Kenkyūjō Kiyō* 10 (November 1956), 359-425.

59. F. W. Mote, "The Transformation of Nanking, 1350-1400."

60. See Ho Ping-ti, *Studies in the Population of China, 1368-1953* (Harvard University Press, Cambridge, 1959).

61. This change in urban consumption patterns was noted in the *K'e tzo chui yü* as quoted in the *Shou-tu chih* [Gazetteer of Nanking] (Cheng-shu shu-chu, Taipei, 1966), II, 1083-87.

62. See Chinese writings of the 1950s such as Fu I-ling, *Ming-tai Chiang-nan shih-min ching-chi shih-t'an* [Exploratory reconnaissance of urban dwellers' economy in the Ming period lower Yangtze region](Jen-min ch'u-pan she, Shanghai, 1957).

63. Matsumoto Toyotoshi, *Jōkamachi no rekishi chirigakuteki kenkyū* [Historical geographical study of castle cities] (Yoshikawa hirobunkan, Tokyo, 1967). Especially useful is part I, chapter 5: "Shoki jōkamachi ni okeru chiiki kōzō ron no sokatsu" [Summary of the explanation of the territorial plan in early castle cities].

64. Matsumoto Toyotoshi, *Jōkamachi no rekishi chirigakuteki kenkyū*, 185-86.

65. See Toyoda Takeshi, *Nihon no hōken toshi* [Feudal cities of Japan] (Iwanami shoten, Tokyo, 1968), 105-12, and also Ono Hitoshi, *Kinsei jōka-machi no kenkyū* [Study of Tokugawa period castle cities] (Kokushi kenkyū sosho, Shibundō, Tokyo, 1928).

66. Watanabe Nobuo, *Bakuhansei kakuritsuki shōhin ryūtsū* [Commercial flow at the time of the establishment of the Bakuhan system] (Hakushobō, Tokyo, 1966).

67. On the development of Japanese commerce read Sasaki Ginya, "Chūsei toshi to shōhin ryūtsū" [Cities and commercial circulation of the Kamakura to Sengoku periods], *Nihon Rekishi 8 Chūsei 4* (Iwanami kōsa, Tokyo, 1963).

68. Harada Tomohiko, *Nihon hōkentaiseika no toshi to shakai* [Cities and society in the feudal system of Japan] (Sanichi shobō, Tokyo, 1960).

69. Some principal fifteenth and sixteenth century cities are listed in Asaka Yukio, ed., *Nihon no rekishi chiri*, 50-52, in Toyoda Takeshi, *Nihon no hōken toshi*, chapter 2, and in Sekiyama Naotarō, *Nihon no jinkō* [Population of Japan] (Shibundō, Tokyo, 1966), 114-15.

70. For a general discussion of the urban policies of the three unifiers see Nakabe Yoshiko, *Kinsei toshi no seiritsu to kōzō*, 225-354.

71. See Toyoda Takeshi, *Nihon no hōken toshi*, 85-86.

72. The pattern of land distribution is discussed in Watanabe Nobuo, *Bakuhansei kakuritsuki no shōhin ryūtsū*, chapter 1.

73. See Honjō Eijirō, *Kyoto* (Shibundō, Kyoto, 1966).

74. Matsumoto Toyotoshi, *Jōkamachi no rekishi chirigakuteki kenkyū*, part 2.

75. It is possible that early Chinese cities were outposts of relatively advanced civilization, but the evidence is not conclusive.

76. In F. W. Mote, "The Transformation of Nanking, 1350-1400," Chinese capital cities are compared with other great historic capitals, which served as more dominant cultural centers of their respective countries.

77. See John W. Hall, "Foundations of the Modern Japanese Daimyo," in John W. Hall and Marius B. Jansen, *Studies in the Institutional History of Early Modern Japan* (Princeton University Press, Princeton, 1968), 65-77.

NOTES TO CHAPTER 2

1. Most data on the distribution of administrative units are taken from the *Ch'ien-lung fu t'ing chou hsien t'u-chih* [Gazetteer of fu, t'ing, chou, and hsien of the Ch'ien-lung period] (Peking, 1789).

2. Diagrams and descriptions of city plans are provided by Chang Sen-dou in "Some Observations on the Morphology of Chinese Walled Cities," *Annals of the Association of American Geographers* 60:1 (March 1970), 63-91, and in "The Morphology of Chinese Walled Cities," which will appear in *The City in Late Imperial China*.

3. See Table 5, p. 102. If the village to population ratio in Chihli province was typical, then there were about 700,000 to 900,000 settlements in China during the early nineteenth century. At that time the figure for Japan was about 65,000, as indicated in Asaka Yukio, *Nihon no rekishi chiri*, 108. Data on the number of Chinese settlements in the twentieth century as well as on the number of standard and intermediate markets are provided by G. William Skinner, "Marketing and Social Structure in Rural China," *Journal of Asian Studies* 24:1, 2 (November 1964 and February 1965).

4. Indications of actual koku figures for han throughout Japan are provided in *Mitoshi shi* [History of Mito city] (Mitoshi shi hensan iinkai, Mito, 1963) II, 64-67.

5. Sekiyama Naotarō, *Nihon no jinkō*, 102.

6. Takahashi Bonsen, *Nihon jinkōshi kenkyū* [Study of the history of the Japanese population] (Nihon gakujutsu shinkōkai, Tokyo, 1955), 4-6.

7. See *Kōtō Nihonshi seizu* [Detailed maps of Japanese history for high schools] (Teikoku shoin, Tokyo, 1968), 48.

8. Nakajima Giichi, "Ichiman koku daimyo no jōka" [Castle cities of daimyo with 10,000 koku], *Shin Chiri* 10:2 (September 1962), 4-5. Nakajima also gives examples of small jōkamachi without markets in "Keizai chiiki no keisei" [The formation of economic areas], in Asaka Yukio, ed., *Nihon no rekishi chiri*, 136.

9. John W. Hall, "The Castle Town and Japan's Modern Urbanization," in John W. Hall and Marius B. Jansen, eds., *Studies in the Institutional History of Early Modern Japan* (Princeton University Press, Princeton, 1968), 182-83.

10. Muramatsu Yūji, "Shin no naimufu shōen 'nei-wu fu tsao-sung huang-ch'an ti-mou ts'e' to shite shiryō ni tsuite" [Estates of the Ch'ing Imperial Household Registry: concerning land records as materials prepared and sent for imperial estates], *Keizaigaku Kenkyū* 12 (Hitotsubashi daigaku, 1961), 1-20.

11. *Ibid.*, 18-19.

12. See Yamori Kazuhiko, "Shōhin ryūtsū to jōkamachi" [Commercial flow and castle cities], Tsujita Usao, ed., *Sangyō chiri no shomondai* [Various problems of commercial geography] (Ryuhara shoten, Tokyo, 1964), II, 145. Also see Nakai Nobuhiko, "Edo jidai no shijō keitai ni kansuru sobyō" [A rough sketch of the Tokugawa period market structure], *Nihon Rekishi* 115 (January 1958), 76-83.

13. Dwight Perkins, *Agricultural Development in China, 1368-1968*, 16.

14. See Asaka Yukio, ed., *Nihon no rekishi chiri*, 108. A detailed discussion of underestimations of arable land is available in English by James I. Nakamura, "Growth of Japanese Agriculture, 1875-1920," in William W. Lockwood, *The State and Economic Enterprise in Japan* (Princeton University Press, Princeton, 1965), 249-324.

15. Patterns of Japanese consumption are described by Ōishi Shinzaburō, "Kyōhō kaikakuki ni okeru Edo keizai ni taisuru Osaka no chii: Kyōhō kaikakuki ni okeru shijō kōzō ni tsuite" [Position of Osaka in the Edo economy during the Kyōhō reform period: concerning the market structure of the Kyōhō reform period], *Nihon Rekishi* 191 (April 1964), 20-21.

16. See Ho Ping-ti, *Studies in the Population of China, 1368-1953*.

17. Sekiyama Naotarō, *Nihon no jinkō*, 69.

18. See the appendices in Dwight Perkins, *Agricultural Development in China, 1368-1968*.

19. See the charts in Sekiyama Naotarō, *Nihon no jinkō*, 80-83.

20. These figures are adopted from Irene B. Taeuber, "Cities and Urbanization in Traditional China: Queries, Dilemma, Approaches"; a paper presented to the conference on Urban Society in Traditional China.

21. The uneven distribution of women was discussed by Irene B. Taeuber at the conference on Urban Society in Traditional China.

22. E. S. Crawcour, "The Tokugawa Heritage," in William W. Lockwood, *The State and Economic Enterprise in Japan*, 30-31.

23. See Chang Chung-li, *The Chinese Gentry: Studies on Their Role in*

Nineteenth Century Chinese Society (University of Washington Press, Seattle, 1967), 116-41.

24. Figures for Manchus in Peking are given in the *Chin Wu shih-li* (Peking, 1851), chuan 3, 15. In addition, some local gazetteers indicate the numbers of bannermen in other cities.

25. The division of bushi into levels is clarified in Hattori Masayuki, "Jōka-machi Tokushima ni okeru toshi kōzō no henyō katei" [The process of the changing appearance of the urban structure in the castle city of Tokushima], *Chiri Kagaku* 5 (Hiroshima chiri gakkai, 1966), 23-36.

26. This figure includes approximately 27,000 serving in official posts plus tens of thousands more with high degrees. See Chang Chung-li, *The Chinese Gentry: Studies on Their Role in Nineteenth Century Chinese Society*, 116.

27. See Sekiyama Naotarō, *Nihon no jinkō*, chapter 5, section 4, 29-55, "Mibun betsu oyobi shokugyō betsu jinkō" [Population according to status and occupation].

28. The emergence of local merchants in the Kantō region is described by Itō Yoshiichi, *Edo chimawari keizai no tenkai* [Development of the economy in the vicinity of Edo] (Hakushobō, Tokyo, 1966).

29. Sekiyama Naotarō distinguishes between those with merchant and artisan statuses and those who were actually employed in commercial activities. The latter figure was about 9 percent in the 1870s, while the former was only 5-6 percent. I have chosen 7 percent as representative of the figures for diverse areas of Japan. See *Nihon no jinkō*, 153.

30. Kawai Masaji, "Jōkamachi seiritsu no mondai—Hiroshima o chūshin to shite" [The problem of the establishment of castle cities—centering on Hiroshima], in Yozumi Shōgorō, ed., *Daimyo ryōkoku to jōkamachi* [Daimyo domains and castle cities] (Tokyo, 1967), 7-8.

31. Figures for the number of rentiers in various Japanese cities are provided in Tanaka Yoshio, *Jōkamachi Kanazawa* (Nihon shoin, Tokyo, 1966), 45.

32. See Sidney Gamble, "Daily Wages of Unskilled Chinese Laborers, 1807-1902," *Far Eastern Quarterly* 3 (November 1943), 41-73.

33. An example of an article which examines Chinese urban disorders is Li Hua's "Shih-lun Ch'ing-tai ch'ien-ch'i ti shih-min tou-cheng" [An attempt to explain the disturbances of urban residents in the early Ch'ing period], *Wen Shih Che* (October 1957, Shantung ta-hsüeh hsüeh-pao).

34. Sekiyama Naotarō, *Nihon no jinkō*, 153.

35. The incorporation of inhabitants with special low statuses into the pao-chia system under the Yung-cheng emperor is described by Hsiao Kung-chuan, *Rural China: Imperial Control in the Nineteenth Century* (University of Washington Press, Seattle, 1967), 47.

36. *Chin-men pao-chia t'u-shuo* (Tientsin, 1846), Vol. 12.

37. Momose Hiromu, " 'Chin-men pao-chia t'u-shuo' ni tsuite: Shindai Tenshin ken ni no nōkōshōko ni kansuru tōkei shiryō" [Concerning the "Explanation of the Tientsin pao-chia plan": statistical materials relating to households of farmers, artisans and merchants in Ch'ing period Tientsin hsien], in

Tōyō Nōgyō Keizaishi Kenkyū: Ono Takeo Hakushi Kanreki Kinen Ronbunshū Kankōkai (Nihon hyōronsha, Tokyo, 1948), 125-34.

38. See Nakai Nobuhiko, "Kinsei toshi no hatten" [Development of Tokugawa cities], *Nihon Rekishi 11: Kinsei 3* (Iwanami shoten, Tokyo, 1967), 54-56.

39. The distinction between residence and abode is made in an article by G. William Skinner, "Chinese Peasants and the Closed Community: An Open and Shut Case," *Comparative Studies in Society and History* (July 1971), 275.

40. Kono Michihiro, "Shindai Santōshō no kansei rikujō kōtsuro" (Ch'ing period Shantung sheng official land communications routes), *Shirin* 33:3 (May 1950), 317.

41. *Ibid.*, 318.

42. Kono Michihiro, "Shindai no maekiro" [Ch'ing period roads with horse stations], *Jinbun Chiri* 2:1 (1950), 13-24.

43. Matsumura Yasuichi, "Kinsei waga kuni no dōro kōtsu: ryūtsū no rekishi chiri" [Road traffic of our country in the Tokugawa period: the historical geography of circulation], *Rekishi Chirigaku Kiyō* 3 (1961), 63.

44. See Harasawa Bunya, "Edo jidai ni okeru shukueki to wakimichi ōkan to no kankei ni tsuite" [Concerning the relationship between post stations and branch road traffic in the Edo period], *Nihon Rekishi* 119 (May 1958), 59-70.

45. See Ho Ping-ti, *Chung-kuo hui-kuan shih-lun* [An historical survey of Landsmannschaften in China] (Hsüeh-sheng shu-chu, Taipei, 1966).

46. G. William Skinner, "Marketing and Social Structure in Rural China," part 2, 195-211.

47. *Ibid.*, part 1, 17-31.

NOTES TO CHAPTER 3

1. See Yamane Yukio, "Min Shin jidai Kahoku ni okeru teikishi" [Periodic markets in North China during the Ming and Ch'ing periods], *Shiron* 8 (1960), 494-95.

2. An article which relates hui-kuan to long-distance commerce is Nakamura Jihei's "Shindai Kokan kome ryūtsū no ichimen: Nankin no Konan kaikan yori mita" [One aspect of the flow of Hukuang rice in the Ch'ing period: seen from the Hunan hui-kuan in Nanking], *Shakai Keizai Shigaku* 18:3 (1952), 53-65.

3. See Wakita Osamu, *Kinsei hōken shakai no keizai kōzō* [The economic structure of Tokugawa feudal society] (Ochanomizu shobō, Tokyo, 1963), 31-32.

4. G. William Skinner, "Marketing and Social Structure in Rural China," parts 1, 2, and 3 (1964-65). Skinner was influenced by the pioneering work of Katō Shigeshi and other Japanese who have examined Chinese local gazetteers and, in turn, has created an impact on Japanese scholarship since 1965. Skinner was also influenced by C. K. Yang's field work as reported in *A North China Local Market Economy: A Summary of a Study of Periodic Markets in Chowping Hsien, Shantung* (Institute of Pacific Relations, New York, 1944).

5. Unfortunately most data on quantities of goods date from the twentieth century. For example, gazetteers of the early 1930s for Hsiang-ho and Ch'ing-yuan hsien in Chihli provide information on the kinds of goods available at many markets.

6. Two sources describing quantities marketed are Yamauchi Kiyoshi, *Shina shōgyōron* (Tokyo, 1942), 274-75, and Amano Motonosuke, "Gendai Shina no 'shih-chi' to 'miao-hui' " [Contemporary Chinese markets and fairs], *Tōagaku* 2 (1940), 109-70.

7. *Man-ch'eng hsien lüeh* (1930).

8. Kato Shigeshi, *Shina keizaishi kōshō*, Vol. ii, "Shindai ni okeru sonchin no teikishi" [Periodic markets in "ts'un" and "chen" during the Ch'ing period], 540-45.

9. Yamauchi Kiyoshi, *Shina shōgyōron*, 277.

10. Examples are given by C. K. Yang, *A North China Local Market Economy: A Summary of a Study of Periodic Markets in Chowping Hsien, Shantung*.

11. See Nakajima Giichi, *Shijō shūraku* [Marketing settlements] (Kokon shoin, Tokyo, 1964), 26-35.

12. See Itō Yoshiichi, *Kinsei zaikatashi no kōzō* [Structure of local markets in the Tokugawa period], chapter 1, section 2, "Hanryōiki shijō no seiritsu to zaikatashi" [Establishment of a han domain market and local markets] (Rinjinsha, Tokyo, 1967), 22-43.

13. The same section in Itō Yoshiichi's book contains a general discussion of the process of establishing han markets. Another description of new markets under jōkamachi control is provided by Yamori Kazuhiko, "Shōhin ryūtsū to jōkamachi," in Tsujita Usao, ed., *Sangyō chiri no shomondai*, 46.

14. Nakabe Yoshiko, *Kinsei toshi no seiritsu to kōzō*, 581.

15. Also turn to Nakabe Yoshiko, *Kinsei toshi no seiritsu to kōzō*, 584-610, for a discussion of marketing policies and central cities.

16. Itō Yoshiichi, "Edo jidai no shijō no hattatsu" [Development of the Tokugawa period market], *Rekishi Kyōiku* 7:11 (November 1959), 27-30.

17. For a discussion of tonya merchants see E. S. Crawcour, "Changes in Japanese Commerce in the Tokugawa period," in John W. Hall and Marius B. Jansen, eds. *Studies in the Institutional History of Early Modern Japan* (Princeton University Press, Princeton, 1968), 189-202.

18. Itō Yoshiichi, *Kinsei zaikatashi no kōzō*, 81-94.

19. Tanaka Yoshio, *Jōkamachi Kanazawa*, 42.

20. See Itō Yoshiichi, *Kinsei zaikatashi no kōzō*, 99-119.

21. Descriptions of Tokugawa merchants in relation to changing patterns in the flow of commerce are provided by Moriya Yoshimi, "Kinsei kōki shōhin ryūtsū kenkyū no hito zentei" [One premise for the study of late Tokugawa commercial flow], *Rekishigaku Kenkyū* 276 (May 1963), 34-45.

22. Nakajima Giichi, "Ichiman koku daimyo no jōka," 1-15 and "Echigo kuni Murakami fukin no teikishi" [Periodic markets in the vicinity of Murakami in Echigo kuni], *Shin Chiri* 10:4 (1963), 32-39.

23. The degree of "urbanness" was discussed by G. William Skinner, "The City in Chinese Society," a paper presented at the conference on Urban So-

ciety in Traditional China and to appear in revised form in his book, *The City in Late Imperial China.*

24. Sekiyama Naotarō, *Nihon no jinkō,* 138-39.

25. Nishimura Mutsuo, "Dentō kōgyō to rekishi jidai no ritchi" [Traditional industry and its historical locations], in Tsujita Usao, ed., *Sangyō chiri no shomondai,* II, 67.

26. Fu I-ling, *Ming-tai Kiang-nan shih-min ching-chi shih-t'an,* chapters 1-5.

27. See Terada Takanobu, "SōSō chihō ni okeru toshi no mengyō shōnin ni tsuite" [Concerning cotton industry merchants in the cities in the Soochow and Sung-chiang areas], *Shirin* 41:6 (November 1958), 52-69.

28. Fujii Hiroshi, "Shin-an shōnin no kenkyū," part 2, 32-61.

29. *Ibid.,* parts 1-4, and Saeki Tomi, "Shincho no kōki to Sansei shōnin" [Rise of the Ch'ing dynasty and Shansi merchants], *Shakai Bunka Shigaku* (1966), 11-42.

30. After deciding that this is the most useful way to group the eighteen Ch'ing sheng, I found a similar approach in Dwight H. Perkins, *Agricultural Development in China, 1368-1968* (Aldine Press, Chicago, 1969).

31. Abe Takeo, "Beikoku jukyū no kenkyū: 'Yung-cheng shih' no isshō to shite mita" [Study of the supply and demand of grains: seen from a chapter of the Yung-cheng history], *Tōyōshi Kenkyū* 15:4 (March 1957), 188-90.

32. See Kitamura Norinao, "Shindai no shōhin shijō ni tsuite" [Concerning the commercial market of the Ch'ing period], *Keizaigaku Zasshi* 28:3, 4; 1-22.

33. Nakahara Teruo, "Shindai ni okeru sōryō no shōhinka ni tsuite" [Concerning the commercialization of the grain transport system in the Ch'ing period], *Shigaku Kenkyū* 90 (October 1958), 44-56.

34. Saeki Tomi, "Shindai Tao-kuang cho ni okeru Huai-nan ensei no kaikaku" [Reform of the Huai-nan salt system during the Ch'ing Tao-kuang reign], *Tōhōgaku Ronshū* 3 (September 1954), 87-120.

35. Ho Ping-ti, *Chung-kuo hui-kuan shih-lun.*

36. Niida Noboru, "Shindai no Kankō SanSensei kaikan to SanSen girudo" [Ch'ing period Shansi and Shensi hui-kuan in Hankow and Shansi and Shensi guilds], *Shakai Keizaishigaku* 13:6 (September 1943), 2-4.

37. See Chang Peng, "The Distribution and Relative Strength of the Provincial Merchant Groups in China, 1842-1911" (Thesis at the University of Washington, Department of Economics, 1957), 67-115. Also see the *Shina shōbetsu zenshi* [Complete provincial gazetteers of China] (Tōa dobun shoin, 1917-20).

38. Chang Peng, "The Distribution and Relative Strength of the Provincial Merchant Groups in China, 1842-1911," 112-62.

39. Note the commentary by Nakai Nobuhiko on the uses of tax revenues, "Edo jidai no shijō keitai ni kansuru sobyō," part 1, 80-81.

40. One figure for the population of Sakai is given by Nakai Nobuhiko, "Kinsei toshi no hatten," 73.

41. Ōishi Shinzaburō, "Kyōhō kaikakuki ni okeru Edo keizai ni taisuru Osaka no chii: Kyōhō kaikakuki ni okeru shijō kōzō ni tsuite," 14.

42. See Wakita Osamu, *Kinsei hōken shakai no keizai kōzō*, 96-119.

43. Nakabe Yoshiko, *Kinsei toshi no seiritsu to kōzō*, 514-32 and 622-36.

44. Ōishi Shinzaburō, "Kyōhō kaikakuki ni okeru Edo keizai ni taisuru Osaka no chii: Kyōhō kaikakuki ni okeru shijō kōzō ni tsuite," 2-29. Also see Suzuki Naoji, "Kinsei ni okeru chūō beikoku shijō no tenkai" [Development of the central grain market in the Tokugawa period], *Nōson Kenkyū* 28 (December 1968), 1-9.

45. See Nakai Nobuhiko, "Kinsei toshi no hatten," 45-50.

46. Tsuda Hideo, *Hōken keizai seisaku no tenkai to shijō kōzō* [Development of feudal economic policies and market structure] (Ochanomizu shobō, Tokyo, 1961), 427-28.

NOTES TO CHAPTER 4

1. Chao Ch'uan-ch'eng, *Ch'ing tai ti-li yen-ko piao* [Chart of successive geographic changes of the Ch'ing period] (Chung-kuo shu-chu, Peking, 1955).

2. Momose Hiromu, "Shinmatsu Chihli sheng Ch'ing hsien shijō kyōdōtai zatsu kō" [A note on the marketing communities of Ch'ing hsien in late Ch'ing Chihli sheng], *Tōyōshi Kenkyū* 27:3 (1968), 72-86.

3. *Feng-jun hsien chih*, 1891.

4. *Pa hsien chih*, 1922.

5. Data on Ch'ing hsien, Shen chou chih-li chou, and Ting chou chih-li chou were shown to me by Shiba Yoshinobu. Momose Hiromu, describes these data on Chihli village populations in "Shinmatsu Chihli sheng ts'un-chen hu-k'ou shōkō" [A short study of late Ch'ing Chihli sheng village and chen population], *Tōhōgakuhō* 12:3 (December 1941), 99-112.

6. Additional information concerning settlement sizes in North China during the twentieth century is provided by Tanaka Shūsaku, "Shūraku mitsudo o kiban o seru jinkō bunpu ni tsuite: Hokushi Kahoku chiiki no baai" [Concerning population distribution which is based on settlement densities: the case of the North China Hopei area], *Osaka Gakugei Daigaku Kiyō* (Jinbun kagaku 1, 1952), 111-23.

7. *T'ung chou chih*, 1773.

8. *Pao-ting fu chih*, 1680.

9. *Ch'ing-yuan hsien chih*, 1874.

10. Momose Hiromu, "'Chin-men pao-chia t'u-shuo' ni tsuite: Shindai Tenshin ken ni no nōkōshōko ni kansuru tokei shiryō," 125-34.

11. Momose Hiromu, "Shinmatsu Chihli sheng Ch'ing hsien shijō kyōdōtai zatsu kō," 72-86.

12. *Sadamotoshi shi* (Ome, 1946), 222.

13. See works by Itō Yoshiichi, including his "Edo jidai no shijō no hattatsu," 27-33.

14. Itō Yoshiichi, *Kinsei zaikatashi no kōzō*, 99-119.

15. Okamura Ichirō, *Kawagoe no jōkamachi* (Kawagoe, 1955), 60-65.

16. Populations of posts are given in Kodama Kōta, *Shukueki* [Post stations] (Shibundō, Tokyo, 1960), 177-230.

17. *Hachiōjishi shi* (Hachiōji, 1963), 12.

18. Muto Tadashi, "Waga kuni kinsei makki ni okeru toshi seiritsu no kihon ni tsuite," 60-96.

19. See Itō Yoshiichi, *Edo chimawari keizai no tenkai*, 152.

20. *Utsunomiyaryō kinseishi* [History of Utsunomiya domain in the Tokugawa period] (Utsunomiya, 1964), 7.

21. *Ibid.*, 38.

22. *Mitoshi shi*, II, 439.

23. *Hitachishi shi* [History of Hitachi city] (Hitachi, 1959), 478.

24. *Mitoshi shi*, II, 71-73.

NOTES TO CHAPTER 5

1. Yamane Yukio, "Kahoku no miao-hui" [Fairs of North China], *Shiron* 17 (March 1967), 1-22, and Yamane Yukio, "Min Shin jidai Kahoku ni okeru teikishi," 493-504.

2. Kono Michihiro, "Shindai Santōshō no kansei rikujō kōtsūro," 317-36.

3. Nakamura Jihei, "Shindai Kahoku no toshi no kokō ni kansuru hito kōsatsu" [An inquiry concerning the population of Ch'ing dynasty North China cities], *Shien* 100 (March 1968), 169-80, and "Shindai Sansei no son to li-chia sei" (Villages and the li-chia system of Ch'ing period Shansi), *Tōyōshi Kenkyū* 26:3 (December 1967), 62-85.

4. Yamane Yukio, "Shantung sheng Tzu-yang hsien hu-ts'e ni tsuite" [Concerning the household register of Tzu-yang hsien in Shantung sheng], *Tōkyo joshi daigaku fuzoku hikaku bunka kenkyūjō kiyō* (June 1963), 23-111.

5. *Ch'ang-chou hsien chih*, 1766.

6. Morita Akira, "Shindai Kokan chihō ni okeru teikishi ni tsuite" [Concerning periodic markets in the Ch'ing period Hukuang area], *Kyūshū Sangyō Daigaku Ronsō* 5:1 (1964), 49-73.

7. G. William Skinner, "Marketing and Social Structure in Rural China," part 2, 207.

8. See an article on Kwangsi by Makino, "Shina no toshi ni okeru hitoko no heikin jinkō" [The average population of a household in Chinese cities], *Shina kazoku kenkyū* [Study of the Chinese family] (Shakatsusha, Tokyo, 1944), 643-85.

9. Kuramochi Tokuichirō, "Shisen no jōshi" [Markets of Szechwan], *Nihon Daigaku Shigakkai Kenkyū Ihō* (December 1957), 2-32.

10. Takahashi Bonsen, *Nihon jinkōshi no kenkyū*, 364-65.

11. *Ibid.*, 154-55.

12. Tanaka Yoshiō, *Jōkamachi Kanazawa*, 44-50.

13. *Ibid.*, 136.

14. Sekiyama Naotarō, *Kinsei Nihon jinkō no kenkyū* [Study of the Tokugawa period Japanese population] (Ryūjinsha, Tokyo, 1948), 236-37.

15. See Nakabe Yoshiko, *Kinsei jōkamachi no seiritsu to kōzō*, 680.

16. Kobayashi Kentarō, "Daimyo ryōkoku seiritsuki ni okeru chūshin shūraku no keisei: Owari heino no jirei kenkyū ni yoru kentō" [The position of central places in the period of the establishment of daimyo domains: con-

sidered through studying the example of the Owari plain], *Shirin* 481:1 (January 1965), 91.

17. Sekiyama Naotarō, *Kinsei Nihon jinkō no kenkyū*, 234. Also see Chihōshi Kenkyū Kyōgikai, *Nihon no machi 3: Bakumatsu, Meijiki ni okeru toshi to nōson* [Settlements of Japan 3: cities and villages in the late Tokugawa and Meiji periods] (Yūsankaku, Tokyo, 1958), 276-89.

18. Nakabe Yoshiko, *Kinsei jōkamachi no seiritsu to kōzō*, 535-52.

19. Tsukushi Nobuzane, "Tōkaidō shukujō no henbō" [Transfiguration of Tōkaidō posts], *Mie no Bunka* 7 (February 1957), 20-28.

20. Nakabe Yoshiko, *Kinsei jōkamachi no seiritsu to kōzō*, 370-402.

21. Taniguchi Sumio, "Jōkamachi Okayama no seiritsu" [The Establishment of Okayama castle city], in Yozumi Shōgorō, ed., *Daimyo ryōkoku to jōkamachi*, 157-58. Similar figures are given in Honjō Eijirō, *Nihon jinkōshi*, 184.

22. *Shinshū Hiroshimashi shi* (Hiroshima, 1959), 104.

23. Furushima Toshio, ed., *Nihon keizaishi taikei* [An outline of the economic history of Japan] (Tokyo University Press, Tokyo, 1965), Vol. 3, 225-26.

24. Kobayashi Kentarō, "Kinsei shotō Hagi hanryō ni okeru shijō no bunpu to ruikei kubun" [Types and Distribution of markets in early Tokugawa Hagi han], in *Hanryō no rekishi chiri: Hagi han* [Historical geography of domains: Hagi han], Nishimura Mutsuo, ed. (Ōmeido, Tokyo, 1968), 307-22.

25. Kobayashi Kentarō, "Kinsei shotō Hagi hanryō ni okeru chihōteki chūshin shūraku no kōzō" [Structure of local central places in early Tokugawa Hagi han], *Jinbun* 14 (Kyoto University, January 1968), 21-52.

26. Hattori Masayuki, "Jōkamachi Tokushima ni okeru toshi kōzō no henyō katei," 23-36.

NOTES TO CHAPTER 6

1. The precise time of Nanking's decline from a city with about one million residents is not clear. In this study I have assumed that the decline began at least by the seventeenth century, but it may not have occurred until the middle of the Ch'ing period. Furthermore the pattern of population growth in Soochow, Wuhan, Canton, and other level 2 cities has not been sufficiently clarified to assert without qualification that Peking was always the most populous city in Ch'ing China.

2. These stages in the history of Edo's development are described by Naitō Akira, *Edo to Edojō* [Edo and Edo castle] (Kojima kenkyūjō, Tokyo, 1966).

3. *T'ien fu kuang chi* (Peking, 1962 edition).

4. Iakinov Bichurin, *Opisanie Pekina* (St. Petersburg, 1829).

5. *Chin Wu shih-li* (Peking, 1851).

6. *Shina shōbetsu zenshi*, Vol. 18 (4th edition), 120.

7. L. S. Yang, "Government Control of Urban Merchants," a paper presented at the conference on Urban Society in Traditional China, 18.

8. *Hung-ya hsien chih*, 1813.

9. *Shun-t'ien fu chih*, chuan 13 and 14, 1885.

10. *Ch'ien-lung Ching-ch'eng t'u* (Peking, 1751).

11. *The Chinese Traveller* [Collected from Du Halde, Le Compte and other modern travellers] (E. C. Dilly, London, 1775), Vol. II, 21.

12. Sasaki Masaya, "Shindai kanryō no kashoku ni tsuite" [Concerning the money-making of Ch'ing officials], *Shigaku Zasshi* 63:2 (February 1954), 34.

13. *Ching-shih fang-hsiang chih* (Peking, about 1900).

14. Ikeda Yasaburō, *Hiroshige no Edo* (Kodansha, Tokyo, 1968), 122.

15. Sekiyama Naotarō, *Nihon no jinkō*, 118.

16. Kingsley Davis, "The Origin and Growth of Urbanization in the World," 133.

Abe Takeo. "Beikoku jukyū no kenkyū—'Yung-cheng shih' no isshō to shite mita" [Study of the supply and demand of grains—seen from a chapter of the Yung-cheng history], *Tōyōshi Kenkyū* 15:4 (March 1957), 120-213.

———. "Hao-hsien t'i-chie no kenkyū" [Study of payments of extra silver], *Tōyōshi Kenkyū* 16:4 (March 1958), 108-262.

Aitō Matsuo. "Gen no Ta-tu" [Yuan Peking], *Rekishi Kyōiku* 14:12 (December 1966), 59-65.

Amano Motonosuke. "Gendai Shina no shih-chi to miao-hui" [Contemporary Chinese markets and fairs], *Tōagaku* 2 (1940), 109-70.

Andō Seiichi. "Hanryōiki keizai to jōkamachi" [Han domain economy and castle city], *Rekishi Kyōiku* 14:1 (November 1966), 136-41.

———. "Kinsei zaikata shōgyō to kyokuchiteki shijōen" [Tokugawa period local commerce and local marketing spheres], *Rekishi Kyōiku* 6:1 (January 1958), 13-19.

———. "Kinsei toshi no shōgyō" [Commerce of Tokugawa period cities], *Shakai Keizai Shigaku* 31:1 (1966), 42-54.

Aoyama Sadao. *Tōsō jidai no kōtsu to chishi chizu no kenkyū* [Study of the communications systems and local maps of the T'ang and Sung periods] (Yoshikawa kōbunkan, Tokyo, 1963).

Armstrong, Alex. *Shantung* (Shanghai, 1891).

Asaka Yukio, ed. *Nihon no rekishi chiri* [Historical geography of Japan] (Ōmeido, Tokyo, 1966).

Asaka Yukio, Naka Eiichi, Mitomo Kunigorō, and Yajima Jinkichi, eds. *Nihon chishi zeminaru—Kantō chihō (jo Tokyo)* [Seminar on Japan's local records—Kantō area, excluding Tokyo] (Ōmeido, Tokyo, c. 1960).

Asao Naohiro. *Kinsei hōken shakai no kiso kōzō: Kinai ni okeru Baku-*

han taisei [Basic structure of the Tokugawa period feudal society: the Bakuhan system in the Kinai area] (Ochanomizu shobō, Tokyo, 1967).

Balazs, Étienne. "Une Carte Économique de la Chine au XIe Siècle," *Annales Économies, Sociétés, Civilisations* 12:4 (October-December 1957), 587-93.

————. "Les Villes Chinoises," *Recueils de la Société Jean Bodin* 6 (1954), 225-40 and reprinted as "Chinese Towns" in *Chinese Civilization and Bureaucracy* (Yale University Press, New Haven, 1964), 66-78.

Chang Chung-li. *The Chinese Gentry: Studies on Their Role in Nineteenth Century Chinese Society* (University of Washington Press, Seattle, 1967).

Chang Kwang-chih. *The Archaeology of Ancient China* (Yale University Press, New Haven, 1968).

————. "Towns and Cities in Ancient China," an unpublished paper prepared for the conference on Urban Society in Traditional China.

Chang Peng. "The Distribution and Relative Strength of the Provincial Merchant Groups in China, 1842-1911" (Thesis at the University of Washington, Department of Economics, 1957).

Chang Sen-dou. *The Chinese Hsien Capital: A Study in Historical Urban Geography* (Thesis at the University of Washington, Department of Geography, 1961).

————. "Historical Trend of Chinese Urbanization," *Annals of the Association of American Geographers* 53:2 (June 1963), 109-43.

————. "The Morphology of Chinese Walled Cities," in *The City in Late Imperial China*, ed. G. William Skinner (Stanford University Press, Stanford, forthcoming).

————. "Some Aspects of the Urban Geography of the Chinese Hsien Capital," *Annals of the Association of American Geographers* 51:1 (March 1961), 23-45.

————. "Some Observations on the Morphology of Chinese Walled Cities," *Annals of the Association of American Geographers* 60:1 (March 1970), 63-91.

Chao Ch'uan-ch'eng. *Ch'ing-tai ti-li yen-ko piao* [Chart of successive geographic changes of the Ch'ing period] (Chung-kuo shu-chu, Peking, 1955).

Ch'i Kung-min. "Ming mo shih-min fan feng-chien tou-cheng" [Anti-feudal struggles of late Ming urban residents], *Wen Shih Che* (Shantung ta-hsüeh hsüeh-pao chih-i, February 1957), 38-46.

Ch'ien-lung Ching-ch'eng t'u [Ch'ien-lung map of Peking] (Peking, 1751).

Ch'ien-lung fu t'ing chou hsien t'u-chih [Gazetteer of fu, t'ing, chou and hsien of the Ch'ien-lung period] (Peking, 1789).

Chihōshi Kenkyū Kyōgikai. *Nihon no machi: sono rekishiteki kōzō* [The cities of Japan: their historic structure] (Yūsankaku, Tokyo, 1958).

——. *Nihon no machi 2: hōken toshi no shomondai* [The cities of Japan 2: various questions about feudal cities] (Yūsankaku, Tokyo, 1959).

——. *Nihon no machi 3: Bakumatsu, Meijiki ni okeru toshi to nōson* [The cities of Japan 3: cities and villages in the late Tokugawa and Meiji periods] (Yūsankaku, Tokyo, 1961).

Chin-men pao-chia t'u-shuo [Explanation of the Tientsin pao-chia plan] (Tientsin, 1846).

The Chinese Traveller (Collected from Du Halde, Le Compte and other modern travellers), Vols. I and II (E. C. Dilly, London, 1775).

Ching-shih fang-hsiang chih (Peking, c. 1900).

Chin Wu shih-li (Peking, 1851).

Crawcour, E. S. "Changes in Japanese Commerce in the Tokugawa period," in John W. Hall and Marius B. Jansen, eds., *Studies in the Institutional History of Early Modern Japan* (Princeton University Press, Princeton, 1968), 189-202.

——. "The Tokugawa Heritage," in William W. Lockwood, ed., *The State and Economic Enterprise in Japan* (Princeton University Press, Princeton, 1965), 17-44.

DaiNihon koku saizu zen [Complete detailed maps of Japan] (Jinbunsha, Tokyo, 1969).

Davis, Kingsley. "The Origin and Growth of Urbanization in the World," *The American Journal of Sociology* 60 (March 1955), 429-37.

Dore, Ronald. *City Life in Japan: a Study of a Tokyo Ward* (University of California Press, Berkeley, 1958).

Eberhard, Wolfram. "Data on the Structure of the Chinese City in the Pre-industrial Period," *Economic Development and Cultural Change* 4:3 (April 1956), 253-68.

Fu I-ling. *Ming Ch'ing shih-tai shang-jen chi shang-yeh tzu-pen* [Merchants and commercial capital of Ming and Ch'ing times] (Jen-min ch'u-pan she, Peking, 1956).

——. *Ming-tai Kiang-nan shih-min ching-chi shih-t'an* [Exploratory reconnaisance of urban dwellers' economy in the Ming period lower Yangtze region] (Jen-min ch'u-pan she, Shanghai, 1957).

Fujii Hiroshi. "Shin-an shōnin no kenkyū" [A study of Shin-an merchants], *Tōyōgakuhō* 36: parts 1-4 (1953-54).

Fujimoto Eijirō. *Chūgoku keizaishi* [Chinese economic history] (Hōritsu bunkasha, Kyoto, 1967).

Fujimoto Tochiharu. *Dōgyōsha chō* [Wards with men of the same trade] (Yūkonsha, Tokyo, 1963).

Fujioka Kenjirō, ed. *Kinai rekishi chiri kenkyū* [Study of the historical geography of the Kinai region] (Nihon kagakusha, Kyoto, 1958).

———. "Nihon ni okeru toshi bunpu no ritchi no hensen" [Distribution of cities and changes in the location of industry in Japan], *Toshi Mondai* 48:1 (January 1957), 55-63.

———. *Toshi to kōtsuro no rekishi chirigakuteki kenkyū* [An historical geographical study of cities and traffic routes] (Ōmeido, Tokyo, 1960).

Fukuda Keitarō. "Kodai Nihon ni okeru ichi no kigen to shokunō" [Origin and function of markets in ancient Japan], *Keizaigaku Kenkyū Fukuda Tokuzo Hakushi Tsuioku Ronbunshū* (Moriyama shoten, Tokyo, 1933), 329-53.

Furushima Toshio, ed. *Nihon keizaishi taikei* 3 [An outline of the economic history of Japan] (Tokyo University Press, Tokyo, 1965).

Gamble, Sidney. "Daily Wages of Unskilled Chinese Laborers, 1807-1902," *Far Eastern Quarterly* 3 (November 1943), 41-73.

Gotō Kimpei. "Wang Ts'ai Ch'eng chou k'ao" [On Ch'eng chou, the metropolis of the Chou dynasty], *Tōyōgakuhō* 44:3 (December 1961), 36-60.

Hachiōjishi shi [History of Hachioji City] (Hachiōji, 1963).

Hall, John W. "The Castle Town and Japan's Modern Urbanization," in John W. Hall and Marius B. Jansen, eds., *Studies in the Institutional History of Early Modern Japan* (Princeton University Press, Princeton, 1968), 169-88.

———. "Foundations of the Modern Japanese Daimyo," in John W. Hall and Marius B. Jansen, eds., *Studies in the Institutional History of Early Modern Japan* (Princeton University Press, Princeton, 1968), 65-77.

———. *Government and Local Power in Japan, 500-1700* (Princeton University Press, Princeton, 1966).

———. "The Traditional Japanese City," a paper presented at the conference on Urban Society in Traditional China.

Hansei Ichiran. (Nihon shiseki kyōkai, Tokyo, 1928).

Harada Tomohiko. "Hōkentoshi no jichi soshiki" [Self-government organizations in feudal cities], *Toshi Mondai* 48:8 (August 1957), 55-61.

———. *Nihon hōkentaisei no toshi to shakai* [City and society in the feudal system of Japan] (Sanichi shobō, Tokyo, 1960).

———. *Nihon hōken toshi kenkyū* [Study of the feudal city in Japan] (Tokyo University Press, Tokyo, 1957).

Harasawa Bunya. "Edo jidai ni okeru shukueki to wakimichi ōkan to no kankei ni tsuite" [Concerning the relationship between post stations and branch road traffic in the Tokugawa period], *Nihon Rekishi* 119 (May 1958), 59-70.

Hartwell, Robert. "A Cycle of Economic Change in Imperial China: Coal and Iron in Northeast China, 750-1350," *Journal of the Economic and Social History of the Orient* 10:1 (July 1967), 102-55.

Hattori Katsuhiko. *Hokugi Rakuyō no shakai to bunka* [The society and culture of Northern Wei Lo-yang] (Mineruva, Tokyo, 1965).

Hattori Masayuki. "Jōkamachi Tokushima ni okeru toshi kōzō no henyō katei" [The process of the changing appearance of the urban structure in the castle city of Tokushima], *Chiri Kagaku* 5 (Hiroshima chiri gakkai, 1966), 23-36.

Hayashi Reiko. "Edo momen tonyanakama to Kantō momen" [Edo cotton wholesale companies and Kantō cotton], *Rekishigaku Kenkyū* 274 (March 1963), 30-42.

———. "Kaseiki ni okeru shōhin ryūtsū" [Commercial flow in the Kasei reign period], *Rekishi Kyōiku* 12:12 (December 1964), 10-15.

Hino Kaisaburō. "Tōdai jōyo no 'fang, shih, no chiao, yü' " ["Fang, shih chiao and yü" in the cities of the T'ang period], *Tōyōgakuhō* 47:3 (December 1964), 1-34.

Ho Ping-ti. *Chung-kuo hui-kuan shih-lun* [An historical survey of Landsmannschaften in China] (Hsüeh-sheng shu-chu, Taipei, 1966).

———. "The Geographic Distribution of Hui-kuan in Central and Upper Yangtze Provinces—With Special Reference to Interregional Migrations," *Tsing-hua Hsüeh-pao*, New Series 5:2 (December 1966), 120-52.

———. *The Ladder of Success in Imperial China: Aspects of Social Mobility, 1368-1911* (Columbia University Press, Science Editions, New York, 1964).

———. "Lo-yang, A.D. 494-534," *Harvard Journal of Asiatic Studies* (1966), 52-101.

———. *Studies in the Population of China, 1368-1953* (Harvard University Press, Cambridge, 1959).

Honjō Eijirō. *Kyoto* (Shibundō, Kyoto, 1966).

———. *Nihon jinkōshi* [History of the Japanese Population] (Nihon hyōronsha, Tokyo, 1941).

Hoshi Ayao. *Mindai sōun no kenkyū* [Study of the Ming period transport system] (Nihon gakujutsu shinkōkai, Tokyo, 1963).

———. "Shindai no sōun kikō ni tsuite" [Concerning the organization of the Ch'ing period transport system], *Yamagata Daigaku Kiyō* 1:4 (1953).

Hoshi Takeo. "Shindai no unrō gasho ni tsuite" [Concerning the government office for Ch'ing period transport provisions], *Yamagata Daigaku* 11 (October 1965), 67-76.

Hsiao I-shan. *Ch'ing-tai t'ung-shih* [Complete history of the Ch'ing period] (Shang wu-yin shu-kuan, Taipei, 1963).

Hsiao Kung-chuan. *Rural China: Imperial Control in the Nineteenth Century* (University of Washington Press, Seattle, 1967).

Hsü Cho-yun. *Ancient China in Transition: An Analysis of Social Mobility 722-222 B.C.* (Stanford University Press, Stanford, 1965).

Hucker, Charles, ed. *Chinese Government in Ming Times* (Columbia University Press, New York, 1969).

———. "Governmental Organization of the Ming Dynasty," *Harvard Journal of Asiatic Studies* 21 (1958), 1-66.

Hyacinthe, Rev. *Description de Pekin avec un Plan de Cette Capitale* (St. Petersburg, 1829).

Iakinov, Bichurin. *Opisanie Pekina* (St. Petersburg, 1829).

Ikeda Shirō. "Bakumatsu no Saga jōkamachi ni tsuite" [Concerning the late Tokugawa period Saga castle city], *Nihon Rekishi* 89 (November 1955), 35-45.

Ikeda Yasaburō. *Hiroshige no Edo* (Kodansha, Tokyo, 1968).

Imahori Seiji. "Shindai ikō Kōga no suirin ni tsuite" [Concerning Yellow river water transportation in the Ch'ing period and after], *Shigaku Kenkyū* 72 (1959), 23-37.

Itō Yoshiichi. *Edo chimawari keizai no tenkai* [Development of the economy in the vicinity of Edo] (Hakushobō, Tokyo, 1966).

———. "Edo jidai no toshi no hattatsu" [Development of Tokugawa period cities], *Rekishi Kyōiku* 7:11 (November 1959), 27-33.

———. *Kinsei zaikatashi no kōzō* [Structure of local markets in the Tokugawa period] (Rinjinsha, Tokyo, 1967).

———. "Minami Kantō ni okeru zaikatashi no suitai" [Decline of local markets in South Kantō], *Chihōshi Kenkyū* 8:6 (December 1958), 20-27.

Kaizuka Shigeki. "Chūgoku kodai toshi ni okeru minkai" [Popular assemblies in ancient Chinese cities], *Tōhōgaku Ronshū* 2 (March 1962), 34-39.

Kanazawa Osamu. "Tokushima ken ni okeru toshi hattatsushi" [History of the development of cities in Tokushima ken], *Shin Toshi* 38:10, 16-23.

Kano Hisashi. "Nihon kodai no toshi to nōson" [Cities and villages of ancient Japan], *Nihonshi Kenkyū* 59 (March 1962), 34-39.

Katō Shigeshi. *Shina keizaishi kōshō* [Studies in the economic history of China] (Tōyōbunko, Tokyo, 1952-53), Vols. I, II.

Kawahara Tairō and Kikuura Sugeo. *Nihon shōgyō hattenshi* [History of the development of Japanese commerce] (Tokyo, 1960).

Kawakami Kōichi. *Sōdai no keizai seikatsu* [Economic life of the Sung period] (Yurasha bunkashi senshū, Yoshikawa kōbunkan, Tokyo, 1966).

Kawasaki Fusagorō. *Edo happyaku hachi chō* [The 808 wards of Edo] (Tōgensha, Tokyo, 1967).

Kishimoto Makoto. "Jinkō idō kara mita kinsei no toshi to sonraku" [Tokugawa period cities and villages viewed from population movements], *Chirigaku Hyōron* 23:12 (December 1950), 23-31.

Kitamura Norinao. "Shindai no shōhin shijō ni tsuite" [Concerning the commercial market of the Ch'ing period], *Keizaigaku Zasshi* 28:3, 4; 1-22.

Kitamura Toshio. "Chihō shijō no hatten, zanzon to sono yoin ni kansuru rekishi chiriteki kenkyū: Omi Yokkaichi o chūshin to shite" [Development of local markets, historical geographical study concerning survivals and their main causes], *Jinbun Chiri* 2:4 (October 1950).

Kiuchi Shinzō. "Hokushi Sanseishō no chihō toshi ni tsuite" [Concerning local cities in North China's Shansi province], *Chirigaku Hyōron* 19:3 (1943), 135-59.

Kiuchi Shinzō. Fujioka Kenjirō, and Yajima Ninkichi, eds., *Shūraku chiri kōsa II: hattatsu to kōzō* [Examination of settlement geography: development and plan] (Chōsō shoten, Tokyo, 1957).

Kobayashi Fumimizu. "Genroku, and Kyōhōki ni okeru zaikata shōnin no seichō" [Growth of local merchants in the Genroku and Kyōhō periods], *Rekishi Kyōiku* 6:1 (1958), 20-24.

Kobayashi Kentarō. "Chūsei jōkan no rekishi chirigakuteki kōsatsu: Sengoku daimyo kuni no chiiki kōzō kenkyu no kokoromi" [Historical geographical examination of castles from the Kamakura to the Sengoku periods: an attempt to study the territorial structure of the Sengoku daimyo lands], *Jinbun Chiri* 15:4 (August 1963), 40-64.

Kobayashi Kentarō. "Kinsei shotō Hagi hanryō ni okeru chihōteki chūshin shūraku no kōzō" [Structure of local central places in early Tokugawa Hagi han], *Jinbun* 14 (Kyoto University, January 1968), 21-52.

———. "Daimyo kyōkoku seiritsuki ni okeru chūshin shūraku no keisei: Owari heino no jirei kenkyū ni yoru kentō" [The position of central places in the period of the establishment of daimyo domains: considered through studying the example of the Owari plain], *Shirin* 48:1 (January 1965), 87-125.

Kobayashi Shigeru. "Kinsei Shimonoseki no hattatsu to sono rekishiteki igi" [Development of Shimonoseki in the Tokugawa period and its historical significance], *Shimonoseki Shōkei Ronshū* 6:2 (November 1962), 35-80.

Kodama Kōto. *Shukueki* [Post stations] Shibundō, Tokyo, 1960).

Kodama Shozaburō. "Kinsei kōki ni okeru shōhin ryūtsū to zaikata shōnin" [Late Tokugawa commercial flow and local merchants], *Rekishigaku Kenkyū*, 273.

Kono Michihiro. "Shindai no maekiro" [Ch'ing period roads with horse stations], *Jinbun Chiri* 2:1 (1950), 13-24.

———. "Shindai Santōshō no kansei rikujō kōtsūro" [Ch'ing period Shantung sheng official land communications routes], *Shirin* 33:3 (May 1950), 317-36.

Kōtō Nihonshi seizu [Detailed maps of Japanese history for high schools] (Teikoku shoin, Tokyo, 1968).

Kozuma Sakae. *Chūgoku shijō no kōzōteki henkaku* [Structural change of the Chinese market] (Hōritsu bunkasha, Tokyo, 1963).

Kubota Shigeharu. "Kinsei jōkamachi Matsuyama no rekishi chirigaku-teki kenkyū" [Historical geographical study of the Tokugawa period castle city of Matsuyama], *Matsuyama Shinonome Gakuen Kenkyū Ronshū* 2:2 (November 1966), 81-123.

Kuramochi Tokuichirō. "Min Shin jidai toshi kukaku ko (1) 'yu' no kōzō to bunpu: Min Shin jidai chishi yori mitaru" [A treatise on urban divisions in the Ming and Ch'ing period (1) the structure and distribution of 'yu': as seen from Ming and Ch'ing period gazetteers], *Nihon Daigaku Shigakkai Kenkyū Ihō* 4 (December 1960), 1-18.

———. "Shisen no jōshi" [Markets of Szechwan], *Nihon Daigaku Shigakkai Kenkyū Ihō* 1 (December 1957), 2-32.

Li Hua. "Shih-lun Ch'ing-tai ch'ien-chi ti shih-min tou-cheng" [An attempt to explain the disturbances of urban residents in the early Ch'ing period], *Wen Shih Che* (Shantung ta-hsüeh hsüeh-pao, October 1957).

Li-shih Yen-chiu. *Chung-kuo ku-tai shih fen-ch'i wen-t'i chi* [Collection of discussions of the problem of the dividing period in the history of ancient China] (San-lien shu-tien, Peking, 1957).

———. *Chung-kuo ti nu-li chih yü feng-chien chih fen-ch'i wen-t'i lun-wen hsuan-chi* [Anthology of essays on the problem of the dividing period between the slave system and the feudal system in China] (San-lien shu-tien, Peking, 1956).

Ma, Lawrence J. C., *Commercial Development and Urban Change in Sung China: 960-1279* (Michigan Geographical Publications, Ann Arbor, 1971).

Masui Tsuneo. "Kantō no hsu-shih: shijō kindaika ni kansuru hito kō-satsu" [The markets of Kwangtung: one consideration concerning the modernization of marketing], *Tōaronsō* 4 (May 1941), 263-84.

Matsumoto Toyotoshi. *Jōkamachi no rekishi chirigakuteki kenkyū* [Historical geographical study of jōkamachi] (Yoshikawa kōbunkan, Tokyo, 1967).

Matsumura Yasuichi. "Kinsei waga kuni no dōro kōtsū: ryūtsū no rekishi chiri" [Road traffic of our country in the Tokugawa period: the historical geography of circulation], *Rekishi Chirigaku Kiyō* 3 (1961), 59-94.

Matsuyama Shinonome and Kubota Shigeharu. "Kinsei jōkamachi Matsu-yama no rekishi chirigakuteki kenkyū" [Historical geographical study of the Tokugawa period castle city of Matsuyama], *Matsuyama Tōun-gakuen Kenkyū Ronshū* 2:2 (November 1966), 81-123.

Meng Wen-tung. "Ts'ung Sung-tai ti shang-shui ho ch'eng-shih k'an Chung-kuo feng-chien she-hui ti tzu-jan ching-chi" [To observe the national economy of Chinese feudal society from commercial taxes and cities of the Sung period], *Li-shih Yen-chiu* 4 (1961), 45-52.

Mitoshi shi [History of Mito city] (Mitoshi shi hensan iinkai, Mito, 1963).

Miura Toshiaki. "Edo jōkamachi no seiritsu katei: kokuyaku futan kan-kei o tsujite mita machi no seiritsu ni tsuite" [The process of establish-ing Edo jōkamachi: concerning the establishment of a city seen through the relationships of corvee burdens], *Nihon Rekishi* 172 (September 1962), 36-55.

Miyazaki Ichisada. "Chūgoku Jōdai wa hōkensei ka toshikokka ka?" [Was the Shang period in China a feudal system or a time of city states?], *Ajiashi Kenkyū* 3 (1963), 63-86.

———. "Chūgoku jōkaku no kigen isetsu" [Hypothesis on the origin of the inner and outer cities in China], *Ajiashi Kenkyū* 1 (1957), 50-65.

———. "Les Villes en Chine a l'époque des Han," *T'oung Pao* 48 (1960), 376-92.

Miyazaki Ichisada. "Rokuchō jidai Kahoku no toshi" [Cities of Six Dynasties China], *Tōyōshi Kenkyū* 20:2 (March 1962), 53-74.

Mizue Tsurako. "Hōken toshi Edo no seiritsu to hatten" [Establishment and development of the feudal city Edo], *Rekishi Kyōiku* 14:11 (November 1966), 19-25.

Mizukami Kazuhisa. "Jōkamachi Kanazawa no shōkugyō kōsei: Bunka 8 Kanazawa machi kata ezu meichō ni yoru kōsaku" [Occupational structure of the castle city of Kanazawa: examination through a register of names with the 1811 map of Kanazawa], *Kanazawa Daigaku Hōbungakubu Ronshū—Tetsugaku Shigaku hen* 9 (1961), 121-62.

Momose Hiromu. " 'Chin-men pao-chia t'u-shuo' ni tsuite Shindai Tenshin ken no nōkōshōko ni kansuru tokei shiryō" [Concerning the "Explanation of the Tientsin pao-chia plan"—statistical materials related to households of farmers, artisans and merchants in Ch'ing period Tientsin hsien], *Tōyōnōgyō Keizaishi Kenkyū Ono Takeo Hakushi Kanreki Kinen Ronbunshū Kankōkai* (Nihon hyōronsha, Tokyo, 1948), 125-34.

———. "Shinmatsu Chihli sheng Ch'ing hsien shijō kyōdōtai zatsu kō" [A note on the marketing communities of Ch'ing hsien in late Ch'ing Chihli sheng], *Tōyōshi Kenkyū* 27:3 (1968), 72-86.

———. "Shinmatsu Chihli sheng ts'un-chen hu-k'ou shōkō" [A short study of late Ch'ing Chihli sheng village and chen population], *Tōhōgakuhō* 12:3 (December 1941), 99-112.

Morita Akira. "Shindai Kokan chihō ni okeru teikishi ni tsuite" [Concerning periodic markets in the Ch'ing perod Hukuang area], *Kyūshū Sangyō Daigaku Ronsō* 5:1 (1964), 49-73.

Moriya Yoshimi. "Kinsei kōki shōhin ryūtsū kenkyū no hito zentei" [One premise for the study of late Tokugawa commercial flow], *Rekishigaku Kenkyū* 276 (May 1963), 34-45.

Mote, F. W. "The Transformation of Nanking, 1350-1400," a paper presented at the conference on Urban Society in Traditional China.

Muramatsu Yūji. "Shin no naimufu shōen 'nei-wu fu tsao-sung huang-ch'an ti-mou ts'e' to shite shiryō ni tsuite" [Estates of the Ch'ing Imperial Household Registry—concerning land records as materials prepared and sent for imperial estates], *Keizaigaku Kenkyū* 12 (Hitotsubashi daigaku, 1961), 1-20.

Murayama Shūichi. *Nihon toshi seikatsu no genryū* [The origins of urban life in Japan] (Seki shoin, Kyoto, 1953).

Muto Tadashi. "Waga kuni kinsei makki ni okeru toshi seiritsu no kihon ni tsuite" [Concerning the foundations for the establishment of cities in late Tokugawa Japan], *Shirin* 48:3 (May 1965), 60-96.

Naba Toshisada. "Toshi no hattatsu to shōnin seikatsu no kōjō" [The development of cities and the advancement of the livelihood of the masses], *Sekai bunkashi taikei no Sō Gen jidai* [The Sung and Yuan periods in an outline of the cultural history of the world] (Seibundō shinkōsha, Tokyo, 1935), 150-201.

Naitō Akira. *Edo to Edojō* [Edo and Edo castle] (Kajima kenkyūjō, Tokyo, 1966).

Nakabe Yoshiko. *Kinsei toshi no seiritsu to kōzō* [Establishment and plan of Tokugawa cities] (Shinseisha, Tokyo, 1967).

Nakahara Teruo. "Shindai ni okeru sōryō no shōhinka ni tsuite" [Concerning the commercialization of the grain transport system in the Ch'ing period], *Shigaku Kenkyū* 90 (October 1968), 44-56.

———. "Shindai sōsen ni yoru shōhin ryūtsū ni tsuite" [Concerning the commercial flow through Ch'ing period grain transport ships], *Shigaku Kenkyū* 72 (1959), 67-81.

Nakai Nobuhiko. "Edo jidai no shijō keitai ni kansuru sobyō" [A rough sketch of the Edo period market structure], *Nihon Rekishi* 115 (January 1958), 76-83; 116 (February 1958), 30-36; 118 (April 1958), 68-74.

———. "Kinsei toshi no hatten" [Development of Tokugawa period cities], *Nihon Rekishi 11—kinsei 3* (Iwanami shoten, Tokyo, 1967), 37-100.

Nakajima Giichi. "Echigo kuni Murakami fukin no teikishi" [Periodic markets in the vicinity of Murakami in Echigo kuni], *Shin Chiri* 10:4 (1963), 32-39.

———. "Ichiman koku daimyo no jōka" [Castle cities of daimyo with 10,000 koku], *Shin Chiri* 10:2 (September 1962), 1-15.

———. *Shijō shūraku* [Marketing settlements] (Kokon shoin, Tokyo, 1964).

Nakamura, James I. "Growth of Japanese Agriculture, 1875-1920," William W. Lockwood ed., *The State and Economic Enterprise in Japan* (Princeton University Press, Princeton, 1965), 249-324.

Nakamura Jihei. "Shindai Kahoku no toshi no kokō ni kansuru hito kōsatsu" [An inquiry concerning the population of Ch'ing dynasty North China cities], *Shien* 100 (March 1968), 169-80.

———. "Shindai Kokan kome ryūtsū no ichimen: Nankin no Konan kaikan yori mita" [One aspect of the flow of Hukuang rice in the

Ch'ing period: seen from the Hunan hui-kuan in Nanking], *Shakai Keizai Shigaku* 18:3 (1952), 53-65.

———. "Shindai Sansei no son to li-chia sei" [Villages and the li-chia system of Ch'ing period Shansi], *Tōyōshi Kenkyū* 26:3 (December 1967), 62-85.

Narakino Sen. "Shindai ni okeru jōshi gōson no chian iji ni tsuite" [Concerning the maintenance of public order in cities and villages during the Ch'ing period], *Shichō* 49 (1953), 35-48.

Niida Noboru. "Shindai no Kankō San Sen sei kaikan to San Sen girudo" [Ch'ing period Shansi and Shensi hui-kuan in Hankow and Shansi and Shensi guilds], *Shakai Keizaishigaku* 13:6 (September 1943), 1-22.

Nishikawa Masao. "Shisen pao-lu undō" [Szechwan pao-lu movement], *Tōyōbunka Kenkyūjō Kiyō* 55 (March 1968), 109-78.

Nishimura Nushiko. "Sengoku jidai no toshi jichi to sono genkai" [City self-government in the Sengoku period and its limits], *Rekishi Kyōiku* 12:8 (August 1964), 30-8.

Nishimura Mutsuo, ed. *Hanryō no rekishi chiri—Hagi han* [Historical geography of a han—Hagi han] (Ōmeido, Tokyo, 1968).

Nomura Kentarō. *Edo* (Shibundō, Tokyo, 1966).

Nomura Shoshichi. "Kamakura no toshiteki henkō" [Urban changes in Kamakura], *Shin Chiri* 4:3, 4, 5 (1949).

Norton, Thomas J. "The Physical Structure of Preindustrial Edo" (University of Washington Department of Urban Planning, Development Series No. 3, Seattle, 1964).

Nouët, Noël. *Histoire de Tokyo* (Paris, 1961).

Ōishi Shinzaburō. "Kyōhō kaikakuki ni okeru Edo keizai ni taisuru Osaka no chii: Kyōhō kaikakuki ni okeru shijō kōzō ni tsuite" [The position of Osaka in the Edo economy during the Kyōhō reform period: concerning the market structure during the Kyōhō reform period], *Nihon Rekishi* 191 (April 1964), 2-31.

———. "Sengoku makki ni okeru jidai keitai oyobi toshi no mondai ni kansuru hito kōsatsu" [One inquiry concerning the form of land rent in the late Sengoku period and the question of cities], *Shisō* 344:2 (1953), 75-86.

Okamura Ichirō. *Kawagoe no jōkamachi* [The castle city of Kawagoe] (Kawagoe, 1955).

Ono Hitoshi. *Kinsei jōkamachi no kenkyū* [Study of Tokugawa period castle cities] (Kokushi kenkyū sosho, Shibundō, Tokyo, 1928).

Perkins, Dwight H. *Agricultural Development in China, 1368-1968* (Aldine Press, Chicago, 1969).

Po Shou-i. *Chung-kuo chiao-t'ung shih* [History of Chinese communications] (Chung-kuo wen-hua tseng-shu, Shang Wu-yin shu-kuan, 1937).

Sadamotoshi shi (Ome, 1946).

Saeki Tomi. "Kinsei Chūgoku no toshi to nōson" [Cities and villages of China during the Sung to Ch'ing periods], *Rekishi Kyōiku* 14:12 (December 1966), 66-72.

———. "Shincho no kōki to Sansei shōnin" [Rise of the Ch'ing dynasty and Shansi merchants], *Shakai Bunka Shigaku* (1966), 11-42.

———. "Shindai ni okeru engyō shihon ni tsuite" [Concerning salt capital in the Ch'ing period], *Tōyōshi Kenkyū* 11:1 (September 1950), 51-65; 11:2 (March 1951), 38-50.

———. "Shindai Tao-kuang cho ni okeru Huai-nan ensei no kaikaku" [Reform of the Huai-nan salt system during the Ch'ing Tao-kuang reign], *Tōhōgaku Ronshū* 3 (September 1954), 87-120.

Saeki Yuichi. "Mindai shōekisei no hōkai to tō kinu orimonogyō ryūtsū shijō no tenkan" [Collapse of the artisan corvée system of the Ming period and development of market circulation of the urban silk goods industry], *Tōyōbunka Kenkyūjō Kiyō* 10 (November 1956), 359-425.

Sasaki Ginya. "Chūsei toshi to shōhin ryūtsū" [Cities and commercial circulation of the Kamakura to Sengoku periods], *Nihon Rekishi 8 Chūsei 4* (Iwanami kōsa, Tokyo, 1963), 109-55.

———. "Kamakura jidai ni okeru ryōshusei to shōgyō no kankei" [Relationship of the domain ownership system and commerce during the Kamakura period], *Rekishi Kyōiku* 7:7 (July 1959), 61-7.

Sasaki Kiyoharu. "Kinsei jōkamachi no shōen: Enshū Hamamatsu o rei to shite" [The commercial sphere of a Tokugawa period castle city: as an example Hamamatsu of Enshū], *Shōkei Kenkyū* 16 (Tōkai Daigaku Ronshū), 25-52.

Sasaki Masaya. "Shindai kanryō no kashoku ni tsuite" [Concerning the moneymaking of Ch'ing officials], *Shigaku Zasshi* 63:2 (February 1954), 22-57.

Sato Taketoshi. "Tōdai no shisei to gyō: toku ni Chōan o chūshin to shite" [T'ang period market system and guilds: especially centering on Ch'ang-an], *Tōyōshi Kenkyū* 25:3 (December 1966), 32-59.

Sekiyama Naotarō. *Kinsei Nihon jinkō no kenkyū* [Study of Tokugawa period Japanese population] (Ryūginsha, Tokyo, 1948).

Sekiyama Naotarō. *Nihon no jinkō* [Population of Japan] (Shibundō, Tokyo, 1966).

Shiba Yoshinobu. "10-13 seiki ni okeru Chūgoku toshi no tenkan" [Conversion of Chinese cities in the 10th-13th centuries], *Sekaishi Kenkyū* 14 (January 1966), 22-37.

———. *Sōdai shōgyōshi kenkyū* [Commercial activities during the Sung dynasty] (Kazama shobō, Tokyo, 1968).

———. "Sōdai shōgyōshi kenkyū no tame no oboegaki" [Notes on the history of Chinese city development), *Rekishigaku Kenkyū* 1-1 (1933), 49-69.

Shida Fudōmaro. "Shina toshi hattatsushi no hito shaku" (A sketch of the history of Chinese city development), *Rekishigaku Kenkyū* 1-1 (1933), 10-18.

Shigeta Atsushi. "Shindai ni okeru Konan beishijō no hito kōsatsu" (One inquiry into the Hunan rice market during the Ch'ing period), *Tōyōbunka Kenkyūjō Kiyo* 10 (November 1956), 427-98.

———. "Shinmatsu ni okeru Konan cha no seisan kōzō: gokō kaikō ikō o chūshin to shite" (Structure of production of Hunan tea during the late Ch'ing period: centering on the time after the five treaty ports opened), *Jinbun Kenkyū* 16-4 (May, 1965), 61-110.

Shina shōbetsu zenshi [Complete provincial gazetteers of China], (Tōa dobun shoin, 1917-20).

Shinshū Hiroshimashi shi [Revised history of Hiroshima city], (Hiroshima, 1959).

Shoji Yoshinotsuke. "Chihōteki shijō keisei no mondai" [Problems of local market formation], *Shōgaku Ronshū* 19:1 (1960), 151-81.

Shou-tu chih [Gazetteer of Nanking] (Cheng-shu shu-chu, Taipei, 1966).

Sjoberg, Gideon. *The Preindustrial City* (The Free Press, New York, 1960).

Skinner, G. William. "Chinese Peasants and the Closed Community: An Open and Shut Case," *Comparative Studies in Society and History*, (July 1971), 271-81.

———. "The city in Chinese society," a paper presented at the conference on Urban Society in Traditional China, and to appear in revised form in his book, *The City in Late Imperial China*.

———. "Marketing and Social Structure in Rural China," parts 1 and 2, *Journal of Asian Studies* 24:1, 2 (November 1964 and February 1965).

Stuzhina, E. P., *Kitaiskoe Remeslo v XVI-XVIII Vekakh* [Chinese crafts in the XVI-XVIII centuries] (Nauka, Moscow, 1970).

———. "Problems of the economic and social structure of the city and of craft production in China during the XIth-XIIIth centuries in contemporary historiography," *Istoriographiia Stran Vostoka* (Moscow University, Moscow, 1969).

Sudō Yoshiyuki. "Sōdai no kyōson ni okeru kotoshi no hatten: toku ni ten, shi, sho o chūshin to shite" [Development of small cities in Sung period settlements: especially centering on t'ien, shih and pu], *Shigaku Zasshi* 59:9, 10 (1950), 25-50 and 16-44.

Suzuki Naoji. "Kinsei ni okeru chūō beikoku shijō no tenkai" [Development of the central grain market in the Tokugawa period], *Nōson Kenkyū* 26 (December 1967), 55-71; 28 (December 1968), 1-9.

———. "Tokugawa jidai no beikoku haikyū soshiki josetsu" [Introduction to the organization of grain distribution during the Tokugawa period], *Chūōgakuin Daigaku Ronsō* 1:1 (November 1966), 201-30.

Tada Kenkai. "Kandai no chihō shōgyō ni tsuite: gozoku to konōmin no kankei o chūshin ni" [Han period local commerce: centering on the relations of wealthy families and small farmers], *Shichō* 92 (July 1965), 36-49.

Taeuber, Irene B. "Cities and Urbanization in Traditional China: Queries, Dilemma, Approaches," a paper presented at the conference on Urban Society in Traditional China.

———. *The Population of Japan* (Princeton University Press, Princeton, 1958).

Takahashi Bonsen. *Nihon jinkōshi no kenkyū* [Study of the history of the population of Japan] (Nihon gakujutsu shinkōkai, Tokyo, 1955).

Takanaka Toshie. "Min Shin jidai no toshi kyōdōtai" [Urban communities of the Ming and Ch'ing periods], *Shigaku Kenkyū* 73 (September 1959), 41-45.

Takeuchi Makoto. "Chihō nōmin no Edo shinshutsu" [The advance of local farmers into Edo], *Rekishi Kyōiku* 12:12 (December 1964), 16-25.

Tanaka Shūsaku. "Shūraku mitsudo o kiban o seru jinkō bunpu ni tsuite: Hokushi Kahoku chiiki no baai" [Concerning population distribution which is based on settlement densities: the case of the North China Hopei area], *Osaka Gakugei Daigaku Kiyō* (Jinbun kagaku 1, 1952), 111-23.

Tanaka Yoshio. *Jōkamachi Kanazawa* (Nihon shoin, Tokyo, 1966).

T'ao Hsi-sheng. "Wu-tai ti tu-shih yü shang-yeh" [Cities and commerce in the Five Dynasties period], *Shih Hua* 1:1 (1935), 31-35.

Terada Takanobu. "SōSō chihō ni okeru toshi no mengyō shōnin ni tsuite" [Concerning cotton industry merchants in the cities of the Soochow Sungchiang area], *Shirin* 41:6 (November 1958), 52-69.

T'ien fu kuang chi (Peking, 1962 edition, originally written about 1671).

Tomioka Gihachi. "Kinsei no neiriku toshi to kōtsūro no mondai: Tōbu Chūgoku chihō no baai" [Problems of inland cities and transport routes of the Tokugawa period: the case of the Eastern Chūgoku region], *Chirigaku Hyōron* 37:8 (August 1964).

Toyoda Takeshi. "Higashi to nishi hōken toshi" [Feudal cities of East and West], *Rekishi Kyōiku* 14:11 (November 1966), 1-11.

———. "Hōken toshi kara kindai toshi e" [From feudal cities to modern cities], *Toshi Mondai* 48:1 (January 1957), 11-21.

———. *Nihon no hōken toshi* [Feudal cities of Japan] (Iwanami shoten, Tokyo, 1968).

Tso Yun-peng. "Lun Ch'ing-tai ch'i-ti ti hsing-ch'eng yen-pien chi ch'i hsing-t'ai" [Discussion of the formation and transformation of Ch'ing banner lands and their nature], *Li-shih Yen-chiu* (May 1961), 44-65.

Tsuda Hideo. *Hōken keizai seisaku no tenkai to shijō kōzō* [Development of feudal economic policies and market structure] (Ochanomizu shobō, Tokyo, 1961).

Tsujita Usao, ed. *Sangyō chiri no shomondai* [Various problems of commercial geography] (Ryuhara shoten, Tokyo, 1964), Vol. II.

Tsukushi Nobuzane. "Tōkaidō shukujō no henbō" [Transfiguration of Tōkaidō posts], *Mie no Bunka* 7 (February 1957), 20-28.

Twitchett, Denis. "The T'ang Market System," *Asia Major* (1966), 202-48.

Umehara Kaoru. "Sōdai chihō kotoshi no ichimen" [One aspect of Sung period small local cities], *Shirin* 41:6 (November 1958), 35-51.

———. "Sōdai no chihō toshi" [Sung period local cities], *Rekishi Kyōiku* 14:12 (December 1966), 52-58.

Utsunomiya Kiyoyoshi. "Shikan no shuto Chōan ni tsuite" [Concerning Ch'ang-an the capital of the Western Han], *Tōyōshi kenkyū* 11:4 (February 1952).

———. *Kandai shakai keizaishi kenkyū* [Study of the social and economic history of the Han period] (Marubundō, Tokyo, 1955).

Utsunomiyaryō kinsei shi [History of Utsunomiya domain in the Tokugawa period] (Utsunomiya, 1964).

Wakamori Tarō, ed. *Jōkamachi* (Yūki shobō, Tokyo, 1962).

Wakita Osamu. *Kinsei hōken shakai no keizai kōzō* [The economic structure of Tokugawa feudal society] (Ochanomizu shobō, Tokyo, 1963).

Watanabe Eisaburō. "Kodai Nihon ni okeru toshi no hattatsu" [The development of cities in ancient Japan], *Toshi Mondai* 48:8 (August 1957), 944-52; 49:5 (May 1958), 546-54.

Watanabe Nobuo. *Bakuhansei kakuritsuki shōhin ryūtsū* [Commercial flow at the time of the establishment of the Bakuhan system] (Haku-shobō, Tokyo, 1966).

———. "Edo jidai kōki ni okeru nōson shijō no keisei to sono kōzō" [The formation of late Tokugawa period village markets and their structure], *Bunka* 23:2 (Tōhoku Daigaku, Summer 1959), 64-95.

Wheatley, Paul. *The Pivot of the Four Quarters: A Preliminary Enquiry into the Origins and Character of the Ancient Chinese City* (Chicago: Aldine Press, 1971).

Wright, Arthur F. "The Cosmology of the Chinese City," a paper presented at the conference on Urban Society in Traditional China.

———. "Symbolism and Function: reflections on Ch'ang-an and other Great Cities," *Journal of Asian Studies* 24 (August 1965), 667-79.

Yajima, Jinkichi. "Kantō Seihokubu no taniguchi shūraku" [River valley settlements in Northwest Kantō], *Shin Chiri* 4:3, 4, 5 (1949).

Yamane Yukio. "Kahoku no miao-hui" [Fairs of North China], *Shiron* 17 (March 1967), 1-22.

———. "Min Shin jidai Kahoku ni okeru teikishi" [Periodic markets in North China during the Ming and Ch'ing periods], *Shiron* 8 (1960), 493-504.

———. "'Shantung sheng Tzu-yang hsien hu-ts'e' ni tsuite" [Concerning the household register of Tzu-yang hsien in Shantung sheng], *Tokyo Joshi Daigaku Fuzoku Hikaku Bunka Kenkyūjō Kiyō* (June 1963), 23-111.

Yamauchi Kiyoshi. *Shina shōgyōron* [Discussion of Chinese commerce] (Tokyo, 1942).

Yamori Kazuhiko. "Hikone jōka ni okeru jinkō dōtai ni tsuite" [Concerning population movements in Hikone castle city], *Ryūtsū no Rekishi Chiri: Rekishi Chirigaku Kiyō* 3 (1961), 129-43.

———. "Jōkamachi kenkyū nōto: sono seika to kadai" [Notes on the study of castle cities: results and problems], *Jinbun Chiri* 11:6 (1959), 563-77.

———. "Jōkamachi no chikisei: sono mensekiteki kōsei" [Land use of a castle city: its areal composition], *Rekishi Chirigaku Kiyō* 5 (Nihon rekishi chirigaku kenkyūkai, 1963), 185-214.

———. "Jōkamachi no jinkō kōsei: Hikone han no rekishi chiriteki kenkyū" [The population composition of a castle city: historical geographical study of Hikone han], *Shirin* 37:2 (April 1954), 64-78.

Yamori Kazuhiko. "Kinsei jōkamachi puran no hatten ruikei hito jōsetsu"

[One introduction to similar types of development of Tokugawa period castle city plans], *Shirin* 41:6 (1958), 561-80.

Yang Ching-kun. *A North China Local Market Economy: A Summary of a Study of Periodic Markets in Chowping hsien, Shantung.* (Institute of Pacific Relations, New York, 1944).

Yang, Lien-sheng. "Government Control of Urban Merchants," a paper presented at the conference on Urban Society in Traditional China.

Yazaki Takeo. *Nihon toshi no hatten katei* (Marubundō, Tokyo, 1962).

———. *Social Change and the City in Japan: From Earliest Times Through the Industrial Revolution* (Japan Publications, Inc. Tokyo, 1968).

Yonekura Jirō. *Tōa nōshūraku Nihon oyobi Chūgoku no shūraku no rekishi chiriteki kenkyū* [Historical geographical study of East Asian village settlements in Japan and China] (Kokon shoin, Tokyo, 1960).

Yozumi Shōgorō, ed. *Daimyo ryōkoku to jōkamachi* [Daimyo domains and castle cities] (Tokyo, 1968).

APPENDIX A

LIST OF GAZETTEERS
FOR CHAPTER 4

Shun-t'ien fu

Chi-fu t'ung-chih, 1735, 1884
Shun-t'ien fu chih, 1593, 1886
Cho chou chih, 1765, 1935
T'ung chou chih, 1783, 1879
Chi chou chih, 1704
Pa hsien chih, 1922
Ch'ang-p'ing chou chih, 1673,
    1886, 1892
Shun-i hsien chih, 1719, 1932
Mi-yun hsien chih, 1882, 1913
P'ing-ku hsien chih, 1667, 1934
Huai-jou hsien chih, 1721
Ta-hsing hsien chih, 1685
Liang-hsiang hsien chih, 1889,
    1923
Fang-shan hsien chih, 1665, 1927
Ku-an hsien chih, 1859, 1927
Yung-ch'ing hsien chih, 1779, 1875
Tung-an hsien chih, 1624, 1677,
    1749, 1913
Wen-an hsien chih, 1703, 1921
Ta-ch'eng hsien chih, 1673, 1897
Pao-ting hsien chih, 1673
Hsiang-ho hsien chih, 1678, 1935
San-ho hsien chih, 1760, 1934
Wu-ch'ing hsien chih, 1881
Pao-ti hsien chih, 1745
Ning-ho hsien chih, 1779, 1880

Pao-ting fu

Pao-ting fu chih, 1680, 1886
Ch'ing-yuan hsien chih, 1677,
    1873, 1933
Man-ch'eng hsien chih, 1751, 1930
An-su hsien chih, 1778, 1931
Ting-hsing hsien chih, 1779, 1891

Hsin-ch'eng hsien chih, 1838,
    1895, 1934
T'ang hsien chih, 1878
Po-yeh hsien chih, 1766
Wang-tu hsien chih, 1771, 1905,
    1933
Jung-ch'eng hsien chih, 1857, 1896
Wan hsien chih, 1732, 1933
Li hsien chih, 1641, 1876
Hsiung hsien chih, 1671, 1929
Ch'i chou chih, 1755, 1882
Shu-lu hsien chih, 1671, 1762,
    1799, 1872, 1905
An chou chih, 1849
Kao-yang hsien chih, 1730, 1932

Cheng-ting fu

Cheng-ting fu chih, 1862
Cheng-ting hsien chih, 1645, 1875
Chin chou chih, 1676, 1860, 1926
Huo-lu hsien chih, 1736, 1881
Kao-ch'eng hsien chih, 1698, 1933
Ching-hsing hsien chih, 1730,
    1876, 1933
Yuan-shih hsien chih, 1758, 1876
Wu-chi hsien chih, 1893
Luan-ch'eng hsien chih, 1847, 1873
Hsing-t'ang hsien chih, 1763
Hsin-lo hsien chih, 1885
Ling-shou hsien chih, 1686, 1873
P'ing-shan hsien chih, 1673, 1854,
    1877, 1898, 1930
Fu-p'ing hsien chih, 1874
Tsan-huang hsien chih, 1672, 1751

Tientsin fu

Tientsin fu chih, 1674, 1899
Tientsin hsien chih, 1739, 1870

Ch'ing hsien chih, 1673, 1803,
  1877, 1930
Ch'ing-yun hsien chih, 1809, 1855,
  1913
Ching-hai hsien chih, 1873
Nan-p'i hsien chih, 1680, 1888,
  1932
Yen-shan hsien chih, 1915
Ts'ang chou chih, 1743, 1932

Ho-chien fu

Ho-chien fu chih, 1677, 1760
Ho-chien hsien chih, 1760
Chiao-ho hsien chih, 1673, 1916
Ching chou chih, 1745, 1931
Wu-ch'iao hsien chih, 1876
Ku-ch'eng hsien chih, 1727, 1886
Hsien hsien chih, 1761, 1924
Fu-ch'eng hsien chih, 1734
Su-ning hsien chih, 1754
Jen-ch'iu hsien chih, 1763, 1837
Tung-kuang hsien chih, 1693, 1888
Ning-tsin hsien chih, 1900

Shun-te fu

Shun-te fu chih, 1750
Hsing-t'ai hsien chih, 1827, 1905
Chu-lu hsien chih, 1661, 1886
P'ing-hsiang hsien chih, 1868
Sha-ho hsien chih, 1757, 1845
Kuang-tsung hsien chih, 1874
T'ang-shan hsien chih, 1881
Nei-ch'iu hsien chih, 1832
Nan-ho hsien chih, 1667, 1749
Jen hsien chih, 1914

Kuang-p'ing fu

Kuang-p'ing fu chih, 1745, 1894
Yung-nien hsien chih, 1758, 1877
Ch'u chou chih, 1747
Fei-hsiang hsien chih, 1732
Chi-tse hsien chih, 1766
Kuang-p'ing hsien chih, 1676
Ch'eng-an hsien chih, 1673, 1802,
  1930
Tz'u chou chih, 1703, 1874
Han-tan hsien chih, 1756, 1933

Wei hsien chih, 1673, 1928
Ch'ing-ho hsien chih, 1718, 1872,
  1883, 1934

Chih-li chou

Ting chou chih, 1733, 1848, 1933
Shen-tze hsien chih, 1735, 1862
Ch'u-yang hsien chih, 1672, 1904
I chou chih, 1747
Lai-shui hsien chih, 1895
Kuang-ch'ang hsien chih, 1875
Tsun-hua chou chih, 1794, 1886
Feng-jun hsien chih, 1755, 1891
Yü-t'ien hsien chih, 1790, 1933
Chao chou chih, 1897
Pai-hsiang hsien chih, 1680, 1767
Kao-i hsien chih, 1685, 1800
Lin-ch'eng hsien chih, 1691
Ning-chin hsien chih, 1679
Shen chou chih, 1900
Wu-ch'ing hsien chih, 1694, 1831
Jao-yang hsien chih, 1749
An-p'ing hsien chih, 1688
Chi chou chih, 1747, 1928
Heng-shui hsien chih, 1767
Hsin-ho hsien chih, 1679, 1876,
  1929
Tsao-ch'iang hsien chih, 1803,
  1876
Nan-kung hsien chih, 1559, 1831,
  1904, 1935

Yung-p'ing fu

Yung-p'ing fu chih, 1711, 1774,
  1879
Lu-lung hsien chih, 1930
Ch'ien-an hsien chih, 1873, 1930
Fu-ning hsien chih, 1682, 1877
Ch'ang-li hsien chih, 1866, 1932
Luan chou chih, 1810, 1898
Lo-t'ing hsien chih, 1755, 1877
Lin-yü hsien chih, 1756, 1878, 1928

Ta-ming fu

Ta-ming fu chih, 1853
Ta-ming hsien chih, 1790, 1933
Yuan-ch'eng hsien chih, 1676,
  1872

LIST OF GAZETTEERS
FOR CHAPTER 5

Shantung

Shantung t'ung-chih, 1910
Li-ch'eng hsien chih, 1772
Lin-ch'ing chih-li chou chih, 1750,
 1785
Tsi-ning chih-li chou chih, 1785,
 1859
Ch'ang-ch'ing hsien chih, 1835
Chi-ho hsien chih, 1737
Hsin-t'ai hsien chih, 1785
Hui-min hsien chih, 1899
I-shui hsien chih, 1827
Kao-t'ang chou chih, 1907
Lin-i hsien chih, 1874
P'eng-lai hsien chih, 1882
T'ai-an hsien chih, 1782, 1867
Te chou chih, 1790
Tzu-yang hsien chih, 1888
Tung-a hsien chih, 1829
Tung-p'ing chou chih, 1825
Yeh hsien chih, 1758

Shansi

Shansi t'ung chih, 1892
T'ai-yuan fu chih, 1783
Ta-t'ung hsien chih, 1871
An-i hsien chih, 1880
Ch'ang-chih hsien chih, c. 1890
Ch'i hsien chih, 1777
Chie-hsiu hsien chih, 1819
Ch'ü-wo hsien chih, 1797
Ho-chin hsien chih, 1797
Hsin chou chih, 1880
Hsü-kou hsien chih, 1712, 1881
Kao-p'ing hsien chih, 1867
Lin-fen hsien chih, 1778
P'ing-ting chou chih, c. 1790,
 c. 1890

P'ing-yao hsien chih, 1883
Shen chou chih, 1771
Shou-yang hsien chih, 1880
Shuo chou chih, 1735
Tai chou chih, 1880
T'ai-p'ing hsien chih, 1825
Yung-chi hsien chih, 1886

Honan

Hsiang-fu hsien chih, 1739, 1898
Lo-yang hsien chih, 1745, 1813
Cheng chou chih, 1748
Chi hsien chih, 1755
Ch'i hsien chih, 1788
Hsi-p'ing hsien chih, 1691
Hsin-yeh hsien chih, 1754
Hsü chou chih, 1838
Huo-chia hsien chih, 1845
Jung-tse hsien chih, 1748
K'ao-ch'eng hsien chih, 1699
Kuang chou chih, 1770
Meng hsien chih, 1790
Nan-yang hsien chih, 1693
Pi-yang hsien chih, 1828
Shang-ch'iu hsien chih, 1705
Shen chou chih, 1892
T'ang hsien chih, 1787
T'ang-yin hsien chih, 1738
Wu-chih hsien chih, 1829
Yü chou chih, 1835
Yü-ch'eng hsien chih, 1745
Yung-ch'eng hsien chih, 1903

Shensi

Sian fu chih, 1779
Ch'ang-an hsien chih, 1815
Hsien-ning hsien chih, 1819
An-k'ang hsien chih, 1815

Ch'i shan hsien chih, 1815
Ching-yang hsien chih, 1911
Feng hsien chih, 1892
Feng-hsiang hsien chih, 1767
Han-ch'eng hsien chih, 1784
Kao-ling hsien chih, 1798
Lin-t'ung hsien chih, 1776
Lung chou chih, 1766
San-yuan hsien chih, 1880
Ta-li hsien chih, 1786
T'ung-kuan hsien chih, 1687

Kansu

Kan-lan hsien chih, 1778
Lan-chou fu chih, 1832
Kan-chou fu chih, 1779
Ning-yuan hsien chih, 1709

Anhwei

Anhwei t'ung chih, 1881
Ch'u chou chih, 1897
Feng-yang hsien chih, 1887
Fu-yang hsien chih, 1829
Ho-fei hsien chih, 1804
Hsin-an hsien chih, 1887
Kui-ch'ih hsien chih, 1883
Liu-an chou chih, 1872
Lu-chou fu chih, 1885
Po chou chih, 1894
Shou chou chih, 1890
Shu-ch'eng hsien chih, 1906
Su chou chih, 1889
Su-sung hsien chih, 1829
T'ai-hu hsien chih, 1872
Tang-t'u hsien chih, 1750
T'ung-ch'eng hsien chih, 1827
T'ung-ling hsien chih, 1757
Wu-hu hsien chih, 1807
Wu-wei chou chih, 1803

Kiangsu

An-tung hsien chih, 1875
Ch'ang chou hsien chih, 1766
Chia-ting hsien chih, 1885
Chiang-tu hsien chih, 1881
Chiang-yin hsien chih, 1878
Chin-kuei hsien chih, 1881

Ching-ch'i hsien chih, 1882
Ch'ing-ho hsien chih, 1879
Feng hsien chih, 1894
Feng-hsien hsien chih, 1878
Fu-ning hsien chih, 1886
Hai chou chih, 1811
Hsin-yang hsien chih, 1880
Hsing-hua hsien chih, 1852
Hua-t'ing hsien chih, 1878
I-cheng hsien chih, 1718
I-hsing hsien chih, 1797, 1882
Ju-kan hsien chih, 1873
Kan-ch'uan hsien chih, 1885
Kan-yü hsien chih, 1888
Kao-cheng hsien chih, 1845
Kao-ch'un hsien chih, 1881
K'un-shan hsien chih, 1880
Liu-ho hsien chih, 1884
Lou hsien chih, 1879
Nan-hui hsien chih, 1879
Pao-shan hsien chih, 1882
Pao-ying hsien chih, 1841
P'i chou chih, 1885
Su-ch'ien hsien chih, 1875
Tan-t'u hsien chih, 1879
Tan-yang hsien chih, 1885
T'ung-shan hsien chih, 1831
Wu-chiang hsien chih, 1747, 1879
Wu-chin hsien chih, 1879
Wu-hsi hsien chih, 1881
Yang-hu hsien chih, 1879
Yen-ch'eng hsien chih, 1895

Chekiang

Chekiang sheng chih, 1891, 1936
Ch'ang-hsing hsien chih, 1885
Chiang-shan hsien chih, 1873
Ch'ien-t'ang hsien chih, 1893
Hai-ning chou chih, 1898
Hsi-an hsien chih, 1811
Jen-ho hsien chih, 1893
Jui-an hsien chih, 1809
Kuei-an hsien chih, 1881
Lan-ch'i hsien chih, 1888
Li-shui hsien chih, 1874
Lin-hai hsien chih, 1683
P'ing-hu hsien chih, 1886

Shan-yin hsien chih, 1803
Sheng hsien chih, 1871
Shih-men hsien chih, 1879
Te-ch'ing hsien chih, 1808
Tz'u-ch'i hsien chih, 1899
Wu-ch'eng hsien chih, 1881
Yin hsien chih, 1788
Yü-yao hsien chih, 1899
Yung-chia hsien chih, 1882

Hupei

An-lu hsien chih, 1843
Chiang-ling hsien chih, 1877
Chien-li hsien chih, 1872
Ching-men chou chih, 1868
Ching-shan hsien chih, 1882
En-shih hsien chih, 1868
Fang hsien chih, 1866
Hankow chen chih, c. 1840
Han-yang hsien chih, 1868, 1888
Hen-yang hsien chih, 1894
Hsi-shui hsien chih, 1880
Hsiang-yang hsien chih, 1874
Hsiao-kan hsien chih, 1883
Hsien-ning hsien chih, 1866
Huang-kang hsien chih, 1881
Huang-p'i hsien chih, 1871
I-ch'ang hsien chih, 1866
I-tu hsien chih, 1866
Kung-an hsien chih, 1874
Pao-k'ang hsien chih, 1866
Ta-chih hsien chih, 1867
Tung-hu hsien chih, 1864
Wu-ch'ang hsien chih, 1885
Yün hsien chih, 1866

Hunan

Hunan t'ung chih, 1914
Ch'ang-sha hsien chih, 1871
Ch'ien-yang hsien chih, 1874
Ch'ing-ch'un hsien chih, 1763, 1869
Heng-shan hsien chih, 1823
Heng-yang hsien chih, 1874
Hsiang-t'an hsien chih, 1818
Hsiang-yin hsien chih, 1881
I-yang hsien chih, 1874

Lei-yang hsien chih, 1886
Lin-hsiang hsien chih, 1892
Ling-ling hsien chih, 1817
Pa-ling hsien chih, 1892
Pao-ching hsien chih, 1872
Shan-hua hsien chih, 1877
Wu-kang chou chih, 1817
Wu-ling hsien chih, 1863

Kiangsi

Chi-shui hsien chih, 1875
Ch'ing-chiang hsien chih, 1870
Kan hsien chih, 1872
Kao-an hsien chih, 1871
Lin-ch'uan hsien chih, 1870
Lu-lung hsien chih, 1781
Nan-ch'ang fu chih, 1873
Nan-ch'ang hsien chih, 1870
Nan-k'ang hsien chih, 1872
P'eng-tse hsien chih, 1819
Po-yang hsien chih, 1871
Shang-jao hsien chih, 1873
Te-hsing hsien chih, 1823
Te-hua hsien chih, 1780
Wan-an hsien chih, 1874
Yü-shan hsien chih, 1873

Fukien

Fukien sheng chih (Japanese), 1908
Chin-chiang hsien chih, 1765
Fu-ch'ing hsien chih, 1898
Hou-kuan hsien chih, c. 1905
Min hsien chih, c. 1905
Nan-p'ing hsien chih, 1872
Shao-wu hsien chih, 1855
T'ung-an hsien chih, 1886

Kwangtung

Kwangtung sheng chih, 1897
Ch'ao-chou fu chih, 1893
Chao-ch'ing fu chih, 1877
Ch'iung chou fu chih, 1890
Fan-yü hsien chih, 1871
Lei-chou fu chih, 1811
Lien-chou fu chih, 1870
Lin-kao hsien chih, 1892

Nan-hsiung chou chih, 1824
Nan-hai hsien chih, 1872
Shun-te hsien chih, 1750
Tung-kuan hsien chih, 1750

Kwangsi

Chao-p'ing hsien chih, c. 1890
Chen-an fu chih, 1892
Ho hsien chih, c. 1890
Hsun-chou chih, c. 1870
Jung hsien chih, c. 1890
Kuei hsien chih, 1894
Kuei-shun chou chih, 1899
Pei-liu hsien chih, 1880
Pin chou chih, 1886
P'ing-lo fu chih, 1805
P'ing-nan hsien chih, 1884
Po-pai hsien chih, c. 1890
Ts'ang-wu hsien chih, 1872
Wu-chou fu chih, 1769
Yü-lin chou chih, 1894

Kweichow

Ch'ien-nan shih-lieh, 1848

T'ung-jen fu chih, 1890
Li-p'ing fu chih, 1892

Yunnan

Yunnan sheng t'ung chih, 1894
Chan-i chou chih, 1886
Wu-ting chou chih, 1883
Yao chou chih, 1885

Szechwan

An-yüeh hsien chih, 1840
Chengtu hsien chih, 1815, 1873
Chien chou chih, 1873
Ch'iung chou chih, 1818
Fu chou chih, 1870
Fu-shun hsien chih, 1882
Hua-yang hsien chih, 1816
Hung-ya hsien chih, 1813
I-pin hsien chih, 1812
Kuan hsien chih, 1886
Kuang-yuan hsien chih, 1757
Lan-chung hsien chih, 1851
Lu chou chih, c. 1890
Pa hsien chih, 1820, 1867
Wan hsien chih, 1866

INDEX

absentee landowners, 15, 54, 85; in China, 24, 73, 76, 87; in Japan, 28, 29, 36-39, 46, 75, 91

administrative divisions, 15, 50, 63-72, 104, 284; changes in Chihli, 150, 162, 169; relation to marketing, 106, 114, 121-27, 156, 201, 219, 262

agriculture: conditions for, 61, 72, 74, 245; improvements in, 18, 32, 38, 44, 107, 118-19; in cities, 19, 22, 34, 83; new crops, 44, 76; new land, 187; origins of, 16, 19-20

America, 62

Amoy, 240

An-ch'ing, 223-24, 235

Anhwei, 65, 130, 212, 217-30, 234, 245, 273, 274; merchants of, 132, 237; places in, 129, 131

An-yang, 16

area of China and Japan, 26, 61, 103

aristocracy: Chinese, 18, 19, 26, 30; Japanese (kuge), 20, 38, 40, 56, 79, 91, 92, 298

artisans, number of, 87-88

Awa, 148

Azuchi, 50

Bakufu: cities of, 50, 70, 71, 192, 270; finances of, 112, 117-18, 135; Kamakura, 36, 56; lands of, 68, 73, 74, 122, 124, 127, 188, 195, 297; Muromachi, 39, 40, 56; Tokugawa, 7, 62, 94, 121, 124, 126, 137, 138, 185, 187, 286-87, 298; vassals of, 83

bannermen, 62-63, 79, 82, 83, 85, 98, 167; in Peking, 73, 292-97

beggars, 91, 197

Biwa Lake, 40, 137

bronze, 18, 53

bureaucracy, 41, 42, 72, 79-80, 82, 103, 279, 297

bushi: levels of, 82-83, 98-99, 266, 268-69; number of, 81, 91, 103; percentage in castle cities, 46-48, 73, 80, 81, 253, 298

canals: inside cities, 35, 227, 286, 287

Canton, 25, 31, 43, 62, 130, 238, 240-44

capital cities: choice of, 41-42, 281; history of, 15-16, 277, 278-84; primacy of, 33, 58, 107

castles: as national administrative centers, 51, 79, 286, 287; functions of, 98-99, 268, 269, 286; number of, 95, 116; pre-Tokugawa, 39-40, 46, 47, 49, 187-88

census of 1953, 146

Central Asia, 22

central marketing towns, 101, 113, 114, 127

INDEX